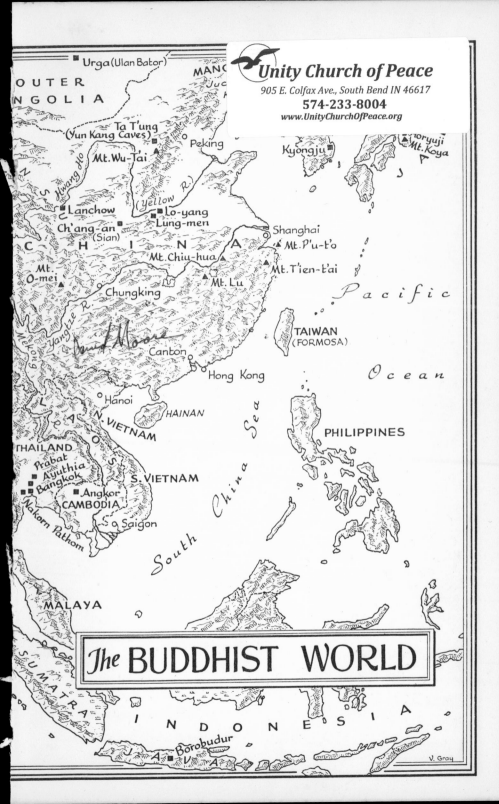

Urga (Ulan Bator)

OUTER
MONGOLIA

MANCHURIA

Ta T'ung
(Yun Kang Caves)

Mt. Wu-T'ai

Hwang-ho

(Yellow R.)

Peking

Kyongju

Horyuji
Mt. Koya

Lanchow

Ch'ang-an
(Sian)

Lo-yang
Lung-men

C H I N A

Mt. Chiu-hua

Shanghai
Mt. P'u-t'o

Mt.
O-mei

Mt. Lu

Mt. T'ien-t'ai

Chungking

Yangtze R.

Mekong

Canton

Pacific

TAIWAN
(FORMOSA)

Ocean

Hong Kong

Hanoi

HAINAN

N. VIETNAM

LAOS

South China Sea

PHILIPPINES

THAILAND

Prabat
Ayuthia
Bangkok

S. VIETNAM

Angkor
CAMBODIA

Nakorn Pathom

Saigon

South

MALAYA

SUMATRA

The BUDDHIST WORLD

BORNEO

I N D O N E S I A

Borobudur

J A V A

V. Gray

Kenneth W. Morgan is Professor of Religion,
Director of Chapel House, and Director of the Fund
for the Study of the Great Religions of the World,
at Colgate University.

Companion Volumes
Edited by Kenneth W. Morgan

ISLAM—THE STRAIGHT PATH
Islam Interpreted by Muslims

THE RELIGION OF THE HINDUS
Interpreted by Hindus

THE PATH OF THE BUDDHA

Buddhism Interpreted by Buddhists

Edited by

Kenneth W. Morgan

COLGATE UNIVERSITY

Contributors

J. Kashyap

U Thittila

B. Ananda Maitreya

Susumu Yamaguchi

Zenryu Tsukamoto

Lobsang Phuntsok Lhalungpa

Shinso Hanayama

Mitsuyuki Ishida

Reiho Masunaga

Shobun Kubota

Hajime Nakamura

THE RONALD PRESS COMPANY · NEW YORK

Library of Congress Catalog Card Number: 56-9981

PRINTED IN THE UNITED STATES OF AMERICA

Preface

This book presents Buddhism from the Buddhist point of view. It is an earnest attempt on the part of eleven devout Buddhist scholars to describe the beliefs and practices of the Buddhist world twenty-five centuries after the Buddha.

Recognition of the need for such a book grew out of conversations among Fellows of the National Council on Religion in Higher Education. It was agreed that a fuller understanding of the leading non-Christian religions requires books written by men speaking from the point of view of their own faith, and edited by a Westerner to make sure that the meaning would be clear to readers brought up in the Greek-Hebrew-Christian tradition. Such books, it was predicted, would be valuable to all who wished to understand the role played by religion in the lives and culture of a greater part of the world.

Thus the approach to the writing of this book is the same as that taken in preparing the two companion volumes—*Islam —The Straight Path* and *The Religion of the Hindus*—and the Edward W. Hazen Foundation again provided necessary financial assistance.

First, I sought the advice of teachers of the history of religions, asking them to help me prepare an outline covering the materials we thought should be included in a fair and representative presentation of Buddhism. Then I visited Japan, Hong Kong, Thailand, Burma, India, and Ceylon, interviewing leading Buddhists in each community, revising the outline in accord with their suggestions, and getting their recommendations for men qualified to write the different sections. On the

iii

basis of their recommendations, the authors of this book were
selected and commissioned to write their chapters following
the outline on which we were all agreed. They were reminded
that they had been chosen by their fellow Buddhists and that
the Buddhist world was expecting them to give a complete and
fair picture of their beliefs and practices. After the manuscripts were written, I visited each writer again to discuss his
section of the book in detail to make sure that the editing
would be done with a clear understanding of the intention of
the writer. The editing has been extensive in order that there
may be no ambiguities and the book may read as one continuous account, not as a collection of essays. We have sought to
avoid comparative judgments, for this is not a study in comparative religion but a straightforward presentation of Buddhism. Statements concerning other religions have been allowed to stand only when they are representative of opinions
widely held among Buddhists. Each writer checked and approved the final form of his chapter before it was printed.

At the outset we had to decide whether or not Southern
and Northern Buddhism should be included in one volume.
We came to the conclusion that there are important advantages in a single volume which introduces the reader to the
whole Buddhist world, showing the great diversity of interpretations of the Buddha's teachings concerning the path to release from suffering—and at the same time making it possible
to see the underlying unity in the Buddhist world, which is
often ignored both in the East and in the West.

Diacritical marks have been omitted in the text, but are
given in the index. New words are defined when they first
appear, and the most commonly used ones are defined in the
glossary as an aid to the reader who may find it difficult to remember the terms which have come into Buddhism from Pali,
Sanskrit, Chinese, Tibetan, and Japanese.

Since the canonical language of Southern or Theravada
Buddhism is Pali and that of Northern or Mahayana Buddhism
is Sanskrit, it does violence to either point of view to insist on
one spelling for the sake of uniformity. Therefore, in the first

three chapters, which are written by Theravada Buddhists, we have used Pali words—*Nibbana* rather than *Nirvana*, for instance—and in the chapters dealing with Mahayana Buddhism the Sanskrit form of the words is used.

The question of chronology is a puzzling one for anyone who tries to fit Buddhism into the Western historical perspective. Because the calendar in the Theravada countries is based on the Buddhist Era, beginning in 544 B.C. with the passing away of the Buddha, in the first three chapters we have given the Buddhist Era dates as well as the dates according to the Western calendar. The Northern Buddhist countries have not accepted the chronology of Southern Buddhism, nor have they agreed upon a common Buddhist calendar, so in the chapters written by Mahayana writers we have followed the Western calendar. The problems of chronology in Buddhism have been discussed by Professor Nakamura in the final chapter of the book.

We have been fortunate in receiving the full cooperation of an able group of writers. Bhikkhu Kashyap is an Indian Buddhist scholar who has devoted his life to the recovery of Buddhist learning in the land of its origin; he is now helping in the rebuilding of Nalanda University, making it again a center of study for Buddhists from all over the world.

U Thittila, Lecturer in Buddhist Philosophy at the University of Rangoon, was the first choice of the Buddha Sasana Council of Burma to write the second chapter of this book. His able presentation of Theravada Buddhism grows out of years of experience in expounding the Path of the Buddha.

Balangoda Ananda Maitreya, the head of a well-known monastery in Ceylon, was recommended by Buddhists in Thailand and Burma as well as his own country as a man who can speak for all Theravada countries. He has traveled widely and writes from a background of years of practice and observation of Theravada Buddhism.

Professor Yamaguchi, who combines the presidency of Otani University with his research and teaching, was recommended again and again as one of the great masters of Mahayana thought; he has recently been honored by his colleagues and students with a commemorative volume as a mark of their respect for him as a scholar whose life is an expression of the ideals he studies.

In these times, when Americans are not permitted to travel freely in China, it was not possible to search there for a Buddhist scholar who would write about those beliefs and practices which are characteristically Chinese. Fortunately, there is in Japan a scholar who is recognized among Buddhists and non-Buddhists alike as one of the great students of Chinese Buddhism in our time, Professor Tsukamoto, President of the Institute of Humanistic Studies at the University of Kyoto and Director of Research in Religion. Out of his background of a lifetime of study, he has written the introduction to Chinese Buddhism which is included in this book.

Tibetan Buddhism is described for us by Lobsang Phuntsok Lhalungpa, an official of the Tibetan government who grew up in Lhasa and lives now in India, at Kalimpong, where he hopes to create a center for Tibetan studies. As he wrote this study of Tibetan Buddhism, he was aided by two scholarly lamas who share his concern for an accurate presentation of Tibetan Buddhism.

The general introduction to Buddhism in Japan was written by Professor Hanayama, the well-known teacher of Buddhism at the University of Tokyo. Because of the distinctive differences between the sects in Japan, we decided to have three of the sects described by members of those sects recommended to us by the leaders in each organization. For the Shin sect, the largest in Japan, we chose Professor Ishida, who teaches Shin thought in Ryukoku University, a Shin college. For Zen Buddhism we asked Professor Reiho Masunaga, who teaches Buddhist philosophy and Zen Buddhism at Komazawa University in Tokyo, to write for us. We chose a writer from Soto Zen because it is the largest Zen sect in Japan and Rinzai Zen has been widely introduced to the West through the writings of Dr. D. T. Suzuki. The Nichiren leaders recommended Professor Kubota, Professor of Sociology at Rissho University in Tokyo and a Nichiren priest who has, by writing, teaching, and example, done much to further the cause of Nichiren in Japan.

For the final chapter, Professor Nakamura, who teaches Indian Philosophy at the University of Tokyo, has undertaken the difficult task of pointing out the common elements and the points of divergence in Buddhism, both Theravada and Mahayana. He is uniquely qualified for this task by his studies in the history of Buddhism and the opportunities he has had to travel in Theravada countries.

For Hinduism, I brought together a collection of colored slides showing the chief pilgrimage places and practices of Hinduism; they have been reproduced by Professor Paul Vieth of the Divinity School of Yale University and are used in many universities throughout the country. A similar collection of slides illustrating contemporary Buddhism is available as a supplement to this book and may be rented or purchased from Professor Vieth.

How can anyone adequately acknowledge his indebtedness in preparing a cooperative volume of this type? I am indebted to the writers for their generous willingness to undertake this task in addition to their pressing duties, and for their cooperation in meeting the schedule required for the production of the book. I am indebted to the Edward W. Hazen Foundation for making the project possible and for the friendly encouragement of their president and trustees. The Fellows of the National Council on Religion in Higher Education have been helpful counselors at every stage of the project. Through their correspondence, conversations, and writings, innumerable Buddhist scholars, both Eastern and Western, have guided me in the preparation of this book.

I am also grateful to the Harvard University Press, the Pali Text Society, and Routledge & Kegan Paul Ltd. for permission to quote from their publications.

KENNETH W. MORGAN

Hamilton, New York

Contents

THE PATH

of

THE BUDDHA

CHAPTER ONE

Origin and Expansion of Buddhism

J. Kashyap

The coming, twenty-five hundred years ago, of Gotama
the Buddha was an epoch-making event in the history of Indian
civilization and culture. He was the first historical figure to
make a profound impression on the Indian mind, to challenge
the thought processes of all India. So great was his influence
that even though Buddhism no longer exists as an organized
religious institution in India his message and personality are
still a living reality in the life of India and will long continue
to be a source of strength. Indeed, it was the Buddha's role to
recast and revitalize for mankind a way of life which can be
applied universally, regardless of time or place or prevailing
culture.

The term *Buddha* means an Enlightened One. It is not a
proper name but an honorary title applied to one who has
reached the very peak of transcendental wisdom through the
practice of the ten great spiritual Perfections in numberless
births during an incomprehensible length of time. A Buddha
is not a person but is rather a personality evolved through the
accumulation of spiritual qualities. The cumulative forces of
virtues and perfections finally bring forth a Buddha, a super-
man, in the world. Although the Buddha is not a man in the
commonly accepted sense of the term, his humanity is so evident that he is and has been a true friend, philosopher, and
guide for mankind. He is a way-finder, a discoverer of the

3

Path of Deliverance which will free men from the ills of the continuing migration through endless series of rebirths.

There have been many Buddhas in the past and many more will follow in the future. As long as there are beings in need of emancipation from the bonds of this inexorable process of life and death, Buddhas will appear with their liberating Truth and will lead beings to deliverance, *Nibbana* (*Nirvana*).

Aeons in the past, when Gotama the Buddha in a previous existence was an ascetic called Sumedha, he met the Buddha of that age, Buddha Dipankara, and as he beheld the majestic personality of the Buddha a transcendental urge stirred him to seek to become a Buddha. His feelings about that exalted state are described in a verse from *The Story of Sumedha* which serves as an introduction to the Jataka tales, a collection of stories about the previous existence of Gotama the Buddha:

> There is, there must be, an escape;
> Impossible there should not be;
> I will make the search and seek the way,
> Which from suffering finds release.

> (Warren, *Buddhism in Translation*, p. 5.)

It was his all-embracing compassion that made Sumedha abandon his personal release from the suffering of worldly existence and sacrifice himself for the welfare and deliverance of all beings. His genuine humanity made him vow at the feet of Buddha Dipankara to become a supreme Buddha himself and solve the riddle of life for all beings, mundane and divine. That vow was a pledge to fulfill the ten Perfections required of a Bodhisattva, that is, one who aspires to become a Buddha. The ten Perfections (*Paramis*) are Liberality, Morality, Renunciation, Wisdom, Energy, Forbearance, Truthfulness, Resolution, Good Will, and Equanimity.

The career of one who aspires to become a Buddha is indeed a hard and painful one, and by the time the future Buddha brought to maturity these spiritual perfections an incalculable period of time had passed during which a numberless series of births were undergone, sometimes as a god, sometimes as a human being, sometimes as an animal. It is a long and arduous training that evolves the personality to holiness, a gradual progress that rises in stages to Buddhahood, to Omniscience.

Vasubandhu, a great Buddhist seer who wrote ten centuries after Gotama the Buddha (fifth century A.D.), gives in his *Abhidharmakosha* an interesting account of the attitude of a Buddha-aspirant, a Bodhisattva:

> But why do the Bodhisattvas, once they have taken the vow to obtain Supreme Enlightenment, take such a long time to obtain it?
>
> Because the Supreme Enlightenment is very difficult to obtain; one needs a vast accumulation of knowledge and merit, innumerable heroic deeds in the course of three immeasurable world cycles (kalpas).
>
> One could understand that the Bodhisattva seeks for the Enlightenment, which is so difficult to obtain, if the Enlightenment were his only means of arriving at deliverance. But this is not the case. Why then do they undertake such infinite labor?
>
> For the good of others, because they want to become capable of pulling others out of this great flood of suffering. But what personal benefit do they find in the benefit of others? The benefit of others is their own benefit, because they desire it.

Our future Buddha, after having fulfilled in countless births the ten Perfections, reached maturity and was born for the last time as Siddhattha Gotama, the son of King Suddhodana who was the ruler of the kingdom of the Sakyas with his capital at Kapilavastu (modern Padaria in southern Nepal). His father called him Siddhattha, "Wish-fulfilling," because he fulfilled the long cherished wish of the barren royal family and because at the time of his birth phenomenal blessings and prosperity had come to the Sakya kingdom.

Seven days after he was born in the beautiful garden of Lumbini near Kapilavastu, his mother, Queen Maha Maya, died leaving him under the care of her sister Maha Pajapati Gotami. As was the vogue in those days, on the sixth day after his birth Brahman astrological experts were called to forecast his future, and it is said they prophesied that the child was destined to become either a universal monarch or an omniscient Buddha. The experts predicted that if the child witnessed the four signs of ill—old age, sickness, death, or a recluse—he would renounce the life of royal pomp and exchange it for the life of a homeless monk.

The king was, of course, anxious that his son should follow in his footsteps and therefore decided that the upbringing of the prince should be in keeping with the highest tradition of regal abundance, pleasure, and magnificence, and that he should be sheltered from seeing any of the four ills of life. Thus as the young prince grew up in the affluent surroundings of the palace he was slowly initiated into the various branches of learning, and since he was exceptionally intelligent he soon mastered the different arts and sciences in the highest traditions of his time. In addition to an aptness for knowledge he also manifested qualities rare and noble. He was extremely tender and kindly toward all beings and also tended to become contemplative and was often serious-minded.

There is a touching account of how the prince in his boyhood saved a swan from his cruel cousin Devadatta who had shot it down. As the beautiful white bird fell fluttering at his feet when he was playing with a playmate in the palace garden, he lifted the frightened creature and tenderly pulled out the arrow and rubbed some healing herbs on the wound. The bird lost its fear and became quite tame. After a time when the prince was going to release the bird, Devadatta the would-be killer demanded it and was promptly refused. Then in the full hearing of the court there ensued a lively debate as to who should get the bird, the killer or the savior. His superior pleading, it is said, won the hearts of all. Thus, even at that tender age and in spite of the rigid surroundings of the palace, he clearly and surely manifested the mission that was his and for which through long aeons he had been preparing himself.

When Gotama was sixteen, his father, who feared that he might become dissatisfied with the world, gave him in marriage to a young maiden who was reputed to be the most beautiful in the land. And thus, amidst a world of pomp and luxury, he remained with only occasional moods of doubt until he witnessed the four great signs which aroused in him his dormant desire to retire from the world to seek the solution for the ills of life. He was twenty-nine when he saw a decayed and frail old man, a loathsome corpse, a sick person wallowing in his own filth, and a calm recluse surrounded by a halo. In his cloistered palace life he had been carefully shielded from these sights, and when he witnessed them for the first time his mature mind must have had a flash of vision into the terrible truth that decay, disease, and death are inherent in every life.

An insatiable longing to escape from that cage of regal pomposity and sumptuous living obsessed him. Just at that time a son was born to him and he called him Rahula, a bond, for he thought that the bondage of his life in the palace would soon grow too strong. On the full-moon night of the month of May, some twenty-five centuries ago, he made up his mind to retire from the world to seek for mankind the ultimate deliverance, and leaving his home secretly he exchanged his royal robes for those of a recluse.

He left the land of his native Sakyas and went over to the kingdom of Magadha, a country which extended along the Ganges valley, making his way to the capital city, Rajagaha (modern Rajgir, some sixty miles west of Patna). There, one day as he was going around for alms, King Bimbisara noticed his noble bearing and was so attracted to him that he begged him to give up the hard life of a recluse, even promising half of his kingdom and his daughter's hand if he would accept. But such offers did not appeal to the future Buddha who had sacrificed all worldly magnificence on the altar of renunciation for the sake of truth; he declined with the promise that when he attained Supreme Enlightenment he would return and preach the truth to the king. He wandered on from place to place in search of a teacher who could guide him to his goal—but none could satisfy him.

He then decided to struggle alone. For six years he gave himself to extreme penances and self-mortifications. He abandoned food until he became a mere skeleton without having achieved anything. One day he fell into a swoon and when he recovered he understood the futility of such extreme practices and decided to strike a middle course and began to eat. While he had been practicing extreme self-mortification five disciples had joined him, but when he gave up the mortifications they deserted him thinking that he had given up the holy life. Even so, he remained firm and unwavering in quest of the highest wisdom.

Then on the full-moon day of May when he was thirty-five years old, having eaten a bowl of nourishing milk porridge given him by the lady Sujata, and having received a few bundles of Kusa grass from the Brahman Sotthiya for a seat, he seated himself at the foot of the bodhi tree in Gaya. He had now reached the climax of his inner struggle. Having seated himself firmly, cross-legged, he made this solemn and historic resolution: "Let my skin, my sinews and bones dry up, likewise my flesh and blood, but until I have achieved the Supreme Enlightenment I will not leave this posture."

It is said that at this point Mara, the personification of evil, tried to dissuade the Bodhisattva and overpower him, but the strength of his perfections from previous births was so great that nothing, no evil power, could prevail. He strove diligently and by the end of the night achieved Omniscience and became a victorious Buddha. He found the sovereign remedy for all the ills of mankind.

With this triumph a new chapter in the history of man's spiritual endeavor opened. He now decided to make known this great truth which he had realized with so much difficulty. After spending about seven weeks at Gaya near the bodhi tree, he set forth toward Banaras where his five former disciples had been living. At the deer park in Banaras—modern Sarnath—he met these renegade monks who seemed indifferent and even disrespectful toward him. After admonishing them he now, for the first time, set in motion "the Wheel of Righteousness" (*Dhammacakka*) as he delivered his first Sermon.

"There are these two extremes," he said. "The one is excessive sensual indulgence and the other is self-mortification, which are vulgar, ignoble, and profitless. Avoiding both these the Perfect Ones teach the Doctrine of the Middle Path which leads to the comprehension of Higher Knowledge and Insight." Thereupon he expounded the Doctrine of the Middle Path comprising the Four Noble Truths and the Noble Eightfold Path. The monks accepted his teaching and by striving diligently each one soon attained the higher wisdom and became an Arahat—that is, a saint who has dispelled ignorance and all other fetters that bind a being to the circle of birth and death; after death he does not take a birth again, he is freed from this bondage.

While the Buddha was still at Banaras, Yasa, the son of a wealthy merchant, visited him with a mind troubled by excessive sexual desire. Buddha having consoled him then preached the Noble Doctrine. In a short while Yasa understood the import of the truth of the Middle Path and became a monk and before long was an Arahat. This was something spectacular and soon created a stir among the people of Banaras who flocked around this new, wonderful spiritual genius. The wealthy father of Yasa and his many wives became the first and principal lay followers of the Master. The conversion of Yasa also brought all his former companions, fifty-four young men of distinguished families, into the new brotherhood. They too became monks and by great efforts soon became Arahats.

Thus in a short while there was a brotherhood of sixty Holy Saints with the Buddha at the head. To them the Master then gave this charge: "Even as I am, monks, you too are freed from all worldly bonds. Go, monks, preach the Noble Doctrine for the good and welfare of the many; go not, two of you, in the same direction." And so saying, he himself set forth toward Gaya. On the way, he preached the Doctrine to thirty young men who had been enjoying a picnic with their women folk and they all decided to become monks. At Gaya he converted the thousand fire-worshiping, matted ascetics (*Jatilas*), by demonstrating his supernatural psychic powers, and accompanied by them he went on to Rajagaha to preach the Doctrine (*Dhamma*) to King Bimbisara as he had promised he would do when he was there before. Inspired by his profound teaching the king and a great multitude of distinguished citizens soon became his faithful disciples.

Near Rajagaha the Buddha accepted from the king a secluded grove and built there a monastery which became one of the most important centers of his activities during the forty-five years of his ministrations. As he wandered from place to place other such centers grew up, at Sravasti (modern Gond district), Kosambi (near modern Allahabad), Vesali (across the Ganges from Patna), and at Banaras. In the time of the Buddha these monasteries were the centers of great spiritual activities from which emanated the Light of the Dhamma to all northern India and even beyond, thus fulfilling the Master's great mission of bringing help and welfare to mankind.

Thus until the ripe old age of eighty years the Buddha taught his followers, and then for the last time he journeyed from Rajagaha to the scene of his final passing away at Kusinara (thirty miles east of modern Gorakhpur, near Kasia). Before leaving Rajagaha for the slow, three-month journey to Kusinara, the Buddha predicted that the time had come for him to enter Parinibbana (final or perfect Nibbana which comes after earthly existence ends). When he could walk no more and lay with his great assembly of monks around him, he retained full vigilance and encouraged them to lead a noble life. He passed away on the same day on which he was born, the same day on which he had attained Omniscience, the full-moon day of May. He was born under a tree in the park at Lumbini, attained Enlightenment under the tree at Gaya, and entered Parinibbana under the shady bough of a tree at Kusinara.

PERSONALITY OF THE BUDDHA

This brief life sketch does not give a full understanding of the towering personality who was the Buddha. Let us turn now to some of the events which illustrate the unruffled calm, the tolerance, the rational and realistic approach of the Great Teacher, the deeds of service, the practicality and ready wit of the Master.

Once the Buddha, accompanied by five hundred monks, left Rajagaha for Nalanda, and as night fell, they took shelter at a wayside grove where there was a spacious public rest house. When they were settled for the night they discovered that Suppiya, a wandering ascetic, and one of his disciples had taken refuge there and, unaware of the Buddha's presence, were engaged in an animated discussion about him. While the ascetic was heaping up false accusations and even slandering the Buddha, the disciple was not only defending him but was even praising him in glowing terms. Both the Buddha and the monks heard the exchange and without any comment passed the night.

Early the next morning as the monks sat in the grove discussing the strange incident of the previous night, the Buddha joined them and after listening to their remarks addressed them thus:

If anyone were to find fault or abuse me or the Doctrine or the Noble Order, do not, monks, for that matter, be offended, displeased, or ruffled. If you by any means become offended or perturbed it will be to your own harm. On the other hand, whenever people hurl abuse and criticize, you should pause and think whether what they say contains some truth or whether what they say is just slander and false. Likewise, monks, if someone were to praise and glorify me, the Doctrine, or the Noble Order, you should not for that matter feel particularly elated or pleased. If you do so it will be to your own harm. On the contrary, in such an event you should pause and examine the truth of the matter. You should find out whether what they say is actually to be found in us and whether they are correct. (Brahmajala Sutta, Digha Nikaya.)

This equanimity, this natural rising above both likes and dislikes, as well as his emphasis on searching for the truth, characterizes the Buddha's toleration toward all men based upon inner strength and firm conviction. For the inherently weak there can be no real toleration, there can be only servility and helplessness. It is only the strong who can possess the noble quality of equanimity, of tolerance toward all men.

There is also the story of Magandhiya, the beautiful Brahman maiden, considered to be the fairest in the land. This maiden, attracted by the noble features of the Buddha, wanted to marry him and when she failed in her design, bore a permanent grudge against him. The fame of her great beauty had spread widely and made her a coveted prize for many princes and soon King Udena of Kosambi married her and made her one of his queens. Having become a queen, she resolved to avenge herself on the Buddha and saw her opportunity when he came to visit Kosambi. With malicious intent she hired some rogues and rival sectarians and set them to vex and molest the Buddha whenever he came into the city. These miscreants followed the Master about the city shouting all kinds of abuse such as, "You are a thief, an idiot, an ass. You will go to hell, you have no chance of salvation," and so on. The Venerable Ananda, the Buddha's constant companion, was hurt when he saw the Teacher being molested publicly like that, so he spoke to the Buddha, "Sir, these citizens are reviling us openly. Let us go elsewhere!"

"Where shall we go?" the Buddha inquired, and the following discussion ensued.

"To some other city, Sir."

"If the people abuse us there, where shall we go?"

"To yet another city, Sir."

"If men revile us there also, then?"

"To still another city, Sir."

"No, Ananda, that is not the proper way. Where a difficulty arises, right there it should be resolved. Only when that is done should one move. Rather, Ananda, I am like a battle elephant whose duty it is to withstand the arrows that are shot from all directions. Even so it is my duty to endure with patience the vile words of wicked men. This will continue only for a week and then the people will know." (Dhammapada Atthakatha.)

As he had prophesied, it is said that the mischief automatically stopped after seven days and the evil design failed as the good people intervened. It is for such astounding calmness that the Buddha is likened to a solid rock which does not shake even when assailed by the heaviest gales.

Not only was he calm in the face of unjust accusations, but he was generous and tolerant toward others, as is shown by his attitude toward the new sect of Jains who, under their leader Mahavira, frequently attacked him. General Siha, from Vesali, which was east of Rajagaha across the Ganges river, was one of the chief supporters of the Jains. On two occasions, after hearing distinguished men praising and glorifying the qualities of the Buddha, he asked Mahavira for permission to visit the Buddha but each time he was forbidden to do so. Finally, however, when he heard the praise repeated he decided to meet the Buddha in spite of any prohibition and to find out for himself

the ground for the charge that the Buddha was the "bewitch-
ing one."

Accordingly Siha visited the Buddha and a lively discussion
followed. Siha quoted all the allegations against the Buddha
and frankly asked him to clarify his position if he thought the
charges were false. To his utter surprise, the Buddha without
any parrying tactics calmly took each accusation and with the
dexterity of a skilled surgeon rationally dissected and analyzed
each charge, gave each a splendid and completely new interpretation, thereby rendering the accusers powerless by making
use of their own words to his advantage for expounding his
Doctrine. Thus, although the Buddha taught the doctrine of
kamma (causality in moral relations), he was accused of being
a pessimistic and fatalistic believer in inaction. To this he replied:

Well, one would quite properly call me an "inactionist" in that I do
teach and train my disciples in a kind of inaction, that is to say, to remain inactive with regard to any misconduct of body, speech, and
mind, which is unwholesome, immoral, and harmful. Contrarily, I
might rightly be called a believer in action in that I do teach and
train my disciples in the performance of such right conduct in body,
speech, and mind as is wholesome, moral, and profitable.

Siha, then, repeated the other charges, such as teaching the
cult of annihilation and penances, austerities, and so on. In a
similar vein the Buddha replied to him saying that it would be
quite right to call him an annihilationist since he did teach the
annihilation of bodily, verbal, and mental misconduct and of
evil, immoral deeds. And that he did, he admitted, teach the
burning away of all evil things by some kind of disciplines.
Siha was undoubtedly moved and fascinated by his sobriety
and complete lack of malice, as well as by his tolerance toward
spiteful rivals. Forthwith he requested the Buddha to accept
him as one of his lay followers.

The Buddha did not accept him at first. He rather advised
him not to make a quick decision but to make further study
and investigation about him and his Doctrine before actually
becoming a follower. This, Siha said, made him more convinced than ever because, he said, "If the other sects were to

secure me as a disciple they would certainly have paraded a banner all around Vesali saying, 'Siha the General has joined the rank of our lay followers.'" After Siha had solemnly repeated thrice that, from that day onward, he would go for refuge only to the Buddha, his Teaching and his Noble Order of Monks, the Buddha admitted him to the lay fold—but on one condition that Siha should not refuse to continue to support the Jain monks with whom he had been associated. To this Siha consented, but he added, "Sir, formerly I was told that the Recluse Gotama teaches that alms and gifts offered to other sects conduce not to true merit but that anything that is offered to the Tathagata, the Perfect One, his Teaching and his Noble Order brings merit unsurpassing. But Sir, now I see quite the contrary."

The Buddha then expounded to him the Doctrine of transcendental wisdom after which he attained that clarity of spiritual vision which leads to the highest realization of Nibbana. (Mahavagga, Vinaya Pitaka.)

There is a similar incident in the case of Upali, the millionaire of Nalanda who was a great benefactor of the Jain sect of naked ascetics and a learned man in whom Mahavira, the leader of the Jains, had full confidence. Once one of Mahavira's trusted lieutenants visited the Buddha and discussed with him certain doctrinal matters and then reported to Mahavira the nature of his conversation with the Buddha. Mahavira, thinking that he had started a controversy with the rival he dreaded most, dispatched Upali as his most trusted exponent to convert the Buddha to his views. Upali, of course, felt a little inflated and with an air declared, "I will put such a question to the Recluse Gotama that he will neither be able to deny or affirm it—just as one with something stuck in the throat is neither able to swallow or vomit. Then I will catch him by the knot, as it were, and swing him around." Boasting thus, he went to the Buddha.

The Buddha, aware of the purpose of his mission, made him agree at the outset to the condition that the discussion should be for the sake of finding the truth and not for the sake of mere argument. On this premise, as the discussion progressed Upali made several contradictions. He maintained that a mental act was of lesser import than a physical act, and that therefore bodily mortification was justified to purify one's being. The Buddha then curtly put the question to this assertion, "Well, householder, even to undertake an action [i.e., bodily mortification] hasn't one to make a resolution or determination at first?"

"That is so, one has to make a resolution," was his reply.

"In that case, what is a resolution, is it not a mental act?"

"It is, Sir."

"Now be careful, householder, think what you have said! Now do you see that a mental act precedes and therefore is of greater import? Now what do you think of this, householder, say a naked ascetic of the Jains mortifies himself to death by refusing to drink cold water; now how does he do that? Is it not through a mental act of resolution that he mortifies himself to death by not drinking cold water where it was essential?"

"Yes, it is so, Sir."

"Now be careful, Upali, for you are contradicting your former assertions."

Thus the discussion proceeded on the same lines as in the case of Siha. Soon Upali found himself in the embarrassing position to which he had boasted that he would drive the Buddha. He was overwhelmed with the Buddha's exposition and he too became a lay follower of the Master. Buddha made the same conditions with him that he made with Siha, that he should continue to support the Jain monks. (Upali Sutta, Majjhima Nikaya.)

The experiences of Siha and Upali show clearly the extent of liberality, broadmindedness, and tolerance that must have been a part of that great personality. There are any number of such instances in the Canon.

The Buddha is not only calm and tolerant, he is also rational in his approach to problems, in his search for truth for its own sake. It was the custom of the Buddha, throughout the forty-five years of his long ministry, to roam all over the country preaching and teaching except for the four rainy months when he remained at one place. While on such a wandering mission he came to a place in the kingdom of Kosala where the intelligent Kalama peoples lived. When it became known that the Buddha had arrived, the Kalamas went in great numbers to greet him and then sat at his feet and the following discussion took place.

The Kalamas said, "Venerable Sir, many religious teachers come to our place from time to time and expound their respective doctrines in detail. All of them say that what they preach is the only truth and the others are wrong. Thus, while glorifying themselves and their doctrines they find fault and despise others. Now, Sir, we are at a loss. How are we to know which of these teachers speak the truth and which speak falsely?"

"Yes, Kalamas," said the Buddha, "it is quite natural to doubt where doubting is proper. Now come, do not accept a thing merely because it has been handed down by tradition or from generation to generation or from hearsay. Do not accept a thing because of mere scriptural sanction, nor by mere logic or inference, nor by superficial knowledge, nor yet because of your fondness for some theory, nor because it seems to be suitable, nor again just out of respect for a certain religious teacher. But, Kalamas, when you know for yourself that certain things are unprofitable, blameworthy, censured by the wise, and when performed or undertaken conduce to loss and suffering, then you should reject them.

"Now what do you think, Kalamas, when greed arises within a person, does it arise to his profit or to his loss?"

"To his loss, Sir."

"Well, by becoming greedy or being overcome by greed and thereby losing balance of mind, does he not indulge in killing, commit theft, go after another's wife, tell lies and not only that, mislead others into evil and immoral acts which lead to his own loss and misery for a long time?"

"Yes, he does, Sir."

"Likewise, when hatred or malice, delusion or ignorance or such other evil states arise do they not make people lose control of their minds and thereby lead them to perform all kinds of evil and immoral acts which end in loss and suffering?"

And when the Kalamas answered in the affirmative as above, the Buddha continued, "It is precisely for this reason, Kalamas, that I told you not to accept a thing merely because it happens to be traditional, and so on, and that you should reject a thing when you know for yourself that a thing is harmful and will bring misery to yourself and to others. On the other hand, when a person is not greedy, nor malicious, nor deluded—that is to say, is liberal, kindly, and wise—what do you think: will not these qualities be to his own profit and happiness?"

"They will, Sir."

"And by being liberal, kindly, and wise will they not become self-controlled and refrain from the immoral acts of killing, and so forth? And will that not be for their own and also for others' profit and happiness?"

"Yes, that is so, Sir." (Anguttara Nikaya, I. 188.)

Indeed, it was with such penetrating realism and rationality that the Buddha drove home the truth to the hearts of his hearers. The teaching of the Buddha was far from being just a religion of dogmas and faiths thriving primarily on rites and rituals. He certainly did not come to add one more theory on top of the already prevailing mass of views in his time. Nor did he subscribe to any sectarian rivalry such as seems to have been so common in those days. His approach was primarily rational, as can be seen from the discussion with the Kalamas; he cut a clear middle course between such existing wild practices as going naked in order to attain mental purity on the one hand and, on the other, the gross sensualism and ritualism developed through a religious hierarchy based on caste by birth. Amidst such religious chaos, his Doctrine of the Middle Way, which is a progressive course of moral, mental, and spiritual development, was indeed a great contrast.

Again, the common-sense realism of the Master is shown in the case of Malunkyaputta. Malunkyaputta, who had been a member of the Order of monks (*Sangha*) for some time, was addicted to all kinds of speculation. One day as he sat in meditation he began speculating on various futile questions such as whether the world is eternal or not, whether it is finite or infinite, whether or not the soul and body are identical, whether the Tathagata (the Perfect One, the Buddha) exists or not after death, and so forth. If, he thought, the Teacher does not elucidate these questions I shall leave his Order. Accordingly, he went to the Buddha and related all his speculations, saying, "If the Blessed One knows, let him elucidate my questions, and if he does not know, let him say so frankly."

"Pray, Malunkyaputta," said the Buddha, "did I ever ask you to lead a holy life under me with a promise to elucidate such questions, or did you ever make such an agreement before entering the Order?"

"No, Sir."

"Well, Malunkyaputta, anyone who demands the elucidation of such futile questions which do not in any way tend to real spiritual progress and edification is like one who has been shot by an arrow and refuses to let the doctor pull it out and attend to the wound. If the wounded man were to say, 'So long as I do not know who the man is who shot me, whether he belongs to the Brahman caste, or the Kshatriya or Vaisya or Sudra caste; and from what clan he hails; and whether he is tall, or medium height, or short; and whether he is fair, black, yellow, or dusky; and what kind of bow and arrow he used, and so on —until then I will not allow the arrow to be pulled out or the wound to be attended to'—that man, Malunkyaputta, will die without ever knowing all these details."

As a practical man he should, of course, get himself treated by the physician at once, without demanding those futile details which will not help him in the least. This was the attitude of the Buddha toward those dogmas and speculations which do not in any way help one toward a genuine spiritual progress. Life is short, and before anything can come from such speculations death will overtake each one of us; and the true purpose of life, that is, the attainment of spiritual perfection, will not be achieved. To stick to the essentials and to eschew non-essentials is the way of the wise.

A holy life, Malunkyaputta, [reiterated the Buddha] does not depend on the dogma that the world is eternal or not eternal and so forth. Whether or not these things obtain, there still remain the problems of birth, old age, death, sorrow, lamentation, misery, grief, and despair—all the grim facts of life—and for their extinction in the present life I am prescribing this Dhamma (Doctrine). Accordingly bear it in mind that these questions which I have not elucidated, such as the dogmas that the world is eternal or not eternal and so forth, I have not elucidated purposely because these profit not, nor have they anything to do with the fundamentals of holy life nor do they tend toward Supreme Wisdom, the Bliss of Nibbana. (Majjhima Nikaya, I. 166.)

Here again the note of rationality strikes right to the point, as it does on another occasion when the Buddha clearly stated that "whether the Buddhas arise or not, the truth remains unchanged."

The Buddhas are not redeemers, messiahs, saviors, incarnations, or avataras—primarily the Buddhas are teachers who have discovered a great truth which, out of great compassion toward all beings, they teach. The Teacher puts the responsibility on the student to learn and live by the lesson taught. "You yourselves must exert; for the Tathagatas [the Perfect Ones] but point out the Way." (Dhammapada 276.) "If you travel on this Path you will put an end to all suffering; this Path have I shown ever since I knew the arrow of suffering." (Dhammapada 275.)

The same teaching is repeated in the conversation with Ananda, shortly before the final passing away of the Master. The Venerable Ananda, the personal attendant of the Buddha, had been found weeping, and the Buddha, knowing of it, called him and after comforting him said, "Ananda, I have fulfilled all the duty of a real teacher. There is nothing that I have left esoteric. I do not have the closed fist of a so-called teacher. Lead the holy life, you will make an end of suffering. Be a light unto yourself, a refuge unto yourself; let the Dhamma be your only light, your only refuge, and naught else." (Mahaparinibbana Sutta, Digha Nikaya.)

In addition to teaching by elucidating the Dhamma, the Buddha taught by example. He was called a perfect Physician who cures all the ills of life with his healing balm of the Dhamma, whose great compassion, guided by wisdom, was revealed again and again in his lifetime. Once, on his round of inspection, he saw a monk very ill, unattended and covered with his own filth, utterly abandoned by his fellow monks because of the unpleasant nature of his illness. He himself attended the monk, washing and nursing him until he was well. Later he called the monks together and taught them, "He who attends the sick, attends me." (Mahavagga.)

The personality of the Buddha is revealed many times by the way in which even under very difficult circumstances he remained utterly unruffled, tranquil, sober, and firm as a rock—and continued to teach with clear insight and cool wit.

The ritualistic Brahmans, the highest caste of the Hindu community, had always been unfavorable toward him. Once the wife of an important Rajagaha Brahman became a firm and devoted follower of the Buddha, and she used to praise, quite openly, the high qualities of the Master. One day, while serving her husband, she gave vent to an inspired utterance, "Glory to the Blessed One, the Noble Teaching and the Noble Order" and repeated that phrase three times. This made the Brahman wild with anger and he shouted at her, "There now! At any and every opportunity must the wretch be speaking the praises of the snivelling monk? Now, wretch, I will give that teacher of yours a piece of my mind!" Thereupon, completely vexed and upset, he went to the Buddha and without ado flung at him the question, "What must we slay if we would live happily?"

The Buddha replied, "Wrath must you slay, if you would live happily."

The truth hit him at once, and his mind became sober. After hearing the Dhamma at some length, he decided to renounce worldly life and so became a monk, and soon attained Arahatship.

When it became known that the Brahman had been ordained by the Buddha, his brother became furious with rage, went straightway to the Buddha, and as soon as he reached his presence he started showering torrents of abuse on the Master in filthy terms. When he had let off his heat and become exhausted with his reviling, the Buddha, unmoved and serene, asked him, "Now Bharadwaja, do you receive visits from your friends and colleagues, relatives and guests?"

"Yes, sometimes I do," said the reviler.

"Well, do you not prepare for them food and a place for rest?"

"Yes, sometimes I do."

"But if they do not accept your hospitality, then whose do these things become?"

"Well, if they do not accept, Venerable Gotama, those things are for us."

"So, then, Bharadwaja, all that wherewith you revile, scold, and abuse us, we do not accept—like the visitor who does not dine with you."

Bharadwaja was highly impressed. Thereupon the Buddha preached to him on the dangers of anger and on the benefits which accrue from the absence of anger. Moved by the teaching, he requested the Master to admit him to the Order and soon attained the highest Wisdom. (Samyutta Nikaya.)

There is yet another remarkable aspect of the Buddha's personality which shows itself in his teaching when he uses some homely illustrations spiced with ready wit in solving the problems of his followers. His method is simple and practical; yet the dramatic effect of his teaching is strikingly effective. Once the Buddha visited the house of one of his wealthiest lay followers, on his routine alms round. The proud and obstinate daughter-in-law of the merchant was wrangling and making a lot of noise when she was told to go and pay respect to the Teacher as is the custom in India. The Buddha asked the merchant, "Why are the people screaming in this house? One would think fishermen had been robbed of their fish."

The merchant poured out his grief as to the undesirable conduct of the young lady, saying that she did not care to listen to anybody in the house.

"Very well, come here, Sujata," the Teacher called to the young lady.

Saying, "Yes, Sir," she immediately appeared in front of the Buddha.

The Buddha then, with typical wit, asked her, "Now, Sujata, there are seven types of wives a man may have. Which seven? One resembles a murderess, another a robber, another a mistress, another a mother, another a sister, another a friend, and another a servant. Which of these seven do you think you resemble?" The effect of this witty question was almost spontaneous. Sujata became modest forever. (Nidanakatha Jataka.)

Then there is the story of Sona the young, overenthusiastic monk who through excessive exertion paced up and down meditating until his feet bled without attaining the desired concentration of mind. Having failed in his attempts, he became disheartened and was thinking of leaving the Order. Through his supernatural psychic powers the Buddha became aware of what was passing through Sona's mind. He went where Sona was meditating and told him about the thoughts which had been passing through his mind, and said:

"Now, Sona, were you not a clever musician and skilled lute player formerly, when you were a layman?"

"Yes, Sir."

"Now what do you think, when the strings of your lute become too tight, could you get the right tune, or was it then fit to play?"

"No indeed, Sir."

"Likewise, when the lute strings become too slack, could you get the right tune or was it then fit to play?"

"No indeed, Sir."

"But when the lute strings were neither too tight nor too slack but were keyed to an even pitch then did it give the right tune?"

"Yes indeed, Sir."

"Even so, Sona, too much zeal conduces to restlessness and too much slackness conduces to mental sloth." So saying, the Master admonished the young monk to strike a balance between these two extremes and develop an even tempo of spiritual equilibrium. (Mahavagga Vinaya Pitaka.)

The canonical literature abounds in similar remarkable anecdotes illustrating the personality of the Master, but one more will have to suffice here, the story of Kisa Gotami. Kisa Gotami lost her only child and became almost mad with grief, not allowing anyone to take away her dead child in the hope that it might revive again through some miracle. She wandered everywhere and at last came into the presence of the Buddha. Buddha understood the deep sorrow that so blinded the poor mother, so after giving her comfort he told her that he could revive the child if she could procure a handful of mustard seeds from the house of one where no death had ever taken place. Hope came to her and she set forth from house to house asking for a handful of mustard seeds. She did receive, everywhere, the seeds with profuse sympathy. But when it came to asking whether there had been any death in the family, everybody universally lamented the loss of a mother or a father or a son or daughter, and so on. She spent hours traveling in search of the precious seeds that promised the revival of her son, but alas, none could give them to her.

A vision arose before her and she understood the implication of the Buddha's hint. She understood that death is inherent in life which is the source of all suffering, all delusion. To overcome life and death is to attain the highest security and freedom from suffering, which is the true significance of the holy life. With the dawn of this insight she felt a great relief, whereupon after having performed the last rites for her child, she went to the Buddha and asked for admission into his Order of Nuns. She was admitted and soon she attained the fruit of the holy life, the Highest Wisdom. (Dhammapada Commentary.)

The Doctrine

Siddhatta Gotama saw the four signs of suffering—old age, disease, death, and a mendicant—and renounced his position as a prince in the Sakya kingdom. For years he sought the answer to suffering through practicing austerities, but without success; and then he turned to the Middle Path, regained his strength, plunged into deep meditation at the foot of the sacred bodhi tree of Buddhagaya, and obtained the Supreme Enlightenment.

Then, at the foot of the bodhi tree, the Blessed One sat cross-legged on one seat for seven days without interruption, experiencing the bliss of emancipation. During the first watch of the night he reflected on the Chain of Dependent Origination (*Paticcasamuppada*), the heart of the Doctrine which he taught.

The cycle of rebirths, in which all existent beings are caught, is governed by the law of kamma. All of a man's good and bad acts leave behind their impressions in his mind; the accumulation of these impressions develops the tendencies and temperament of his personality. This process continues for the whole span of his life. At the moment of his death he falls into a sort of swoon in which this whole process of personality formation is summed up. At his death the process of his consciousness flows on into another life on a plane corresponding to the level of mental development in his past life.

Thus, for instance, the man whose actions have been bestial and irrational will get animal tendencies and temperament and will be reborn as an animal. There is no gap between the moment of death in one life and the moment of birth in the next; the two births are in the same process of life, often explained by the simile of the advancing flame of fire, ever consuming and ever renewing. With the arising of the first moment of consciousness in the womb of the mother there also arises the first seed of his physical existence which goes on developing with the nutriment received from different sources, developing the different organs of sense. The child is born, and as he grows he engages in all sorts of activities, good and bad. Thus, the cycle of life goes on and on from one birth to another, experiencing old age, decay, death, and misery.

The Doctrine (Dhamma) taught by the Buddha is based on a conception of all existence as impermanent and substanceless. Whatever exists is in a state of constant flux, through and through, like the flame of the lamp. All existence is a process which continues without a break, constantly renewing itself. The hardest stone is even of the same fleeting nature. It is due to our ignorance, rooted in attachment, that things are thought to have identity.

The logical corollary that follows from the principle of the impermanence, the dynamic nature of all existence, is that all existence must be substanceless. By substanceless is meant that there is no substratum, no identical factor which serves as the basis of the qualities, and there is no individual whole that exists apart from the sum of its parts. A thing is a mere conglomeration of parts, regardless of how minutely it is viewed.

From the conventional point of view, things in the world do exist as permanent substance, as lasting entities for the possession of which we all strive and to which we keep clinging. But to the seer, the man of wisdom, they are fleeting phenomena having no stability in them. Thus, there are two grades of reality: conventional and metaphysical. It is only from the point of view of conventional truth that entities are cognized as a substance or a unity; but seen from the point of view of metaphysical truth, free of attachment rooted in ignorance, all things are impermanent and substanceless.

Because all things are impermanent and substanceless, they cannot be a solace to us. Men, out of ignorance and attachment, try to cling to them, but they fall into despair and disappointment as all things glide away. When, however, a man obtains an insight into the true nature of all existence—that it is impermanent (*anicca*), substanceless (*anatta*), and is ultimately suffering (*dukkha*)—an insight which is possible only in the mystic state called *samadhi*, his ignorance (*avijja*) is dispelled and his attachment, or desire (*tanha*), is uprooted. He becomes free from all passions and then his actions no more accumulate the potentiality of kamma that causes birth after death. He becomes a saint, an Arahat, who is free from all bondage of the cycle of birth and death.

This is called the principle of dependent origination, which is formulated in this manner:

Depending on ignorance, there arise kamma-formations;

Depending on kamma-formations, there arises the moment of consciousness that links one birth with another;

Depending on that moment of consciousness, there arises psycho-physical (mind-body) existence;

Depending on psycho-physical existence, there arise the six organs of sense;

Depending on the six organs of sense, there arises contact;

Depending on contact, there arise feelings;

Depending on feelings, there arises desire;

Depending on desire, there arises grasping;

Depending on grasping, there arises the process of life;

Depending on the process of life, there arises birth;

Depending on birth, there arise old age, death, sorrow, lamentation, pain, grief, and despair.

When the same chain of dependent origination is stated in the following manner, the path to freedom from bondage to the cycle of birth and death is clearly seen:

With the complete and final cessation of ignorance, the kamma-formations do not arise;

With the cessation of the kamma-formations, the moment of re-birth-consciousness does not arise;

With the cessation of rebirth-consciousness, the psycho-physi-cal existence does not arise;

With the cessation of the psycho-physical existence, the six organs of sense do not arise;

With the cessation of the six organs of sense, contact does not arise;

With the cessation of contact, feelings do not arise;

With the cessation of feelings, desire does not arise;

With the cessation of desire, grasping does not arise;

With the cessation of grasping, the life process does not arise;

With the cessation of life process, birth does not arise;

With the cessation of birth, old age, death, sorrow, lamentation, pain, grief, and despair do not arise. Thus, the entire mass of suffering ceases.

Thus it is clear that an understanding of the chain of dependent origination is central to the Enlightenment of the Buddha.

The first thought of the Buddha after the Enlightenment was, "To whom must I preach the Doctrine that is so deep and profound?" It occurred to him that the five ascetics who had waited upon him while he practiced austerities were deserving persons to receive the teachings, so he set out for Sarnath, the deer park near Banaras, where they were living. The five ascetics saw the Buddha coming and, remembering that he had given up austerities, they resolved, "Look, the ascetic Gotama is coming; let us not rise from our seats when he comes; rather, we shall only leave a seat for him." But, as the Buddha approached they could not keep their resolve, and they stood up, greeted him, washed his feet, and honored him. They gave him the seat of honor and sat in a circle to receive his instructions.

The Buddha said:

Monks, these two extremes should be avoided by one who has gone out from home to the homeless life. What two? The giving up to the pleasures of sense, which is low, vulgar, worldly, unworthy, and harmful; and the giving up to self-mortification which is painful, unworthy, and harmful. Monks, by avoiding these two extremes the Tathagata has found that Middle Path which gives vision, which gives knowledge, which tends to peace, higher wisdom, enlightenment, and Nibbana.

Now this, monks, is the Noble Truth of Suffering: birth is suffering, decay is suffering, disease is suffering, death is suffering; to be conjoined with things which one dislikes is suffering; to be separated from things which one likes is suffering; not to get what one wants, that also is suffering. In short, these five aggregates which are the objects of grasping are suffering.

Now this, monks, is the Noble Truth of the Origin of Suffering: it is this craving that leads back to birth, along with the lure and the lust that finds pleasure now here, now there, namely, the craving for sensual pleasure, the craving to exist, the craving for annihilation.

Now this, monks, is the Noble Truth of the Cessation of Suffering: verily it is the utter passionless cessation, the giving up, the forsaking, the release from, the detachment from this craving.

Now this, monks, is the Noble Truth of the Path Leading to the Cessation of Suffering: verily it is this Noble Eightfold Path, namely, right view, right-mindedness, right speech, right action, right livelihood, right effort, right mindfulness, and right concentration. This, monks, is that Middle Path which is found out by the Tathagata, which gives vision, which gives knowledge, which tends to peace, higher wisdom, enlightenment, and Nibbana.

When, monks, my knowledge and insight of these Four Noble Truths, under their three aspects and twelve modes, in their essential nature, was quite clear to me, then only, monks, did I proclaim, in this world that I had gained the incomparable Supreme Enlightenment; and there arose in me knowledge and insight. Sure is my heart's release. This is my last birth. There is no more becoming for me.

Thus spake the Blessed One; and the company of five monks was glad and rejoiced at the words of the Blessed One. When this discourse was being expounded there arose in the Venerable Monk Kondanna the pure and stainless Eye of Truth: "Whatsoever is of an originating nature is subjected to cessation."

When the foundation of the Kingdom of Righteousness had been thus established by the Blessed One, the devas (deities) of the earth raised the cry: "Near Banaras at Isipatana, in the deer park, has been established by the Blessed One the unsurpassed Kingdom of Righteousness which has not been established before either by an ascetic, a Brahman, a deva, a mara [demon], Brahma, or by anyone whatsoever in the world." (Samyutta v. 420.)

The sermon in the deer park which the Buddha preached to the five monks is known as the Discourse of the Setting in Motion of the Wheel of Righteousness.

The Middle Path

The Noble Eightfold Path, the Buddha said, is the Middle Path which leads to the complete and final cessation of evils, to the attainment of the Sublime, to Nibbana. The first two steps are called the Higher Wisdom—right understanding and right-mindedness. The next three steps are known as Ethical Discipline—right speech, right action, right livelihood. And the final three steps are known as Mental Discipline—right efforts, right mindfulness, and right concentration.

The Higher Wisdom begins with right understanding, which consists of a clear comprehension of the principles of Buddhism, usually included under three heads: (1) understanding of the impermanence, substancelessness, and suffering of existence; (2) understanding of the Four Noble Truths; (3) understanding of kamma and the chain of dependent origination. A clear understanding of these basic principles will keep before the eye of the disciple the ideals he is aspiring to realize.

The second step in the Higher Wisdom is right-mindedness, which is an act of will, a firm determination to renounce all the things that stand as obstacles to the realization of one's ideals. It is the recognition that it is not possible for one leading the household life to fulfill the pure life of holiness and that it is necessary to renounce worldly life and become a member of the Order. That renunciation is right-mindedness.

The Ethical Disciplines, comprising the next three steps in the Eightfold Path, are based on the Buddha's teaching that one who has taken up the life of holiness must avoid both the extreme of "Eat, drink, and be merry" and the ascetic extreme of indulging in self-torture. As a prince, he had had all the mundane pleasures at his disposal, and as an ascetic he had practiced extreme penances—he had seen that neither of these could give him the peace he sought. Rather, one must follow the Middle Path of self-discipline and self-conquest. The three forms of ethical discipline are: (1) Right speech, which consists in refraining from falsehood, from back-biting, from harsh speech, and from idle gossip; (2) Right action, which consists in refraining from taking life, from taking a thing that is not given, and from sexual misconduct (all defined clearly in the Vinaya Pitaka, the rules of the Order); (3) Right livelihood, which consists in refraining from all sorts of ignoble occupations, such as trading in arms, in living beings, in flesh, in intoxicants, and in poisons. These are not merely guides to good conduct, but are rules which, if violated, will give rise to complications in man's psychic life making it difficult to attain that concentration of mind which is necessary if the true wisdom is to dawn. The Buddha said, "The practice of Ethical Disciplines is conducive to the attainment of Mental Discipline, and the practice of Mental Discipline is conducive to the attainment of the Higher Wisdom."

Mental Disciplines, the last three steps in the Eightfold Path —right efforts, right mindfulness, and right concentration— must be based on pure conduct, the Buddha taught. Right efforts are four in number—the effort to prevent the arising of evil thoughts that have not arisen, the effort to eliminate evil thoughts that have already arisen, the effort to cultivate good thoughts that have not arisen as yet, and the effort to conserve the good thoughts that have already arisen.

Right mindfulness, the seventh step, is based on a constant awareness which the disciple is taught to develop within himself, an unfailing vigilance over the states of his own personality. This constant awareness has been compared to the vigilance of a doorkeeper who does not fail to notice anyone who comes in or goes out. The Maha Satipatthana Sutta of the Digha Nikaya describes in full how this mindfulness must be developed and perfected. The four steps in right mindfulness, in developing this constant awareness, are reflection on the states of the body, on the states of feeling, on the states of mind, and on the states of things.

In reflecting on the states of the body the practitioner is taught to start with focusing his attention on his own respiration. He is not required to exert, even in the least, any effort to make his breath long or short but has simply to watch it as it goes in and comes out. This practice, when followed peacefully for some time, makes his mind serene and he feels very light. It is prescribed for those who are of distracted mind and weak memory. The practitioner also is taught to be aware of the movements of his own body, to be ever aware of the slightest movement of his limbs or of all his body. When he walks, stands, sits, sleeps, eats, drinks, or does anything, he learns to be constantly aware of it. Such watchfulness should become so ingrained in him that it becomes second nature to him. This is beneficial in everyday life, but it is absolutely necessary for the practice of the higher stages of mental discipline.

The disciple must also learn to be constantly aware of his feelings, whether pleasant, painful or neutral, as they arise and pass away. People are often carried away by a pleasurable feeling and disturbed by a painful one. The practice of constant awareness keeps one aware of the coming of such feelings and enables the disciple to maintain his equilibrium of mind.

The practitioner must also be constantly aware of the states of his mind, the love, hatred, joy, depression, hope, fear, and all such states which arise and exercise a dominating influence on men and make them forget themselves. Any such distraction is a hinderance to mental discipline and can be overcome by the practice of constant awareness. One who has developed constant awareness, for instance, is fully aware when anger arises in him, and thus is not led away by it but overcomes it like a charioteer who reins back his steeds when they become restive and try to run away. The power of an emotion over us decreases as our mindfulness increases. In addition, awareness of the states of mind makes it possible to control the mind when sitting in meditation, for the mind often tends to be more restless than a monkey.

The fourth stage in right mindfulness is reflection on the states of things. This requires the practitioner to be constantly aware of the nature of the Four Noble Truths, of the nature of the six spheres of sense and of the five aggregates of which all things are compounded. It means, in short, the practice of constant awareness of the Truth taught by the Buddha about man and the universe, for this kind of awareness is necessary to keep the disciple from being misled by wrong views.

The final step in the Eightfold Path is right concentration. With the mental discipline achieved by the practice of right efforts and right mindfulness the practitioner sets himself to the attainment of a state which transcends the normal discursive understanding, he seeks to reach a mystic state of mind known as samadhi. We have already seen that it is our desire (tanha) which is the root of all evils. It is due to desire that a man accumulates *kamma* and is born and reborn again and again and has to undergo all sorts of suffering. How can this desire be annihilated? This can be done, says Buddhism, only by realizing that all existence is impermanent, substanceless, and suffering.

By studying religious books, or even by independent thought, one can understand, without any doubts, that everything is transitory, substanceless, full of misery, and not worth pursuing. But this understanding alone is not sufficient to give us deliverance from the bondage of desire. A great scholar or a wise philosopher is quite liable to fall victim to the temptations of desire. This is so because although he has correct understanding, he does not have the "realization" of it. This realization dawns upon the practitioner in his samadhi in which he gets an immediate intuition of the truth.

The Buddha has taught how to attain samadhi. First, the practitioner must overcome the distracting factors that stand in the way of attaining the concentration necessary for samadhi. These distracting factors are sensual passion, ill will, sloth and torpor, distraction and worry, and perplexity. Under their influence it is not possible to concentrate upon anything. In order to overcome them and attain samadhi one has to undergo a long and strenuous training. Buddhism teaches fully how to do it. Then, when samadhi is realized, the practitioner is able to perform many miracles, but these miraculous powers, which come automatically with the perfection of concentration, have little spiritual significance for the attainment of Nibbana. Buddhism teaches the practitioner not to be allured by them but to strive on for the attainment of the passionless state of mind in which he is free from the bondage of all types of desire and thus attains Nibbana.

The disciple who has followed the Noble Eightfold Path, who has learned the Higher Wisdom and has followed the Ethical and Mental Disciplines, is able to destroy the fetters that keep man in bondage, to attain Nibbana. Of the Arahat thus freed, the Buddha says:

> The old is withered out, the new becomes not;
> The mind desireth now no future birth.
> Whoso have utterly destroyed the seeds
>   Of all existence, whose desires are quenched,
> Extinguished are those wise ones as this lamp.
>
> (Ratana Sutta, Sutta Nipata)

THE SANGHA

The Order of monks established by the Buddha is commonly called the Sangha. It is made up of the disciples of the

Buddha who tread their Master's path of the homeless life in order to achieve, here in this life, the deathless state of Nibbana. Thus, the Sangha forms the living example to laity who may not be able to reach that highest goal in one life due to their worldly preoccupations.

The Sangha was established when the first disciples were ordained after the Master had delivered his first sermon setting in motion the wheel of righteousness at the deer park near Banaras. Soon after, as we have seen, Yasa and his fifty-three close friends became monks and with vigilance attained the highest fruit of the holy life. These, with the Buddha at the head, formed the first sixty holy Arahats in the world. Then the thirty young men whom he met on the road to Gaya joined the order, followed by the thousand fire-worshiping Jatilas at Gaya. At Rajagaha, King Bimbisara and a very large following became lay supporters of the Sangha, and there the Buddha received into the Order his two chief disciples, Sariputta and Moggallana and their two hundred and fifty followers. So rapidly did the fame of the Buddha spread and so great was the number of men who joined the Sangha, that soon people began to ask each other whose turn it would be next to be ordained by the Buddha. Sectarian rivals among the Jains and Hindus spread the rumor that the Buddha sought to make womankind barren by bringing their husbands under his spell so that they would renounce the life of a householder.

On one of his wandering tours the Buddha visited his former home and preached to his royal father and other relatives of the Sakya clan. Many outstanding Sakyans became important members of the Sangha, such as the Buddha's son, Rahula; Ananda, called the storekeeper of the Dhamma because of his ability to memorize the entire teaching of the Master; Upali, a former barber of the Sakyan nobles who became the chief exponent of the rules of monastic discipline; and Nanda and Anuruddha and others who were proficient in some particular aspect of the Teaching. Other outstanding figures in the Sangha who played key roles in this great spiritual movement were such men as the Venerable Sariputta, who was second only to the Master and was called by him the Captain of the Dhamma; the Venerable Maha Moggallana, famous for his supernatural psychic powers and next to the Buddha in that sphere; Maha Kassapa, noted for his asceticism; Maha Kaccana, famous for his analytical knowledge. Infamous among that group of early followers was Devadatta, of the Sakya clan, who left the Sangha and sought to oppose it.

Wherever the Buddha went he attracted large gatherings of hearers, and among his many very faithful lay and monastic devotees were great kings, nobles, powerful Brahmans, and former religious teachers. Within the forty-five years of the Teacher's ministrations, yellow-robed, clean-shaven monks of the Sangha wandered untiringly on foot preaching the Doctrine of Deliverance throughout the length and breadth of northern India.

At first, the ordination was done by the Master himself with the exhortation, "Come, monks, well taught in the Doctrine. Live the holy life for the utter destruction of suffering." After that they took the simple pledge, "I take refuge in the Buddha, I take refuge in the Dhamma, I take refuge in the Sangha." There was no caste or class barrier and no special privilege within the Sangha, a daring innovation at a time when the evil of untouchability and caste were the very core of Indian social life. But as the numbers swelled and people from all levels of society entered the Order, complications and slackness arose, and a code of moral discipline had to be promulgated for the guidance of the growing Sangha. Some among the monks had not attained sufficient maturity and were not restrained enough. People who admired the calm and restrained deportment of the Buddha and his Arahat disciples were displeased to see some of the monks lacking in proper conduct and complained to the Master. To safeguard the Sangha, the Buddha set up regulations governing the ordination, probation, and proper training of novices, and placed the task of monastic management in the hands of the monks themselves.

A body of able monks formed a chapter and took responsibility for ordination, probation, censuring, looking into disputes, management of monasteries, and all the business of the Sangha. The Buddha required the monks to have preceptors who would be responsible for their moral, mental, and spiritual training. Each community of monks had to elect by common consent an able, wise, and noble Elder (*Thera*) to be their preceptor. This arrangement was based on the principle of mutual responsibility, for while the pupils had their duties toward their preceptors, the preceptors also had their duties toward the novices. And all of them had a common responsibility toward the Supreme Teacher, the Buddha, for maintaining the high standard of purity expected of them. Within the lifetime of the Buddha, the rules governing the Sangha—not only for the individual but also for the community as a whole —had been so framed and the conduct so perfectly outlined, that there was no need to have a supreme chief, or so to say, a Buddhist Pope, after the passing away of the Master.

At a later date, the Buddha enjoined the observance on each new-moon and full-moon day of the fortnightly confessions called *Uposatha*, at which the code of moral conduct (*Patimokkha*) is recited. This ceremony impressed upon the monks their obligations and responsibilities and kept their moral and mental solidarity unimpaired. Also required was the observance of the period of retirement during the four months of the rainy season when the monks had to keep themselves confined to one place and devote the whole time to the pursuit of Higher Wisdom. At the conclusion of this period of intensive spiritual training the members of the Sangha assembled in the chapter house and invited censure for any act of omission or commission. These gatherings, together with the regular fortnightly confessions, had a great psychological effect and created a sense of unity and brotherhood within the Sangha. Even to this day this noble spirit continues without a break among the Buddhist monks in the various Buddhist countries.

During the Master's lifetime a similar Order was established for nuns with all the same rules and such additional ones as were required for women.

Historically, the Buddhist Sangha is the earliest monastic institution governed by perfect democratic principles which continues to the present day. When a great part of humanity was still groping in the darkness of ignorance, the Master

Architect built up a magnificent organization of spiritual experts which has never been equaled.

THE COUNCILS

After the Master entered Nibbana, a lax old monk named Subhadda said, "Now that the Great Recluse has passed away, let us live as we please and not be bound by multiple precepts." Maha Kassapa, who was head of the Sangha, since the two chief disciples—Sariputta and Moggallana—had already preceded the Buddha into Nibbana, decided that a Great Council should be called at Rajagaha to decide upon the authoritative teachings of the Buddha. Under the patronage of the ruler of the Magadhan empire, five hundred leading Arahats met at the Sattapanni cave near Rajagaha to preserve for all time the noble Dhamma by reciting and compiling the teachings systematically.

Thus, with the formation of the words of the Buddha at this First Great Council, a faithful version of the entire Teaching was enshrined in the canon called the *Tipitaka* (*Tripitaka* in Sanskrit). Those who followed this true version became the custodians of the Doctrine. As the Buddha had enjoined, just before his final passing away, "Let the Dhamma be your only guide, your only refuge," the Sangha thereafter was guided entirely by the principles of Dhamma and rules of conduct rather than by any single person. The entire Tipitaka was transmitted by memory until the time of the Fourth Great Council.

The Second Great Council was held one hundred years after the Buddha, at Vesali. Several lax monks who lived there tried to abrogate some of the rules and to incorporate new heretical practices which went against the spirit of the Dhamma and the holy life. In order to uphold the pure Dhamma, the elders of the Order, some of whom were direct Disciples who had been living in the time of the Buddha, challenged the lax monks to an open debate and when these schismatics had been completely defeated, the Second Great Council was convened under the patronage of King Kalasoka, and the canon was recited by seven hundred Arahats who were the wisest in the entire Sangha.

The Third Great Council was held in the third century after the Buddha, during the reign of Emperor Asoka. The Emperor had become a Buddhist and was doing everything in his power to aid Buddhism throughout his empire. This royal patronage had attracted many thousands of heretical followers of other sects who joined the Sangha as a means of gaining a living, but who preached their own fanciful theories and thereby brought confusion to the minds of the faithful followers of the Buddha. To put an end to such malicious misrepresentations, the Emperor Asoka convened the Third Great Council and purified the Sangha of all masquerading heretics. At this council, which was held at Pataliputra (*Patna*), a thousand Arahats recited the entire canon during a period of nine months, the Sangha was purified, and plans were laid for sending missionaries throughout the empire and to other lands.

Emperor Asoka, who ruled the Kingdom of Magadha from Kashmir to the Ganges valley and south almost to Madras during forty years of the third century B.C., was one of the most influential figures in the history of Buddhism. He was a devout Buddhist who supported the Sangha and sought to extend the Dhamma, the Way of Righteousness, throughout his empire; even today we have several of the rock edicts and pillars on which he inscribed the messages encouraging his people to follow the way of the Buddha. On the advice of the Venerable Moggaliputta Tissa who headed the Third Great Council, he sent Messengers of the Dhamma to the various foreign countries known at that time. The Truth, he felt, should not be confined to his own domain but should be known by everyone all over the world.

With the convening of the Third Great Council and the sending of missionaries abroad, Asoka undoubtedly kept Buddhism from perishing from the face of the earth, for after some centuries when Buddhism was lost from the land of its birth —through the actions of the Islamic vandals whose fanatical zeal made it a point to destroy all magnificent monasteries and burn the innocent monks alive—it was these foreign countries such as Ceylon, Burma, and Thailand, which had received the Dhamma from Asoka's noble missionaries, which ardently preserved the teachings of the Buddha.

The Fourth Great Council, according to the reckoning of the Theravada Sangha—the Southern Buddhism which followed the pure Dhamma as found in the Pali Tipitaka—was held in Ceylon early in the sixth century after the Buddha (around 25 B.C.), when the Tipitaka, which had been transmitted in the Pali language by memory from the time of the Buddha, was committed to writing for the first time. "Then," says the Mahavamsa, the Great Chronicle of Ceylon, "the most wise Bhikkhus [monks] who had passed down the Tipitaka and the commentaries thereon orally in former times, since they saw that the people were less righteous, assembled and, in order that the true Doctrine may endure, wrote them down in books."

The Tipitaka is the canon of the Three Baskets which include the Baskets (*Pitaka*) of Vinaya, Sutta, and Abhidhamma. The Vinaya Pitaka deals with the monastic rules and moral disciplines and consists of five books. The Sutta Pitaka contains all the discourses, or popular teachings, of the Buddha and is divided into five Nikayas, or sections. The Abhidhamma Pitaka deals with the higher philosophy of the Buddha.

The Fifth Great Council was held in Mandalay, Burma, early in the twenty-fifth century after the Buddha (A.D. 1871) with the support of King Mindon. At that time the Pali text of the canon was inscribed on 729 marble slabs placed at the foot of Mandalay Hill.

The Sixth Great Buddhist Council was held in Rangoon, beginning with the full-moon day of May, 2,498 years after the passing away of the Buddha and ending on the twenty-five hundredth anniversary (May, 1956). At that Council the Tipitaka was recited in Pali and steps were taken toward translating it into some modern languages.

King Kaniska, who ruled a kingdom extending from northern India through what is now Afghanistan, called a Council in the first century A.D. which is not recognized by the Theravada Sangha but which seems to have influenced Buddhism as it developed in China and Tibet. At this Council, a version of the Dhamma in Sanskrit was approved, with many additions and interpolations and many commentaries.

BUDDHIST SCHOOLS

In modern times, there are only two major schools of Buddhism—Theravada, which is found chiefly in Ceylon, Burma, Thailand, Cambodia, and Laos; and Mahayana, which is found in China, Tibet, and Japan. A third type of Buddhism, Tantrayana, is not a separate school but is an added characteristic of the Mahayana Buddhism of Tibet.

The original tradition was that of Theravada (the Way of the Elders), the orthodox followers whose tradition has been maintained in Pali and whose rules and teachings go back to the earliest times. The first break with the Theravada tradition came at the time of the Second Great Council with the formation of the Mahasanghika school, a precursor of Mahayana. The second major school to arise was Sarvastivada, which differed from Theravada in only minor details at first, divided into several subsects, and eventually contributed many of its followers to Mahayana. According to the accounts of early Buddhism, there were at one time eighteen schools of Buddhism, including the original tradition of the Theras. The differences among these eighteen schools in early Buddhism were not fundamental but generally related to superficial beliefs and practices.

In due course, the centers of Theravada moved toward the south and flourished outside India. Amaravati and Conjeeveram in South India became great centers for the study of the Dhamma and also for training missionary monks who spread the pure Doctrine among the countries of southeastern Asia as far as Indonesia and Borneo. By about the ninth century after the Buddha (fourth century A.D.), it is evident that the Pali tradition existed in only a few monasteries throughout India as is shown by the fact that such an important center as Buddhagaya had to send the disciple Buddhaghosha to Ceylon to bring the vast literature of the Pali commentaries to India.

In the meantime, the Buddhism of northern India was made up of many sects separated by only minor differences and related either to the Sarvastivada or Mahasanghika traditions. The two major traditions which have today become known as Theravada and Mahayana, flourished side by side for centuries, but eventually Mahayana became the dominant form of Buddhism in northern India. The sects which finally developed into the Mahayana slowly turned the original scriptures into Sanskrit, the language of the intellectuals, which the Buddha had expressly prohibited as, he said, the Dhamma was meant for all, not merely for a few intellectuals. When the Teaching was put into Sanskrit, it was given a slight esoteric gloss, like the Vedas of Hinduism. In the course of time many new ideas came to be put into the mouth of the Buddha as sect after sect grew up among the Mahayanists. When the sects which followed the Sanskrit tradition became powerful, they chose the name of Mahayana (Great Vehicle) for themselves, and called those who followed the orthodox tradition Hinayana (Little Vehicle), a contemptuous term almost amounting to abuse.

Mahayana Buddhism differs from Theravada in its use of Sanskrit rather than Pali sources, in its elaborate philosophical speculations, and in its emphasis on various Bodhisattvas rather than on Gotama the Buddha and the ideal of the Arahat which he taught.

In the Mahayana centers in northern India the chief activity was philosophical inquiry, technical and intricate, primarily to meet the criticism of the orthodox Brahman scholars. Thus at Nalanda the great Buddhist logicians like Nagarjuna, Dharmakirti, and others wrote voluminous critical works defending the Buddhist idealistic position in logic and epistemology against the realistic Nyaya position propounded at the Brahman center across the Ganges in Mithila. The logical controversy between Nalanda and Mithila was kept alive for about seven hundred years without a break, giving rise to many valuable philosophical contributions. Philosophical discussions and studies continued with zeal and vigor for centuries in numerous great monasteries in the northwestern part of India, in Kashmir, and what is now Afghanistan. The two great Mahayana schools which grew out of these philosophical speculations were the Madhyamika and the Yogacara—also called Vijnana-vada—which both play an important part in the growth of Buddhism in China, Japan, and Tibet.

Among the great scholars in the Mahayana tradition were Asvaghosha, who lived in the seventh century after the Buddha (early second century A.D.) and wrote some of the first Mahayana commentaries; Nagarjuna, who probably lived half a century later and first formulated the Madhyamika doctrines; and the two brothers, Asanga and Vasubandhu from Peshawar, who were converted from the Sarvastavadins to Mahayana and founded the Yogacara school late in the ninth century after the Buddha (fourth century A.D.).

After a time, in the Mahayana tradition, the philosophical speculations were symbolized by various Bodhisattvas and gods such as Avalokitesvara (the Bodhisattva of Great Compassion), Tara (the goddess of mercy), Manjusri (the Bodhisattva of Meditation), and Amitabha (the Buddha of the Happy Western Paradise). Grand temples were built in their honor and elaborate ceremonies were performed which naturally attracted large congregations from all levels of society and encouraged different superstitious beliefs and modes of worship.

This multiplication of Mahayana deities with the various images and types of worship formed the basis of a cult which later came to be called Tantrayana. Tantric practices consisted of special, secret ways of worshiping the tantric deities and of using magical charms; a new literature grew up, unknown in earlier Buddhism, to explain this mode of worship. Tantric mystics were accepted as great leaders who professed to have discovered the shortest cut to Deliverance; they openly ridiculed the hard ethical discipline of the early Buddhist monks and even on occasion propagated mass indulgence in wine and women. In some quarters it was believed that the "grace of the *guru* (teacher)" was sufficient for the realization of the Sublime. These decadent and perverse forms did great harm to the good name of Buddhism and contributed to the weakness which made it impossible for Buddhism to revive after the

Mahayana temples and monasteries were destroyed by the Muslim invaders.

BUDDHIST ART

Very early, the religious devotion and fervor in the Sangha gave birth to schools of arts and architecture which expressed the inner devotion of the followers of the Buddha. The artists chose to depict in stone and in plaster reliefs important scenes from the life of the Buddha such as the birth, the great renunciation, the attainment of Enlightenment, the first sermon—that is, the setting in motion of the wheel of Dhamma—and the great Demise.

In the earliest period, up to about the end of the fifth century after the Buddha (the middle of the first century B.C.) the Buddha was symbolically represented in the scenes from his life, but never shown as a man. For instance, his birth was represented by a garden in the midst of which stood a tree and his mother, the renunciation was symbolized by a horse, the Enlightenment by the bodhi tree, the first sermon by a wheel flanked by deer. Such very early works were found at Sarnath, Nalanda (the great university center which grew up not far from Rajgir), and at Amaravati (near the Kistna river in Andhra, southern India). The next stage added pictorial representation of the Jataka tales, the stories of the lives of the Buddha in his previous existences, as are found in the bas-reliefs of Bharhut and Sanchi (in north central India). It was at this time that Asoka erected his famous pillars throughout India; the lion capital from the pillar at Sarnath, because it is an exquisite piece of ancient art, has been adopted as the national emblem of India.

In this early period the first shrines were built of wood and then copied in many details in stone in the rock-cut temples which still exist near Bombay at Bhaja, Karli, Ellora, and Ajanta; later the shrines were built as stone buildings. Another characteristic structure of the early period was the monastery (*vihara*) which was an unpretentious building, often merely a row of cells built around a central court, and little changed in form down to the present time. Also found in the earliest period was the stupa, a memorial mound built over a relic of the Buddha or of one of his disciples; notable examples to be found in modern times are the stupas at Sanchi and Sarnath, and the many variations of that form found in the dagobas of Ceylon and the pagodas of Burma, Thailand, Cambodia, China, and Japan.

The first sculptural representations of the Buddha in human form date from about the seventh century after the Buddha (first century A.D.) in the art of the Gandhara school which was primarily Mahayana and shows Greco-Roman influence. Gandhara, which lies in the Peshawar valley in northwestern India, was the center from which this new development in Buddhist art spread into Afghanistan and Central Asia and southward to Mathura (Muttra) and Amaravati. Examples of this period may still be seen at Bamiyan, in north central Afghanistan, where temples were carved from the face of the cliffs and there are two great standing Buddhas, one 120 feet and the other 175 feet high. The bas-reliefs decorating the great stupa at Amaravati, dating from the eighth century after the Buddha (second century A.D.) show a development of the Gandhara art which was both Theravada and Mahayana and influenced Buddhist art as far away as Indo-China. But the greatest development of Gandhara art took place at Mathura where the next steps were taken which led to the flowering of Buddhist art in the Gupta period.

The Gupta period, which extends from the crowning of Chandragupta in 864 B.E. (A.D. 320) to the end of the reign of Harsha in 1191 B.E. (A.D. 647), brought the Buddhist art of India to its highest perfection as an expression of the inner feelings of devotion and zeal of the artists. Examples of the painting have been preserved at the Ajanta caves, and of the sculpture at Mathura and Sarnath.

The influence of the Buddhist art of India spread south and east to Ceylon, Burma, Thailand, Cambodia, and on to Java and northward through Afghanistan and Central Asia to China and Japan. In all Buddhist lands, Theravada and Mahayana Buddha images were accepted and worshiped in four postures (*mudras*) of giving benediction, dispelling fear, setting the

wheel of Dhamma in motion, and Enlightenment. The Mahayana followers took a special interest in the creation of art,
producing wonderful works of painting, sculpture and architecture wherever their teachings spread.

In modern times, a pilgrimage to the sites where great art
inspired by Buddhism might still be seen would take one from
Afghanistan to Japan. Such a pilgrimage might start at Bamiyan in Afghanistan and continue to Sanchi and Ajanta in India,
to Polonnaruwa and Anuradhapura in Ceylon, to Pagan in
northern Burma, and the Shwedagon Pagoda in Rangoon, to
Bangkok, to Angkor in Cambodia, to Borobudur in Indonesia;
then to China to visit the caves at Tun Huang, in Kansu Province, the Yun Kang caves at Ta T'ung near Peking, and the
cave temples of Lung Men near Loyang in Honan; and finally
to Nara, Kyoto, and Kamakura in Japan. In these places, as in
countless others, are inspiring examples of the ways in which,
through the ages, men have expressed the inspiration which
has come to them from the Master who set in motion the wheel
of the Dhamma twenty-five centuries ago.

HINDUISM AND BUDDHISM

The Buddha taught the Dhamma, and the Sangha developed
in a predominantly Hindu environment in which the orthodox
religious community opposed Buddhism. The five distinctive
features of Buddhism in its relations with Hinduism, aptly
summarized by the famous Buddhist logician, Dharmakirti, in
the twelfth century after the Buddha (*ca.* A.D. 600), may serve
as a guide for a discussion of the ways in which Buddhism
differs from Hinduism.

1. Buddhism, as opposed to Hinduism, discards the blind
acceptance of the authority of the Vedas as divine revelation.
From the earliest times in India, the Vedas, the scriptures of
the Hindus, have been the source of religious authority and
inspiration, looked upon as divine, infallible revelation. The
Buddha preached against the acceptance of the blind authority
of the Vedas, or of any book, or even of the Buddha himself,
as harmful to spiritual progress. "O ye Kalamas, do not accept
a thing merely because it has been handed down by tradition."

The Pali Tipitaka are not scriptures for Buddhists in the sense that the Vedas are for Hindus, but are the most faithful record of the words of the Buddha—to be studied, practiced, and realized.

2. Buddhism differs from Hinduism concerning belief in a creator God. Buddhism, based on the principle of the dependent origination of all existence, cannot accept a first cause, a creator. Some Hindus say that God dwells in heaven—a deistic conception; others say that God pervades each atom of existence—a pantheistic conception; still others believe in a personal God, such as Rama, Krishna, or Siva. These different conceptions of God are unacceptable to the Buddhist. In Buddhism, the gods are celestial beings on different subtle planes of existence where they are born, live, and die at the end of their span of life. Human beings are also born on these planes at certain stages of mystic realization in the course of their religious practices. Many Buddhist gods like Viswakarma the world master-builder, and Prajapati, the lord of creatures, have their origin in the Vedas, but while they represent presiding deities of the different spheres of nature for the Hindus, in Buddhist writings they are regarded as highly moral, subtle beings on a different plane of existence. They are considered to be devotees of the Buddha and his disciple Saints, for the Saints in the Holy Order of the Buddha are regarded as spiritually higher than these gods. The Buddha taught his disciples to preach the Dhamma to men and gods alike.

3. Buddhism also rejects the spiritual efficacy of external rites and rituals, performed earnestly by Hindus, such as taking dips in the river Ganges to wash off all sins, bearing a pattern of holy marks on the body to ward off evil forces, observing untouchability, purifying the body by fasting, or practicing austerities. Buddhism believes in the possibility of self-purification only through self-culture, self-discipline, and self-realization; no external rites will help inner purity. The spirit of Buddhism is shown in the story narrated in the Therigatha, one of the books in the Tipitaka, of the discussion between a nun and a Brahman concerning bathing in the river on a cold winter night. The nun said, "If you could go to heaven by

bathing in the river, then surely the fish, tortoises, frogs, water snakes, and crocodiles too will attain heaven. Moreover, if the sins are washed off by bathing, the merits too will be washed off by the water. . . . O Brahman, if you are afraid of sins, it is better not to commit them at all."

4. Buddhism differs from Hinduism in that it rejects the caste system and untouchability. From the beginning, Hindu religious authority has emphasized the hierarchy of castes, having the sanction of the Hindu scriptures for their insistence on privilege. Twenty-five centuries ago the Buddha raised the first voice of protest against this demoralizing practice when he said, "It is not by birth that one becomes a Brahman or an untouchable, but it is through one's acts that one becomes a Brahman or an untouchable."

5. Finally, Buddhism opposes self-mortification and the practice of austerities, as commonly accepted by the Hindus and Jains. Even today one can see Hindu ascetics who believe that they are cleansing their souls and securing salvation by smearing their naked bodies with dust and ashes, sitting in the scorching sun in summer, lying flat on thorns, or piercing the body with spikes. The Buddha himself had practiced such austerities and he saw that they were of no help in the realization of the Truth; rather, they make a man more disturbed and restless. For Buddhism, austerity is the burning up of one's own mental defilements, not the inflicting of physical pain.

The time of the Buddha was an age of philosophical renaissance in India with different leaders offering varying interpretations of the universe and of man and his ethical values. There were six distinct philosophies in those days, in addition to the orthodox Vedic schools, which argued in one way or another for ethical nihilism, accidentalism or chance, determinism, materialism and moralism. The Buddha had to combat all these arguments and propound his own doctrines of nonsubstance, impermanence, and dependent origination—doctrines which brought a new profundity in thought, a new discipline in practice, and a renaissance of the spirit in man.

The philosophical view expressed in the Vedas is primarily monistic, grounded in the recognition of a basic spiritual existence called Brahman. The Buddha challenged this monistic position by saying that it was merely an imaginary construction to believe in a Brahman of which we have no real comprehension. He said that such a belief is like a man who tries to climb a ladder to the sky to reach a place he knows nothing about, or is like a man who falls in love with a beautiful queen whom no one has seen.

Buddhism's revolutionary position is unique in the history of religious thought in India, bringing to the traditional faiths a challenge which compelled them to strengthen their defenses. Religious superstition and blind faith, carried down through the ages, were shaken to their roots, and all the systems of Indian philosophy did their best to meet the rational arguments raised against them by the Buddha.

In considering the relations between Hinduism and Buddhism, it should be remembered that there were similarities as well as differences. Both Hinduism and Buddhism existed in a common culture for many centuries; there never was a distinctly separate Buddhist society isolated from the rest of the community. It should not be thought that Buddhism had a disrespect for the Vedas; the Buddha referred to the Vedas and the Hindu sages with due honor in the course of his sermons to Brahman scholars on several occasions. The Vedic Sages and Buddhist Saints had much in common in their practice of yoga. The Buddha emphasized the need for the mystical realization of the sage through deep meditation and called upon his disciples to follow the path of renunciation and yogic discipline; many Buddhist saints possessed supernatural powers through yoga.

The Buddha also taught that all existence is subject to the law of kamma, that rebirth is the lot of man, and that suffering is due to attachment—beliefs which were commonly held in his time by followers of the Vedas.

DECLINE OF BUDDHISM IN INDIA

The virtual disappearance of Buddhism from India is one of the most baffling problems in the history of that land. Why did Buddhism disappear from the land of its birth, after disseminating the Doctrine to all the parts of the then known world? Of the various reasons suggested, many of them having some truth in them, the most important were the decline of vigor in the Sangha, the Muslim invasion, and the opposition of the Hindu community.

The decline of vigor in the Order was a major cause of the decline of Buddhism. The vitality of the Sangha lay in the spirit of renunciation, self-discipline, broadmindedness, liberality, service, and sacrifice for the many; when those characteristics were weakened and lost, the influence of the Order disappeared. The Buddha himself, right up to the last days of his life, went on from one place to another arousing the people and leading them to the noble Path of Righteousness. Sariputta, Moggallana, and numerous other Arahat disciples of his followed the same ideals. As time went on, the Buddhist monks did their best to live up to those high principles and succeeded in converting the major part of the known world to the sublime Doctrine of the Buddha. In India, great kings and emperors embraced Buddhism and with zealous devotion sacrificed for the preservation and spread of the Dhamma.

By the eleventh century after the Buddha (sixth century A.D.) there were great universities and centers for study throughout the country, some with as many as 10,000 students from every Buddhist land. Kings, nobles, merchants, and the common people all contributed their share toward the maintenance of these institutions, but although these rich endowments and the royal patronage made the Buddhist organizations strong and prosperous, they at the same time gradually undermined the high ideals of renunciation and sacrifice on which the Sangha and the universities were founded. The monks gradually became used to an easy life devoted primarily to academic pursuits and religious celebrations; they grew lax and accepted perverse and worldly practices and beliefs which were opposed to the earlier ideals. This led to the disintegration of the Order into diverse sects, to the weakening of the moral standards of the Sangha, and to a corresponding waning of the religious fervor, faith, and devotion of the laity.

The Muslim invasion played an important part in the disappearance of Buddhism from India for, just as the Sangha began to decline in vigor, the Muslim vandals invaded the country, indiscriminately massacring the people and burning and destroying the shrines, monasteries, and schools in their path. Especial ferocity was directed toward Buddhist institutions with huge Buddha images, many of gold and precious stones. The shaven-headed monks wearing distinctive saffron robes were easily spotted and cruelly murdered as idolaters. In the destruction of the University of Nalanda, it is recorded by the Turkish historian Minhazad, in his book *Tavakata-I-Nasiri*, that thousands of monks were burned alive and yet more thousands beheaded, and the burning of the library continued for several months.

This extermination of the monks gave a fatal blow to the organization of the Sangha from which it never recovered. There was no one left to carry on the organization or to lead the bewildered laity who in their helplessness were exposed to the forcible proselytization of the Muslims and the slow but steady absorption by the Hindus. Although the Hindus and Jains were subjected to the same persecution, since their priests and leaders were scattered among their people and not easily singled out for destruction, they could survive and gradually rebuild the communities. With the destruction of the Sangha, the Buddhists were left without leaders, and Buddhism did not recover.

The third important factor in the decline of Buddhism in India was the strong opposition from the orthodox Hindu tradition. The orthodox members of the community had always, in their hearts, been against Buddhism—chiefly because of criticism of the caste system. During the glorious days of Buddhism, under the protection of royal patronage, the sectarian Hindus could not raise their voice against Buddhism, but after the invasions the orthodox community was able to move without restraint and slowly converted Buddhist temples which had escaped destruction into Hindu temples. The Buddhists, lacking strong leadership and subject to community pressures, were slowly absorbed. In those parts of India not brought under the control of the invaders, the pressure of the caste system slowly brought about the end of Buddhism.

Thus these three factors—the disintegration of the Sangha, external invasion, and internal opposition—together contributed to the decline of Buddhism in the land of its birth.

BUDDHISM IN INDIA TODAY

The disappearance of Buddhism in India has been almost complete, so much so that even in such places as Patna, Rajgir, and Muttra, which were Buddhist strongholds for centuries, the people today cannot recognize the Buddhist relics which are discovered there. Most of the Buddhist images which were not destroyed came to be worshiped as Hindu deities. The Buddha image of Lumbini temple, the very site of his birth, became the deity Rumin Dai; the holy images at Buddhagaya were converted into the five Pandava brothers; at Nalanda and Kusinara, the huge black stone images of the Gupta period became known as Teliya Baba (the oil-accepting deity) and Dheliya Baba (the stone-accepting deity).

In spite of the long period of oblivion, however, the high personality of the Buddha hovered so strongly in the minds of the people that they had to accept him as an incarnation of their god Vishnu and even today the Hindu priest in his daily worship recites, "In this age of the incarnation of the Buddha (Buddhavatara) I offer this oblation. . . ." There is no denying that the present form of Hinduism definitely bears marks of Buddhist influences. There are small pockets of people throughout the country whose worship includes Buddhist meditation not yet beyond the possibility of recognition. For instance, the Tharus of the Tarai area in the United Provinces, the Dharma worshipers of Bengal and Orissa, and the Ayyappan cult of Malabar in southern India are undoubtedly the remnants of the old Buddhists of India. There are still small groups of people in Kashmir, Assam, and Chittagong who have not lost their identity as Buddhists.

The darkest period of Buddhism in India lasted from the eighteenth to the middle of the twenty-fourth centuries after the Buddha (thirteenth to the nineteenth centuries A.D.). The first glimpse of the rays of a Buddhist revival in India dawned with the enthusiastic efforts of Western archeologists and historians who contributed much to bringing to light this lost culture. One of the heroes of the Indian War of Independence of 1857, Babu Amar Singh, started the revival of the Sangha tradition in India by going to Ceylon for training as a monk and to Burma for instruction in the methods of meditation and then returning to Kusinara to establish a monastery at the place of the great Demise of the Master. This monastery of Kusinara has formed the nucleus for the modern Buddhist movement in India, winning a handful of Indian monks who, as renowned scholars of Pali, Sanskrit, Hindi, and English, are giving their lives to the revival of Buddhism in India. Buddhist centers now exist at Nalanda, where the University has been revived by the Government, and at Lucknow, Calcutta, and Chittagong. Twenty-one centuries after the Arahat Mahinda took the Pali Tipitaka to Ceylon, the Buddhists of Ceylon sent back to Nalanda copies of the Pali Tipitaka to be restored to the script and language of India. Scholars from all Buddhist countries have come once more to Nalanda to study, making it again the unique meeting place of Mahayana and Theravada Buddhism, as it was centuries ago, according to the reports of Chinese scholars like Hsuan-tsang.

About a century ago the Ceylon Buddhist Mission to India established the Maha Bodhi Society which has organizations in Calcutta, Sarnath, and Buddhagaya and other important places in India. This society has been primarily concerned with the protection of pilgrimage places in India, with assisting pilgrims and with publishing books for the benefit of Indian readers. Ceylonese, Chinese, Burmese, Tibetan and Japanese Buddhists have built rest houses for pilgrims at various shrines for the benefit of their people as they visit India.

Thus, to the rest of the Buddhist world, India has become in modern times an important place of pilgrimage. The chief places of Buddhist pilgrimage are:

1. Lumbini, the birthplace of the Master, is the modern village of Rummindei in Nepal, a few miles inside the border,

north of Gorakhpur. There is an Asokan pillar, a small temple, and a rest house at Lumbini.

2. Buddhagaya, near modern Gaya, where the Buddha achieved Supreme Enlightenment under the bodhi tree, is the most important Buddhist pilgrimage center in India with thousands of pilgrims from all over the Buddhist world coming every year. In front of the venerable tree stands the massive temple—erected originally by Asoka—which, together with the many votive stupas, pillars, and gates that surround it are splendid masterpieces of ancient Indian workmanship. For a long time this sacred place was owned and managed by a Hindu Saivite sadhu who appointed Brahman priests on contract to conduct Hindu ritualistic services there. Since independence, the government has entrusted the management of this holy site to a responsible board consisting of Indian Buddhists and Hindus and has spent large sums for the restoration of the temple area.

3. At Sarnath, near Banaras, where the Buddha delivered his first sermon, the most important ancient structure is the stupa which marks the exact spot where the sermon was delivered. There, also, is the famous Asokan pillar with the lion capital, which is now the national emblem of the Government of India, and the column bearing the inscription reminding the monks of the high standard of monastic discipline to be observed.

4. At Kusinara, the place where the Buddha finally passed away, there now stands a great stupa and a shrine in which there is a most beautiful and majestic image of a reclining Buddha. The atmosphere in the temple vibrates with a strange solemnity and tranquillity which envelops the visitor as soon as he enters the building. About a mile away is the place where the Buddha was cremated. Kusinara is near Kasia, which is a few miles east of Gorakhpur.

5. Rajagaha, the modern Rajgir, about seventy miles from Patna, is the place where the Buddha had his first monastery, where he spent much of his time, where the First Great Council was held; it is believed by the Mahayanists that on a hill near Rajagaha the Buddha preached the famous Mahayana Sutra, the Lotus of the Wonderful Law, the Saddharma Pundarika Sutra.

6. Nalanda, about eight miles from Rajgir on the Patna road, was the birthplace of Sariputta and Moggallana who were

two of the leading disciples of the Buddha. At that holy site was founded the famous Nalanda University which was for centuries one of the most influential and active of all Buddhist centers. The outlines of the old University buildings can still be seen and many valuable antiquities have been recovered and preserved in the museum.

7. Sravasti is sacred because there the Buddha spent twenty-four rainy seasons during his ministry, and it was the site of two famous ancient monasteries built by two of his lay disciples. It is now in disrepair but still has the bodhi tree planted there by Ananda 2,500 years ago. It is located seven miles from Balarampur, which is about a hundred miles northeast of Lucknow.

8. Sanchi is the hill on which magnificent stupas and viharas were built to enshrine the holy relics of Sariputta and Moggallana, the two chief disciples of the Buddha. The great stupas, beautiful railings, and the magnificent gates of Sanchi, dating back to the time of Asoka, are among the finest examples of early Buddhist art. Sanchi is near Bhopal, in north central India.

The famous caves at Ajanta, Ellora, and Kanheri are not, strictly speaking, places of pilgrimage, but are famous for the majesty of their frescoes, the wonderful temples cut from the rock, and the stupas which have immortalized the inspiration and devotion of those great masters of ancient times. Pilgrims from all over the world come to marvel at their beauty.

Thus, although Buddhism has virtually disappeared from the land of its birth, the sacred places of Buddhism in India are once more being recovered and the land of the Buddha is again a land of inspiration to the Buddhists throughout the world.

Spread of Buddhism Outside India

Over twenty-two centuries ago, Asoka, at the instruction of the Arahat Moggaliputta Tissa, who was president of the Third Great Buddhist Council, sent able and wise missionaries abroad to the foreign countries of the world to preach the noble Dhamma "for the good and welfare of the many," as the Master had urged in his lifetime. Undoubtedly it is this unprecedented act which has made India the center of a glorious culture which has spread to most of the eastern half of the globe. There had been political and commercial ties between India and various other countries from time to time, but none of them were as lasting as this cultural relationship which was founded on true good will and spiritual insight. Regardless of any temporary setbacks, so long as this Message of Peace and Good Will exists on the face of the earth, nothing can break the relationship between these countries.

According to the Ceylonese *Great Chronicle* (*Mahavamsa*) and the Burmese *Chronicle of the Dispensation of the Buddha* (*Sasanavamsa*), the great Buddhist emperor sent messengers of the Dhamma to northern India, Afghanistan and Central Asia, Syria, Egypt, Nepal, Tibet, Burma, Ceylon, and the countries of southern India which lay outside Asoka's realm. As a background for understanding the later developments of Buddhism, let us consider briefly the history of the spread of Buddhism outside India.

Ceylon. Asoka's son Mahinda carried the message of Buddhism to Ceylon, arriving at Mihintale, a hill a few miles from the then capital city of Anuradhapura, at a time when King Tissa was on a hunting excursion there. There was a pact of friendship between the king and Asoka, so the Arahat Mahinda was given a good reception. A lively discussion took place between them, and finding the king to be very intelligent, the Venerable Mahinda preached the Dhamma to him and to his followers in a manner which so impressed them that they all embraced the great teaching. The monastery which was built for the Sangha in the royal park became the citadel of Theravada Buddhism in Ceylon, and from it, with the aid of the royal family and the nobility, Buddhism spread so rapidly that within the lifetime of Mahinda, Ceylon became a stronghold of the Dhamma.

When the daughter of King Tissa wished to dedicate her life to the noble cause of the Dhamma and become a nun, Arahat Mahinda had the king request Asoka to send Mahinda's sister, who was a nun and an Arahat, to found the order of nuns (*Bhikkhuni*) in Ceylon. Emperor Asoka sent his daughter together with a group of nuns and with them sent a sapling from the sacred bodhi tree which was planted with great pomp and jubilation near the monastery in Anuradhapura. This venerable tree still is to be seen in Anuradhapura and is today one of the holiest objects of Buddhist worship. Also received during the reign of King Tissa were relics of the Buddha which were housed in a great stupa now known as the Thuparama Dagoba.

The next great event in the history of Buddhism in Ceylon was the holding of the Fourth Great Council in the fifth century after the Buddha (first century B.C.) to preserve the Dhamma in its pristine purity by committing it to writing for the first time. The Council was held under the Sinhalese Sangha in the rock caves of Matale with five hundred monks in attendance.

The ninth century after the Buddha (fourth century A.D.) was a period of importance in Buddhist thought. It was the time when Buddhaghosha—an Indian monk from a Brahman family of Gaya—came to Ceylon to translate the commentaries back from Sinhalese into Pali, the language of the canon; he also wrote a résumé of the entire teaching of the canon in one volume, the Visuddhi Magga. Other commentators about that time were Dhammapala, Mahanama, and Kassapa, who gave final form to the commentaries as we have them today.

Seven centuries later (eleventh century A.D.) the capital was removed to Polonnaruwa, and a new impetus was given to Buddhism in Ceylon. The Sangha was reformed and purified, many great temples (viharas) and dagobas (stupas) were built, and Buddhist emissaries were sent to Burma and Thailand. Under the Venerable Sariputta, the subcommentaries were translated into Pali; the Venerable Anuruddha at this time wrote valuable commentaries on the Abhidhamma section of the canon, which are in use today. From this time until the arrival of the Portuguese in A.D. 1505, Ceylon was the beacon light of Buddhism, and her supremacy in learning and piety was recognized by all the neighboring Buddhist countries.

After the foreign occupation by the Portuguese, Dutch, and British, Buddhism became weak and once was so nearly lost that it was necessary to bring ordained monks from Thailand to restore the Sangha in the island. After that, the Sangha grew to the strength and influence which is recognized today.

The sacred places of pilgrimage and worship in Ceylon to-day are Anuradhapura, Mihintale, Polonnaruwa, Matale Rock Temple, Dambulla Rock Temple, the Temple of the Sacred Tooth in Kandy, Adam's Peak, and Kelaniya. Tradition says that the Buddha visited Ceylon three times during his ministrations.

Burma. The account of the early history of Buddhism in Burma is rather uncertain, based on tradition; it is only from the time of King Anawrahta of Pagan, sixteen centuries after the Buddha (A.D. 1044–1077) that we stand on the firm ground of history.

The Vinaya Pitaka mentions two merchants, Tapassu and Bhallika, who happened to pass Buddhagaya and being prompted by a deity went to the Buddha and offered him his first food after his Enlightenment. Buddha, having accepted them as disciples, gave them a few hairs from his head as a relic. Burmese tradition holds that these two merchants were residents of Dagon, now called Rangoon, and that they returned to their native town and enshrined the hair relic of the Master in a *cetiya* (pagoda) which later came to be called the Shwedagon Pagoda, now one of the wonders of the world. It towers majestically with solid gold plated pinnacles in the heart of Rangoon and is perhaps the most frequented holy shrine of the Buddhist world.

According to tradition, Buddhism flourished at what is now called Prome from the time of the Second Great Council, a century after the Buddha, until the country was laid waste three centuries later.

Thaton, in lower Burma, was the capital of the kingdom of the Mons, who were probably originally a Telegu people from India. Tradition holds that the Buddha visited Thaton in the eighth year of his enlightenment, and one of his monks returned in the year the Buddha passed away and stayed for eight years laying the foundation for Buddhism there. Subsequently, in the time of Asoka, the two monks, Sona and Uttara, visited Thaton and preached to the multitude. Tradition holds that for the next eight centuries Buddhism flourished in Lower Burma with Thaton as its center. Since Thaton was a regular port of call on the route between India and the countries of southeastern Asia, missionaries visited regularly from the famous mission training centers of Amaravati and Conjeeveram and went on from there to Thailand, Cambodia, and Java. Although these missionaries were Theravada Buddhists and the area around Thaton remained Theravada, it should be remembered that side by side with the spread of Theravada there was also a strong Mahayana movement from China, Cambodia, Malaya, and northern India.

When King Anawrahta came to the throne in Pagan in northern Burma, he was not pleased—so it is said—with the religion of his people, which was a strange mixture of Tantrism, Mahayana, and Hinduism. So when he met the Arahat Shin Arahan and heard the simple yet profound teaching of the Theravada, he was immediately converted and requested the Arahat to remain at Pagan for the establishment of the Dhamma. At Arahan's suggestion, King Anawrahta asked the king of Thaton for some relics and copies of the Tipitaka, and when he was refused, he attacked and conquered Thaton and brought to Pagan all the relics and copies of the Tipitaka as well as a large number of monks to preach the Dhamma. He ruled over most of Burma, established communications with the Buddhists of Ceylon, and started a great building program at Pagan which continued for two centuries until the country was overrun by the armies of Kublai Khan.

During the two centuries after the destruction of Pagan the life of the people was unstable and the Sangha lost much of its effectiveness, but with the coming of King Dhammaceti (A.D. 1472-1492) a zealous reform movement was instituted. The Burmese Sangha had become corrupted, so in order to keep the tradition pure he sent a mission to Ceylon where learned Theras (Elders) re-ordained the Burmese monks.

As noted above, the Fifth Great Council was held in Mandalay under King Mindon in 1871, giving new life to religion which was threatened by the materialistic influences of the Western invaders. In modern times, after seventy years of occupation by the British, and later by the Japanese, Burma remains a Theravada Buddhist country and has demonstrated its zeal by convening the Sixth Great Council, which ended in Rangoon on the twenty-five hundredth anniversary of the Buddha's Great Demise (May, 1956).

Thailand. The Mons of Thailand had maintained trade relations with India from pre-Buddhist times, and there were many colonies of Indian traders among them. Traditionally, the arrival of Buddhism in Thailand is attributed to the two celebrated Asokan missionaries, Sona and Uttara, who are said to have brought Buddhism to Burma. The Mons of Thaton and the Mons of Thailand were of the same stock, which made it quite natural for the Theravada Buddhism of Thaton to have spread to Thailand, aided by the missionaries who came from Amaravati and Conjeeveram in India. At the same time, Mahayana Buddhism was introduced from Java and Malaya and from Cambodia.

When the Khmer culture of Cambodia superseded that of the Mons in the tenth century A.D., it brought in a highly Indianized culture which was more Hindu than Mahayana. That lasted until the Thai race, driven southward from China by the armies of Kublai Khan, overran the country about the end of the thirteenth century. The early Thai kings were impressed by the Theravada culture of Pagan and turned to Ceylon as the seat of the Pure Dhamma for guidance in establishing Theravada Buddhism in their kingdom. Their influence extended to Cambodia and Laos. Throughout all the dynastic changes in Thailand, their adherence to Theravada Buddhism remained strong, as it is to this day.

Cambodia. The area which now includes Cambodia, Laos, and Viet Nam, as well as the further areas of Malaya, Sumatra, Java, Borneo, and Bali were at one time so completely colonized by Indians that they were commonly known as "farther India." Until about the eighteenth century after the Buddha (thirteenth century A.D.) the Hindu influence was strong in these areas, with Hindu dynasties at various times and an extensive trade with India. The remains of Hindu temples, images of Hindu gods, and numerous inscriptions give evidence of the extensive Hindu culture in southeastern Asia.

The Khmers of Cambodia were related to the Mons and seem to have had cultural and political relations with the people of Burma in early times. According to the account of I-Ching, the Chinese pilgrim who traveled throughout southeast Asia on his way to India, there were Theravada Buddhists in Cambodia at least until the beginning of the eleventh century after the Buddha (fifth century A.D.). According to Chinese and early Cambodian accounts, an Indian Brahman established a dynasty in Cambodia about the seventh century after the Buddha (late first century A.D.), which was the beginning of a series of Hindu rulers who dominated the culture of the area for almost twelve centuries. During this Brahmanical period, Mahayana Buddhism was found in Cambodia but was so closely allied with the culture that it was scarcely distinguishable as a separate religion.

The renaissance of Theravada in Ceylon in the Polonnaruwa period (sixteen centuries after the Buddha—eleventh century A.D.) had set in motion currents which came in waves, one after another, to the far shores of Burma, Thailand, Cambodia, and Laos. Within two centuries, all these countries became fervent followers of Theravada Buddhism and have remained so to this day. In Cambodia, this influence was felt first through Thailand, and then directly from Ceylon and Burma. As in Thailand, traces of Hinduism still remain in court ceremonials, but the ruler is the defender of Buddhism and the government lends its aid to the Sangha. It was in the years between the fifteenth and twentieth centuries after the Buddha (ninth to fourteenth centuries A.D.) that the beautiful Buddhist architecture flourished at Angkor.

Laos. The people of Laos are chiefly from the same tribes which came south from China to settle as Shans in Burma and Thais in Thailand, but they have kept some traces of the early inhabitants who must have been related to the Mons since the script of their Tipitakas closely resembles modern Burmese rather than the script of Thailand and Cambodia which seems to have been acquired from the Khmers. The history of Buddhism in Laos closely parallels that of Cambodia, with Theravada Buddhism coming in about two centuries after its renaissance at Polonnaruwa in Ceylon and continuing as the chief religion to the present time.

Viet Nam. While this area was originally chiefly Hindu, the closer ties with China brought Mahayana Buddhism to what is now Viet Nam. Within the past century there has been a movement, starting in Cambodia, to revive Theravada in Viet Nam and there is now a Sangha at Saigon.

Malaya, Sumatra, Java, Bali, Borneo. Since this area was a chain of prosperous Indian colonies closely linked with India by commerce and culture, it was natural that Buddhism should spread to these countries at a very early date. Both Theravada and Mahayana Buddhism were found here, sometimes aggressively repressed by Hindu rulers and sometimes favored by rulers who were Buddhist. Chinese pilgrims came to Java and Malaya to study with famous Buddhist scholars, and the great temples at Borobudur—one of the finest examples of Buddhist art—indicate the important role which Buddhism played there at one time. Twenty centuries after the Buddha (fifteenth century A.D.) the Islamic traders began to settle in Malaya and the islands and slowly penetrated the Buddhist and Hindu communities by matrimonial alliances and by exerting economic pressure. Later, when they became powerful they gained political control and today these areas are Muslim except for Bali which remains Hindu, and for small groups of Buddhists, chiefly Mahayana, who have held to their faith.

Central Asia. By the time of Asoka in the third century after the Buddha, the Dhamma had spread to Kashmir and what is now known as Afghanistan; by the sixth century after the Buddha (first century A.D.) Buddhism was playing an important role in the area north of Afghanistan along the Oxus river valley almost to Samarkand, and eastward toward the Gobi desert. At this time, King Kaniska ruled from his capital at Peshawar a kingdom extending from Muttra on the Indian plains through Kashmir, Khotan, Afghanistan, and west to the borders of modern Iran. The western and northern limits of his kingdom mark the approximate extent of the spread of Buddhism in those directions in Central Asia, but for a thousand years Buddhism moved eastward from Central Asia along the trade routes to China, Korea, and Japan.

From very early times the area extending from the Peshawar valley through Kashmir, Afghanistan, and northward was a stronghold of Buddhism, with Mahayana predominating but with a large representation of Sarvastivada sects. Fa Hsien, the Chinese pilgrim who traveled this way in the tenth century after the Buddha (around A.D. 400), found both schools of Buddhism throughout Central Asia and extensive monasteries and temples with many beautiful works of art. Hsuan-tsang, some two centuries later, also found Buddhism flourishing in this area with some monasteries having as many as three thousand monks.

The Sarvastivadins, called "Little Vehicle" Buddhists by the Mahayanists, would fall between Theravada and Mahayana. They held some beliefs similar to those of the Theravada school in the South, but they used Sanskrit instead of Pali and had very little to do with the Theravada Buddhism of Ceylon and Burma. Ultimately, the Sarvastivadins were absorbed in Mahayana schools or destroyed by invaders.

The Mahayana schools trace their origin to the time of the Second Great Council, a century after the Buddha. After several centuries of development two major schools of Mahayana became prominent, the Madhyamika system of Nagarjuna and the Yogacara system of Asanga and Vasubandhu. These schools prospered in Kashmir and Afghanistan and were influential in shaping the Buddhism of China, Korea, and Japan.

It is likely that about the twelfth century after the Buddha (seventh century A.D.) the invasions of the White Huns in Central Asia devastated some of the monasteries. The end of Buddhism in Kashmir, Afghanistan, and the Central Asian area came with the Muslim invasions three centuries later.

The Mongols from Central Asia who are Buddhists today trace their conversion to Buddhism to about the time of Kublai Khan who favored Tibetan Buddhism and brought this form of Buddhism to China in the eighteenth century after the Buddha (thirteenth century A.D.). Three centuries later the Dalai Lama made a special effort to instruct the Mongols in Tibetan Buddhism and since that time there has been a loyal band of Mongolian Buddhists looking to Lhasa for their guidance.

China. It was the Mahayana Buddhism of northern India and Central Asia which spread to China, Tibet, Korea, and Japan, following the trade routes northward from India and eastward through the Gobi desert. It is likely that Buddhism had been known in China among travelers and traders by the sixth century after the Buddha (first century B.C.), but Chinese tradition says that Buddhism was brought to China early in the seventh century after the Buddha by Emperor Ming, who as a result of a dream, dispatched an envoy of eighteen men to India to bring back the teachings of the Buddha. After studying eleven years in India, they returned with a collection of Buddhist books, some images of the Buddha, and two great Buddhist scholars. They founded a monastery which became the center for Buddhist studies in China and in the following years were joined by other monks from India who helped in the translation of the Sanskrit Buddhist books into Chinese. Reports of their early successes in China inspired in the Buddhist missionaries of India a burning zeal to devote their lives to translating books and propagating the Dhamma in this great country. Within three centuries, more than 350 books had been translated.

About a thousand years after the Buddha (fifth century A.D.), Kumarajiva, a noted monk and scholar from Kashmir who was living in Central Asia, was captured by Chinese soldiers at the express order of the Emperor and brought to China to organize a Buddhist mission there. With the help of Chinese scholars, he became a master translator of Sanskrit Buddhist books into Chinese, helping to originate the style of classical Chinese which has continued to modern times. His book on the lives of Asvaghosha and Nagarjuna, the two great Mahayana teachers, is a masterpiece in Chinese, and his translation of the Saddharma Pundarika Sutra (The Lotus of the Wonderful Law) superseded the earlier translation because of the quality of the language and became one of the most influential books in the history of Buddhism in China. His disciple, Fa Hsien, visited India and wrote an account of his travels which is one of the chief sources of Buddhist history of that period.

At the earnest invitation of the Chinese Emperor, the Venerable Gunavarman, an illustrious Indian monk who had converted Java to Buddhism, came over to China in this same century and propagated the teachings of The Lotus of the Wonderful Law among the masses; he also established the Order of Buddhist Nuns there.

In the next century (sixth century A.D.), the great Buddhist mystic and saint, Bodhidharma, came to China and animated the entire country with a life of spirituality. Though for the major part of his stay in China he kept himself in seclusion as he followed his meditative practices, the very name of Bodhidharma was a magically stirring force in the religious life of the country and continues to be so even today.

The great Chinese scholar and traveler, Hsuan-tsang, visited India in the twelfth century after the Buddha (629 A.D.) and spent many years traveling throughout the country, talking with famous scholars and collecting manuscripts to take back to China. When he returned he was given a royal reception and was aided by the Emperor and many scholars in translating the Sanskrit works which he brought from India. Many of his translations of Buddhist Sanskrit books are available even today and are regarded as the summit of religious and literary scholarship.

The last recorded Buddhist missionary from India was the famous logician from Nalanda, Jnanasri, who visited China at the end of the sixteenth century after the Buddha (the middle of the eleventh century A.D.). After that the stream of Indian monks to China ceased to flow, partly because missionary activities had shifted to Tibet, but chiefly because the Buddhist centers in India had been weakened or destroyed by the Muslim invaders.

During these centuries, Buddhism in China had sometimes been aided by devout Buddhist emperors and at other times was subjected to violent persecution. During the reign of

Kublai Khan, thirteen centuries after Buddhism came to China (thirteenth century A.D.), the government census recorded 213,148 Buddhist temples in China.

Korea. About four centuries after Buddhism came to China (the fourth century A.D.), Buddhism traveled eastward from China to Korea, carried by missionaries whose zeal drove them on through Manchuria and across the Yalu river, carrying valuable Buddhist images and religious books. A Chinese monk, Sundo, is the first missionary known to have reached northern Korea, where he established two large monasteries and converted many people without opposition. About the same time, other monks from China carried Buddhism to the rest of Korea with such success that within a few generations the whole country was Buddhist. That same zeal for missionary activity carried Buddhism from Korea to Japan 150 years after it came from China. Eleven hundred years after Buddhism came to Korea, late in the fifteenth century, the ruler of Korea banished all Buddhist monasteries and temples from the cities of his country and from then until the present century, organized Buddhism existed in Korea in monasteries hidden in the valleys and in rural areas.

Japan. It was almost exactly 1,100 years after the Buddha (A.D. 552) that Buddhism was introduced to Japan by the king of Korea who sent a delegation with an image of the Buddha to the emperor of Japan. It is likely that some Buddhist influence from Korea existed in Japan before this time and certain that for several centuries Korean Buddhists made a determined drive to establish Buddhism in their neighboring country of Japan. It is interesting to note that much of the success of the Buddhists mission to Japan was due to the zealous efforts of the nuns of Korea who penetrated the inner apartments of the Japanese families and converted them to Buddhism.

One of the first Buddhist temples in Japan was built at Horyuji near Nara, in A.D. 587, thirty-five years after the royal message was sent from Korea, and it is still standing today, probably the oldest wooden building in the world. The Horyuji temple was built by Shotoku Taishi, the regent who did more than anyone else to establish Buddhism in Japan; he was a devout

Buddhist, a great scholar, a lover of the arts, and a wise and benevolent ruler whose role in Japanese history is similar to that of Asoka in India.

Although Buddhism seems to have come to Japan from Korea, it was to China that the Japanese Buddhists turned for guidance. Within a century, missions were being sent to China to study and bring back Buddhist books and images; in A.D. 654 Dosho returned from China, where he had studied with the great Chinese traveler, Hsuan-tsang; two centuries later, Ennin journeyed through China as Hsuan-tsang had in India and returned to be recognized as a master of Buddhist scholarship. Buddhist monks from China and even from India also visited Japan from time to time. As a result of this close relationship with China, all schools of Chinese Mahayana thought were found in Japan, centering first at Nara, then at Kyoto, and finally at Kamakura.

Tibet. Although only the Himalayas separate Tibet from India and there had been several attempts by Indian monks to introduce Buddhism into Tibet, it was not until the twelfth century after the Buddha (seventh century A.D.) that Buddhism was officially introduced into Tibet, making it the last of the modern Mahayana countries to accept Buddhism.

The cultural relations between India and Tibet began during the reign of Songtsan-Gampo. The king had two queens, one from Nepal and the other from China, both of whom were devout Buddhists who used their influence to convert the king to Buddhism. Thereafter, he sent Tibetans on missions to India to study Buddhism, invited learned monks from foreign countries to propagate the Dhamma in Tibet, and established many temples and monasteries. Even today in Tibet, he is looked upon with great honor and depicted in portraits as one turning the wheel of righteousness.

A century later (eighth century A.D.) King Trisong-Detsan sent a royal invitation to the great Buddhist saint and philosopher Santarakshita, who was at that time Principal of the famous Buddhist University at Nalanda, asking him to teach the Dhamma to the people of Tibet. Unfortunately, soon after the arrival of Santarakshita the country was subjected to several calamities such as epidemics, floods, storms, and famine, which the people attributed to the arrival of the Indian teacher, and the king had to send him to Nepal for a time. Santarakshita advised the king to invite the great Indian mystic, Padmasambhava, who, he thought, might be able to quell those calamities with his spiritual and yogic powers. Soon after his arrival the disturbances ended and Padmasambhava was hailed as their deliverer. He established a monastery near Lhasa which was modeled after the famous University of Odantapuri near Nalanda. After he returned to India, Santarakshita carried on the mission to Tibet, aided by other monks from India, and through their efforts they translated many books from Sanskrit into Tibetan, including a most perfect Tibetan version of the entire Buddhist Tripitaka.

Late in the seventeenth century after the Buddha (A.D. 1038), the great Indian Buddhist saint and scholar Atisha came to Tibet as a royal guest and abolished the heresies which had arisen as a formidable challenge to Buddhism. He established a number of monasteries, ordained many able Tibetan scholars as monks, and wrote valuable books on Buddhism for the benefit of the people of the country. From that time on, the people of Tibet have been Buddhist.

As we have looked back over the twenty-five centuries since the Dhamma was first taught to men, we have seen how Buddhism has spread from the deer park at Sarnath west to the borders of Iran, northward to the Gobi Desert, eastward to Japan, and throughout all of southeastern Asia to Borneo and Java. Today, only ancient ruins remain at Bamiyan and in Central Asia, at Pagan in Burma, at Angkor Wat in Cambodia, at Borobudur in Indonesia, and at the historic pilgrimage sites in India; but the Light of the Dhamma still shines in Asia, in Ceylon, Burma, Thailand, Cambodia, and Laos, in Nepal, Tibet, China, Korea, and Japan. Today, as for uncounted generations in the past, tens of millions of men and women follow the teachings of the Buddha, the Enlightened One.

CHAPTER TWO

The Fundamental Principles of
Theravada Buddhism

U Thittila

All the teachings of the Buddha can be summed up in one word: Dhamma. The Sanskrit form of the word is *Dharma*, but in the Pali language, which the Buddha spoke and in which all the Buddhist scriptures were written, it is softened to Dhamma. It means truth, that which really is. It also means law, the law which exists in a man's own heart and mind. It is the principle of righteousness. Therefore the Buddha appeals to man to be noble, pure, and charitable not in order to please any Supreme Being, but in order to be true to the highest in himself.

Dhamma, this law of righteousness, exists not only in a man's heart and mind, it exists in the universe also. All the universe is an embodiment and revelation of Dhamma. When the moon rises and sets, the rains come, the crops grow, the seasons change, it is because of Dhamma, for Dhamma is the law residing in the universe which makes matter act in the ways revealed by the studies of modern science in physics, chemistry, zoology, botany, and astronomy. Dhamma is the true nature of every existing thing, animate and inanimate.

If a man will live by Dhamma, he will escape misery and come to Nibbana, the final release from all suffering. It is not by any kind of prayer, nor by any ceremonies, nor by any appeal to a deity or a God that a man will discover the Dhamma which will lead him to his goal. He will discover it in only one way—by developing his own character. This development comes only through control of the mind and purification of the emotions. Until a man stills the storm in his heart, until he extends his loving-kindness to all beings, he will not be able to take even the first step toward his goal.

THE SCRIPTURES

The Teachings of the Buddha were called Dhamma because they enable one to realize truth. The doctrinal aspect of the Buddha's Teachings has been preserved in the Pali scriptures called Tipitaka, which means the Three Baskets of the Canon. In English translation, they would fill more than a dozen large volumes. The Three Baskets are known as the Basket of Discipline (Vinaya Pitaka), the Basket of Discourses (Sutta Pitaka), and the Basket of Ultimate Things (Abhidhamma Pitaka).

The Basket of Discipline (Vinaya Pitaka) deals mainly with the rules and regulations which govern the conduct of monks (Bhikkhus) and nuns (Bhikkhunis). It also gives a detailed account of the life and ministry of the Buddha and the development of the Sangha. This Pitaka is divided into five books:

1. Major Offenses (Parajika)—including an explanation of how each rule was promulgated and listing special cases and exceptions

2. Minor Offenses (Pacittiya)—also with explanations and exceptions

3. The Great Section (Mahavagga)—giving the rules for admission to the Sangha, ordination, dress, residence, and the rules for the performance of special monastic activities

4. The Small Section (Cullavagga)—dealing with the treatment, offenses, and duties of teachers and novices, with special rules for nuns

5. Epitome of the Vinaya Pitaka (Parivara)—containing a commentary primarily on the Great Section (Mahavagga) and telling important stories about the events following the Enlightenment of the Buddha

The Second Basket, called the Basket of Discourses (Sutta Pitaka), contains the discourses delivered by the Buddha on various occasions. It is divided into five Nikayas or Collections:

1. Collection of Long Discourses (Digha Nikaya)—thirty-four discourses in three series, many dealing with the training of the disciple

2. Collection of Medium-Length Discourses (Majjhima Nikaya)—152 discourses, many of which tell of the Buddha's austerities, his Enlightenment, and early teachings

3. Collection of Kindred Sayings (Samyutta Nikaya)—these are divided according to subject:
   Sagathavagga—discourses in verse, or containing verses
   Nidanavagga—beginning with discourses on the chain of causation
   Khandhavagga—on the five aggregates and on heresies
   Salayatanavagga—beginning with discourses on the six senses
   Mahavagga—the great series, on the Noble Eightfold Path

4. Collection of Gradual Sayings (Anguttara Nikaya)—in eleven divisions, beginning with discourses dealing with one thing—such as a quality—and going on with lists of pairs, then threes, and up to lists of eleven things

5. Collection of Short Discourses (Khuddaka Nikaya)—This is the biggest volume, made up of fifteen books which contain the most exquisite parts of the entire canon:

Shorter Texts	(Khuddaka Patha)
The Way of Truth	(Dhammapada)
Heartfelt Sayings	(Udana)
"Thus Said" Discourses	(Iti-vuttaka)
Collected Discourses	(Sutta Nipata)
Stories of Celestial Mansions	(Vimana Vatthu)
Stories of Departed Spirits	(Petavatthu)
Psalms of the Brethren	(Theragatha)
Psalms of the Sisters	(Therigatha)
Birth Stories	(Jataka)
Expositions	(Niddesa)
Analytical Knowledge	(Patisambhida)

Lives of Saints	(Apadana)
The History of the Buddha	(Buddhavamsa)
Modes of Conduct	(Cariya Pitaka)

The discourses in the Sutta Pitaka, the Second Basket, are given to suit the understanding and temperament of ordinary, untrained people and are therefore in conventional, simple language in the form of prescriptions.

The Third Basket, the Basket of Ultimate Things (Abhidhamma Pitaka), deals with the higher philosophy of the Buddha and contains these seven books:

Enumeration of Phenomena	(Dhammasangani)
Book of Analysis	(Vibhanga)
Treatise on the Elements	(Dhatukatha)
Book of Human Types	(Puggalapannatti)
Points of Controversy	(Kathavatthu)
Book of Pairs	(Yamaka)
On Relations	(Patthana)

The Abhidhamma Pitaka, the Third Basket, is the most interesting to a deep thinker. It is a philosophy inasmuch as it deals with the most general causes and the principles which govern all things. It is also an ethical system because it enables one to realize the ultimate goal, Nibbana. And because it deals with the working of the mind, with thought processes and mental factors, it is also a system of psychology. Abhidhamma is therefore generally translated as the Psycho-ethical Philosophy of Buddhism. In the Abhidhamma Pitaka all the basic doctrines of Buddhism are systematically elucidated from the philosophical, psychological, and physiological standpoint. A knowledge of the Abhidhamma is therefore essential to a clear understanding of the Buddhist Doctrine.

Abhidhamma is highly prized by the profound students of Buddhist philosophy, but to the average student it seems to be dull and meaningless. This is because it is so extremely subtle in its analysis and technical in its treatment that it is very difficult to understand without the guidance of an able teacher. That is probably why the Abhidhamma is not so popular as the other two Pitakas among western Buddhists.

The versions of the Pali texts extant in Theravada Buddhist countries such as Burma, Ceylon, Thailand, Cambodia, and Laos differ only in a few unimportant grammatical forms or spellings of words. In substance and in meaning, and even in the very phrases employed, they are in complete agreement; there is no doubt that these versions represent the true Teaching of the Buddha as he originally gave it. The Tipitaka contains everything necessary to show forth the path to the ultimate goal, to Nibbana.

In addition to the Pali texts, there are commentaries on all of them by the early elders of the Buddhist Order and also subcommentaries written on the commentaries in the course of the centuries. It is true that these extracanonical works sometimes introduce a great deal of speculative matter, but they have remained faithful to the original Doctrine and often give highly illuminating illustrations. The works of Buddhaghosha Thera (Elder) rank very high in exegetical literature.

RATIONALITY OF BUDDHISM

Buddhism is not a religion in the sense in which that word is commonly understood, for it is not a system of faith and worship. In Buddhism, there is no such thing as belief in a body of dogmas which have to be taken on faith, such as a belief in a Supreme Being, a creator of the universe, the reality of an immortal soul, a personal savior, or archangels who are supposed to carry out the will of the Supreme Deity. It is true that there are different types of devas or spiritual beings mentioned in Buddhism, but they are beings like ourselves, subject to the same natural law of cause and effect. They are not immortal, nor do they control the destiny of mankind. The Buddha does not ask us to accept belief in any supernatural agency or anything that cannot be tested by experience.

Buddhism begins as a search for truth. It does not begin with unfounded assumptions concerning any god or First Cause, nor does it claim to present through any form of divine revelation the whole truth of the absolute beginning and end of mankind's spiritual pilgrimage. The Buddha himself searched with direct insight and discovered the nature of the cosmos, the causes of its arising and of its passing away, the real cause of suffering and a way in which it can be brought to an end. Having made those discoveries he proclaimed for the sake of all human beings the principles on which he had conducted his research so that all who wished to do so could follow his methods and know the final truth themselves.

Because the Buddha's way is the way of rationality, he did not ask for absolute faith in himself or his teachings. Rather, as he instructed the Kalamas, he said that we must not believe anything merely because it was handed down by tradition, or said by a great person, or commonly accepted, or even because the Buddha said it. The Buddha taught that we should believe only that which is true in the light of our own experience, that which conforms to reason and is conducive to the highest good and welfare of all beings. The follower of the Buddha is invited to doubt until he has examined all the evidence for the basic facts of the teaching and has himself experimented with them to see if they are true. Having proved by these means that they are true, he is able to accept them. One of the qualities of the Dhamma, the path of the Buddha, is that it is "Ehi Passiko"—"That which invites everyone to come and see for himself."

The Buddha teaches men to rely upon themselves in order to achieve their own deliverance, not to look to any external savior. He never puts himself forward as a mediator between us and our final deliverance, but he can tell us what to do, because he has done it himself and so knows the way. Unless we ourselves act, the Buddha cannot guide us to our goal. Even though a man may "take refuge in the Buddha," as he expresses his intent in the simple ceremony of pledging himself to live a righteous life, it must not be with any blind faith that the Buddha can save him. The Buddha can point out the path; he can tell us of its difficulties and of the beauties which we will find as we tread the path; but he cannot tread it for us. We must tread the path ourselves. No one can purify or defile another person; each of us is responsible for his own purification or defilement. The Buddha says, "By oneself, indeed, is evil done; by oneself is one defiled; by oneself is evil left undone;

by oneself, indeed, is one purified. Purity and impurity depend upon oneself—no one purifies another." (Dhammapada.)

BUDDHIST DEVOTION

The rationality of Buddhism is not by itself enough—there must also be devotion in order that the truth may be realized. In Buddhism, mere belief is dethroned and replaced by confidence (*saddha*) based on knowledge of truth. Reason enables man to arrange and systematize knowledge in order to find truth, while confidence gives him determination to be true to his high ideals. Confidence or faith becomes superstition when it is not accompanied by reason, but reason without confidence would turn a man into a machine without feeling or enthusiasm for his ideals. Reason seeks disinterestedly to realize truth, but confidence molds a man's character and gives him strength of will to break all the barriers which hinder his progress in achieving his aims. While reason makes a man rejoice in truths he has already discovered, confidence gives him fresh courage and helps him onward to further conquests, to aspire to work strenuously for the realization of what has not yet been attained. It is this saddha which has the power to transform cold abstract rationalism into a philosophy of fervent hope, love, and compassion. It is also this saddha which is the basis of the loving devotion to the great teacher, the Buddha, his teaching and his holy Sangha.

The object of devotion, in which every faithful follower of the Buddha puts his whole hope, is known as the Threefold Refuge: the Buddha—the Enlightened One; the Dhamma—his Doctrine; and the Sangha—the Order of his Noble Disciples. Every Buddhist religious meeting begins with the recitation in Pali of the formula of the Three Refuges:

> I go to the Buddha for refuge.
> I go to the Doctrine for refuge.
> I go to the Sangha for refuge.

These three are also known among Buddhists as the Triple Gem, or the Three Jewels, using the word *Gem* or *Jewel* in the sense of that which pleases, that which gives delight, that which is precious, that which can give to humanity the real spiritual pleasure of a refuge against the evil powers of greed, ill will, and delusion.

The Buddhist takes refuge in the Buddha because the Buddha had boundless compassion for man's weakness, sorrow, disappointment, and suffering, and because he found for all beings the path of deliverance by his own ceaseless effort through a long and painful struggle. The Buddha gave to men great encouragement and inspiration to fight against evil until it is overcome.

The Buddhist takes the Second Refuge, in the Dhamma, because it enables one who follows it to bring an end to all dissatisfaction and suffering through the attainment of Enlightenment, perfect wisdom and perfect equanimity. The best way to follow the Dhamma is to practice it in one's daily life. As we are all subject to birth, old age, sickness, dissatisfaction, sorrow, and death, we are all sick people. The Buddha is compared to an experienced and skillful physician, and the Dhamma is compared to the proper medicine. However efficient the physician may be, and however wonderful the medicine may be, we cannot be cured unless and until we take the medicine ourselves. Realization is possible only through practice. The practice of the Dhamma is the only way in which one can truly express one's gratitude and veneration for the Buddha who, with infinite compassion, showed us the way to the end of all suffering. The Buddha said, "He honors me best who practices my teaching best."

The Buddhist takes the Third Refuge, in the Sangha, because the Sangha is the living stream through which the Dhamma flows to humanity. *Sangha* literally means group, congregation, and is the name for the community of Noble Ones who have reached the stages of sanctity of which the last is perfect sainthood. It is also the name for the community of monks (Bhikkhus) who are striving to attain Arahatship by following the Dhamma. The Sangha is the point at which the Dhamma makes direct contact with humanity, it is the bridge between living man and absolute truth. The Buddha strongly emphasized the importance of the Sangha as a necessary institution for the good of mankind. If there had not been the Sangha, the Dhamma would have been a mere legend and tradition after the demise of the Buddha—it is the Sangha which has preserved not only the Word of the Master, but also the unique spirit of the Noble Teaching since the Master's passing away.

Non-Buddhists often ask whether or not Buddhists worship images. The answer is that the true Buddhists know who and what the Buddha is. They do not worship an image nor pray to it expecting any worldly boons or sensual pleasures while they are living or a pleasurable state of existence, such as heaven, after death. The images before which they kneel are only representations of one to whom they pay their homage in gratitude because he, through his own efforts and wisdom, discovered the way to real peace and made it known to all beings. The offerings they make are but symbols of their reverence for the Buddha and are a means of concentrating their minds on the significance of the words they are reciting. Just as people love to see the portrait of one dear to them when separated by death or distance, so do Buddhists love to have before them the representation of their Master, because this representation enables them to think of his virtues, his love and compassion for all beings, and the doctrine he taught.

The words they recite are meditations and not prayers. They recite to themselves the virtues of the Buddha, his Dhamma, and his Holy Order so that they may acquire such mental dispositions as are favorable to the attainment of similar qualities in their own minds, in however small a degree. The things they offer as they kneel are object lessons of the truth they are trying to realize in their meditation. This is one of the meditations used in the offering of flowers:

These flowers I offer in memory of the Buddha, the Holy One, the Supremely Enlightened One. These flowers are now fair in form, glorious in color, sweet in scent. Yet all will soon have passed away, their fair form withered, the bright hues faded, their scent gone. It is even so with all conditioned things which are subject to change and suffering and are unreal. Realizing this, may we attain Nibbana, perfect peace, which is real and everlasting.

The external forms of homage are not absolutely necessary for an intellectual who can easily focus his attention and visualize the Buddha, but they are very useful for the average man because they tend to concentrate his attention on the Buddha.

There are no prayers in Buddhism. Instead of prayers there are meditations for purifying the mind in order that truth can be realized. According to Buddhism, the universe is governed by everlasting, unchangeable laws of righteousness—not by any god or any Supreme Being who can hear and answer prayers. These laws are so perfect that no one, no god or man, can change them by praising them or by crying out against them. Sin is the direct consequence of man's ignorance of these laws. Ignorance creates sin, sin begets sorrow; this is an eternal sequence.

Buddhists do not believe that there is any creator god who has made his laws so imperfectly that they require continual rectification through the prayers of men. If one believes that the universe is governed by a changeable and changing god—rather than by eternal laws—one will have to try to persuade him to make it better. Such a belief in a changeable god would mean a belief that his will is not always righteous, that his wrath has to be appeased, his mercy has to be aroused, his partiality has to be overcome. But for a Buddhist, the laws of righteousness which govern the universe are the same for all, the same forever. A man's duty, therefore, is not to break those laws, nor to try to change them by prayers or any other means, but to try to understand them and to live in harmony with them.

All through the Buddha's teaching, repeated stress is laid on self-reliance and resolution. Buddhism makes man stand on his own feet, it arouses his self-confidence and energy. The Buddha again and again reminded his followers that there is no one, either in heaven or on earth, who can help them or free them from the result of their past evil deeds. "It is through unshaken perseverance, O monks, that I have reached the light, through unceasing effort that I have reached the peace supreme. If you also, O monks, will strive unceasingly, you too will within a short time reach the highest goal of holiness by understanding and realizing it yourselves."

Understanding that neither a god nor ceremonies can help or save him, the true Buddhist finds no place for prayer; he feels compelled to rely on his own efforts and thus gains self-confidence. He sees that the tendency to rely on a god or any other imaginary power weakens man's confidence in his own power and lessens his sense of responsibility; he sees that blind faith in any authority leads to stagnation and spiritual lethargy. The Buddhist reaches his goal through perseverance in meditation rather than through prayer.

DEPENDENT ORIGINATION

Through twenty-five centuries, Buddhism has combined rationality with devotion. A freedom of thought which rejects dogmatism has released mankind from the fetters of ignorance, and the practice of meditation has made possible the realization of Nibbana. Let us consider now the insights which the Buddha taught as a result of his great efforts which led to Enlightenment.

Buddhists believe that life is beginningless, that it has no ultimate origin, for the cause ever becomes the effect and the effect becomes the cause, and in the circle of cause and effect a First Cause or beginning is inconceivable. The Buddha positively states, "The origin of phenomenal existence is inconceivable, and the beginning of beings obstructed by ignorance and ensnared by craving is not to be discovered." (Samyutta Nikaya, II. 178.) For all beings, the cause becomes the effect and the effect becomes the cause, and thus birth is followed by death and death is followed by birth. Birth and death are two phases of the same life process.

According to Buddhism the universe evolved, but it did not evolve out of nothingness; it evolved out of the dispersed matter of a previous universe, and when this universe is dissolved, its dispersed matter—or, its residual energy which is continually renewing itself—will in time give rise to another universe in the same way. The process is therefore cyclical and continuous.

The universe is composed of millions of world-systems like our own solar system, each with its various planes of existence.

There are altogether thirty-one planes of existence in which beings are born according to their kammic energy, that is, according to the creative energies generated by their thoughts, words, and deeds. The four lowest planes are known as the Four States of Unhappiness: the plane of woeful states which are temporary, not everlasting; the animal kingdom; the plane of ghost beings; and the plane of demons. Just above the four lowest planes are the Seven Happy States, made up of the plane of human beings and above them the six planes of the lower heavenly beings. These eleven lowest planes are all planes of desire. Above them are the twenty planes of existence of the higher heavenly beings.

The Wheel of Life, the process of life and death in the thirty-one planes of existence, is explained by the chain of causation, by the dependent origination (*paticcasamuppada;* in Sanskrit, *pratîtyasamutpada*) of all physical and psychical phenomena. Nothing exists independently; all phenomena, all beings and things, are effects which result from a complex of causes; they are dependent in their origination upon that combination of causes and have no identity apart from them.

This interdependence of all things, this process of dependent origination, operates in a universe governed by five orders:

1. The physical inorganic order—The unchanging order of seasons which cause wind and rains, and the nature of heat would belong to this order.

2. The order of germs and seeds, the physical organic order, may be illustrated by rice growing from rice seed, or the particular characteristics of certain fruits or trees. The scientific theories concerning cells deal with this order.

3. The order of act and result—In this order it is clear that desirable and undesirable acts produce corresponding good and bad results. As surely as water seeks its own level, so do acts produce inevitable results, not in the form of rewards or punishments, but as an innate sequence. This sequence of deed and result, known as kamma, is as natural and necessary as the way of the sun and the moon.

4. The order of the norm—Gravitation and other similar laws of nature, or the reasons for being good, may be included in this group. The order of the norm explains the natural phenomena occurring at the advent of a Bodhisattva in his last birth.

5. The order of mind or psychic law includes the processes of consciousness, the arising and perishing of consciousness, the constituents of consciousness, the powers of the mind and such mental powers. Telepathy, telesthesia, retrocognition, premonition, clairvoyance, thought-reading, and all psychic phenomena which are inexplicable to modern science are included in this order.

These five orders embrace everything in the world and every mental or physical phenomenon can be explained by them. They are laws in themselves and require no lawgiver. Within a universe governed by these five orders, life goes on in a cycle which is governed by the law of dependent origination, the twelve links in the chain of causation:

1. Ignorance is the first link in the chain of causation. It is ignorance of what things truly are and especially ignorance of the Four Noble Truths concerning the origin and cessation of suffering. Ignorance is the primary root of all evil; greed and anger, for instance, are always accompanied by ignorance. If a man could see clearly, he would do right, but in his ignorance he does evil things which prolong his wandering in the world of rebirths.

2. Through ignorance arise volitional activities, that is, all moral and immoral actions of body, speech, and mind arise through ignorance. Note that this second link in the causal chain includes moral as well as immoral actions, for both tend to prolong the cycle of rebirths.

3. Through volitional activities arises relinking consciousness, that is, the consciousness which is relinked to another existence. The moral and immoral actions are the causes of rebirth of a being, after death, in a new mother's womb.

4. Through relinking consciousness arise mind and matter. This is because without relinking consciousness there can be no continuing process of mental and physical existence.

Mind and matter mean here the kamma-determined results of mental and physical phenomena.

5. Through mind and matter arise the six senses, that is, the five physical sense organs and the mind.

6. Through the six senses arise the impressions, sensory and mental. Without the five physical sense organs there can be no sense impressions, and without the mind there can be no mental impressions.

7. Through impression arises feeling. Any feeling, whether agreeable, indifferent, or disagreeable, whether bodily or mental, is conditioned by impression.

8. Through feeling arises craving or desire (tanha). It is because of agreeable feelings that craving arises for pleasant, delightful sights, sounds, smells, tastes, contacts, and ideas.

9. Through craving arises attachment. There are four types of attachment common to man, attachment to sensuality, to false views, to wrong rites and ceremonies, and to self-deception.

10. Through attachment arises the process of becoming; that is, the attachment gives rise to the current of becoming which manifests itself as the life force for future rebirth.

11. Through the process of becoming arises rebirth. Without the process of the life force generated through attachment, there could be no rebirth. This process of becoming is compared to the seed which generates the new being.

12. Through rebirth arise old age and death. Without rebirth there could be no old age and death with the inevitable consequences of sorrow, lamentation, pain, grief, and despair.

Of the twelve links in the chain, the twelve steps in dependent origination, note that the first two are determined by past experiences and are identical with past volitional activities performed under the influence of ignorance. The next four—relinking consciousness, mind and matter, six senses, sense impressions and feelings—are concerned with the present existence of a being, but are the results of past existence or past actions. The next three—craving, attachment, and the process of becoming—are also concerned with the present existence and are going on from moment to moment. From this we see that although our present position in character and circumstances is the result of our past actions, what we shall be in the future depends upon what we do now, upon how we face circumstances in the present. Thus it is within our power to alter or modify the quality of the life force that continues in the next birth. The last two links are the result, the sum total, of our present activities.

In this process of becoming, the turning of the Wheel of Life, cause and effect, past and present, birth and death, are dependent phases of the same process. This cycle continues until the two factors, ignorance and craving, which are the key-points of the Wheel, are totally annihilated. Of these two, ignorance is the main cause of the present existence and, therefore, if it is destroyed, the subsequent links all cease to arise in the future and the chain is broken. Since craving is the main cause of present activities, if it is destroyed, there will be no future birth and the life process ends; the Wheel of Life no longer turns. It is only when this great task is accomplished that the goal of Nibbana is won.

The understanding of dependent origination is basic to an understanding of Buddhism. The Buddha said, "Whoso understands the dependent origination, understands the Law; and whoso understands the Law, understands dependent origination." (Majjhima Nikaya 28.) This understanding of dependent origination makes clear the three fundamental characteristics of all existence—that existence is impermanent (anicca), substanceless (anatta), and full of suffering (dukkha).

The Buddha has summed up all physical and mental phenomena of existence in five groups, called the five aggregates or *khandhas* (*skandhas* in Sanskrit). "And what, in brief, are the Five Groups of Existence? They are corporeality, feeling, perception, mental formations, and consciousness." (Digha Nikaya 22.)

Corporeality, or matter, is the visible form of the four invisible qualities or forces which are known as the essential elements:

1. The element of extension is the fundamental principle of matter. It is this element which enables objects to occupy

space and which gives material objects the qualities of hardness and softness. It can be found in water, earth, fire, and air, but it is preponderant in earth and therefore is called the element of earth.

2. The element of cohesion is the one which coheres the scattered atoms of matter and forms them into mass or bulk. It is known as the element of water since it is preponderant there.

3. The element of heat matures all objects of matter; it includes cold since heat and cold are two phases of the same element. The preservation and decay of all material objects are due to this element. It is called the element of fire since it is preponderant in fire.

4. The element of motion is the power of supporting or resisting. It is the cause of movement and vibration and is known as the element of air.

These four elements are interrelated and inseparable. All forms of matter are composed of these elements; every material object is simply a combination of them in one proportion or another. When the same matter is changed into another form, the composite things formed are held to be mere conceptions presented to the mind by the particular shape or form. A piece of clay, for example, may be called a cup, a plate, or a pot, according to the several shapes it assumes, but these objects can be analyzed and reduced to the fundamental elements which alone exist in an ultimate sense. The terms *cup*, or *plate*, are mere conceptions which have no separate essential substance other than the elements of which they are composed.

Mind, which is the most important part of a being, is essentially a stream of consciousness which is best described as thought. Thought, however, is not simply a physiological function but is a kind of energy, something like electricity. Thoughts and radiations of currents of thought are mental elements of the mental world which correspond to the four material elements of the world of matter. A being is essentially a manifestation of its thought forces which are in a state of flux.

If the forces of the thoughts are developed, they become, through the degrees of perfection which they attain, finer and higher energies of thought; and if they are further developed, they become sufficiently strong to overcome the gravitational sphere of the earth. The currents of thoughts which are not capable of overcoming the gravitational sphere of the earth remain within that sphere, within the sphere of existent things. But they will form a new type of life, for a current of thought, though subject to change, is not lost. It will continue to exist and will manifest itself in a new being of some kind according to its tendencies. In this way, this circulation of life and death goes on forever until it is checked by the development of the mind.

The Buddha's analysis of the mind shows that the mind consists of four mental aggregates (khandhas): sensations or feelings; perceptions of sense objects or reaction to the senses; fifty types of mental formations, including tendencies and faculties; and consciousness, which is the fundamental factor of all the other three.

Thus a being is a composition of the five aggregates of the mental and material forces which are changing all the time, not remaining the same for two successive moments. The Buddha said:

All corporeal phenomena, whether past, present or future, one's own or external, gross or subtle, lofty or low, far or near, all belong to the group of corporeality; all feelings belong to the group of feeling; all perceptions belong to the group of perception; all mental formations belong to the group of formations; all consciousness belongs to the group of consciousness. (Majjhima Nikaya 109.)

Existing beings are made up of these five basic elements, and nothing else.

Is any one of the five aggregates the self or soul (*atta*)? The Buddha's answer is "No." Then what remains to be called the self or the soul? As has been said above, apart from the five aggregates there remains nothing to be called the soul. This is one of the three fundamental characteristics of all existence, the characteristic of substancelessness, of anatta, the absence of a permanent unchanging self or soul, the absence of any underlying substance which exists apart from the elements of which any existent thing is composed. It is this doctrine of anatta, no-soul, for which Buddhism stands and on which Buddhism differs from other religions. If the wheels and axles, the floorboards and sides, the shafts and all other parts are removed from a cart, what remains? The answer is nothing, and the combination of these parts is called a cart. In exactly the same way, the combination of the five aggregates is called a being which may assume as many names as it has shapes of forms and may vary as its physical and mental makeup changes.

If there is no self or soul, what is it that moves from life to life, growing all the time until it enters into the state of Nibbana which is the only unchanging reality?

The answer is that the uninterrupted process of psychophysical phenomena, which is composed of the five aggregates and is called a being, moves from life to life. The process of uninterrupted psycho-physical phenomena is constantly moving and changing like the current of a river. This state of constant change, this impermanence (anicca) is also one of the three fundamental characteristics of phenomenal existence. What is constantly changing cannot be restful, peaceful or satisfactory; and this unsatisfactory nature, this state of unrest or non-peace (dukkha) is the other fundamental characteristic of all phenomenal existence.

Returning now to the chain of interdependent causation, it is clear that phenomenal existence is only a combination of the basic elements, the aggregates, which are constantly combining and recombining with no underlying unchanging substance or soul to give them permanence. The main cause of the restlessness, the suffering, which is the lot of beings turning on the Wheel of Life, is craving or selfish desire for existence, which is one of the fifty mental formations. It is this desire which sets the life force in motion, which stimulates the mind and manifests itself in action. This action, called kamma, is in reality volition or will power, which is responsible for the creation of a being, for the binding of the five aggregates together. Without desire (tanha), however, the whole process would not be possible; therefore tanha is the real creator of a being, the chief builder of the house of the five aggregates which is called man, woman, I. It is only when this fact is realized and the main cause, desire, is annihilated that a being which is composed of the five aggregates, a being which is a process of psycho-physical phenomena, enters into the everlasting peace of Nibbana.

KAMMA

In this universe in which nothing is permanent, in which every existent being is a changing combination of the five aggregates, all change is governed by kamma.

Kamma (*karma* in Sanskrit) is a Pali word meaning action. In its general sense, kamma means all good and bad actions. Kamma refers to all kinds of intentional actions whether mental, verbal, or physical, that is, all thoughts, words, and deeds. In its ultimate sense kamma means all moral and immoral volition. The Buddha says, "Mental volition, O Bhikkhus, is what I call action [kamma]. Having volition, one acts by body, speech, and thought." (Anguttara Nikaya III. 415.)

Kamma, the order of cause and effect in action, is not determinism, nor it is an excuse for fatalism. The past influences the present, but does not dominate it. The past is the background against which life goes on from moment to moment; the past and the present influence the future. Only the present moment exists, and the responsibility for using the present moment for good or for ill lies with each individual.

We have seen in the discussion of dependent origination how the origination of existent things is a continuous process in which every existent being is an effect of previous causes. Every action produces an effect—it is cause first and effect afterwards. We therefore speak of kamma as "the law of cause and effect." Throwing a stone, for example, is an action. If the stone strikes a glass window and breaks it, the break is the effect of the action of throwing, but it is not the end, for the broken window will now be the cause of further trouble. Some of one's money will have to go to replace it, depriving one of the opportunity to save it or to use it for a desirable purpose, and the effect upon one is a feeling of disappointment. This may make one irritable and if one is not careful the irritability may become the cause of doing something else which is wrong.

There is no end to the result of action, no end to kamma, so we should be very careful about our actions, making sure that their effect will be good. It is therefore necessary for us to do a good, helpful action which will return to us in good kamma and thus make us strong enough to start a better kamma.

Throw a stone into a pond and see how the rings around the place where it strikes grow wider and wider until they become too wide for our eyes to follow. The little stone disturbs the water of the pond, but its action is not finished yet. When the tiny waves reach the edges of the pond, the water moves back until it pushes the stone that has disturbed it. The effects of our actions come back to us just as the waves do to the stone; and as long as we do our actions with evil intention, the new waves of effects come back to beat upon us and disturb us. If we are kind and keep ourselves peaceful, the returning waves of trouble will grow weaker and weaker until they die down and our good kamma will come back to us in blessing.

If we sow a mango seed, a mango tree will come up and bear mangoes, and if we sow a chili seed, a chili plant will grow and produce chilis. The Buddha says:

> According to the seed that's sown,
> So is the fruit ye reap therefrom.
> Doer of good will gather good,
> Doer of evil, evil reaps.
> Sown is the seed, and thou shalt taste
> The fruit thereof.

(Samyutta Nikaya)

Everything that comes to us is right. Whenever anything pleasant comes to us and makes us happy, we may be sure that our kamma is indicating that what we have done is right. When anything hurts us or makes us unhappy, our kamma is showing us our mistake. We must never forget that kamma is always just—it neither loves nor hates, it does not reward or punish, it is never angry, never pleased. It is simply the law of cause and effect.

Kamma knows nothing about us. It does not know us any more than fire knows us when it burns us. It is the nature of fire to burn, to give out heat; and if we use it properly it gives us light, cooks our food, burns up things we want to destroy —but if we use it wrongly it burns us and our property. It is the nature of fire to burn and it is our responsibility to use it the right way. It is foolish to grow angry and blame fire when it burns us because we made a mistake. In this respect, kamma is like fire.

In the world around us there are many inequalities in the lot of man—some men are inferior and some superior, some perish in infancy and others live a full eighty years or more, some are handsome and others ugly, some are rich and others are paupers. What is the cause of the inequalities that exist in the world? Buddhists cannot believe that this variation is the result of blind chance for, like modern scientists, Buddhists believe that the world works in accordance with the laws of cause and effect. Nor can Buddhists believe that this inequality is due to a creator god.

One of the three divergent views that prevailed at the time of the Buddha was the belief that, "Whatsoever happiness or pain or neutral feeling the person experiences, all that is due to the creation of a Supreme Deity." Commenting on this fatalistic view the Buddha said:

So, then, owing to the creation of a Supreme Deity men will become murderers, thieves, unchaste, liars, slanderers, abusive, babblers, covetous, malicious, and perverse in views. Thus for those who fall back on the creation of a God as the essential reason, there is neither the desire to do, nor the effort to do, nor necessity to do this deed or abstain from that deed. (Anguttara Nikaya I. 158.)

According to Buddhism, the inequalities which exist in the world are due, to some extent, to the environment—which is itself shaped by cause and effect—and to a greater extent to causes, that is kamma, which are in the present, in the immediate past, and in the remote past. Man himself is responsible for his own happiness and misery; he creates his own heaven and hell. Shaped by the past, man chooses in the present those causes which shape his future. Man is master of his own destiny, child of his past, and parent of his future.

Kamma is classified in four ways, with four subdivisions in each group:

I. Kamma is classified according to the time in which results are produced. There is kamma which ripens in the same lifetime, kamma which ripens in the next life, and kamma which ripens in successive births. These three types of kamma are as bound to produce results as a seed is to sprout. But for a seed to sprout, certain auxiliary causes such as soil, rain, and sun are required. In the same way, for a kamma to produce an effect, several auxiliary causes such as suitable circumstances and surroundings are required. It sometimes happens that for want of such auxiliary causes kamma does not produce any result. This fourth type of kamma is called ineffective kamma.

II. Kamma is also classified according to its particular function. There is reproductive kamma, which conditions the future birth; supportive kamma, which assists or maintains the results of kamma which already exists; counteractive kamma, which suppresses or modifies the result of reproductive kamma; and there is destructive kamma, which destroys the force of existing kamma and substitutes its own resultants.

III. Kamma is classified according to the priority of results.

1. There is serious or weighty kamma, which produces its results in the present life or the next. When the kamma is moral, the highly refined mental states called ecstasies are weighty because they produce results more speedily than the ordinary unrefined mental states. When the kamma is immoral, the five kinds of immediately effective serious crimes are weighty. These serious crimes are matricide, patricide, the murder of an Arahat, the wounding of a Buddha, and the creation of a schism in the Sangha.

2. Death-proximate kamma is the action which one does at the moment before death, either physically or mentally by thinking of one's own previous good or bad actions, by having good or bad thoughts. It is this kamma which, if there is no

weighty kamma, determines the conditions of the next birth.

3. Habitual kamma is the action which one constantly does. This kamma, in the absence of death-proximate kamma or weighty kamma, produces and determines the nature of the next birth.

4. Reserved kamma is the unexpended kamma of a particular being, and it conditions the next birth if there is no habitual kamma to operate.

IV. Kamma is classified according to the plane in which the results are produced—the plane of misery, the plane of the world of desire, the plane of form, and the plane of the formless.

1. Immoral kamma produces its effect in the plane of misery. Immoral kamma is rooted in greed, anger, and delusion and is expressed in ten immoral actions—killing, stealing, unchastity (these three are caused by deed); lying, slandering, harsh language, frivolous talk (these four are caused by word); covetousness, ill will, false view (these three are caused by mind). The evil effects of killing are short life, disease, constant grief caused by the separation from the loved ones, and constant fear. The evil effects of stealing are poverty, wretchedness, unfulfilled desires, and dependent livelihood. The evil effects of unchastity are the having of many enemies, getting undesirable wives, birth as a woman or as a eunuch. Lying results in being tormented by abusive speech, being subject to vilification, incredibility, and a stinking mouth. Slandering results in the dissolution of friendship without any sufficient cause. Harsh language results in being detested by others, although blameless, and a harsh voice. The effects of frivolous talk are deformities of the bodily organs and unacceptable speech. Covetousness leads to unfulfilled wishes. Ill will leads to ugliness, various diseases, and a detestable nature. False view means seeing things wrongly without understanding what they truly are, and it leads to base attachment, lack of wisdom, dull wit, chronic diseases, and blameworthy ideas. (Niddesa, Khuddaka Nikaya.)

2. Good kamma produces its effect in the plane of desires. There are ten moral actions which produce good kamma—

generosity, morality, meditation, reverence, service, transference of merit, rejoicing in the merit of others, hearing the Doctrine, expounding the Doctrine, forming correct views. Generosity yields wealth; morality causes one to be born in noble families and in states of happiness; meditation gives birth in planes of form and formless planes and helps to gain higher knowledge and Nibbana. Reverence is the cause of noble parentage; service is the cause of a large retinue; transference of merit causes one to be able to give in abundance in future births; rejoicing in the merit of others is productive of joy wherever one is born. Both hearing and expounding the Doctrine are conducive to wisdom.

3. Good kamma which produces its effect in the planes of form is purely mental and is created in the five stages of the process of meditation:

> The first stage of ecstasy (*jhana*), which is made up of initial application, sustained application, rapture, happiness, and one-pointedness of mind;
>
> The second stage of ecstasy, which occurs with sustained application, rapture, happiness, and one-pointedness of mind;
>
> The third stage of ecstasy, which occurs with rapture, happiness, and one-pointedness of mind;
>
> The fourth stage of ecstasy, which occurs with happiness and one-pointedness of mind;
>
> The fifth stage of ecstasy, which occurs with equanimity and one-pointedness of mind.

4. Good kamma which produces its effect in the formless plane is of four types, which are also purely mental and done in the process of meditation—moral consciousness dwelling in the infinity of space, dwelling in the infinity of consciousness, dwelling on nothingness, and moral consciousness in which perception is so extremely subtle that it cannot be said whether it is or is not.

Kamma, as has been stated above, is not fate; it is not irrevocable destiny; it is not blind determinism. Nor is one bound to reap in just proportion all that one has sown. The actions of men are not absolutely irrevocable; in fact, only a few of them are. For example, when one fires a bullet from a rifle, one cannot call it back or turn it aside from its mark. But if, instead of a bullet through the air, it is an ivory ball on a billiard table that one sets moving with a cue, another ball can be sent after it to change its course, or, if one is quick enough, one might even get around to the other side of the table and send against it a ball which would meet it straight in the line of its course and bring it to a stop on the spot. With one's later action with the cue one modifies, or even in favorable circumstances entirely neutralizes, one's previous action. Kamma operates in the broad stream of life in much the same way. There, too, one's kamma of a later day may modify the effects of one's action—kamma—of a former day. If this were not so, there would be no possibility of man's ever getting free from all kamma; life would be a perpetually self-containing energy which could never come to an end.

Man has, therefore, a certain amount of free will and there is every possibility to mold his life or to modify his actions. Even the most vicious person can by his own free will and effort become the most virtuous person. One may at any moment change for the better or for the worse. But everything in the world, including man himself, is dependent on the conditions surrounding him, and without those conditions nothing whatsoever can arise or enter into existence. Man therefore has only a certain amount of free will and not absolute free will. According to Buddhist philosophy, everything mental or physical arises and passes away in accordance with the laws governing the conditions of his existence. If that were not so, there would be only chaos and blind chance. That this is not such a world of chaos and blind chance is shown by all the laws of nature which modern science has discovered.

The real, essential nature of action, that is, of kamma, is mental. When a given thought has arisen in one's mind a number of times, there is a definite tendency toward the recurrence of that thought. When a given act has been performed a number of times, there is a definite tendency toward the repetition of that act. Thus, each act, whether mental or physical, tends consistently to produce its like and to be in turn produced. If a man thinks a good thought, speaks a good word, does a good deed, the effect upon him is to increase the tendencies to goodness present in him, to make him a better man. If, on the contrary, he does a bad deed in thought or in speech or action, he has strengthened in himself his bad tendencies; he has made himself a worse man. Having become a worse man, he will gravitate to the company of worse men in the future and incur all the unhappiness of varying kinds that attends life in such company. On the other hand, the man whose character is continually growing better will naturally tend to the companionship of the good and enjoy all the pleasantness and comforts and freedom from the ruder shocks of human life which such society provides.

In the case of a mentally cultured man, even the effect of a greater evil may be minimized, while the lesser evil of an uncultured man may produce its effect to the maximum according to the favorable and unfavorable conditions of his existence.

The Buddha said:

"Here, O Bhikkhus, a certain person is not disciplined in body, is not disciplined in morality, is not disciplined in mind, is not disciplined in wisdom, is with little good and less virtue, and lives painfully in consequence of trifles. Even a trivial evil act committed by such a person will lead him to a state of misery.

"Here, O Bhikkhus, a certain person is disciplined in body, is disciplined in morality, is disciplined in mind, is disciplined in wisdom, is with much good, is high souled, and lives without limitation. A similar evil act committed by such a person is expiated in this life itself and not even a small effect manifests itself (after death), not to say a great one.

"It is as if, O Bhikkhus, a man were to put a lump of salt into a small cup of water. What do you think, O Bhikkhus? Would now the small amount of water in this cup become saltish and undrinkable?"

"Yes, Lord."

"And why?"

"Because, Lord, there was very little water in the cup, and so it became saltish and undrinkable by this lump of salt."

"Suppose, O Bhikkhus, a man were to put a lump of salt into the river Ganges. What think you, O Bhikkhus, would now the river Ganges become saltish and undrinkable by the lump of salt?"

"Nay, indeed, Lord."

"And why not?"

"Because, Lord, the mass of water in the river Ganges is great, and so it would not become saltish and undrinkable."

"In exactly the same way, O Bhikkhus, we may have the case of a person who does some slight evil deed which brings him to a state of misery; or again, O Bhikkhus, we may have the case of another person who does the same trivial misdeed, and expiates it in the present life. Not even a small effort manifests itself (after death), not to say of a great one." (Anguttara Nikaya.)

The more we understand the law of kamma, the more we see how careful we must be of our acts, words, and thoughts and how responsible we are for our fellow beings. Living in the light of this knowledge, we learn certain lessons from the doctrine of kamma.

From an understanding of kamma we learn patience. Knowing that the law of kamma is our great helper if we live by it, and that no harm can come to us if we work with it, knowing also that it blesses us just at the right time, we learn the grand lesson of patience, we learn not to get excited, and we learn that impatience is a check to progress. In suffering, we know that we are paying a debt, and we learn, if we are wise, not to create more suffering for the future. In rejoicing, we are thankful for its sweetness, and we learn, if we are wise, to be still better. Patience brings forth peace, success, happiness, and security.

From an understanding of kamma we learn confidence. The law of kamma being just and perfect, it is not possible for an understanding person to be uneasy about it. If we are uneasy and have no confidence, it shows clearly that we have not grasped the reality of the law of kamma. We are really quite safe beneath its wings, and there is nothing to fear in all the wide universe except our own misdeeds. The law of kamma makes a man stand on his own feet and arouses his self-confidence. Confidence strengthens and deepens our peace and happiness and makes us comfortable and courageous. Wherever we go, kamma is our protector.

We gain self-reliance from an understanding of kamma. As we in the past have caused ourselves to be what we are now, so by what we do now will our future be determined. A knowledge of this fact, and that the glory of the future is limitless, gives us great self-reliance and takes away that tendency to appeal for external help which is really no help at all.

We also learn restraint when we understand kamma. Naturally, if we realize that the evil we do will return and strike us, we will be very careful lest we do or say or think something that it is not good, pure, and true. Knowledge of kamma will restrain us from doing wrong for our own sake or the sake of others.

The understanding of kamma gives us power. The more we make the doctrine of kamma a part of our lives, the more power we gain, not only to direct our future, but also to help our fellow beings more effectively. The practice of good kamma, when fully developed, will enable us to overcome evil and limitations, and to destroy all the fetters that keep us from our goal, Nibbana.

UNIVERSAL LOVE

In order to create good kamma, to perform good actions, Buddhism emphasizes the importance of universal and all-embracing love—called *metta* in Pali. Metta is much deeper than good will. Some scholars interpret the meaning of metta as generous-mindedness, kindheartedness, or the sending out of thoughts of love to others. But, in the words of the Buddha, metta has a far wider significance and a more extensive application. It means a great deal more than loving-kindness, harmlessness, and sympathy. It is not a mere feeling but a principle; it is not merely the radiating of benevolent thoughts but it is the doing of charitable actions.

In the Metta Sutta, the Discourse on Universal Love, the Buddha says:

As a mother, even at the risk of her own life, protects and loves her child, her only child, so let a man cultivate love without measure toward all beings. Let him cultivate love without measure toward the whole world, above, below, and around, unstinted, unmixed with any feeling of differing or opposing interests. Let a man remain steadfastly in this state of mind all the while he is awake, whether he be standing, walking, sitting, or lying down. This state of mind is the best in the world.

This is the model held up to mankind by the Buddha. This is the ideal of what man should be to man. This is an appeal to every mind and every heart and a call to service. Consider the Buddha's illustration of a mother's love for her child. It is not mere loving-kindness, a mere expression of good will toward the child. Can language express the deathless love in a mother's heart? Is not this a love which will be expressed even at a peril to her own life?

Metta, therefore, is not simply a brotherly feeling; it is active benevolence, a love which is expressed and fulfilled in active ministry for the uplifting of fellow beings. Universal love goes hand in hand with helpfulness and a willingness to forego self-interest in order to promote the welfare and happiness of mankind. As explained in the Digha Nikaya, metta embodies the virtues of unselfishness, charity, and active loving care for others. It is metta which in Buddhism is the basis for social progress.

It is metta which attempts to break all the barriers separating one from another. There is no reason to keep aloof from others merely because they belong to another religious persuasion or nationality. The true Buddhist exercises metta, universal love, toward every living being and identifies himself with all, making no distinction whatsoever with regard to caste, color, class, or sex. This practice is not the result of blind obedience to a religious commandment; it is the outcome of the understanding that all living beings, including animals, are subject to the same laws and conditions of existence. "As I am, so are they; as they are, so am I; thus one should identify oneself with all that lives, and should not kill, nor hurt any living being."

The whole human family is so closely knit together that each unit is dependent upon other units for its growth and development. Life is a mighty wheel of perpetual motion. This wheel contains within it numberless small wheels, corresponding to the lives of individuals, each of which has a pattern of its own. The great wheel and the smaller wheels, the whole world and the individuals, are intimately and indissolubly linked.

To bring out the goodness in us, each one of us has to try to reproduce in his own wheel of life that pattern which is in harmony with the pattern of the great universal wheel. For all the wheels to revolve in harmony, the highest good in each must be developed. This is possible here and now by the performance of daily duties with kindness, courtesy, and truthfulness. The ideal that is placed before us is that of mutual service and practical brotherhood. Men, being in need of each other, should learn to love each other and bear each other's burdens. Mutual service is a perpetual call upon humanity, for we are bound alike by the bonds of humanity. To do good for the welfare of humanity is our holiest work.

REBIRTH

The principle of dependent origination and the law of kamma provide the background for understanding the nature of rebirth. According to Buddhism, death is "the temporary end of a temporary phenomenon." It is not the complete annihilation of the being, for although the organic life has ceased, the kammic force which hitherto actuated it is not destroyed. Our physical forms are only the outward manifestations of the invisible kammic force. This force carries with it all the characteristics which usually lie latent but may rise to the surface at any moment. When the present form perishes, another form takes its place according to a good or bad volitional impulse— the kamma that was the most powerful—at the moment before death.

At death the kammic force remains entirely undisturbed by the disintegration of the physical body and the passing away of the present consciousness creates the conditions for the coming into being of a fresh body in another birth. The stream of consciousness flows on like a river which is built up by its tributaries and dispenses its water to the countryside through which it passes. The continuity of flux at death is unbroken in point of time; there is no breach in the stream of consciousness, and therefore there is no room whatever for an intermediate stage between this life and the next. The only difference between the passing of one ordinary thought moment—or one unit of consciousness—to another and the passing of one dying thought moment to the rebirth-consciousness is that in ordinary thought the change is invisible, and in the death-rebirth moment a perceptible death occurs. Rebirth takes place immediately.

It may be asked whether the new place is always ready to receive this rebirth. The answer is yes, just as a point in the ground is always ready to receive the falling stone, so there is always an appropriate place to receive the rebirth which is conditioned by the natural law of kamma.

Death being a momentary incident, rebirth is immediate. The transmission of the life force, the kammic force, may be compared to the sound wave which makes the tuning fork vibrate in response to a particular note. So long as the musical note sets up vibrations in the air, so long will the tuning fork which is responsive to that particular note vibrate in unison. When the vibrations of the musical note cease, the tuning fork will cease to vibrate to that particular note. And so it is with that restless kammic force which continues to bring about births through appropriate germ plasms or other life conditions until that restless kammic force ceases to exist in the peace of Nibbana.

In the words of the late Bhikkhu Silacara:

This new being which is the present manifestation of the stream of kamma energy is not the same as, and has no identity with, the previous one in its line; the aggregate that makes up its composition being different from, and having no identity with, those that make up the being of its predecessor. And yet it is not an entirely different being, since it has the same stream of kamma energy, though modified perchance just by having shown itself in that last manifestation, which is now making its presence known in the sense-perceptible world as the new being.

If we were to obtain a quick motion picture of any particular individual's life from his birth to his death, the most striking fact that would attract our attention would be the changefulness that we would find running right through the series of pictures. The infant changes to the child, the child to the adult, and the adult to the decrepit old person who collapses in death. This change goes on in every part of the individual's body, and not only in the body but in the mind also. So much so that any adult who surveys his own existence will realize that the child that was is now no more. That child had a different body, in size as well as form, different likes and dislikes, different aspirations, and was almost a stranger to the present adult. And yet the adult is responsible for whatever he has done in his childhood because there is a continuity or identity in the process of life force from childhood to manhood.

In exactly the same way, the new being has the same stream of kammic energy or life force as its predecessor, and thus it is responsible for whatever its predecessor has done. This new being has as much identity with the previous one as the adult of today has with the child that he was; nothing less and nothing more.

This is well expressed in the *Milinda-panha*, the *Questions of King Milinda*. King Milinda asked Arahat Nagasena whether he who is reborn remains the same or becomes another.

"Neither the same nor another," was the answer he received. "Suppose O King, that a man were to light a lamp, would it burn the night through?"

"Yes, it might do so, Venerable Sir."

"Now, is it the same flame that burns in the first watch of the night, Sir, as in the second?"

"No, Venerable Sir."

"Or the same that burns in the second watch and in the third?"

"No, Venerable Sir."

"Then is there one lamp in the first watch and another in the second and another in the third?"

"No, the light comes from the same lamp all the night through."

"Just so, O King, is the continuity of a person or a thing maintained. One passes away, another comes into being; and the rebirth is, as it were, simultaneous. Thus, neither as the same nor as another does a man go on to the last phase of his self-consciousness."

Asked for another illustration, Arahat Nagasena gives that of milk which, once it is taken from the cow, after a lapse of time turns first to curds, then from curds to butter, and then from butter to ghee. Just as it would not be correct to say that the milk was the same thing as the curds, or the butter, or the ghee, but that they are produced out of it, so, he points out, the continuity of a person or a thing is maintained in the same way.

There is also the illustration of the wave of water in the lake or the ocean. A certain mass of water is raised up as a wave. As the wave passes on, or seems to pass on, a moment or so later it is not the same mass of water that forms the wave, but a different mass altogether. And yet we speak of the wave "passing on."

The present being, present existence, is conditioned by the way one faced circumstances in the last and in all past existences. One's present position in character and circumstances is the result of all that one has been up to the present—but what one will be in the future depends on what one does now in the present. The true Buddhist regards death as a momentary incident between one life and its successor and views its approach with calmness. His only concern is that his future should be such that the condition of that life may provide him with better opportunities for perfecting himself. Holding, as he does, the great doctrine of kamma, he perceives that it is within his power to alter or modify the quality of the life force that continues in the next birth, and that his future environment will depend entirely on what he does, on how he has behaved in this and in his previous lives.

Buddhism teaches that with the practice of meditation and concentration the memory can be trained. By meditation and mind culture one can acquire the power to see one's rebirth as a link, or a succession of links, in a chain of births; one can also acquire the power of looking back into one's previous lives. Not only this, but Buddhism goes further and teaches that with the attainment of Nibbana in this life itself, through enlightenment or true wisdom, one can reach the end of this chain of rebirths.

There are on record instances of people who have possessed wonderful memories, some for what they had once read, others for music, others for names. There are still others who have remembered their past lives. The average person's memory is very bad indeed, but the fact that they do not remember an activity in their past does not prove that it did not happen. The same is true of the memory of past lives. Some people, simply because they cannot remember past lives, deny that there have been any previous births.

To students of Buddhism this seems a very foolish position, for we are taught neither to accept nor reject any teaching until we have examined all the evidence for it and have experimented with it ourselves to see if it is true. Having proved by these means that a thing is true or untrue, a Buddhist should live according to the evidence; but he must never judge others or be impatient if they cannot see things as he does. He must be tolerant of all, even the intolerant, and he must always remember that what is proof to one is not proof to another. What each person needs is experience—to see, to hear, and to feel for himself—and he has no right to ask others to believe before they have also had experience.

It is common to read in the Buddhist literature the remarks of the Buddha and many of his disciples concerning their own past lives and those of others, and often, too, of their future lives. Having attained his final Enlightenment and developed higher spiritual powers, the Buddha declared, "I recall my varied lot in former existences as follows—first one life, then two lives, then three, four, five, ten, twenty, up to fifty lives; then a hundred, a thousand, a hundred thousand, and so forth." He also said, "With clairvoyant vision, I perceived beings disappearing from one state of existence and reappearing in another. I beheld the base and the noble, the beautiful and the ugly, and the happy passing according to their deeds." (Sutta 36, Majjhima Nikaya I. 248.)

There are several discourses in which the Buddha clearly states that the beings who have done evil are born in woeful states, and those who have done good are born in blissful states. All the Jataka stories, which are not only interesting but are of psychological importance, deal with the Buddha's disciples who also developed certain higher spiritual powers and were able to remember their past lives to a great extent.

From the foregoing we can now answer the following three questions.

Whence come we?

We came out of the past, out of the things which we have done before, out of the past vices and virtues, out of the labors unfinished, out of the darkness of our own ignorance, out of our own desires. Thus we come down to the present, bringing with us the virtues and the vices of the past.

Why are we here?

We are here because of the past, for the past gives birth to the present and from the present is born the future. We were brought here by our own joys and our own sorrows, and most of all we were led here by our own desires and we will remain here until the last selfish desire is annihilated. To the wise man, the life he lives here is an opportunity to rid himself of the burden which he has accumulated in the past, to rid himself of his wrong notions, his wrong viewpoints, to rid himself of his wrong concepts of life and death—and, leaving them all behind, to place his feet upon the Middle Path.

Whither are we going?

We go to the effects of our causation. Those whose labors are unfinished merely go around the Wheel of Life and return again to labor toward fuller completion. Those who have followed the Middle Path and finished their labors reach the state of Nibbana, the complete cessation of sorrow. To unmask the great illusion is the labor of man. To stand in equilibrium in the midst of worldly things is the way of the Buddha. To contemplate life but never to be enmeshed within worldly life is the law of the Buddha. To go forth out of worldly life into the higher spiritual life is the advice of the Buddha. To be absorbed into what is real, permanent—into Nibbana—is the end of the Buddhist way of life, the path of the Buddha.

The Four Noble Truths

The Buddha, after his Enlightenment, showed the way all men can follow to bring an end to kamma, to attain Nibbana. The Four Noble Truths, which explain that way, are given here in the words of the Buddha, brought together from various sources in the Pali canon.

It is through not understanding, not realizing four things that I, Disciples, as well as you, had to wander long through this round of rebirths. And what are these four things? They are—

The Noble Truth of Suffering (dukkha);

The Noble Truth of the Origin of Suffering;

The Noble Truth of the Extinction of Suffering;

The Noble Truth of the Path that leads to the Extinction of Suffering.

As long as the absolutely true knowledge and insight as regards these Four Noble Truths was not quite clear to me, so long was I not sure whether I had won that supreme Enlightenment which is unsurpassed in all the world with its heavenly beings, evil spirits, and gods, amongst all the hosts of ascetics and priests, heavenly beings, and men. But as soon as the absolutely true knowledge and insight as regards these Four Noble Truths had become perfectly clear to me, there arose in me the assurance that I had won that supreme Enlightenment unsurpassed.

And I discovered that profound truth, so difficult to perceive, difficult to understand, tranquilizing and sublime, which is not to be gained by mere reasoning, and is visible only to the wise. The world, however, is given to pleasure, delighted with pleasure, enchanted with pleasure. Truly, such beings will hardly understand the law of conditionality, the Dependent Origination of everything; incomprehensible to them will also be the end of all formations, the forsaking of every substratum of rebirth, the fading away of craving, detachment, extinction, Nibbana. Yet, there are beings whose eyes are only a little covered with dust—they will understand the truth.

What, now, is the Noble Truth of Suffering? Birth is suffering; decay is suffering; death is suffering; sorrow, lamentation, pain, grief, and despair are suffering; not to get what one desires is suffering; in short, the five aggregates of existence are suffering.

What, now, is the Noble Truth of the Origin of Suffering? It is that craving which gives rise to fresh rebirth, and, bound up with pleasure and lust, now here, now there, finds ever fresh delight. But where does this craving arise and take root? Wherever in the world there are delightful and pleasurable things, there this craving arises and takes root. Eye, ear, nose, tongue, body, and mind are delightful and pleasurable—there this craving arises and takes root. Visual objects, sounds, smells, tastes, bodily impressions, and mind objects are delightful and pleasurable—there this craving arises and takes root. Consciousness, sense impression, feeling born of sense impression, perception, will, thinking, and reflecting are delightful and pleasurable—there this craving arises and takes root. This is called the Noble Truth of the Origin of Suffering.

What, now, is the Noble Truth of the Extinction of Suffering? It is the complete fading away and extinction of this craving, its forsaking and giving up, the liberation and detachment from it. But where may this craving vanish, where may it be extinguished? Wherever in the world there are delightful and pleasurable things, there this craving may vanish, there it may be extinguished. Be it in the past, present, or future, whosoever of the monks or priests regards the delightful and pleasurable things in the world as impermanent (anicca), miserable (dukkha), and without a self (anatta), as a disease and cancer, it is he who overcomes craving. This, truly, is Peace, this is the Highest, namely the end of all kamma formations, the forsaking of every substratum of rebirth, the fading away of craving, detachment, extinction, Nibbana. The extinction of greed, the extinction of anger, the extinction of delusion—this is indeed called Nibbana.

And for a disciple thus freed [the Arahat], in whose heart dwells peace, there is nothing to be added to what has been done, and naught more remains for him to do. Just as a rock of one solid mass remains unshaken by the wind, even so neither forms, nor sounds, nor odors, nor tastes, nor contacts of any kind, neither the desired nor the undesired, can cause such a one to waver. Steadfast is his mind, gained his deliverance. And he who has considered all the contrasts on this earth, and is no more disturbed by anything whatever in the world, the peaceful one, freed from rage, from sorrow and from longing, he has passed beyond birth and decay.

To give oneself up to indulgence in sensual pleasure, the base, common, vulgar, unholy, unprofitable; and also to give oneself up to self-mortification, the painful, unholy, unprofitable: both these two extremes the Perfect One has avoided and found out the Middle Path, which makes one both to see and to know, which leads to peace, to discernment, to Enlightenment, to Nibbana.

What, now, is the Noble Truth of the Path that Leads to the Extinction of Suffering? It is the Noble Eightfold Path, the way that leads to the extinction of suffering, namely: Right Understanding, Right Thought, Right Speech, Right Action, Right Livelihood, Right Effort, Right Mindfulness, Right Concentration. This is the Middle Path which the Perfect One has found out, which makes one both to see and to know, which leads to peace, to discernment, to Enlightenment, to Nibbana. Free from pain and torture is this path, free from groaning and suffering; it is the perfect Path. Truly, like this Path there is no other path to the purity of insight. If you follow this Path, you will put an end to suffering. But each one has to struggle for himself; the Perfect Ones have only pointed the way. Give ear, then, for the Immortal is found. I reveal, I set forth the Truth. As I reveal it to you, so act. And that Supreme Goal of the holy life, for the sake of which sons of good families rightly go forth from home to the homeless state: this you will in no long time, in this very life, make known to yourself, realize, and make your own.

THE MIDDLE PATH

The Eightfold Path is the Middle Path by which beings reach the goal of Nibbana.

1. Right understanding is understanding of the Four Truths —understanding the nature of suffering, the origin of suffering, the extinction of suffering, and the Path that leads to the extinction of suffering.

2. Right thought is thought which is free from lust, free from ill will, and free from cruelty. We should think about right things and not about wrong things; we should always keep in our minds thoughts which are high and beautiful. Right thought must never have the slightest touch of evil in it. There are some people who would not deliberately think of anything impure or horrible, and yet they will cherish thoughts which are on the brink of impurity and horror—not definitely evil, but certainly a little doubtful. Whenever there is anything which seems in the least suspicious or unkind, it must be shut out of thought. We must be quite sure that our thoughts are kind and good.

Another meaning of right thought is correct thought. Often we think untrue or wrong thoughts about persons just because of prejudice or ignorance; we think that a person is bad and therefore conclude that his actions must be evil. When we attribute motives to another person without foundation, we are thinking untruly about him, and our thought is not right thought. When we fix our attention on the evil in a man instead of the good, we strengthen and encourage the evil, while with right thought we would strengthen and encourage the good.

3. Right speech is abstaining from lying, from talebearing, from harsh language, and from vain talk. A man who abstains from lying speaks the truth, is devoted to the truth, is reliable, worthy of confidence, is not a deceiver of men. When at a meeting, or among people, or in the midst of his relatives, or in society, or in the king's court and called upon as a witness to tell what he knows, if he knows nothing he says, "I know

nothing"; if he has seen nothing, he answers, "I have seen nothing." Thus, he never knowingly speaks a lie either for his own advantage, or for another person's advantage, or for any advantage whatsoever.

Right speech requires that a man avoid talebearing. What he has heard here, he does not repeat there, so as to cause dissension. Thus he unites those who are divided, and those who are united, he encourages. Concord gladdens him; he rejoices in concord and spreads concord by his words. He also avoids harsh language—rather, he speaks such words as are gentle, soothing to the ear and loving, words which go to the heart, are courteous and friendly and agreeable to many. And, finally, he avoids vain talk; he speaks at the right time, in accordance with the facts, speaks what is useful, speaks about the law and the discipline. His speech is like a treasure, uttered at the right moment, accompanied by arguments which are moderate and full of sense.

4. Right action is abstaining from killing, from stealing, and from unlawful sexual intercourse. The man who follows the path does not kill living beings; he has no stick or weapon, is conscientious, full of sympathy, and is anxious for the welfare of all living beings. He does not steal—what another person possesses of goods and chattels in the town, village, or in the jungle, that he does not take away with thievish intent. He avoids unlawful sexual intercourse; he has no intercourse with such persons as are still under the protection of father, mother, brother, sister, or relatives, nor with married women, nor with female convicts, nor with betrothed girls.

5. Right livelihood is the right way of earning a living, that which causes no harm to any living thing. It affects such trades as those of the butcher or fisherman, but reaches much farther than that. We should not obtain our livelihood by harming any creature, and therefore the selling of alcohol is not a right means of livelihood because the seller is living on the harm he does to other people. Further, the merchant who in the course of his trade is dishonest, who is cheating the people, is not following the right means of livelihood. The merchant has a right to a reasonable profit, the lawyer and doctor have a right to a

reasonable fee, but all must be trustworthy and look to their duties.

6. Right effort includes four great efforts, the efforts to avoid, to overcome, to develop, and to maintain. The disciple must strengthen his will to avoid the arising of evil, unwholesome things that have not yet arisen. Thus, when he perceives a form with the eye, a sound with the ear, an odor with the nose, a taste with the tongue, an impression with the body, or an object with the mind, he neither adheres to the whole or its parts. He watches over and restrains his senses, striving to ward off that through which evil and unwholesome things might arise. When he has control over the senses, he experiences an inward feeling of joy into which no evil thing can enter. In addition to the effort to avoid, the disciple must make the effort to overcome the evil, unwholesome things which have already arisen. He must also make the effort to arouse wholesome things which have not yet arisen, and, finally, to maintain the wholesome things that have already arisen, not let them disappear but rather bring them to growth, to maturity, and to the full perfection of development.

7. Right mindfulness is contemplation on the four fundamentals of mindfulness—contemplation on the body, feeling, mind, and mind objects. The only way that leads to the attainment of purity, to the overcoming of sorrow and lamentation, to the end of pain and grief, to the entering upon the right path and the realization of Nibbana, is the contemplation on the four fundamentals of mindfulness. Vigilant attention leads us to see correctly and to attain a point of view from which we can see beyond the pairs of opposites. He who does not practice attention is the plaything of the multiple influences with which he comes in contact, he is like a drifting cork which is at the mercy of the waves, he unconsciously submits to the action of his physical and psychical environment; he is a corpse.

We must be conscious of our movements and acts, both physical and mental. Nothing of what goes on in us should escape attention. We must be conscious of the feelings which are occurring in us; we must investigate them and search for their causes. We must be aware of anger when we are angry, find its cause, and foresee its results. In this way we can check all feelings such as envy, sensuality, and anxiety. When we perform a charitable deed, we must also question ourselves as to our motives. The result of this kind of question will often be a changing of selfish moral values. The practice of perfect attention is a means of learning to know oneself, to know the world in which one lives, and consequently to acquire right understanding.

8. Right concentration is concentration on a single object which is associated with wholesome consciousness. The four fundamentals of mindfulness which constitute the seventh step of the Path are the objects of concentration, and the four great efforts of the sixth step are the prerequisites for concentration. The practicing and cultivating of mindfulness is the development of concentration.

THREE STAGES OF DEVELOPMENT

All the teachings of the Buddha can be summed up in one verse which embodies the three stages on the grand path that leads to Nibbana:

> To refrain from all evil,
> To do what is good,
> To purify the mind,
>   This is the teaching of the Buddhas.

There are three stages of development for a Buddhist—morality is the first stage, concentration the second, and wisdom the third. The eight steps of the Eightfold Path are classified under these three stages. Morality includes right speech, right action, and right livelihood; concentration includes right effort, right mindfulness, and right concentration; and wisdom includes the first two steps, right understanding, and right thought. Although wisdom is in one sense the beginning of the Eightfold Path, in a more important sense it is the outcome.

There are three stages of development because there are three stages of defilement which must be overcome. In the first stage, defilements are not manifest in words or deeds, but lie latent in each being; in the second stage they come up from the latent state to the level of thoughts, emotions, and feelings when they are awakened by an object, pleasant or unpleasant; in the third stage they become fierce and ungovernable and produce evil actions.

The three stages of development dispel the three stages of defilement. Morality can dispel only the defilements of evil actions, but leaves untouched the defilements of the two lower levels, so they could rise again. Therefore, morality is called the temporary putting away of defilements. The development of concentration can dispel only the second defilements of thoughts, emotions, and feelings. It can be effective for a considerable time, for it is more powerful than morality; but since the defilements which are latent are not dispelled, the defilements of the second level could arise again. Therefore the putting away by concentration is called the putting away to a distance.

The defilements of the first level, the latent defilements, are dispelled by wisdom, by insight. They are untouched by morality or concentration, but when dispelled through insight will never arise again. Getting rid of them by wisdom is like cutting a tree by the root; therefore, the putting away by insight is called the cutting away.

Since the three stages of development are interdependent and interrelated, they should be practiced at the same time. For example, when living a moral life, it is easier to have right concentration and right understanding. The practice of right concentration helps one to live rightly and to understand things rightly; and in the same way, the practice of right understanding helps one to live rightly and to concentrate rightly. On the other hand, they cannot be practiced separately, for it is impossible to live a moral life without concentration—which is mind control—and without right understanding; in the same way, concentration and wisdom always require the other two stages.

The first of the rules of discipline (morality) prescribed for the lay disciples are the Five Precepts: not to kill, not to steal, not to commit any sexual misconduct, not to lie, and not to take any intoxicating liquor or drugs. These are not the Buddha's commandments, which it would be considered a sin to break. They represent the preliminary ideals of a virtuous life which a man will accept wholeheartedly if he is to call himself a Buddhist. He does not make a promise to the Buddha to obey the precepts; he gives the promise to himself. The pledge is phrased, "I accept the precept to refrain from taking life." Each man who repeats the precepts puts himself on his honor to do his best not to break them. And if he breaks them the only repentance which is constructive is to make the pledge to himself again as many times as is necessary, day after day, month after month, year after year, until he wins the struggle against his lower nature. A man must win the goal of purity and nobility by himself. Neither the Buddha, nor angels, nor any god can bring a man to deliverance. The practice of the moral life is the very core and essence of Buddhism. A person of right understanding who realizes the law of cause and effect may accept the precepts and then go on a step further and cultivate sense restraint, since he realizes that overindulgence in sensual pleasures is a hindrance to moral and spiritual progress.

The spiritual man who has learned to practice morality and master his senses is inclined to move to the second stage on the path to Nibbana, the stage of control and culture of the mind which brings a higher and more lasting happiness through concentration. This higher happiness can be attained through *jhanas* (*dhyanas* in Sanskrit). The word *jhana* comes from a root which may mean "to think closely of an object," or "to burn adverse things which hinder spiritual progress." It has been translated as trance, absorption, or ecstasy, but it is best thought of as a special, extramundane experience.

The spiritual man who seeks the second stage of development selects one of the recommended objects of concentration which appeals to his temperament and concentrates on it for days, weeks, months, or even years until he is able to visualize it without difficulty. When he can visualize it without looking at it, he continues concentration on it until he develops it into a conceptualized object, at which stage he has attained proximate concentration. At that point, he can overcome temporarily the five hindrances of sensual desires, hatred, sloth, restlessness and worry, and doubts. By continuing in the discipline of concentration he eventually attains the five stages of jhana and easily develops the five supernormal powers: celestial eye, celestial ear, remembrance of past births, reading thoughts of others, and various psychic powers.

The mind of the spiritual man who has reached such high levels of experience through the jhanas is highly refined; yet that man is not entirely free from evil tendencies because concentration can only overcome temporarily the evil tendencies of the second stage of defilements. Since the evil tendencies of the first stage—the latent defilements—still remain untouched, the defilements of the second stage—the thoughts, emotions, and feelings aroused by sense objects—would arise again.

Morality makes a man gentle in his words and deeds; concentration controls the mind and makes him calm, serene, and steady; and wisdom enables him to overcome all the defilements completely.

The spiritual man who has reached the third stage on the path to Nibbana, the stage of wisdom or insight, tries to understand the real nature of his self and of the things of the world in general. With his highly purified mind he begins to realize that there is no ego-principle or persistent identity of a self or substratum in either internal or external phenomena. He perceives that both mind and matter, which make up his personality, are in a state of constant flux; he sees that all conditioned things are impermanent (anicca), subject to suffering (dukkha), and void of self-existence (anatta). To him then comes the knowledge that every form of worldly pleasure is only a prelude to pain and that everything is in a state of flux and cannot be the source of real, permanent happiness.

The aspirant then concentrates on the three characteristics of existence—impermanence, suffering, and non-ego. Having neither attachment nor aversion for worldly things, he intently keeps on developing insight into both internal and external phenomena until he eliminates the three fetters of self-illusion, doubts, and clinging to vain rites and rituals. It is only when he destroys these three fetters completely that he realizes Nibbana, for the first time in his existence. At this stage he is called one who has entered the stream that leads to Nibbana, for just as a stream flows inevitably toward the ocean, so the aspirant will with certainty attain his final enlightenment. But because he has not eradicated the remaining seven fetters, he may be reborn as many as seven times.

When the aspirant has developed deeper insight and weakened the next two fetters—sensual craving and ill will—he becomes a Once-returner because if he does not obtain final release in this present life he will be reborn in the world of desires only once. When those two fetters are completely discarded, the aspirant becomes a Non-returner, one who will not be reborn in this world or any of the realms of sense pleasures, but if he does not attain his final Enlightenment in this life he will be reborn in one of the higher, suitable planes and pass from there to Nibbana.

The fourth stage is that of Arahat, the perfected saint who completely annihilates the remaining five fetters of craving for existence in the world of form, craving for existence in the immaterial world, pride or conceit, restlessness, and ignorance. He then realizes that rebirth is exhausted, the Holy Life is fulfilled and what was to be done has been done. This is the highest, holiest peace and end of greed, hatred, and delusion. The Arahat stands on heights more than celestial, realizing the unutterable bliss of Nibbana. There is nothing in him to cause him to be born again, or grow old again, or die again. There is nothing more for him to do, for he has shown that man can follow the Path of the Buddha to Nibbana.

NIBBANA

Nibbana is the result of the cessation of craving, of selfish desires. It may also be defined as the extinction of lust, hatred, and ignorance. The Pali word Nibbana is formed of *ni* and *vana*. *Ni* is a negative particle and *vana* means craving or selfish desire. Nibbana therefore literally means the absence of craving. The Sanskrit word Nirvana comes from the root *va* which means to blow, and the prefix *nir* which means off or out. Hence, Nirvana in its Sanskrit form means "the blowing out."

It is understood to mean the blowing out of the flame of personal desire.

The predominance of the negative explanation of Nibbana resulted in the mistaken notion that it is "nothingness" or "annihilation." However, in the Pitakas we find many positive definitions of Nibbana, such as Highest Refuge, Safety, Unique, Absolute Purity, Supramundane, Security, Emancipation, Peace, and the like. Nibbana is therefore not a negative concept because it is the cessation of craving, a "blowing out," for it is a blowing out of man's desires, and that blowing out of desires leaves a man free. Nibbana is freedom, but not freedom from circumstances; it is freedom from the bonds with which we have bound ourselves to circumstances. That man is free who is strong enough to say, "Whatever comes I accept as best."

Freedom does not mean that one can do everything that can be imagined, that one can defeat a lion with a slap of the hand. Freedom to do anything we wish is not freedom, for that means a return to the bondage of our wishes, our desires. Freedom means that one cannot be made a slave to anyone or anything, because one is free from personal desire, free from resentment, anger, pride, fear, impatience—free from all craving. Such a man's binding emotions have been blown out like so many candles. That man is free here on earth. He has reached Nibbana in this world.

CHAPTER THREE

Buddhism in Theravada Countries

B. Ananda Maitreya Nayaka Thero

Against the background of the history of Buddhism told by the Venerable Bhikkhu Kashyap of Nalanda and the outline of the beliefs of Theravada Buddhism by the Venerable Bhikkhu Thittila of Rangoon, let us consider in more detail the influence of Buddhism in Theravada countries and the practices of the people who follow Theravada—that is, who follow the Doctrine of the Elders as determined by the five hundred Arahats at the First Great Council.

When, at the end of the Third Great Council, the bearers of the Dhamma were sent by Asoka to the countries of southern Asia, they went forth representing a simple and sincere teaching which had spread throughout much of India. As in the Buddha's time, the Buddhist community consisted of four groups of people—the monks (*Bhikkhus*), nuns (*Bhikkunis*), male lay devotees (*Upasakas*), and female lay devotees (*Upasikas*).

There was no Buddhist patriarch or religious head who had power over the Sangha in those days. Every group of monks was under the guidance of a qualified elderly monk, and the power of governing the whole Sangha was vested in the community of elderly monks who headed the local groups. Every fortnight the monks and nuns gathered to recite the rules of conduct (Patimokkha), and every rainy season they gathered in one place for three months of study and meditation. During

113

the months between rainy seasons the members of the Sangha wandered from place to place along with their guiding elders. The fortnightly recitation of the rules of conduct and other duties of the Sangha, such as ordination, were carried on at a place called a *seema*, a small area marked off by pillars to indicate that it was set aside for such ceremonies. Nuns lived apart from the monks except when they came to receive instruction from one of the elders. In the early days there were no rituals, no images to worship, no elaborate religious festivals. In short, they lived a very simple life with the sole aim of attaining Arahatship as soon as possible.

Although at the time that Asoka's bearers of the Dhamma were selected the Mahasanghika school had broken away from the Theravada position and was beginning to use Sanskrit as the means of instruction, there was no serious difference among Buddhists as to doctrine. The teachings which prevailed at the time when Buddhism spread to southern Asia were concerned with impermanence, suffering, nonsubstantiality; the Four Noble Truths; the Eightfold Path; dependent origination—the Buddha's exposition of how one's past, present, and future lives are connected by the law of cause and effect; the thirty-seven constituents of Enlightenment—such as meditations, will, energy, mindfulness, and so on; and kamma and rebirth—making clear that kamma is not mere outward action but includes the volition which rouses one to do a deed and which causes rebirth.

It is from this simple Indian background and with these beliefs that the bearers of the Dhamma set out two and a half centuries after the Buddha to carry his teachings to the North, the West, the South, and the East.

CEYLON

Arahat Mahinda came to Ceylon with six companions and was received with great honor by King Tissa. He taught the Dhamma with such energy and appeal that before long almost the whole of Ceylon had embraced Buddhism, many men had joined the Sangha, many monasteries and stupas had been built,

including the famous Mahavihara monastery and the Thuparama stupa in which were enshrined the Buddha's collarbone
and other relics. When some royal ladies also wished to join
the Sangha, Emperor Asoka sent, at Arahat Mahinda's request,
the nun Sanghamitta to found the order of nuns. She brought
with her the shoot from the sacred bodhi tree at Buddhagaya
which was planted at Anuradhapura and is still there to this
day.

For more than a century after Arahat Mahinda passed away
—toward the end of the third century after the Buddha, or
early in the third century B.C.—the rulers of Ceylon did their
best to bring in a golden era of Buddhism in Ceylon. They
were interrupted by two invasions by the Dravidian Hindu
forces of southern India, but were finally successful in driving
them back and were able to devote their attention to uplifting
Buddhism in the island. There followed several centuries in
which many pious kings caused monasteries to be built and
maintained and did much for the progress of Buddhism in Ceylon. In those days there were large numbers of monks and nuns
with some monasteries caring for as many as a thousand Bhikkhus. The majority of the Bhikkhus and Bhikkhunis devoted
their whole time to the practice of yoga and, it is said, there
were many Arahats in those days.

In the ninth year of the reign of King Kit-Sirimevan, 854
B.E. (A.D. 310) the tooth relic was brought to Ceylon from
India and received by the king with highest honors. He had it
placed in an urn of pure crystal in the Temple of the Tooth
Relic in Kandy, where it is the object of pious pilgrimage to
the present day. His benevolent rule was followed by that of
his son, Buddhadasa, who led an ideal Buddhist life, treating his
subjects as a mother would treat her children. The Mahavamsa,
the Great Chronicle, says of him, "He fulfilled the wishes of
the poor by gifts of money, those of the rich by protecting
their property and their life. Great in discernment, he treated
the good with winning friendliness, the wicked with sternness,
and the sick with remedies." His son, King Mahanama, who
ruled from 953–975 B.E. (A.D. 409–431), was ruler when Cey-

lon was visited by Buddhaghosha, the famous Indian scholar, and by the early Chinese scholar, Fa Hsien.

Buddhaghosa was, according to the Mahavamsa, born a Brahman in a village near Buddhagaya and later converted to Theravada Buddhism. He became a great scholar, grammarian, linguist, and philosopher. Urged on by his teacher, he came to Ceylon to translate the commentaries from Sinhalese into Pali. He settled at Mahavihara monastery and not only wrote a commentary called *Visuddhi Magga* but also translated most of the Sinhalese commentaries into Pali. When he had finished his work, he returned to India and, according to the Burmese tradition, he returned to Burma by way of Thaton. About one hundred years after Buddhaghosa another famous Indian scholar, Dhammapala, wrote additional commentaries which are in use today.

For almost five hundred years, from the twelfth to the seventeenth centuries after the Buddha (sixth to eleventh centuries A.D.), Ceylon experienced a period of disturbances due to Indian invasions and internal disruptions which disorganized the government and forced the removal of the capital from Anuradhapura to Polonnaruwa. During this time the order of nuns ceased to exist, and Buddhism was so degenerate that when King Vijaya-bahu in 1609 B.E. (A.D. 1065) sought to restore Buddhism, hardly five duly ordained monks were to be found. The king corrected the situation by bringing ordained Bhikkhus from southern Burma to restore the ceremony of ordination in Ceylon, and thousands of pious people joined the revived Sangha. There followed a period of two centuries in which the doctrinal divisions within the Sangha were curbed by the rulers, Buddhism became once more influential, and many new commentaries were written. During this period, the first *Sangharaja* or ruler of the entire Sangha, was appointed by the king; he was Sariputta Sangharaja, noted for his commentaries and other religious writings.

From the beginning of the nineteenth century after the Buddha until the coming of the Portuguese (around A.D. 1250 to 1505), the invasions from India which disturbed the country made it difficult for Buddhism to continue its growth, but it maintained its strength in the face of many obstacles. It was during this period, in 2019 B.E. (A.D. 1475), that a delegation of Bhikkhus came from Burma to receive the higher ordination and took back to Burma copies of all the available Pali scriptures.

The situation of the Buddhists worsened after the arrival of the Portuguese in Ceylon, for the invaders exploited the internal rivalries in the country and in the areas which they controlled attempted to force conversions to Catholicism. Under the Portuguese the people were miserable, and the progress of the nation was stopped. At one point, monks were again brought from Burma to restore the higher ordination, and thus the struggle to maintain the national religion and culture continued.

In an attempt to overthrow the Portuguese, the Dutch were invited to the island, but when the Portuguese left the island forever in 2200 B.E. (A.D. 1656) the Dutch took their place. They sought to establish Protestantism and to prohibit Buddhism but were not successful. Urged on by the pious and energetic Bhikkhu Saranamkara, the king in 2294 B.E. (A.D. 1750) sent an embassy to Thailand to bring back a delegation of ten Bhikkhus who held an ordination ceremony in Kandy at which over three thousand persons were ordained. At the same time, Bhikkhu Saranamkara was appointed Sangharaja by the king.

The British displaced the Dutch rule in the maritime provinces in 2340 B.E. (A.D. 1796), and nineteen years later the British rule was extended throughout the island. At first this gave greater freedom to the Sangha and in the course of the next few years several groups of Bhikkhus went to Burma to receive higher ordination and returned to establish centers in Ceylon where the ordination could be continued. The British during the first half century of their rule were responsible by treaty for the internal protection of Buddhism, but owing to the opposition of Christian authorities the government gave up all connections with Buddhist affairs, and Christian missionaries became very active, even criticizing Buddhism publicly. The reaction which set in has stimulated revival of Buddhism which continues in Ceylon to the present.

Buddhism in Ceylon has suffered a great deal from the anti-Buddhist movements encouraged by foreign governments for more than three hundred years. It was an understanding of this situation which led many Buddhists, who are a majority in Ceylon, to seek independence for the sole purpose of gaining back their national religion. But the Buddhist public today does not feel that its government has been sufficiently active in supporting Buddhism. Even so, the vitality and enthusiasm of Buddhism in Ceylon is such that the more there is opposition from anti-Buddhist or political bodies, the more energetic the Buddhist leaders become in protecting their national religion and culture.

Buddhism in Ceylon has always been predominantly Theravada. Arahat Mahinda brought the pure Theravada teachings direct from the Third Great Council, and there was no division until late in the fifth century of the Buddhist era (first century B.C.), when a monk who had been disciplined for breaking some minor rules of conduct withdrew and later formed a school associated with the Mahasanghikas. Three hundred years later the king had the books of the heretical sects examined and destroyed, and the monks who professed heretical doctrines were banned from the island. About a generation later a heretical monk from India persuaded the king to accept the doctrines of a Mahayana sect and to seek to impose them on the Sangha, but he was not successful and the queen had the heretical books burned. Some remnants of Mahayana Buddhism remained in Ceylon until 1700 B.E. (A.D. 1156), when it was overcome largely due to the vigorous preaching of a learned Theravada Bhikkhu who came to Ceylon from southern India.

About 1400 B.E. (A.D. 856), a tantric monk from India made a vigorous attempt to establish tantric Buddhism in Ceylon and converted the king, but his efforts were unsuccessful and Tantrayana was never an important part of Buddhist practices in the island.

The minor differences within Theravada Buddhism in Ceylon are historical in origin, depending on whether the higher ordination came back to Ceylon from Thailand or from Burma.

BURMA

Historians differ as to when Buddhism came to Burma. The chronicles of Ceylon and an ancient commentary say that the two Asokan bearers of the Dhamma, Sona Thera and Uttara Thera, evangelized Suvanna-Bhumi. Some scholars identify Suvanna-Bhumi with Thaton in southern Burma while others identify it with Nakorn Pathom in Thailand. Inscriptions in Pali found in southern Burma indicate that Theravada Buddhism was known there by the sixth century after the Buddha (first century B.C.). This is supported by the Tibetan historian Taranatha who states that Theravada was preached from the time of Asoka onward in Pagan, Burma, and in Indo-China. Somewhat later the pupils of Vasubandhu introduced his Mahayana system to Burma, and Mahayana and Theravada existed side by side for centuries.

Apart from these details, nothing important is mentioned in Burmese history until the year 946 B.E. (A.D. 402), when it is said in the Burmese chronicles that Buddhaghosha visited Ceylon and after finishing his task returned to Burma, bringing his commentaries and the original texts of the Tipitaka. After that many Pali scholars appeared in Burma and wrote books on Pali grammar and Abhidhamma.

Burma was first united into one country under King Anawrahta (Anuruddha) of the fabulous city of Pagan, which was a great center of Buddhist culture from 1588 B.E. (A.D. 1044) until it was abandoned after the invasion by the forces of Kublai Khan in 1831 B.E. (A.D. 1287). In King Anawrahta's time—he died in 1621 B.E. (A.D. 1077)—the prevailing religion in northern Burma was Mahayana with a considerable amount of Tantrayana from Tibet and a background of Hinduism. Under the guidance of a Theravada Bhikkhu, he decided to bring Theravada to his kingdom and asked for copies of the Dhamma from the ruler of Thaton in southern Burma. When the request was refused, he conquered Thaton and brought back to Pagan thirty sets of the Tipitaka and 30,000 captives. Part of the building which was used as a library for the Tipitaka still exists in the abandoned capital of Pagan.

Although there is evidence in the ruins of Pagan that Theravada existed for a time side by side with Mahayana, Tantrayana, and Hinduism, it slowly became the chosen path of the people of Burma. At the height of Pagan's influence, several Bhikkhus went to Ceylon to study and returned to found schools of Theravada which continued for several centuries. After the fall of Pagan, although the country was in disorder, Theravada Buddhism continued to grow and experienced a major revival under King Dhammaceti who ruled from 2004 to 2035 B.E. (A.D. 1460 to 1491). In his time there were six schools of Theravada Buddhism, one from Cambodia and five from Ceylon, so he brought Bhikkhus from Ceylon and had all the Burmese Bhikkhus reordained in one sect. After that time Buddhism was firmly established in Burma and the study of Abhidhamma flourished.

Two centuries later a controversy grew up which caused a serious division among the Bhikkhus. It had always been the custom for Bhikkhus to go out fully clad, with both shoulders covered, but some began to keep the right shoulder bare when they walked on the streets. A bitter controversy grew up which divided the monks into the rival one-shouldered and fully-clad sects. After a public hearing before the king, he ruled in favor of the fully-clad sect and appointed a Sangharaja to maintain discipline in the Sangha.

During the last century the vitality of Buddhism in Burma was such that Bhikkhus came from Ceylon to receive higher ordination and take it back to their country; the four great Nikayas were translated into Burmese; the Fifth Great Council was held in Mandalay, and the Tipitaka was inscribed on stone tablets sheltered in shrines at the foot of Mandalay Hill. For a time the Sangharaja was elected, but since the coming of the Burmese Republic the government has appointed a Superior for each of the three Burmese sects. During all this time a great many books on Buddhism have been written by Burmese scholars.

THAILAND

According to the traditions of Thailand, Buddhism was first introduced to Nakorn Pathom in Siam around 300 B.E. (244 B.C.) by the Asokan bearers of the Dhamma, Sona and Uttara. An inscription of about the tenth century after the Buddha (fourth century A.D.) found at Kedah indicates that there was Buddhism in Thailand at that time. The Chinese pilgrim I-Ching, four centuries later, reports that Buddhism had been prevalent there in early days but was destroyed by a wicked ruler.

The Siamese—who call themselves Thai (free)—were Buddhists even before they established themselves in their present country in the nineteenth century after the Buddha (thirteenth century A.D.). They had been influenced by Hinduism and Mahayana Buddhism, according to some historians, when they were under Cambodian rule. Theravada Buddhism was re-established in the Siam area under Burmese rule in the seventeenth century after the Buddha (eleventh century A.D.), before the Thais came to power. Ever since the establishment of the Thai government at Ayuthia at the beginning of the twentieth century after the Buddha (middle of the fourteenth century A.D.), Thailand has been a Buddhist land.

At the time that Ayuthia became the capital, the ruler sent a mission to Ceylon to bring back a learned Bhikkhu who was a master of the Tipitaka and qualified to bring the Theravada ordination to the Bhikkhus of Thailand. Step by step the Theravada temples increased in number and the ancient Hindu temples were adapted to Buddhist uses. The remnants of Mahayana Buddhism were converted to Theravada, and the fame of the Thai Buddhists spread throughout the Buddhist world. Three centuries after the founding of Ayuthia as the capital of Thailand, in 2294 B.E. (A.D. 1750), when the king of Ceylon wished to revive Buddhism in his land, he sent to Thailand for

Bhikkhus who could re-establish the higher ordination, and the Siamese ordination has been in use in Ceylon to the present time.

A few years later, in 2310 B.E. (A.D. 1766), after the Burmese invaded Thailand, there followed a period in which the country was disorganized and Buddhism declined. Ayuthia fell, and when the Burmese were repelled, the new capital was established at Bangkok. After the new capital was built, a convocation of Bhikkhus was held there for the study and preservation of the Tipitaka. From that time to the present, the rulers of Thailand have encouraged and aided Buddhism by building and maintaining monasteries, by having the Tipitakas transliterated into Thai characters, and by reforming the Sangha and appointing able Sangharajas to govern the order. During all these years, the people of Thailand have fortunately been free from outside political domination. The Portuguese and French held concessions in Thailand temporarily, but they were soon expelled; able diplomatic negotiations with China from the time of the Ming Dynasty forestalled invasions from that side.

Theravada Buddhism is the state religion of Thailand with the king as the hereditary Upholder of the Faith; his spiritual counterpart is the Sangharaja who is appointed by the king and given jurisdiction over the monks. The Sangharaja appoints a council of ten members which includes the heads of the four administrative boards: Sangha Administration, Propaganda, Education, Public Works. There is also a Consultative Assembly of forty-five members which acts in an advisory capacity as representatives of the 165,000 monks from 20,000 monasteries in Thailand. The Government Department of Religious Affairs is responsible for the promotion of religious projects and the care of monasteries and monks. It has a large printing plant for publishing books on Buddhism; it makes an appropriation for the upkeep of temples and the provision of hospitals for Bhikkhus; it operates centers of higher learning for Buddhist monks as well as an institute for training Bhikkhus in administration, education, and evangelization. Free passes are given to Bhikkhus on public transportation to aid them in carrying out their religious duties. The National Institute of Culture, supported by the government, seeks to foster Buddhist culture in Thailand by all suitable means.

LAOS AND CAMBODIA

There is little known about the history of Buddhism in Laos which would distinguish it from Cambodia and Thailand. Today, Laos is a strong Theravada country, very similar to Cambodia in its practices.

The Khmer culture, which formed the basis for the country known today as Cambodia, extended at one time from the Bay of Bengal to the Chinese sea, and while it shows evidences of influence by the Chinese, the Hindus, and the Mons, it was a distinctive culture which is revealed in the ruins and art objects which are still available for study. As long ago as the fifth century after the Buddha (first century B.C.), Hindu traders had settled in the area which is now known as Cambodia. Images of Vishnu and the Buddha have been found which can be dated as early as the tenth century after the Buddha (fifth century A.D.), indicating that Buddhism was established in Cambodia by that time, at least. Examples of Gupta art from northern India have been found, dating back to the eleventh century after the Buddha (sixth century A.D.). The peak of the culture in Cambodia was reached in the days of Angkor, the great city which existed from the fifteenth century after the Buddha (ninth century A.D.) until it was abandoned in 1976 B.E. (A.D. 1432).

Mahayana Buddhism and Hinduism existed side by side during the Angkor period in Cambodia, sometimes living peacefully together and sometimes in conflict. Theravada Buddhism, which had been strong in the early centuries, was almost lost from Cambodia before the founding of Angkor, but returned in the eighteenth century after the Buddha (thirteenth century A.D.) and two centuries later had supplanted Mahayana Buddhism—which before that time had overcome Hinduism in Cambodia. Theravada Buddhism has been the religion of Cambodia ever since, accepting the Pali Canon for its authority and following practices similar to those of Burma and Thailand.

There are numerous monasteries in which from thirty to fifty monks lead an excellent way of life which has won the high regard of the laity. They observe the rules of the discipline, serve as schoolmasters and scholars, and meditate daily before the image of the Buddha which is placed in the shrine room of each monastery.

THE SANGHA

The strength of Theravada Buddhism in Ceylon, Burma, Thailand, Laos, and Cambodia lies in the Sangha, the Order which was established by the Buddha twenty-five hundred years ago. According to the Buddha, rapid progress in spiritual life and the handing down of his doctrine to posterity are not easy for a layman who is leading a household life with all the impediments it places in the way of spirituality. He saw that only an order of monks who devoted their whole lives to the Dhamma could successfully transmit the teachings and attain Arahatship. Therefore he founded the Sangha, the Order of monks who break away from all worldly bonds, the Order made up of the homeless ones.

As the occasion demanded, the Buddha promulgated a code of discipline for the internal government of the Sangha, the admission to the Order, the duties of the Bhikkhus, the annual place of residence at the rainy season, and the like. There are also the thirteen practices which are to be followed, according to the inclination of each Bhikkhu, as a means of creating in the follower of the Buddha such qualities as fewness of wishes, contentment, a desire for solitude, easiness of support by others, and similar ones which should be characteristic of a Bhikkhu.

Anyone worthy of admission is welcome to enter the Sangha and to leave it whenever he wishes; he need only be in good health, neither blind nor deaf, and to have the permission of his parents. Before a member of the Sangha receives full ordination he is known as a novice; then he is called a Bhikkhu. After ten years he becomes a Thera, or Elder, and twenty years after he receives full ordination he is known as a Maha Thera, or Great Elder. In Ceylon, a person who joins the Sangha is expected to remain in the Order for life, and it is considered a disgrace to leave the robe; but in the other Theravada countries it is common for people to enter the Sangha for a few months or years and then return to the life of a householder. In Thailand and Cambodia in particular all young men are urged to spend at least one rainy season in the Sangha receiving their moral instruction from the Elders of the Order.

A person who joins the Sangha repeats the Three Jewels: I take refuge in the Buddha, I take refuge in the Dhamma, I take refuge in the Sangha. Bhikkhus are not bound by any vow of obedience to a higher supreme authority, nor by a creedal statement, nor by rituals. Bhikkhus should have complete mastery over themselves; and if they fail in achieving such mastery, there is no absolution, and no form of creed or ritual can bring them salvation. The obedience expected of a Bhikkhu is to the Dhamma; to his seniors in the Sangha he owes only a respectful submission. The rules governing his life in the Sangha are clearly stated in the Vinaya Pitaka and regularly recited. In all Theravada countries the Pali Canon is the guide for monks and laymen.

Whenever there is a group of Bhikkhus, the ordained members should meet together twice a month on every new-moon day and full-moon day, within the boundary of the seema which has been marked off as a suitable place, and there recite together the 227 precepts and prohibitions by which their lives are governed and confess their failures. In some monasteries it is customary for the novices to assemble once a day to recite the rules governing their lives and to confess any lapses on their part. In the early days Bhikkhus were expected to wander from place to place, except during the rainy season when they were to remain in one place and spend their time in meditation and self-examination. From the Buddha's point of view, a lonely life in a forest or in an empty room or under a tree is the most convenient and suitable for a Bhikkhu, but because the pious laymen wished to provide suitable monasteries near villages, the Buddha permitted his disciples to accept them. In modern times the Bhikkhus use monasteries as permanent residences and travel about only when they wish to; but in all

Theravada countries they observe the three months of residence during the rainy season. Although some Buddhist monasteries have become wealthy, the majority of the monks in Theravada countries observe their religious vows quite well.

Bhikkhus must abstain entirely from drugs and intoxicating liquors; some permit themselves to use tobacco, but most do not. Neither monk nor novice should eat solid food between noon and the following morning—if he becomes hungry he may drink tea and eat sugar, honey, or butter. The usual way for a monk to get his food is to go bowl in hand from house to house on his silent begging rounds. He is to accept whatever food is given him, but should not eat meat which has been specially prepared for him; otherwise he can eat meat when it is given to him. All members of the Sangha must, of course, remain chaste in thought and deed. A Bhikkhu may not touch a woman nor converse with a woman unless a third person is present.

A monk can rightfully keep as his personal possessions eight articles: one undergarment, two robes, a belt, an alms bowl, a small knife or razor, a needle, and a water strainer. His robes should be prepared from cloth offered to him by the laity or from castoff rags. First they must be torn into pieces and then sewed together and dyed yellow or yellowish brown to render them commercially valueless. Books and other things, including even houses and land, may be accepted and used as the common property of the Sangha. Some Bhikkhus, in Thailand for instance, never touch money; if a layman wishes to put money at their disposal, he gives it to a keeper who spends it as directed.

If a Bhikkhu contravenes a rule, he must confess it at the daily or fortnightly chanting of the rules governing the Sangha. If it is a minor departure, the confession is sufficient; if it is a transgression of some weight, a slight penance which he willingly observes will be imposed upon him. If it is one of the four major transgressions—sexual intercourse, stealing, killing a human being, or deceiving by claiming trances or attainment of sainthood or higher spiritual qualities—the punishment is to require him to leave the robe and return to the household life.

If a charge is to be brought against a Bhikkhu, first his consent must be taken and then the charge must be examined by a chapter of Bhikkhus. Their decision must be determined by the Dhamma, for no one can change or add to the existing Law.

The structure of the Sangha is basically democratic with decisions reached by the assembled Bhikkhus acting in accord with the Dhamma. When there is a difference of opinion as to the interpretation of any of the Teachings recorded in the Tipitaka or commentaries, the Sangha must follow the eight rules for correct interpretation as given by the Buddha. The Dhamma of the Buddha is:

1. The Dhamma that will eliminate pleasure in anything.
2. The Dhamma that will eliminate attachment to worldly things.
3. The Dhamma that will not make you accumulate sins or worldly things.
4. The Dhamma that will make you moderate in your desires.
5. The Dhamma that will make you satisfied with what you have.
6. The Dhamma that will make you like solitude.
7. The Dhamma that will make you persevere, be diligent, to attain Nibbana.
8. The Dhamma that will make you easy to be fed, will keep you from requiring luxuries.

The Bhikkhus of a monastery select a senior monk to head their organization and look after the details of monastic life. Monasteries which are associated in a school may select a Maha Thera to serve as the guiding head for all of their institutions. There is no one office which oversees all monasteries which follow Theravada Buddhism. In Ceylon each sect has its own head, and there is consultation between them on common concerns. In Burma the Sasana Council, which is made up of leading Buddhists, monks and laymen, serves as an advisory body for all followers of the Dhamma. In Thailand they have a Sangharaja who is chosen by the heads of the major monastic groups, approved by the Ministry of Education, and appointed by the king. In turn, the Sangharaja chooses Bhikkhus who will fill the chief positions in the Sangha, and they are approved by the government.

SECTS IN THERAVADA

The sectarian differences within Theravada Buddhism have no particular significance either for organizational responsibility or for beliefs—they reflect historical origins and minor variations in practices. While in Mahayana Buddhism the various sects reflect different rituals, philosophies, and scriptures, in Theravada there is a unity throughout Ceylon, Burma, Thailand, Laos, and Cambodia based on the Pali Tipitaka and commentaries which are accepted in the same way by all Buddhists.

In Ceylon the Sangha is divided into three sects—Siamese, Amarapura, and Ramanya—named after the countries from which their ordination was introduced to Ceylon. The Siamese sect was started in 2297 B.E. (A.D. 1753), when the king of Ceylon brought a delegation of ten Bhikkhus from Ayuthia in Thailand, and over three thousand people were ordained at Kandy. That sect is sometimes called the Upali-vamsa since the leader of the Thai Bhikkhus was Phra Upali. The Amarapura sect was founded when a group of novices went to Amarapura in Burma and after receiving higher ordination there returned to establish the Amarapura sect in Ceylon in 2345 B.E. (A.D. 1801). The Ramanya sect was founded a few years later by seven novices who went to the Ramanya country of southern Burma and returned to establish a new center for ordination in Ceylon.

Although all three sects accept the same rules of discipline, the Amarapura sect is stricter in practice than the Siamese sect, and the Ramanya sect, in appearance, is the strictest of all. All these sects are practically alike except for a few minor details regarding the use of robes and umbrellas. One division of the Siamese sect requires its members to cover only the left shoulder when they are in the temple premises or when they go out from the monastery. The members of one branch of the Ramanya sect do not use the ordinary umbrella used by Bhikkhus of the Amarapura sect and by the other branch of the Ramanya, but they use a special umbrella made of palmyra leaves. The Siamese sect ordains only the people who belong to the highest level of society, called Govi-gama, while the other two sects do not regard caste distinction as a rule. But all monks are hospitably received in all monasteries, regardless of their sect affiliation.

In Burma, in the reign of King Dhammaceti in the twenty-first century after the Buddha (fifteenth century A.D.) the five existing sects—one from Cambodia and four from Ceylon—were combined by the king in one sect which received its higher ordination from Ceylon. In modern times there are three sects in Burma—Sudhamma, Swedjin, and Dvara. The Swedjin sect is somewhat stricter than the Sudhamma, and the Dvara sect follows the strictest discipline of all. The Dvaras never use umbrellas; instead they use a large fan made of palmyra leaf. Apart from this there is no important difference between these sects.

In Thailand there are two sects, the Maha Nikaya (Great Sect) and the Dhammayuttika Nikaya (Sect of the Followers of the Dhamma). The Dhammayuttikas are a reform sect, about a century old, smaller and more strict; they will not touch money, are not permitted to prepare their own food, go where liquor is served, ride on trolleys, or wear shoes, but they may carry an umbrella. The members of the Maha Nikaya are more lax in these matters. Both sects follow the 227 rules of the Vinaya Pitaka but have slight differences in their everyday life. The monks of the Maha Nikaya confess twice a day, morning and evening, while the monks of the Dhammayuttika Nikaya make their confession only when they feel guilty of a transgression of the rules. Maha Nikaya monks recite the Patimokkha at the fortnightly service in a closed room while the Dhammayuttikas chant and confess publicly.

In Cambodia there is no sect distinction worth mentioning.

In times past both Tantrayana and Mahayana have been found in some of the Theravada countries, but today the Buddhism of Ceylon, Burma, Thailand, Laos, and Cambodia is almost exclusively Theravada, based on the Pali Canon. The only Mahayana deity that has entered the worship of ordinary Buddhists in Theravada countries is Bodhisattva Avalokitesvara. In Ceylon he is known as Natha-deva and mistaken by the majority for the Buddha yet to come, Bodhisattva Maitreya. The figure of Avalokitesvara usually is found in the shrine room near the Buddha image.

The Bhikkhus in Theravada countries spend their time in the observance of the discipline of the Vinaya Pitaka, in study of the Tipitaka and the commentaries, in meditation, in teaching novices and laymen, and in various forms of service to the community. The members of the Sangha bend all their energies toward following the path to Enlightenment which was taught by the Buddha.

IMAGES AND SHRINES

In the self-discipline of the monk, in the following of the Dhamma, the most important activity is meditation, which is described in detail at the end of this chapter. Meditation is an active striving toward the goal of Nibbana; it is not worship in the sense in which that word is normally used in the English language. But some people mistake Buddhists for idol worshipers because there are images of the Buddha in the shrines. That is quite far from the truth. Not a single Theravada Buddhist deifies the image of the Buddha. The respect paid to the Buddha image is nothing more than the general practice of cultured people to honor a statue or monument of a great personage with flowers, incense, and similar signs of veneration. The words said by a Buddhist before the image are a meditation on the virtues of the Buddha, an expression of aspiration for similar virtues. The respect and honor paid to a bodhi tree, also, is an expression of gratitude, for it was under the shadow of a bodhi tree that the Bodhisattva attained Buddhahood.

According to the Pali Canon, there are three objects which may properly be objects of devotion—the relics of the body of the Buddha, the things constructed on his account, such as images, and the articles the Buddha used, such as his girdle or his alms bowl.

The relics of the body of the Buddha—such as his collarbone, or locks of his hair—have been enshrined in stupas, dagobas, or pagodas in Theravada countries. Perhaps the most famous of the relics is the Sacred Tooth which has been at Kandy in Ceylon for over fifteen centuries.

The greatest number of pagodas have been erected in Burma where the extremely religious and pious Burmans have added to the beauty of the landscape by building numerous pagodas throughout the countryside. The structure of a pagoda is made up of four parts: the square terrace, usually made of brick; then the polygonal plinth on which rests the bell-shaped body divided into two parts by an ornamental band; finally, there is the cone-shaped spire which often has a metal crown and is gilded. Symbolically, the base of the pagoda represents Mount Meru with its five terraces; the plinth and the two sections of the bell-shaped body represent the three realms of the sensual, corporeal, and immaterial; the spire represents the Buddha. Another interpretation of the symbolism of the pagoda in Burma is that the square base represents the heavens of the four guardian deities of the four directions, the eight-sided plinth represents the Tushita heaven where the future Buddha resides, and the upper part of the pagoda represents Nibbana.

The veneration of the footprint of the Buddha is regarded by the common folk of Buddhism as next in importance to the veneration of relics. In almost every country in Asia where Buddhism has prevailed there is at least one of the supposed impressions of the Buddha's foot. According to the Buddhist tradition of Ceylon, the Buddha was supposed to have impressed his footprint on the bank of the Narmada river in South India, on Mount Elumalei near Tirupati in South India, on Adam's Peak, Sri-Pada, in Ceylon, and in Yonaka-pura, which is probably Gandhara. There is a sculpture of the footprint marked with a wheel symbol on one of the gateways at Sanchi, and there are sculptured footprints at Amaravati, indicating that the veneration of the footprint came into Buddhism very early. In many temples in all Buddhist lands there are facsimiles of the Buddha's footprint as objects of veneration.

It is said that the first statue of the Buddha was made of sandalwood at the order of a king during the life of the Buddha. Fa Hsien, the Chinese pilgrim who visited India in the tenth century after the Buddha (fifth century A.D.), said that he saw that image and that it was the model for all statues of the Buddha made after that time. This account, however, is rejected by scholars, for they find no evidence for any Buddha statues until at least three centuries after the demise of the Buddha. Some scholars say that the first Buddha images were made six centuries after the Buddha (first century A.D.), during the time of King Kaniska of Gandhara, and were of Bactrian-Greek origin; and other scholars say that prior to the images which show Greek influences there were large, fine Buddha images in Madhura, Sarnath, Anuradhapura, and many other places. However that may be, it seems certain that the erecting of Buddha images started after the time of Asoka.

Before the time of Asoka, the representations of the Buddha were symbolic, using a lotus, a bodhi tree, a wheel, or a stupa whenever the Buddha's presence was to be indicated. Examples of the symbolic representations of the Buddha have been found at Amaravati, Sanchi, and Bharhut. When the anthropomorphic school of Buddhist art arose, it spread quickly throughout the Buddhist world and has been the basis for the great art which has been inspired wherever Buddhism is known. Although the use of stone and brick in building was known in India long before the Asokan era, it was the genius of Buddhism that inspired a new art and architectural development. The image of the Buddha expresses the deep-rooted inspiration which moved the followers of the Buddha to create glorious stupas, pagodas, images, and paintings as monuments to the Enlightened One. The creative energy of Buddhism transformed the literature and arts of all the countries where it prevailed.

One result of the widespread adoption of the image of the Buddha as an object of veneration was that each nation seems to have created its images according to its own ideas of beauty. There is the early Grecian form of Gandhara and the characteristic Gupta image, and it has been noted that in Burma and Thailand especially the images resemble a well-proportioned native of those countries. In Mahayana countries, too, images typical of Tibet, China, and Japan have been created.

In all the Buddhist world there is a recognizable similarity in the postures of the Buddha images. The standing figures in Burma and Thailand commonly have the right hand on the chest and the left hand holding the skirt of the robe; some have both hands open and pointing down with palms in the front. In Ceylon the standing figures usually have the right hand held up with the open palm to the front in the blessing posture.

Seated images are the most common, showing the Buddha seated cross-legged with the soles of the feet upward, often with an aureole behind the head. The position of the hands indicates the different moods of the Buddha. When the left hand is lying open upon the upturned soles of the feet and the right hand rests over the right knee with palm down and fingers pointed downward, it is known as the Earth-touching mood, indicating the strength which comes from the earth. When the palms are held upward on the lap, one over the other, it is known as the Meditation mood. The Blessing mood is indicated by sitting with the left palm upward on the lap and the right hand with open palm uplifted to about the level of the chin. The Teaching mood is shown by a figure which has the thumb of the right hand touching the tip of the forefinger with the other fingers straightened and pointed upward. It is also known as the Teaching mood when both palms are held together in front of the breast with the little finger of the left hand held between the thumb and forefinger of the right hand.

The third characteristic posture of Buddha images is the reclining Buddha, showing the Buddha at the moment of his passing into Parinibbana, the Nibbana of no return. It is an image which, by its very nature, is a great inspiration to the followers of the Buddha.

A feature of the Buddha images which varies from country to country is the dress. Almost all of the ancient Buddha figures in Ceylon have only their left shoulder covered—the only exception being one figure with both shoulders fully covered painted on the wall of the shrine room of Dambulla. In all other countries Buddha figures are seen either with the left shoulder covered or with both shoulders fully covered. The ancient Buddha figures found in China, Tibet, Burma, and Thailand have the covering that is characteristic of the Kaniskan era; but in later times the covering of the body of the Buddha images has varied considerably.

Shrines also contain images of Arahats whose accomplishments are such that meditating on them will be an encouragement to members of the Sangha and laymen as well. Frequently the walls of the shrines are adorned with pictures illustrating the Jataka tales and episodes from the life of the Buddha and his Arahat followers. Such works of art serve as objects of devotion and as a means of instruction for the laymen who visit the shrines.

LAY FOLLOWERS

While a lay follower does not expect to attain Nibbana in this life, he can hope to attain the first stage of the Holy Path to Nibbana in his present existence. The most obvious practices of a lay follower of the Buddha would be the repetition of the Triple Refuge formula on various occasions, the keeping of the five precepts—refraining from killing, stealing, unlawful sexual indulgence, bad speech, and drinking liquor—and, on the fortnightly Uposatha days when the monks recite the rules of conduct, keeping the eight precepts—that is, the five precepts including celibacy, plus refraining from taking food after noon, enjoying music, garlands, perfumes, and the like, and using high or luxurious seats or beds. The lay followers strive for peace and tranquillity in their domestic life and seek to follow the instructions concerning their duties given by the Buddha. A brief summary of those instructions, taken from the Vyagghapajja and the Sigalovada Sutta, is given here by way of illustration:

Four requisites for earning wealth: dauntless energy in wealth, mindfulness in keeping what is earned, simple living, and keeping company with good people.

Four bad actions to be avoided: killing, stealing, unlawful sexual indulgence, and falsehood.

Four ways of doing injustice to be avoided: doing injustice due to partiality, or due to hatred, or due to fear, or due to ignorance (that is, through deception).

Six things leading to loss of wealth which are to be avoided: addiction to drinking liquor, to walking in the streets at untimely hours, to visiting feasts, to gambling, to bad companions, or to laziness.

Ministry to parents: a child should minister to his parents by supporting them, doing his duties, continuing the family line, acting in such a way as to be worthy of his inheritance, and offering alms in honor of the departed parents.

Ministry of parents to their children: restraining them from the bad, exhorting them to do good, giving them a good education, arranging a suitable marriage in due time, handing over the inheritance to them at the proper time.

Ministry of students to teachers: rising before the teacher, attending to the needs of the teacher, listening attentively, doing personal service to the teacher, and carefully receiving instruction.

Ministry of teachers to students: giving the students the best training, showing them how to grasp things well, teaching them suitable arts and science, introducing them to their friends and companions, keeping them safe in every way.

Ministry of husband to wife: honoring her, avoiding disrespect, being faithful to her, entrusting his treasure to her custody, providing her with garments and ornaments.

Ministry of wife to husband: doing her duties in perfect order, treating the friends and relatives of her husband generously and hospitably, being faithful to him, protecting carefully the treasure entrusted to her, and doing all her duties diligently.

Ministry to friends and companions: showing generosity, speaking courteously, promoting good, treating them with equality, and being truthful to them.

Ministry of friends and companions in return: looking after him when he is careless, safeguarding his property when he is negligent, rendering assistance when he is in trouble, and protecting his children and advancing their welfare.

Ministry to servants and employees: apportioning work to them according to their strength, providing them with food and wages, tending them in sickness, sharing special dainties with them, and giving them rest and holidays at the proper times.

Ministry of servants and employees to their master: rising before him, going to sleep after him, taking only what is given, carrying out his orders promptly and with pleasure, and giving him a good report.

Ministry to members of the Sangha: speaking to them with affection, showing friendliness in deed, thinking of them respectfully, being generous in supplying their wants readily, providing them with their material needs.

Ministry of members of the Sangha to a lay devotee: dissuading him from evil, exorting him to the good, loving him with a kind heart, teaching him what he has not heard and making clear what he has already heard, pointing out to him the path to a happy state.

In addition to these obligations, it is customary for devout lay followers to have a small shrine in their homes as a reminder of the Dhamma, to visit the temple to pay respect to the Buddha because of his excellent virtues, and on occasion to go to the preaching hall near the monasteries to listen respectfully to the teachings expounded by the Bhikkhus. As the opportunity arises, the lay follower or Bhikkhu may make a pilgrimage to one of the many places of pilgrimage in India and the Theravada countries such as the Temple of the Tooth in Kandy, the bodhi tree at Anaradhapura, the Shwedagon Pagoda in Rangoon or the beautiful temple of the Emerald Buddha in Bangkok. Pilgrimages are not only taken for the purpose of acquiring merit, but also as an expression of devotion and a means of strengthening one's resolve to follow the Path which was taught by the Master.

CEREMONIES

The most important of the many ceremonies associated with one's life from birth to death are the tonsure and cremation. At the age of puberty it is customary to have a ceremony which indicates that a child has reached a new period of life. In Thailand, for instance, it takes the form of the tonsure ceremony. On the first day, Buddhist monks are invited to the home and seated on a raised platform. The child then enters dressed in his best clothes and accompanied by appropriate music and, after saluting the monks, places his head upon a cushion while the leading monk ties a cotton cord around the topknot. Then all the people repeat the Triple Refuge and the Five Precepts. After that religious ceremony, all the guests are entertained for the rest of the day. On the second day the Bhikkhus return and chant Parittas, the sayings of the Buddha which have been selected because they create in the hearers a suitable psychic condition. On the third day, again, the monks chant passages from the Canon, and the topknot is cut off by the guest of highest rank. In Thailand the long hairs severed from the head are saved until the child makes his first pilgrimage to the shrine of the Buddha's footprint at Prabat, and then they are offered to the footprint to be used as a brush for sweeping the holy shrine; the short hairs are put in a tiny boat made from banana leaves and cast into the nearest stream to float to the sea.

The people of Theravada countries, being staunch followers of the Buddha, are able to look at death in a way which controls their sorrow. They see that death is inevitable, that the body dies but the process of mind joins another body prepared by the force of the kamma of the dying person and appears in a new form. They know that it is the nature of all composed things to be decomposed. In Ceylon the body is put in a coffin and taken to the cemetery in a procession which sometimes is accompanied by special, solemn music. It may be either buried or cremated. Monks are invited to lead the assembled people in repeating the Triple Refuge and the Five Precepts. After this, all the monks chant the famous verse which expresses the nature of the impermanence of all component things. Then a piece of cloth is offered to the Sangha in the name of the departed one, which is followed by consoling talk. Then they bury the coffin, or have some near relative of the departed one set fire to the funeral pyre.

In the other Theravada countries the body is usually cremated, but the body of a man who has committed suicide is buried. The body of a monk or a man of high rank is cremated with much honor. Immediately after death the body is bathed, embalmed, and put in an urn where it may be kept at the most as long as two years. The funeral ceremonies last for at least three days. A special wooden pavilion is erected for the cremation; other buildings are erected for the guests and for theatrical plays and music programs. Before the cremation the coffin is usually placed within the temple premises, and monks read verses from the Tipitaka. On the third day the guest of highest rank leads the way to the funeral pyre and sets fire to it. After the cremation the ashes are collected and put in an urn which is kept by the relatives in a special place reserved for it in their home.

The most elaborate funeral ceremonies are reserved for a monk or a very religious person, and in Burma these ceremonies are the most elaborate of all. As soon as the body is embalmed it may sometimes be gilded and placed in a coffin or chest and exposed to the veneration of the people. If it is kept for some months or a year or so, during that time there will be a continual festival of music and plays with people flocking day and night to participate in the festival. They offer money, foods, and other necessities to defray the expenses of the festival. Finally, the coffin is carried in a great procession to the cremation ground. An offering of cloth and other necessities is made to the monks, after which the coffin is placed on the pyre and burned.

Marriage is a family ceremony, not a religious ceremony. Often the parents arrange the marriage, although sometimes the initiative is taken by a young man with the consent of his parents. Although the ceremony is not religious, it is not held during the three months of the rainy season when the monks are not moving about, and frequently monks are invited to the ceremony to chant from the Canon and to give their blessings to the young couple. The ceremony is performed by the elder men of the family.

When a young man enters the Sangha, or when there is an ordination, elaborate ceremonies are held at the monastery, gifts are given to the monks, and the scriptures are chanted. There are other special ceremonies at the monastery or temple for the erection of a Buddha image, for the opening or marking of the eyes of such an image, and in some places there is an annual day for gifts when the villagers collect all things necessary for the monks and take them to the monastery in a grand procession. On all these occasions the monks chant from the Tipitaka and bless the people.

FESTIVALS

Of all the Buddhist festivals, Wesak is the highest. It comes at the full-moon time which usually falls in May and is in memory of the birth, Enlightenment, and passing away of the Buddha. Houses and even streets are decorated, many people observe the eight precepts, make offerings to monks, give alms to the poor, and receive instruction from the monks. It is observed usually for at least two days.

The rainy season festival is held in all Theravada countries beginning in July and ending on the full-moon day which usually falls in October. During those three months the monks retire to a monastery and do not travel; their time is spent in study and meditation. The laymen in Burma, Thailand, Cambodia, and Laos take much more interest in the rainy season than they do in Ceylon, for in those countries it is a time which is earnestly devoted to the Dhamma. Many men join the order for the three months and spend a solemn time mostly devoted to meditation. No social life, no marriages, no feasts take place at this time. When the three-month period ends, the greatest feast of the year is held together with an offering of alms and robes to the monks. This festival of offering the robes to the monks who observed the rainy season retreat may last as long as a month in some countries. The ceremony is performed in Ceylon but not on such a grand scale as in the other Theravada countries.

The New Year festival, which is held in March or April, comes at the time of the Hindu New Year based on the old solar calendar and is more national in character. In Ceylon it begins with a visit to the temple and then lasts for three days with every kind of amusement. In the other Theravada countries it is a water-throwing festival at which the main function is the throwing of water at each other whenever the people meet. On this occasion they entertain Bhikkhus and their relatives with much honor and respect. In Laos and Cambodia there are processions headed by young men with sacred umbrellas and with the chief monk followed by the rest of the monks from the local monastery; as they pass along the street, women on both sides throw water on the procession. They come at last to the pagoda, pay honor to the Buddha, and then fall back and watch the dances, which are mostly national.

There are other local festivals in each country, such as those in Ceylon which commemorate the arrival of the Arahat Mahinda, the arrival of the Buddha in Ceylon, and the festival of the tooth relic of the Buddha in Kandy. In Thailand there are annual pilgrimages to ancient Buddhist sites, and in October the big fairs at the Golden Mount and Nakorn Pathom. Similar festivals in other countries fill the year with occasions which serve as reminders of the teachings of the Dhamma and its glorious history.

Non-Buddhist Customs

Many examples of Hindu influence and of spirit worship can be found in Theravada countries among the common people. The Buddhists who pay respect to nature spirits, the spirits of the deceased, and Hindu deities such as Brahma or Ganesha, and who consult astrologers and sorcerers know that none of these deities or practices have anything to do with the Buddhist way of life. They know that this paying of honor to such deities does nothing for them on their way to Nibbana; they only expect from them some little help in living this present life with success. They look to these deities and these practices for help in their worldly needs in this life in much the same way that the strong might be expected to help those of lower rank. They understand that to keep such practices is not against the Buddha's teachings, for they remember his admonition to the Vajjins, "So long, Ananda, as the Vajjins honor, esteem, revere, and support Vajjian shrines in town and country and allow not the proper offerings and rites, as formerly given and performed, to fall into desuetude . . . so long may the Vajjins be expected not to decline but to prosper." (Mahaparinibbana Sutta.)

In the courtyards of many ancient Buddhist temples there is a shrine housing such Hindu deities as Siva, Vishnu, Vibhishana, or Ganesa. In some places the Hindu image may be under the same roof as the Buddha image, sometimes with the Hindu deities standing on both sides of the Buddha image saluting the Buddha. In some temples in Thailand the stories from the Ramayana epic of the Hindus are told in pictures on the walls. These Hindu deities are honored as beings on a plane higher than the human plane, capable of aiding the worldly aims of the present existence.

Many customs inherited from the Indian settlers in Theravada countries are still practiced today. For instance, in Thailand when a child is born, they first wash it and then bind its arms with consecrated cotton and get its horoscope cast by an astrologer. The first name given the child is an ugly one so that it may be preserved from the jealousy of evil spirits; an amulet in the shape of a metal plate with a diagram of mystic signs is hung around its neck. From the astrologer they learn the auspicious times for naming the child, feeding it rice for the first time, teaching it the alphabet, and such other acts, just as the custom is in India. Many people in all Theravada countries consult astrologers for advice as to auspicious times for new undertakings, and palmistry and kindred arts are commonly resorted to.

At times of illness, medical practices learned from the Ayurvedic medicine of Hinduism are often followed. It is a common practice when someone is ill to invite a Bhikkhu to come and chant Parittas, appropriate passages from the Canon, but not for the purpose of warding off evil spirits as some people think; it is done to create a healthy psychic condition which will bring relief and confidence to the patient.

Hindu practices are still retained in the coronation ceremonies of Thailand and Cambodia, together with Buddhist customs which have been added. The same tendency is found in the law, as in Burma, where the ancient Hindu code of Manu was revised, omitting the Hindu rites, and then improved step by step through the centuries by the addition of Buddhist interpretations.

It is only natural that the area which was for centuries known as Farther India should retain Indian customs which do not conflict with the Buddhist culture of those lands today.

Paying honor to spirits as well as to deities is found in almost all Buddhist countries. These are the nature spirits inhabiting trees, mountains, rivers, and the like; they are not evil, but are sometimes vindictive. According to Buddhist commentaries, almost all trees are inhabited by some sort of spirit or ghost whether weak or powerful. Some people light a lamp regularly every day under a tree or in a particular reserved place in honor of such a spirit, for they believe that the spirit will sometimes give help when needed. The most famous spirit of this type in Ceylon is Sumana, the deity of Sri-Pada, the mountain popularly known as Adam's Peak.

These spirits are known as *nats* in Burma and as *phis* in Thailand. Some are the spirits dwelling in trees and in houses; others are heroes who have passed away and live on a higher plane. In Thailand the spirits of those who have passed away may be good or bad—the bad spirits may be the kind who can be kept under control by sorcerers, they may be the ghosts of departed persons, and they may be the deities of the higher realms who cannot be easily seen by men. In Cambodia the spirit worship is very similar to that in Thailand. In Ceylon an example of a spirit which is a hero who has passed away is Vibhishana, venerated at Kelaniya and other shrines.

In Thailand it is believed that the spirits of departed persons are mostly harmful and always do more harm than good. Ignorant folk believe that the ghosts of infants who died immediately after birth might sometimes do much harm to the mother; the ghosts of those who died a violent death are horrible. Sorcerers in Thailand make use of them for various purposes and make them familiar. The good spirits are honored with shrines; in Thailand and Cambodia there is a shrine at the top of a pole at most houses to honor the spirit which protects the house. Some of the spirits in Cambodia and Thailand are known by ancient Hindu names. To quench their wrath or to gain their favor for the purpose of gaining some success in this very life, the people make a variety of offerings to them.

There are also many kinds of sorcerers who practice black magic. In Thailand they are astrologers who sometimes are able to make the spirits under their control enter another's body and do much harm to him. In Cambodia they practice astrology and prepare charms against black magicians. The worst kind of sorceresses are known as Srei Ap in Cambodia and as Sung-ma in Burma; their heads along with their alimentary canals, so they say, move about and feed on excrement; they are very much dreaded by people and if found are exiled or punished severely. There are also sorcerers who prepare amulets as protection against illness and misfortune; some are made of consecrated cotton threads or of gold or silver plates with Buddhist formulas or a symbolic design engraved on them. In Burma, Thailand, and Cambodia there are those who believe that a ball of solidified mercury, prepared according to some secret alchemic system, will bring them various powers, such as invulnerability.

Many practices associated with the worship of spirits and deities are designed to bring success in agricultural activities. In Cambodia the Kradak festival is held in the eighth month in ordinary years; food is offered at night to the moon, and then the women kneel on the ground and salute the moon three times and pray to all deities to accept their offerings. In October they celebrate the water festival, praying that the river will overflow and fertilize the country. In Thailand they hold a Brahmanic ceremony in the beginning of May before they begin plowing and sowing grain. In this festival the minister of agriculture goes to a chosen field in procession and puts his hands on a plow drawn by two white oxen and breaks the earth; then four elderly women of the royal family sow the first grain. After the harvest, grains of rice are burned and offered to the deities. It is common in all Theravada countries to have a festival and to venerate the deities at the time of plowing, planting, and harvesting, but these ceremonies are not Buddhist in origin.

Although many people are blinded by attachment to worldly things and seek success in their worldly objectives by calling upon deities and spirits for help in this life, all Buddhists recognize that the attainment of the ultimate goal can come only by following the Eightfold Path which culminates in meditation.

MEDITATION

Two things, O brethren, are conducive to knowledge. What are the two? Tranquillity and insight. When tranquillity is developed, what happens? Mind is developed. When mind is developed, what happens? Whatever passion there is is abandoned. When insight is developed, what happens? Right understanding is developed. When right understanding is developed, what happens? Whatever ignorance there is is abandoned. The mind soiled with passion is not freed. When there is soiling through ignorance, right understanding is not developed. Thus through unstaining of passion there is freedom of mind, and through unstaining of ignorance there is freedom of right understanding. (Anguttara Nikaya.)

These words of the Buddha make it clear that the only way to culture and the perfection of the mind is meditation, and that meditation is of two kinds—the kind which leads to tranquillity (*Samatha*) and the kind which leads to insight (*Vipassana*).

The meditation which leads to tranquillity is based on practices which were to a large extent known and used by ascetics before the appearance of the Buddha. Because such practices bring a calmness and serenity to the mind and help to turn the mind away from depravities, and because the habit of fixing the mind on an object is useful for the development of mental processes, the Buddha recommended to his followers the way of meditation which leads to tranquillity. By itself, this method is not sufficient, but it serves as a useful preparation for the second kind of meditation, the meditation which leads to insight.

According to *The Path of Purity* (*Visuddhi Magga*), by Buddhaghosha, there are forty subjects of meditation suggested to followers of the Dhamma for the development of tranquillity. The disciple should choose for his meditation the subjects which suit his temperament and character, making the selection under the guidance of a competent teacher if possible, but in the end relying upon his experience as a guide. People are divided into six classes according to their temperament—the lustful, the hot-tempered, the easily deluded, the self-confident, the quick-witted, and those of discursive mind.

The forty subjects of meditation are divided into the ten devices, the ten impurities, the ten recollections, the four sublime states, the four immaterial states, the one notion, and the one analysis.

The ten devices:

1. Earth device—a circle made of dawn-colored clay, generally a span and four inches in diameter
2. Water device—a bowl of clean water
3. Fire device—a bright flame appearing through a hole
4. Air device—the perception of air shaking and swaying the top of a tree
5. Blue device—a circle of blue cloth or the like
6. Yellow device—a circle of yellow cloth or the like
7. Red device—a circle of red cloth or the like
8. White device—a circle of white cloth or the like
9. Light device—a light falling through a circular hole
10. Space device—a limited space of a prescribed dimension, seen through an opening

The ten impurities:

1. A swollen corpse
2. A discolored, blue-green corpse
3. A corpse full of pus
4. A fissured corpse
5. A corpse mangled by dogs or other animals
6. A corpse with dismembered limbs
7. A corpse with its limbs partly destroyed and scattered
8. A corpse covered here and there with blood
9. A worm-infested corpse
10. A skeleton

The ten recollections are the recollection of:

1. The virtues of the Buddha
2. The merits of the Dhamma
3. The Order of the Holy Disciples of the Buddha
4. The merits of the observance of the precepts
5. The merits of liberality
6. The equality between one's self and the deities in regard to the virtues
7. Death—that is, mindfulness of the fact that everyone is subject to inevitable death
8. The body—that is, mindfulness regarding the body
9. Respiration—that is, mindfulness of respiration
10. Peace of mind—that is, cognition of the attributes of peace of mind

The four sublime states are the development of:

1. Universal love, amity (*metta*)
2. Compassion (*karuna*)
3. The happiness of others
4. Equanimity

The four immaterial stages are the attainment of:

1. Infinite space
2. Infinite consciousness
3. Nothingness
4. Neither perception nor nonperception

The one notion is meditation on the loathsomeness of food.

The one analysis is the analysis of the four primary elements.

Of these forty exercises in meditation which lead to tranquillity, the ten impurities and the mindfulness regarding the body are suitable for a person of lustful temperament. The four sublime states and the four color devices are suitable for the hot-tempered. The mindfulness as to respiration is suitable for men of discursive mind and for those who are easily deluded. The first six recollections are suitable for the person to whom confidence comes easily. For those who are quick-witted, the suitable exercises are mindfulness as to death, the cognition of the attributes of peace of mind, meditation on the loathsomeness of food, and the one analysis. The remaining exercises are suitable for all. In choosing a device as an object of meditation, those who are easily deluded should choose a wide one, and a person of discursive nature should choose a little one of a span and four inches in diameter.

There are three stages of the meditation which leads to tranquillity. The first stage is called the preliminary stage and can be attained by any one of the forty meditations. The second stage is called the accessory stage and can be attained through the first eight recollections, the one notion, and the one analysis. The third stage is called the stage of absorption and can be attained through using the rest of the forty meditations. There are nine levels of the stage of absorption (*jhana*), five (or four, according to another classification) belonging to the realm of form, and four belonging to the formless realm. The levels of absorption pertaining to the realm of form can be attained through the ten devices and the respiration exercise. Meditation on the ten impurities and mindfulness concerning the body will attain only the first level of the realm of form; meditation on the first three sublime practices—love, compassion, and the happiness of others—will attain only the first four levels of absorption in the realm of form; meditation on the fourth sublime practice—equanimity—will bring attainment of the fifth level of absorption in the realm of form. Meditation which relies on the four immaterial states will attain the four levels of absorption belonging to the formless realm.

As an example, let us now consider a brief account of the way in which meditation on the earth device is used in the meditation which leads to tranquillity.

First, the beginner must establish himself perfectly in pure conduct so there will be no distractions caused by his actions, and he will be sure that his self-restraint is not endangered from any side. At the same time, he should so guard the gates of his senses that he may not be attracted or fascinated by anything which is perceived by his senses. Then he should be constantly mindful of himself and be self-possessed in all his movements. By such preliminary practices he reaches the state of being content with whatever happens to be his lot, and his mind becomes inclined toward simplicity and fewness of wants. It is only after that preparation that he can select a proper object for meditation, as recommended by his spiritual teacher, and begin to practice meditation.

If he selects the earth device for his object, he must make the device with clay the color of the dawn which he smears on a piece of cloth or some convenient surface in a circle a span and four inches in diameter. Then he places the circle at a distance of about a yard and a half from his seat. He gazes at it and repeats its name all the time, trying to grasp it by the mind. When it is thoroughly grasped by the mind, an image of it appears before the mind, and as he continues to look at it and grasp it the after-image arises. The after-image then appears to be bursting the grasped mental image and is a thousand times more brilliant than it was at first; this is called the transformed after-image. By a repetition of the process of grasping the image of the earth device and then the after-image, the process of mental hindrances subsides.

When he sees in himself the absence of mental hindrances, joy arises and, because of the joy, interest arises. When the mind is interested, the body becomes calm. When he experiences the calmness, he experiences comfort, and his mind becomes concentrated. Then, free from low and sensuous mental states, he enters upon the first absorption (jhana) which is endowed with initial and sustained application, interest, and comfort born of quietude. After mastering this absorption, he goes on further in his practice and brings about the quiescence of initial and sustained application and attains to the second level of absorption which is endowed with inward placidity, unification of the mind, interest, and comfort born of concentration. This, too, he masters and continues his practices and attains to the third level of absorption at which interest fades and he becomes equable and mindful and feels bodily comfort. Again, as a result of further practice, he rejects ease and pain and enters upon the fourth level of absorption which is endowed with equanimity and individualization.

When he has elevated his mind by passing through those four levels of absorption, he can, if he likes, develop his supernormal powers such as clairvoyance, thought reading, remembrance of past lives, levitation, and such. Whether or not he decides to develop these powers, he can go on with his meditation, for those powers are not of any help in attaining the next levels of absorption. A person who sees the evils of the physical body, whether gross or subtle, and prefers to exist purely in a mental state—to be a spirit—follows the path that leads to such a state. Such a person sees the disadvantages even of the level of absorption he has thus far attained and attempts to go farther.

To attain the next levels of absorption, he spreads the object of the previous absorption—that is, the transformed after-image —as far and wide as possible throughout the space he can imagine; then he removes it so that he may see the empty space. Then he fixes his mind on the very same mental space and repeatedly turns to it and impinges on it until his mind becomes firmly fixed in the mental space, and thus he attains to the first level of the formless absorption. He masters that level by entering it and rising from it over and over again, and then if he wishes to rise higher, he takes for his object the consciousness which was fixed on the infinite space and attempts to fix the mind on this new object. After some effort, he succeeds in fixing his mind on the consciousness with which he viewed the mental space and attains the second level of absorption in the realm of the formless. After the mastery of this level, he tries to elevate the mind to a more subtle level. He stops attending to the object of infinite consciousness and attempts to fix his mind on its absence—on "nothingness." When he is successful, he attains the third level of absorption in the formless, known as the realm of nothingness.

When he has mastered the third level, he attempts to attain the fourth stage of formless absorption which is the culmination of the meditation which leads to tranquillity. He enters the third level of formless absorption and rises from it and observes the condition of his immediately previous absorption-consciousness. As he repeatedly reflects upon that condition, his mind becomes most subtle and he attains to the state of mind which is called "neither consciousness nor unconsciousness." It is called that because the grossness of consciousness is absent, and it exists in the most subtle form ever possible.

The persons who have attained to any of the four levels of the formless absorption are destined to be reborn in comparable pure mental states or realms. When the force of their meditation which elevated them to that state has been exhausted, they will come down again and be born among men. Thus it is seen that the attainments of the method of meditation which leads to tranquillity are still worldly, and that is why they were not highly praised by the Buddha.

Thus far we have described the first of the two kinds of meditation, the meditation which leads to tranquillity. Let us turn now to the second kind of meditation, the meditation which leads to insight. This is Buddhist meditation, the meditation which leads the follower further and further away from worldliness and awakens the mind to awareness of the real nature of the living being. Some persons develop insight and attain Arahatship by starting with the meditation which leads to tranquillity and gaining insight from one of the levels of absorption—they are known as those who have made tranquillity of the mind their vehicle. But none of the levels of absorption discussed above is absolutely necessary to Arahatship because even without it some are able to attain Arahatship—they are called the dry-visioned, the ones who attained Arahatship by the meditation which leads to insight.

In the meditation which leads to tranquillity there are forty exercises, but in the meditation which leads to insight, there are only three—meditation on the impermanence, suffering, and nonsubstantiality (anicca, dukkha, and anatta) of life in the world.

The meditator who seeks to practice the meditation which leads to insight, if he has already developed any of the levels of absorption, enters any stage of absorption and from it analyses the factors and qualities of that stage and tries to understand their impermanence, suffering, and nonsubstantiality. If he has not attained any level of absorption, he will analyze his own life. Either way, he will see by analyzing his own self that the so-called being or self is nothing but a process or flux of mental and material states which are interdependent. By analysis he sees that they are but a stream of causes and effects. Then he examines and scrutinizes the nature of the causes and effects very minutely, and at last he realizes the voidness or emptiness of the life of all living beings, either human or divine. The whole universe appears to him as a mere flux, as mere vibrations which are void of any entity. With the attainment of this realization, craving for such an existence wanes, vanishes, and ceases to be. The opposite side of this illusory existence dawns before his mind, and the path which he has been following reaches its culmination. This, in Buddhist terminology, is the Realization of the Four Truths.

The Realization of the Four Truths occurs four times. On the first occasion, the meditator discerns the ill, the suffering, of life; then the false view concerning the ego-entity and any scepticism concerning the Buddha and all his teachings vanish away from him forever, Nibbana gleams before his mind, and all the eight factors of the Path appear together in his mind. This experience is called the Entering of the Stream, for anyone who reaches this state will never fall back into worldliness and is destined to become an Arahat. That fourfold experience —the understanding of suffering, loss of false views, glimpse of Nibbana, and grasping of the Eightfold Path—occurs within one flash of thought and is immediately followed by two or three thought-moments in which he experiences the bliss of Nibbana. Those moments are called the fruit-consciousness of the Stream-winner's Path. After those thought-moments he engages in retrospection, reviewing the Holy stage of the Path which has been attained, the fruits enjoyed, Nibbana intuited, the mental depravities already got rid of in the first stage, and the depravities to be got rid of in the future.

When in that retrospection he sees the depravities to be removed, he goes on with his practice of contemplation, and on the second occasion he discerns once more the ills of existence and consequently slackens his sensual attachment, his anger, and delusion; he sees Nibbana and develops the Path. When one has attained this second stage, he is called a Once-returner because, since he has lessened his attachments that much, he will be reborn only once in the sensual world. This brief thought-moment is followed by its fruit-consciousness two or three times, and then he engages in the process of retrospection as before. As he sees in his retrospection that his realization is still not perfect, he continues his contemplation, and at the moment of reaching the next stage he sees the ills of existence clearer than before, eradicates desire for sensual pleasure, and ends all ill will; he sees Nibbana face to face, and the factors of the Path appear unitedly in his mind at one moment. Because he will never be reborn to the sensual plane after this insight, he is called a Never-returner. This thought-moment at the third stage of progress is followed by its fruit-moments and by the process of retrospection.

Through the process of retrospection after attaining the third stage of insight he sees that there are still some mental depravities to be removed, so he returns to his usual practice of meditation. Now at last he reaches the culmination of his meditative practice; he realizes perfectly the ills of existence, eradicates all the remaining weaknesses of the mind, sees Nibbana as it is, and all the factors of the Path appear in his mind simultaneously. This stage is called the Path of Arahatship. It also is followed by its fruit-consciousness two or three times, and then follows the process of retrospection upon the Path, its fruition, Nibbana, and the eradication of all passions.

A person who has attained to this final stage has become an Arahat and has nothing more to do for he has now reached the end of the Path. He is free of passion and lives a selfless life doing his pure service to frail mortals. This stage of insight is the goal of the Path expounded by the Buddha.

CHAPTER FOUR

Development of Mahayana
Buddhist Beliefs

Susumu Yamaguchi

Translated by Shoko Watanabe

FUNDAMENTAL TEACHING OF THE BUDDHA

As the Indian metaphysical speculations became more profound, they showed a tendency to seek the deliverance of the individual self from the world of suffering. Each of the Hindu philosophical schools sought deliverance from the world of suffering through its own method—the Sankhya through differentiating consciousness (*purusha*) from matter (*prakriti*), the Vedanta through identifying the Brahman and Atman, and the Vaiseshika through the knowledge of the categories. Such ideas form the basis for the metaphysical speculations through which the people of India created their own spiritual civilization which has played a characteristic role in the cultural history of the world.

Buddhism as preached by Sakyamuni (the wise man, *muni*, of the Sakya clan) cannot be grasped apart from these speculations of Hindu scholars. It goes without saying that one who would account for Sakyamuni's renunciation of the world cannot ignore his natural talent for religion, nor the environment in which he grew up as a child; but one cannot deny that the Hindu conception of deliverance from the world of suffering, which had reached its most influential heights in the Upanishad period, had much to do with his adoption of the ascetic's life.

The Buddha reflected very earnestly upon suffering and found that birth is suffering, disease is suffering, death is suffering, association with the unpleasing is suffering, separation from the pleasing is suffering, and not to get what one wants is suffering. In the Four Noble Truths Buddhism has discovered the real cause of human suffering and shows human beings the right and effective way to the deliverance from suffering, just as a doctor finds the cause of illness and administers medicine to cure the disease. Therefore we must regard Buddhism as the flower of the culture of ancient India which considered deliverance from suffering to be the ultimate objective of human beings. We can understand Buddhism only as we recognize it as a religion aiming at complete emancipation from suffering.

The doctrine of the Four Noble Truths tells exactly the way in which Sakyamuni sought the cause of suffering and how he realized its annihilation. As he sat under the bodhi tree, he searched for the destruction of suffering by meditating on the Twelve Links in the Chain of Causation—ignorance, will-to-action, consciousness, psycho-physical existence, six organs of sense, contact of subject and object, feeling, desire, grasping, existence, birth, decay, and death. According to the Sutras, he found that birth is the cause of such suffering as decay and death and traced the chain back to ignorance. Then he contemplated on the way in which ignorance gives rise to will-to-action (*samskara*, or karmic formations), which in turn produces consciousness and so on through the chain of causation until in his contemplation he saw birth as the cause of decay and death. Working backward, he saw that destruction of birth is the cause of the destruction of suffering and, finally, he discovered that the destruction of ignorance is the ultimate cause of the destruction of the whole chain. He is said to have become the Buddha by means of this twofold contemplation up and down the chain of causation.

In other words, he analyzed the way to deliverance from suffering and found that the cause of suffering is ignorance and that by extinguishing ignorance suffering is extinguished. Then, what is this ignorance? It is a lack of the right intuition, that is, not knowing the truth of interdependent causation. Thus, the way to deliverance from suffering taught by the Buddha is nothing other than the right knowledge of the truth of interdependent causation (*pratityasamutpada*). This truth is generally expressed by the formula, "When this exists, that occurs; when this does not exist, that does not exist; when this is destroyed, that is destroyed." This truth is also seen through the twofold contemplation, up and down the twelve links in the chain of causation.

The right knowledge of the truth of interdependent causation must lead to a recognition of the interdependent relations of various aspects of actual human existence because, as expounded by Mahayanists, the truth of interdependent causation must lie in the principle of negation of the very existence of things that are transient and void—since they, being interdependent, do not exist independently. So far as the truth of interdependent causation has such a meaning, suffering is the necessary consequence of attachment to the existence of things and of claiming their unvarying eternity in defiance of the truth.

If, on the contrary, one realizes the truth as it is and knows the vanity of the existence of things, one will not be afflicted by suffering when experiencing decay, disease, and death. Sakyamuni is to be thought of as having freed himself from suffering by thoroughly realizing the truth of interdependent causation in this sense.

In the theory of the Twelve Links in the Chain of Causation (*Nidanas*), which is the plainest expression of the truth of interdependent causation, consciousness and psycho-physical existence (*nama-rupa*) hold important places, for they form the active moments of human existence. Psycho-physical existence includes the four non-material elements or aggregates —feeling, cognition, will-to-action, and consciousness—on the one hand, and the four material elements—earth, water, fire and air—and their compounds on the other. Psycho-physical existence, which is the fourth link in the chain of causation,

refers to the human individual composed of various psychological elements and a physical body.

It is consciousness which unifies the individual. The importance of the relation between consciousness and the psycho-
physical existence in the chain of interdependent causation is
made clear by the stress the Buddha laid on the interdependent
relation between these two links. Since psycho-physical existence is the individual and consciousness is its unifier, the causal
relation between the two explains how the human individual
comes into existence. And if we regard consciousness, insofar
as it is the unifier of the individual, as the "internal," and
psycho-physical existence as the "external," we may interpret
the relation between the two as the relation between the internal and the external in general, which is the interdependent
relation to be found in the actual concrete world we live in.

Thus we may interpret the theory of the Twelve Links in
the Chain of Causation in this way: we are lost in ignorance of
the interdependent relation of our internal and external worlds
and are incurring suffering by incessantly clinging to (or pant-
ing after, or grasping—*trishna*) the external things.

The theory of the Twelve Links in the Chain of Causation
admits of various interpretations and seems to have been a
cause of the development of different Buddhist doctrines in
later ages. At any rate, there is no doubt that the main point
of the Buddha's theory of interdependent causation was the
understanding of the interdependent relation between consciousness (*vijnana*) and psycho-physical existence (*nama-
rupa*), the internal and the external. The validity of the theory
of interdependent causation is expressed in the well-known
statement, "The eternal conformity to the dharma does not
change either in the presence or in the absence of the Enlightened Ones," which is found in many passages of the Sutras,
including the old one which records the event of Sakyamuni's
Self-awakening. The following famous exposition of the teaching, known as "the universal Buddhas' stanza," also expresses
the theory of interdependent causation:

> The Buddha hath the causes told
> Of all things springing from causes;
> And also how things cease to be—
> 'Tis this the Mighty Monk proclaims.
>
> (Mahavagga i. 23, modified from
> Warren's translation; p. 89.)

The way to deliverance from suffering by awakening to an understanding of interdependent causation, as shown by the Buddha, is characteristic of Buddhism and not to be found in any other philosophical system in India. The Buddhist teachings evolved around this theory of interdependent causation.

The idea of karma existed before the Buddha, but he is the first person to understand karma as interdependent causation. The two terms could be equivalent if they are understood as terms which explain human existence, for karma, in broad meaning, is our conduct, including its consequences. In Buddhism, the Twelve Links in the Chain of Causation are concerned with human conduct because if reality is to have any meaning it must be related to human beings—the ways of nature do not matter to the Buddhist. The Buddha dealt only with matters of human conduct. The view of karma as a strict moral law of cause and effect is not fundamental to Buddhist thinking. Karma is a deed which has inevitable consequences; it is not a law of morality.

It is an open question as to whether or not primitive Buddhism believed in rebirth. There is a great deal about rebirth in Buddhist literature, but it has been a question through the centuries, and remains a question in modern times, as to whether or not the idea of rebirth is required by karma, by action and its inevitable consequences.

What is essential to an understanding of Buddhism is a grasping of the truth of interdependent causation.

SCHOOLS OF ABHIDHARMA BUDDHISM

Little is known of the development of the Order in the period following the Buddha's death. We can well imagine, however, that the Order made efforts to arrange and transmit the Master's teaching, and especially that, as the Order grew, it added many new rules of discipline for the purpose of maintaining its authority and controlling the members. This tendency is clear in the record of the First Council which is said to have been held immediately after the Buddha's decease. But after a time, as the Order grew and its authority was established, it became more rigid in organization and formal in doctrine, which led to division in the Order as an attempt was made to counteract the growing conventionalism.

Thus the historians assume that a schism occurred prior to the time of Emperor Asoka, and the two major schools came into being—the Sthaviravadins (conservatives), and the Mahasanghikas (progressives). Schism followed schism until nearly twenty schools were created within two centuries after Asoka's time, a period in which Buddhism is known as Buddhism of the schools, or Abhidharma Buddhism. The word *Abhidharma* consists of two parts— *abhi* (toward) and *dharma* (teaching) —which together mean the study and exposition of the Buddha's teaching. Buddhism in this period is called Abhidharma Buddhism because, whether conservative or progressive, all the schools showed a tendency to expound the Buddha's words and to explain their logical significance. At no other time in its history was Buddhism so divergent in its interpretation as at this period. The argumentative trend of that time seems to have given birth to a considerable number of Abhidharma works, but the works of only a few schools are extant. For instance, the treatises of the Mahasanghikas have been lost except for some fragments from the writings of one minor school which was merged with Mahayana Buddhism. Consequently, we have only scanty materials for the study of Buddhism in this stage, and much remains still in the dark. Depending, then, on the few materials available, let us try to give an outline of how Buddhism at that time understood the theory of interdependent causation, which is regarded as the fundamental teaching of the Buddha.

Among the Abhidharma schools, the Theravadins in Ceylon are today the most influential and the best equipped with treatises. But in the early days it was the Sarvastivadins, also conservative, who became the target of criticism from Mahayana Buddhism and who directly influenced Mahayana in later ages. *Sarvastivadin* means "those who argue that everything (every dharma) exists," that is, that the essences of all things, whether empirical or absolute, worldly or unworldly, did exist, do exist, and will exist. This seems to have been the position of the conservatives who took the Buddha at his word and believed in the existence of everything he mentioned.

This school maintained the existence of all things—such as the five skandhas, the six organs of sense and their six objects of sense, and the six consciousnesses—which the Buddha made use of when he explained his doctrine of interdependent causation. The existing things were classified as seventy-five dharmas, which were divided into five categories—form, mind, function of mind, action not connected with the mind, and the nonphenomenal element. Such was the attitude most characteristic of Abhidharma Buddhism which was eager to expound the Buddha's teaching.

The major efforts of the Sarvastivadins were directed to explaining the essential characteristics of the seventy-five dharmas, not to expounding the intrinsic meaning of the theory of interdependent causation. Their theory is that the cycles of our existence can be explained by means of mental impurity (the outcome of ignorance), clinging to existence, and suffering; they regard the Twelve Links of the Chain of Causation as simply describing the incessant flux of impurity, clinging, and suffering.

In all schools, except the Sarvastivadins, stress was laid on consciousness among the Twelve Links, interpreting it in a variety of ways: the Mahisasakas considered consciousness to be an element which continues to exist as long as human beings exist; the Sthaviravadins considered consciousness to be the life continuum, the constituent of becoming; the Sautrantikas thought of consciousness as an element which continues to exist without change as long as human beings exist; the Vatsiputriyas said that consciousness is the element which transmigrates. Other schools, which are said to belong to the Mahasanghikas, emphasized the character of interdependent causation and transiency of all things. What is remarkable in Abhidharma Buddhism is that all the schools that were called Sthaviravadins —not only the Sarvastivadins who asserted the existence of all things, but also the schools which laid stress on the character of consciousness as unifier—were disposed to maintain the existence of the elements (dharmas). On the other hand, the schools of the Mahasanghikas were inclined to hold the theory of nonexistence of the elements by emphasizing their interdependent and transient character.

At any rate, we may conclude that the theory of interdependent causation implies negation of the existence of elements or a substratum of reality because what is caused interdependently is transient, selfless, and void, and accordingly, it is contradictory to speak of the theory of causation from the standpoint of simple realism. Yet it would be going to extremes to emphasize the significance of transience and voidness in the theory of interdependent causation as excessively as some Mahasanghikas did. The theory of interdependent causation which seeks to express the truth as it is, is to be distinguished from one-sided nihilism. Thus, the nihilism of the Mahasanghikas is no more faithful to the original meaning of interdependent causation as conceived by the Buddha than is the realism of the conservative schools. They held a prejudice either for existence or nonexistence. The Madhyamika school of Mahayana Buddhism to which we shall now turn is historically significant because its followers explain properly the original meaning of interdependent causation, free from the bias of existence or nonexistence.

MADHYAMIKA AS MAHAYANA

It may be said that the fundamental principles of the Mahayana spirit were established by the Prajnaparamita Sutras. A Sutra is simply a discourse by the Buddha or his disciples which now holds the status of a scripture. Prajnaparamita is the wisdom (*prajna*) that has attained the Other World (*Paramita*), that is, the perfect wisdom that has reached the World of Awakening by destroying illusions. What is the wisdom of the awakening? It is the unrestricted wisdom that makes one contemplate everything as being void and incomprehensible, a kind of wisdom which was no novelty in the Prajnaparamita Sutras, for it was expounded in primitive Buddhism. The word *prajna* is known both in the scriptures of primitive Buddhism and in the later Abhidharma works—it means "looking at things as they are," which is wisdom.

Abhidharma Buddhism, however, was likely to be biased toward either the realistic or the nihilistic view and to fail to give due consideration to the wisdom which looks at things as they are. The Prajnaparamita Sutras are regarded by Mahayana Buddhists as an attempt to bring into clear relief and to restore the original form of Buddhism which had degenerated into Abhidharma. The Prajnaparamita Sutras deny completely the substantiality of all the conceptions established in Abhidharma, not excepting even those of Buddha and Bodhisattva, which they say are void and incomprehensible. Such wisdom of voidness and incomprehensibility may be called the true wisdom because it accords with the truth that everything is void (*sunyata*) because it is caused interdependently.

The concept of voidness and incomprehensibility which was taught in the Prajnaparamita Sutras was systematized by the rare thinker named Nagarjuna, whose main work, Mulamadhyamaka Sastra, opens with the following stanzas:

> The perfect Buddha,
> The foremost of all teachers I salute;
> He has proclaimed
> The Principle of (Universal) Relativity;
> 'Tis like blissful (Nirvana)
> Quiescence of Plurality.
> There nothing disappears,
> Nor anything appears,
> Nothing has an end,
> Nor is there anything eternal,
> Nothing is identical (with itself),
> Nor is there anything differentiated;
> Nothing moves,
> Neither hither nor thither, . . .

(Translated by Th. Stcherbatsky)

As is clear from these lines, Nagarjuna claims to have inherited from Buddha Sakyamuni his fundamental doctrine of interdependent causation which was embodied in the truth of voidness and incomprehensibility—nonappearance and nondisappearance, noncessation and noneternity, nonidentity and nondifferentiation, noncoming and nongoing-forth. The Mulamadhyamaka Sastra by Nagarjuna consists only of verses and was commented on later by scholars of the Madhyamika school, so that the import of the work may be studied in detail. Let us consider briefly why Nagarjuna explained interdependent causation as nonappearance, nondisappearance, and so on.

Insofar as the truth of interdependent causation means that things exist interdependently and relatively to each other, the notion of the appearance of things-in-themselves is denied. Accordingly, the appearance of things does not mean the appearance of any substantial things, nor can there be things that might be destroyed. Thus the notion of destruction is also denied. Thus, the truth of interdependent causation of things implies nonappearance and nondisappearance.

According to the theory of interdependent causation, it is inconceivable that there can be any active subject which might act of its own accord. In other words, the subject of a substantial action is denied by this theory, and there can be no action such as coming or going which might be conceivable as the action of a subject of substantial actions. Therefore, there is noncoming and nongoing-forth. Furthermore, the theory of interdependent causation does not admit that a constant cause develops in continuous succession into the effect which is identical with the cause, nor that an effect exists apart from a cause which has ceased to exist. Therefore, the truth of interdependent causation implies nonidentity and nondifferentiation, noncessation and noneternity in causal relations.

Accordingly, the standpoint of interdependent causation is incompatible with the notion of the phenomenal world emerging from an ante-phenomenal active cause, such as prakriti, as claimed by the Hindu Sankhya system, which advocates the theory of evolutionism or the unity between cause and effect—

a theory which holds that the phenomenal world is latent in prakriti and is destined to develop from it.

The doctrine of interdependent causation is also incompatible with the pluralistic realism of the Hindu Vaiseshika philosophy which regards all existences as an inorganic assemblage of the six categories and upholds the theory of the distinction between cause and effect, denying organic development from cause into effect.

The evolutionism of the Sankhya philosophy may be called an idealism that neglects the substantiality of things, since it looks upon the actualities as revelations of an ante-phenomenal active substance. On the other hand, pluralistic realism, the inorganic outlook on actual things of the Vaiseshika philosophy, deservedly is called materialistic because it disregards the organic independence of mind. Therefore we have to conclude that the subjective mind as well as objective matter acquire a concrete significance in the light of the theory of interdependent and interrelated causation and that they reveal their true character only when viewed as nonidentical and nondifferentiated, noninterrupted and noneternal.

Nagarjuna gives several instances to show that a concrete significance is gained if the subjective and objective, the internal and external, the active and passive are recognized as interdependent and interrelated. For example, he argues in the tenth chapter of the Mulamadhyamaka Sastra that if fire (the subjective) exists anterior to fuel (the objective), the absurdity of fire burning without fuel would follow, and if fuel existed before fire, it would imply the preposterousness of fuel that does not burn. This argument enables us to conclude that the truth of interdependent and interrelated causation which implies nonidentity and nondifferentiation, noncessation and noneternity, indicates a standpoint superior to both idealism and materialism because it confirms that the actual things are neither at the beck and call of our subjective mind nor unrelated to it.

By these arguments Nagarjuna seeks to show us the world of wisdom of voidness and inconceivability where the restrictions of our minds are removed. It is needless to say that the negation of appearing and disappearing things-in-themselves and the negation of the subject of movements is a means of pointing out the world of wisdom of voidness and inconceivability. At the very beginning Sakyamuni made it clear that the truth of dependent origination was tantamount to the denial of the theories of a substantial soul (*atman*) and of an independent existence for a thing-in-itself and that interdependent causation is incompatible with evolutionism or pluralistic realism. It is, however, a matter of great significance that Nagarjuna paraphrased the theory of dependent origination by means of the eightfold negation—nonappearance and nondisappearance, noncessation and noneternity, nonidentity and nondifferentiation, noncoming and nongoing-forth—and declared at the beginning of his chief writing that the eightfold negation was the fundamental characteristic of his doctrine. It is quite possible that but for Nagarjuna the Buddhism propounded by Sakyamuni might not have been able to explain logically its standpoint which is unique in the history of Indian philosophy. This is why he was called the second Sakyamuni.

Nagarjuna explained the truth of the voidness and inconceivability of existence by paraphrasing the theory of dependent causation by means of the eightfold negation. The voidness and inconceivability of the extinction of subject and object may be regarded as the same as the "Quiescence of plurality" quoted above from the introductory verse of his main work. He calls this truth of the voidness and inconceivability the voidness (sunyata) and the absolute truth. This indicates that the voidness represents the truth of absolute and supreme significance. On the other hand, he uses the term "phenomenal truth" to refer to the things—interdependently caused dharmas—recognized for what they are through an understanding of interdependent causation. Thus the voidness stands for the unqualified truth which transcends our subject-object consciousness, while phenomenal truth refers to the qualified truth which is comprehended by our subject-object consciousness.

The void and absolute truth is absolutely negative and defies all attempts to express it, while the interdependent world,

which is described by the formula "when this exists that occurs," is the practical world whose positive existence is known
through phenomenal truth. Therefore the phenomenal and
interdependent world is an aspect of the nonqualified world
which is tantamount to the void and absolute truth and is called
the "worldly practices" of the nonqualified world. This aspect
of worldly practices does not exist in substance; it is only an
aspect of the nonqualified world, an aspect of the void and
absolute truth. Existence in the phenomenal world is called
nominal existence, similar to actions based on phantoms, dreams,
or mirages.

Thus nominalism has become the most important principle
in the philosophy of Nagarjuna because, if the interdependent
world is a nominal aspect of the void and absolute truth, the
doctrine of interdependent causation preached by Sakyamuni
is made self-conscious on the basis of the void and absolute
truth. This would mean that the realistic view of interdependent causation is rejected and the nihilistic conception of interdependent causation is refuted by revealing the actual and
positive significance in which the void and absolute truth is
made accessible to the practical world. Nagarjuna said in his
work called Sunyatasaptati, "The absolute truth denotes nothing other than the voidness by nature of all things caused
interdependently; but the Buddha admitted the nominal existence of all things from the practical standpoint of interdependent origination." The world of interdependence is free from
the realistic view because its voidness in the light of the
absolute truth is implied; and, at the same time, it is also free
from the nihilistic view because it is the real and positive
practical expression of the supreme voidness.

Again, Nagarjuna explained his position by saying, "What
is the interdependent causation that we call the voidness? Interdependent causation is a nominal expression; it is the middle
way itself." In his first sermon, the middle way was described
by the Buddha as being free from the two extremities of pleasure and pain, as being the righteous and unbiased standpoint.
But now Nagarjuna relates the middle way to interdependent
causation, the essence of the Buddha's awakening, freeing it

from the realistic view insofar as it is void, and freeing it from the nihilistic view insofar as it is nominal. Such an interpretation of interdependent causation by means of the middle way shows Nagarjuna's position, unique in the history of Buddhist thought.

Thus the world of interdependent causation is nothing other than a practical aspect of the voidness. We who belong to the practical world have to grasp the voidness through this interdependent world; we have to grasp the negative voidness in the positive and actual world of interdependent causation.

As the most concrete example of such a middle way of thinking, we may mention the perfection of liberality, one of the six perfections. The perfection of liberality consists of three factors of which the decisive natures are inconceivable—giver, gift, and receiver—and is called "the pure threefold circle." The circle represents the interdependence of the three factors as in forming a circle. The act of giving, which is supreme, void, and inconceivable, is carried out in the practical world of interdependence and becomes purified. This is the perfection of liberality. Accordingly, the perfection of liberality is a nonrealistic and nonnihilistic practice of the middle way in which the negative, supreme, and void truth is grasped by means of, and in the locality of, the practical phase of interdependent causation.

Such a practical comprehension of the middle way between realism and nihilism is nothing other than what is called the perfect wisdom (*prajnaparamita*). Therefore, the perfect wisdom is not a wisdom transcending the practical world, but a wisdom to be revealed in our practical world. Nagarjuna's doctrine may be regarded as aiming at a systematic interpretation of the perfect wisdom advocated in the Prajnaparamita Sutras as the wisdom with the significance of the middle way.

VIJNANAVADA—THE CONSUMMATION OF MAHAYANA

The Madhyamika theory which was systematized by Nagarjuna sought to present the right view of the doctrine of interdependent causation which was preached by the Buddha, so that this doctrine might become the true principle of our right practice. Upon careful consideration, however, it must be acknowledged that although Nagarjuna indeed admits the empirical existence of the interdependent world, he denies its existence from the viewpoint of ultimate truth because from the standpoint of the middle way he asserts the identity of the empirical and absolute truths, showing the absolute truth of the voidness by affirming—that is, negating the nonexistence of—the interdependent world as the worldly construction of the absolute voidness. In other words, the empirical interdependent world will be reduced to nothingness from the standpoint of Nagarjuna's Madhyamika theory. In fact, some of his followers, Madhyamika scholars in later ages, seem to have turned to such a nihilism.

It is for this reason that there appeared another doctrine which was willing to affirm the real absolute truth of the nominal interdependent world by criticizing the nihilistic view which denied the worldly existence. This trend of thought was developed in the so-called middle-stage Mahayana Sutras such as Samdhinirmocana, Srimaladevisimhanada, Lankavatara, and the like and was made into a philosophical system of Vijnanavada or Yogacara by Asanga and Vasubandhu who are believed to have lived early in the fourth century A.D.

According to the Samdhinirmocana Sutra, the Sutras on which the realistic doctrine of Abhidharma is based are called "the first wheel of the law"; the Prajnaparamita Sutras on which Nagarjuna's nihilistic teaching is founded are named "the wheel of the law without characteristic"; and the Samdhinirmocana and the other Sutras which give a basis for the Yogacara position are said to be "the last wheel of the law" which synthesizes the realistic and nihilistic views. The Samdhinirmocana Sutra is quite properly called the last wheel of the law which synthesizes the realistic and nihilistic views because it gives an explicit explanation of the voidness and substancelessness of all things, while the second wheel of the law, the wheel of the law without characteristic, suggests the same idea only implicitly. This is what is called "the division of the Buddha's teachings into three stages."

This threefold division of the Buddha's teaching is logically systematized as the theory of the threefold existence, that is, the subjective construction, the relative existence, and the absolute reality. The subjective construction is false because the truth of dependent origination is not grasped in this stage and obstinacy ensues. The relative existence refers to "the dependently originated things" relying on causes and conditions separate from themselves. The absolute reality is the perfectly accomplished real state where dependent origination is truly comprehended as such. Accordingly, dependent origination is represented as a false subjectivity in the empirical world, but its real aspect is the absolute reality which assumes temporarily the shape of a false subjectivity in the empirical world. In other words, the dependently originated things are contingent and have an imaginary existence.

According to the theory of the three stages of the Buddha's teachings which we referred to above, the first stage—the realistic view—reveals this imaginary existence which is caused contingently. The second stage—the nihilistic view—makes it clear that the dependently caused things which have only an imaginary existence are void insofar as they are subjectively imagined. The third stage—the Samdhinirmocana Sutra— teaches the middle way which says that the dependently caused things are imaginary and void insofar as they are subjectively imagined, but they are, at the same time, the absolute reality which is affirmatively accomplished in the voidness.

Thus, the empirical world of interdependent causation, which was thought to be imaginary and was denied absolute reality by Nagarjuna, who maintained the Madhyamika theory, was regarded by the followers of Vijnanavada as being made up of dependently caused things which are affirmatively recognized to be the absolute reality. That is to say, the empirical world was now revived as the substratum of identification of the empirical and the absolute world. The world of interdependent causation is one actual existence.

The one actual existence of the world of interdependent causation is called fundamental consciousness (*alayavijnana*) by the Vijnanavada school. This expression is used to show the truth of interdependent causation. Thus, fundamental consciousness denotes our active mental world which is caused interdependently. Now, fundamental consciousness as an actual existence is a kind of subjective consciousness similar to the ideas mentioned above as characteristic of the Abhidharma schools—the foundation of consciousness, the element which continues to exist as long as human beings exist, the constituents of becoming. It is clearly stated in the treatises of the Vijnanavada school that the concept of fundamental consciousness is an offspring of those Abhidharma ideas.

Fundamental consciousness, however, has the character of interdependent causation and accordingly must be regarded as void in the sense of the doctrine of voidness. In a verse from the Mahayanabhidharma Sutra quoted in the Mahayanasamgraha, the character of the interdependent causation of the fundamental consciousness is described as follows:

All things abide in the consciousness,
And this abides in them also in the same way;
(The things and the consciousness) become the effects
    of each other
And they become always the causes (of each other).

The character of the interdependent causation of this fundamental consciousness is stated in verse seven of the Alambanapariksha of the famous fifth-century logician, Dinnaga, in this way:

As the consciousness arises in the shapes of the objects, it is established as representing the objects insofar as the shapes of the objects are present. When the shapes of the objects are present, the consciousness arises in the shape of the subject accompanied by the shapes of the objects as its objective condition. And the perceivable appearance or the consciousness representing the objects becomes habitual and this habit remains as the potency [or seed] of developing the consciousness into the perceivable shape. Such a succession of cause and effect has existed from eternity.

This is the so-called theory of the evolution of the consciousness, advocating the interdependence and interrelation of subject and object. It is, however, an idealistic theory of the interdependent causation, because the empiric subject-object aspect of the interdependent causation is represented as the fact of the consciousness. The negative character of fundamental consciousness is quite evident in the practical approach of the Vijnanavada theory, called "the means to enter into the state without characteristic," which is explained in this way: "From the discernment of the pure consciousness ensues the nondiscernment of the outer world, and from the nondiscernment of the outer world ensues the nondiscernment of the pure consciousness, too."

Nondiscernment even of the pure consciousness is attained at the stage of the voidness where useless arguments cease to exist. Here lies the negative aspect of the theory of Vijnanavada.

It is worthy of notice, however, that the negative aspect of this theory, unlike the absolutely negative voidness maintained by the Madhyamika school, denotes an affirmative and accomplished state of fundamental consciousness, what is called "the existence of the nonexistence" by the Vijnanavada school. This is called "existence of the nonexistence" because the false and defiling aspect of fundamental consciousness, which develops into the subject-object relation and interdependent causation, is denied (negative), and its real and pure aspect as the negation of the defilement is affirmed (affirmative) and accomplished. According to the terminology of the Vijnanavada school, such a negative transition of fundamental consciousness from defilement to purity is called the transformation of the consciousness into the intelligence, or the change of the substratum of fundamental consciousness; that is, the movement of fundamental consciousness from the state of erroneous consciousness to the state of awakened intelligence.

In this manner, the Vijnanavada school has accomplished, by means of fundamental consciousness, the way from defilement to purity, from the worldly existence to the absolute reality. While the Madhyamika school intended to realize the absolute voidness by negating the empirical world of interdependent causation, the Vijnanavada school has succeeded in establishing the way to the absolute reality on the foundation of the empirical world of interdependent causation which is fundamental consciousness, thus making this the basis of mediating between the empirical and the absolute. Here lies the standpoint of the Vijnanavada school which is unique in the history of thought.

VOIDNESS AND MERCY

It is the fundamental attitude of Buddhism to regard our world as the interdependent world and thus to realize the truth of the voidness (sunyata) here. Mahayana Buddhism reflected profoundly on this fundamental Buddhist attitude. Since the world of interdependent causation is an actual world as well as a void world because it is originated interdependently, we ought to be biased neither realistically nor nihilistically. We should not forget that the actual world of interdependent causation becomes the void world through the principle of the identity of affirmation and negation.

These reflections were materialized by Nagarjuna as his doctrine of the middle way which explained the world of interdependent causation through the twofold logic of the nominal practice and the absolute voidness, or negation of nihilism and negation of realism. The same reflections were also expounded as the doctrine of the threefold existence by Asanga and Vasubandhu, who were willing to acknowledge the absolute reality of the world of interdependent causation by way of the positive affirmation of negation. Above all, those reflections found a fuller expression in the idealistic doctrines of Asanga and Vasubandhu, who maintained positively the way to the supreme voidness by means of the fundamental consciousness (alayavijnana) which is identical with the world of interdependent causation. In fine, the fundamental notion of the Mahayana doctrines was that our actual and empirical world is nothing other than the basis for realization of the negative and absolute world.

Now, if the actual and empirical world is regarded as the basis for realization of the negative and absolute world, the empirical world is an existence standing for the absolute world and is to be comprehended as an empirical form of the absolute. And the manifestation of the negative absolute in the empirical world may attest the reality of the negative absolute, because, unless the negative absolute reveals itself in the empirical world, it will remain alien to our practical life and its reality will be entirely imperceptible to us.

Such a comprehension of the negative absolute was expressed in the well-known phrase "the teaching of *visuddhi-dharma-dhatu-nishyanda*." *Dharma-dhatu* may be translated as "the world of the cosmic law" because it is the mine (dhatu) where the truth (dharma) is mined, that is, the source of the cosmic law. Thus is it a synonym for the Suchness (*tathata*), the indescribable source of the truth. *Nishyanda* means "flowing into" or "necessary result" and *visuddhi* means "purity." Therefore, the phrase which explains the negative absolute may be translated, "the purity of the flowing of the Suchness into the empirical world," or "the purity of the necessary result of the world of the cosmic law." In other words, the truth of the negative, void, and absolute reality must necessarily reveal itself as the actual empirical world, and it is the Buddhist teaching that explains this necessary revelation. This is the meaning of the phrase "the teaching of the purity of the necessary result of the Suchness."

If, in this way, the truth of the void and absolute reality necessarily reveals itself in our empirical world by means of the teaching, our actual, empirical world will be flooded with and cherished by the light of the void and absolute reality. The revelation of the void and absolute reality in the empirical world means the realization in the empirical world of that perfect wisdom which has reached the World of Awakening by destroying illusions (prajnaparamita)—that is, it means the salvation of this world. Therefore, according to Mahayana Buddhism the revelation in the empirical world of the void and absolute reality is called mercy (*karuna*). It is also called *upaya*, which means "the way" or "the means," to show how the void and absolute reality reaches the empirical world so that, on its impulse and by its means, the empirical world may be enabled to approach the void and absolute reality. The word *upaya*, the way, clearly expresses the character of the mercy which takes the form of the revelation in the empirical world of the void and absolute reality.

Such being the case, the real awakening consists in the realization of the void and absolute reality which has the character of mercy—a realization which comes in the form of the empirical revelation of the teaching. The realization of the void and absolute reality without the character of mercy cannot be the real awakening. As a matter of fact, there cannot indeed be any awakening without such mercy; but we might suppose a kind of awakening which is restricted to the Theravada salvation of one's own soul, as if the void and absolute reality could be comprehended in part without mercy. After all, the wisdom of the void and absolute reality must inevitably be learned in the course of the practice of altruistic mercy.

The necessary, practical way in which wisdom and mercy are inseparably combined is called the Original Vow of a Bodhisattva. There can be no activity of a Mahayana Bodhisattva other than the fulfillment of such a vow. This idea is summarized in the famous Four Great Vows:

> Sentient beings are innumerable: I vow to save
> them all.
> Our evil passions are inexhaustible: I vow to
> extinguish them all.
> The holy doctrines cannot be measured: I vow to
> study them.
> The path of the Buddhas is hard to reach (or, the
> awakening is supreme): I vow to attain it.
>
> (Translated by Sir Charles Eliot,
> *Japanese Buddhism*, p. 407.)

Such an inseparable accomplishment of wisdom and mercy found an appropriate expression in the term *tathagata*. This word may be analyzed and interpreted in various ways, of which the two most typical interpretations are that it means "one who has gone thus" or "one who has come thus." "One who has gone thus" means one who has attained and realized the Suchness; this interpretation emphasizes the wisdom of the realization of the voidness. "One who has come thus" means one who was reborn in this world emerging from the Suchness, and emphasizes the mercy revealed in the empirical world through the teaching which aims at the saving of all sentient beings.

In other words, Suchness in its entirety is to be realized through the inseparable connection of coming and going, that is, of entering into and emerging from, the Suchness. This is what is called the altruistic Nirvana (literally "nonresident Nirvana"), the Nirvana of one who does not reside in the world of transmigration because he is wise, and does not reside in Nirvana either, because he is merciful. Such an inseparable connection between wisdom and mercy is a belief running through all Mahayana Sutras.

This concept of the inseparable connection between wisdom and mercy is, above all, clearly represented by the idea of Amida, which is said—by Vasubandhu in his treatise on the Sukhavativyuha Sutra—to be "of boundless splendor" (*amitabha*) and "of infinite duration of life" (*amitayus*). By boundless splendor is meant the attainment of the wisdom which penetrates into sunyata, the void; it is called boundless because in Buddhist teaching the void is compared to the atmosphere which is uniform everywhere without distinction or limitation. Just as there is no distinction or limitation and accordingly no obstruction or resistance to our activities in the atmosphere, so it is the same with the accomplishment of the wisdom which penetrates into the void, realizing the void and absolute reality. This is why the wisdom is said to pervade the whole atmosphere, or to "run through the dharmadhatus in the ten directions."

This wisdom is free from the concepts which attribute substantiality to subject and object and is free from the impediment which comes from the determination to surmount substantiality. In this sense, the wisdom which penetrates into the void may be compared to the sunshine which removes mists, clouds, and darkness. This wisdom is verily a splendor. Thus the wisdom which penetrates into the void is called the boundless splendor (amitabha) insofar as it pervades the whole atmosphere and runs through the dharmadhatu in the ten directions infinitely.

It is by means of this wisdom which penetrates into the void that the false concept of the realistic determination of a subject and object in sentient beings is destroyed repeatedly; that is, the infinite world of existence is destroyed. This is the identity of wisdom and mercy. Since all sentient beings develop an infinite human history, the great mercy which develops with the infinite historical development is what is called the "infinite duration of life (amitayus)."

There is a very famous parable of the lotus in the mud, told in the Saddharma Pundarika and many other Sutras; it emphasizes the point that the merciful Mahayana Bodhisattvas who are born in the world of sentient beings are free from the defilement of the world of sentient beings because of their wisdom, just as the lotus flower is untouched by the mud and water in which it blooms.

It is also on the basis of this recognition of the inseparable connection of wisdom and mercy that Mahayana Buddhism developed the idea of the Threefold Body of the Buddha: *Dharmakaya, Sambhogakaya,* and *Nirmanakaya.* Dharmakaya, or the Body of the Law, is the very wisdom of the void and absolute reality; it is the formless reality beyond our words and thoughts. Sambhogakaya, or the Body of Enjoyment, means that the void and absolute reality has taken a merciful vow to live amid the empirical world, to enjoy it, and to save it by leading it into the wisdom which penetrates the void. Therefore, the Body of the Law, (*Dharmakaya*) which is the void and absolute reality, implies the significance of the Body of Enjoyment (*Sambhogakaya*), and there is no distinction between these two Bodies. In status, however, there is a difference, for the Body of Enjoyment is characterized by the vow, and this Body consists of the Original Vow and is at the same time the result of its vow.

The Body of Enjoyment is not visible to sentient beings in the empirical world for it moves in the sphere of the Pure Realm (or Pure Land). When the Buddha of the Body of Enjoyment reveals himself as a corporeal, preaching Buddha in our empirical world, he is called Nirmanakaya, or the Body of Transformations—this is, for instance, the Buddha Sakyamuni. Thus it is by Buddha Sakyamuni, or the Body of Transformations, that the merciful vow of the Body of Enjoyment to lead the empirical world into the wisdom which penetrates the void is accomplished. If Sakyamuni had not appeared at Gaya and preached the Law, the merciful vow of the Body of Enjoyment would never have reached the empirical world of human beings so that they might be favored with the Buddha's mercy. Therefore, Buddha Sakyamuni is the realized aspect of the Body of Transformations, Sambhogakaya, and accordingly of the Body of the Law, Dharmakaya, also. It is the fundamental creed of the Mahayana Buddhists that the Body of the Law, which is the void and absolute reality, revealed itself as the Body of the Enjoyment and also as the Body of Transformations, or Buddha Sakyamuni.

ESOTERIC BUDDHISM

In the eighth century and afterward, Buddhism in India displayed a pronounced tendency to realize the ultimate truth of the void and absolute reality by means of esoteric practices and mantras. As the unique way of the Prajnaparamita, the wisdom which penetrates the void, was difficult for people in general to comprehend, the popular means of elevating one's spirit to the ultimate reality by means of esoteric practices and mantras may have been welcome to them. This form of Buddhism is generally known as tantric Buddhism.

The method of realizing the ultimate reality by means of esoteric practices and mantras is not peculiar to Buddhism, for Tantrism is a religious method which has been current in India since ancient times and was adopted by Buddhists who were influenced by Hindu Tantrists. In the tenth century, Tantrism prevailed throughout Buddhism and a great number of tantric works were written, such as the Mahavairocana Sutra, the Guhyasamaja, and the Sarvatathagatatattvasamgraha, among others. By adopting Tantrism, later Buddhism created an atmosphere considerably different from the Buddhism of the earlier days.

A dogmatic characteristic that distinguishes tantric Buddhism from earlier Mahayana Buddhism is that the new form of Buddhism comprehends the voidness through the notion of *Vajrasattva*. *Vajra* means diamond, characterized as solidity and brilliance; *sattva* is a Hindu term for one of the three subtle elements that make up primal matter and means purity, illumination, and wisdom. From the standpoint of tantric Buddhism, the voidness which is the ultimate reality is not a negative fact but has a positive significance of solid and substantial existence.

In other Mahayana Sutras the Tathagata's Body of the Law (Dharmakaya) was called *Vajrakaya*, and tantric Buddhism is given the name of *Vajrayana*. The basic characteristic of Vajrayana is the description of the void as a positive, substantial existence. This point of view was explicitly expressed in the Mahavairocana Sutra: "The truth is identical with the actualities and the way is inseparable from the aspects." In other words, from the viewpoint of tantric Buddhism, the aspects of actual phenomena are described as they really are through the realistic and positive term *vajrasattva*—diamond wisdom—rather than through the negative term *sunyata*—voidness.

It was the ultimate objective of tantric Buddhism to realize personally the vajrasattva, which may be translated "the identity of actualities and truth." This realization comes when we are free from the discrimination of subject and object and attain the absolutely free and pure consciousness. That realization is also called *bodhicitta*, the Buddha-mind or Buddhanature. The esoteric practices and mantras resorted to by the followers of esoteric Buddhism were supposed to be the means for realizing the Buddha-mind, which is the absolutely positive state.

These esoteric practices include various kinds of special gestures of the hands and special postures (called *mudras*), the offering of flowers, water, and incense, and the playing of musical instruments. The esoteric practices also include the use of sounds (called *dharanis* and *bija-mantras*) which have the power to bring about changes in the empirical world and to aid the realization of the ultimate existence. A dharani is often claimed to be the quintessence of a Sutra—for instance, the prajnaparamita dharani is the quintessence of the Prajnaparamita Sutras, and its repetition refers to the entire contents of those Sutras. Bija-mantras are simple syllables—like *ya, a* or *ba* —which represent the immeasurable virtues. *Ya* stands for Akshobhya (the Buddha of the East), *a* for Vairocana (the Great Bodhisattva of Light), and *ba* for Amitabha (the Buddha of the West). Thus, bija-mantras are shorter forms of dharanis which are summaries of Sutras. By reciting these dharanis and bija-mantras or using the various recommended specific gestures (mudras), the followers of esoteric Buddhism aim at elevating themselves to the world of inspiration where they can realize the reality of the identity of actualities and truth, which is the ultimate and real existence.

Esoteric Buddhists also make use of mandalas. Mandalas are systematically arranged configurations of pictures of Buddhas and Bodhisattvas which represent a meritorious deed which has been accomplished. Mandalas are used as the object of meditation to elevate the follower to the realization of ultimate existence.

While the methods adopted by Mahayana Buddhists in earlier ages were intellectual, those chosen by tantric Buddhists were sensual. It is probably for this reason that esoteric Buddhism speaks of the ultimate state or realization as "supreme bliss," which sounds very sensual.

Tantric Buddhism, which sought to realize the ultimate reality by means of the corporeal body and the senses, came under the influence of Sakta worship in Hinduism—the Hindu school which worshiped the female, creative, and destructive principle in nature and confused realization of ultimate reality with sensual excitement and consequently indulged in indecent practices. Nevertheless, the most important teaching of tantric Buddhism is the notion of the union of wisdom and of the way which brings about its attainment, a union which is compared to the mixture of water and milk. It goes without saying that the sensualism was not the original aspect of tantric Buddhism. In tantric Buddhism, the Buddha-mind, which is identical with the realization of the identity of actualities and truth, is referred to in the sense of tranquil wisdom of the voidness by which the discrimination of subject and object is negated. At the same time, it means also the compassion (karuna) which motivates the positive way of salvation with a view to leading troubled sentient beings to the ultimate reality. The realization of the reality of the identity of actualities and truth is the state of the supreme awakening where self-interest and the interests of other people are equally realized and one does not reside in the world of rebirth because he has attained wisdom; nor does he reside in Nirvana, because he is compassionate and active. In this point, tantric Buddhism does not deviate from the fundamental idea of Mahayana Buddhism.

SCRIPTURES

The literature dealing with the fundamental thought of Mahayana Buddhism consists of Sutras and sastras. Sutras are the principal scriptures, accepted and handed down among the Mahayana followers, in which the essence of the Buddha's Enlightenment is described. Sastras, the introductions to the Sutras and the commentaries on them, have been written by great spiritual leaders who have been followers of the Buddha.

The Prajnaparamita Sutras—the Discourses on Perfect Wisdom—and the sastras written by Nagarjuna are the most important for the Madhyamika doctrines. The Samdhinirmocana Sutra is the basis for the Vijnanavada-Yogacara theories, especially as interpreted in the sastras written by Asanga through the inspiration of Maitreya Bodhisattva. Sastras written by Asanga's brother, Vasubandhu, and by Dinnaga, are also important for an understanding of Vijnanavada doctrines.

Other Sutras which have been influential in Mahayana Buddhism are Srimaladevisimhanada Sutra, Lankavatara Sutra, Avatamsaka Sutra, Sukhavativyuha Sutra, and Saddharma Pundarika Sutra, the Lotus of the Wonderful Law.

BODHISATTVAS

In Mahayana Buddhism a Bodhisattva is a person who regards being free from attachment to all things and being free from resistance to all things as the aim on which his mind is fixed. Now, one who is free from attachment and resistance in every way must be one who leads all other sentient beings to the same state of mind.

In this sense, a Bodhisattva means "a truly religious-minded person" in Mahayana Buddhism. Mahayana followers believe that there are many Bodhisattvas engaging in the practice of the way of freedom from attachment and from resistance in this dharma world where the Buddhist truth should be revealed. However, the personality, character, and task of these Bodhisattvas are not the same, for there are innumerable sentient beings of many different types, all of whom need to be guided by different Bodhisattvas. This is why so many Bodhisattvas are mentioned in Mahayana literature. The presence of these innumerable Bodhisattvas signifies that the message of the Buddha is being revealed to the whole world. Mahayana Buddhism claims that the Buddha's message should be revealed in different ways without limit.

The following Bodhisattvas are among those who represent the fundamental teachings of Mahayana which have been explained in this chapter:

Manjusri Bodhisattva is the Bodhisattva of Wisdom, the prajna of the Madhyamika theory which was set forth in history by Nagarjuna. Manjusri is said to represent the wisdom of the Buddha. The sharp sword which he holds in his hand symbolizes wisdom which cuts through the cloud of ignorance, which cuts away human attachment to the illusion of subject and object.

Samantabhadra Bodhisattva stands for the mercy (*karuna*) of the Buddha. He has vowed to serve all sentient beings by guiding them to a happy life which is attained by the profound intention to be free from all attachment and resistance to things. In him, action is identical with his vow.

Mahasthama-Prapta represents the wisdom and mercy of the Buddha. *Maha* means great, *sthama* means power, and *prapta* means to reach. The power of wisdom is supposed to run through the dharma world in ten directions and to cut off the attachment of the ignorant. He especially represents the wisdom of Amida Buddha.

Avalokitesvara is one who observes (*avalokita*) the world and saves all sufferers freely (*isvara*). Avalokitesvara represents the mercy, the compassion, of Amida Buddha.

Maitreya Bodhisattva has not yet arrived at this earth. His abode is in the Tushita heaven. He is supposed to be a future Buddha who is to come to this world to preach the dharma when the teaching delivered by Sakyamuni Buddha decays. *Maitreya* literally means benevolent, and he will come to the world as an incarnation of great benevolence, just as Sakyamuni Buddha did.

CHAPTER FIVE

Buddhism in China and Korea

Zenryu Tsukamoto

Translated by Leon Hurvitz

The doctrine of the Indian teacher Sakyamuni is now followed in three religious systems—based on versions of the scriptures in Pali, Tibetan, and Chinese—which developed and still maintain themselves outside India. The story of the progress of Theravada or Pali Buddhism has been told in the earlier chapters. The teachings based on the Tibetan Tripitaka spread from Tibet through Central Asia and, after the conquest of China by the Mongols in the latter half of the thirteenth century, came to China as the faith of the Mongol conquerors and later of the Manchus. It was then, and remains to this day, an important religion in China's northwestern areas.

The third system, based on the scriptures in Chinese translation, became the religion of the Chinese nation, converted the people of such non-Chinese nations as the Khitans and Juchens from southern Manchuria, and spread to Korea and Japan where it is one of the most important of the existing religions.

Although these three systems are now virtually three separate religions, different both in form and content, it is still true that they trace their origin back to the same Founder and have a great deal in common in the area of scriptural literature and doctrine. This consciousness of fellowship in a common religion has given the Asian people from India eastward a reciprocal feeling of intimacy which has been an important tie binding together the hearts of the people of these various countries.

The diffusion of the Pali and Tibetan Tripitakas are examples of the spread of a so-called higher civilization into areas of so-called lower civilization. The importation of Buddhism into China and its development there, on the other hand, took place under manifestly different circumstances. In China, long before the coming of Buddhism, there had existed the old, highly developed, and unique civilization of the Chinese people, with its own revered saints and sages and its own canonized classics. The classics had already become the basis for the organization of society and the maintenance of order, serving as guides in politics and ethics.

In India, separated from China by the vast Central Asian deserts, almost impassable mountain ranges, and an apparently boundless ocean, there was also a very old and advanced civilization. Confucianism, based on canonical works ascribed to ancient sages, symbolized the civilization of China; Brahmanism, based on the Vedas which were similarly ascribed to the seers of former times, represented the cultural heritage of India. China and India were alike in their contempt for other peoples and cultures; both were self-centered and exclusive, with a strong feeling of superiority, and both lacked any inclination to appropriate the doctrines of any distant country or people.

However, Buddhism, the Path to the status of the Enlightened Being—denying the authority of traditional Brahmanism, challenging the scriptural position of the Vedas and Upanishads, and founded by the non-Brahman Sakyamuni—was not so much the heir as the stepchild of Indian thought, and a rebellious stepchild at that. This Buddhism, in particular the more highly developed Mahayana Buddhism, mediated between India and China, these two countries which in spite of their nearness had for centuries turned their backs toward each other and lived in proud cultural isolation. It mediated between them and made them friends in the spirit. But it was more than a mediator, for it expedited the transmission into the Chinese cultural sphere of ideas and objects of art from India and areas even further west and brought about a great change in the religion, philosophy, art, literature, and even the habits of the Chinese people.

BUDDHISM COMES TO CHINA

There is a tradition concerning the introduction of Buddhism to China which until recently was believed by both the faithful of China and the scholarly world in general. Emperor Ming of the Latter Han Dynasty (A.D. 58–75), so we are told, saw in a dream a golden man with sunlight issuing from the back of his neck who flew about in space and came to earth. Upon being advised by a court scholar that the man in the vision was probably the Indian Buddha, he dispatched an envoy to India to bring the Buddhist religion back to China. The envoy returned to the court at Lo-yang accompanied by two Indian monks who brought with them images of the Buddha and religious scriptures. They were favorably received by the Emperor and housed in the White Horse Temple, supposedly in A.D. 67, and there they translated into Chinese the Sutra in Forty-two Articles—a Sutra made up of selections from several sources. So much for the story.

This tale of the Emperor's dream appears to have originated about A.D. 200. It was invented and propagated by Buddhists for the purpose of spreading their religion in a cultural atmosphere in which the strength of traditional ideas was very great. By pretending that Buddhism was received at the center of government by command of the Emperor, they sought to invest their religion with an authority that the people of China could not easily deny. It is difficult to ascribe to it any value as historical fact.

On the other hand, we are told in explicit terms, not by Buddhist documents but by an official Chinese history written by scholar officials, that in the neighborhood of Lo-yang the family of the half-brother of this very Emperor Ming, at a time prior to the reputed visit of the envoy and the two Indian monks, were believers in Buddhism, worshiped Buddhist images, and honored foreign monks and novices—and that the Emperor gave his approval to these practices. Another old historical document tells us that in A.D. 2 an envoy of the King of Bactria preached the doctrine of Buddha at the Chinese court. Quite apart from this evidence, it is reasonable to assume that the introduction of a religion such as Buddhism to a foreign land would be achieved through the conversion of a part of the populace before it would ever be introduced to the imperial court.

It is no longer possible to determine with precision the time of the introduction of Buddhism into China, but one may be reasonably certain, in view of the political situation which existed in China and the circumstances of the Buddhist community in India, that the event took place at a time at least not much this or that side of the beginning of the first century A.D.

To begin with the Chinese situation, in the latter half of the second century B.C. the Chinese empire adopted an aggressive political and commercial policy toward its Western neighbors. As this new policy was carried out, it opened up traffic routes over the Sinkiang desert, north of Tibet. These "silk routes," so beloved of the Western merchants, became at the same time the routes over which India was introduced to China. It was along these routes that the evangelists of Indian Buddhism spread their teachings all over Central Asia.

The Indian Buddhist community, on the other hand, had spread beyond the borders of India to the areas of her northwesterly neighbors at the time of Asoka in the third century B.C. About 100 B.C. there came the noteworthy new movement, the so-called Mahayana, which began to circulate a new evangelistic literature of its own. This movement was initiated by a new breed of men within the Buddhist community, men who were given pause by the sectarian splintering of Buddhism, by the atmosphere of pedantry and hair-splitting sophistry in which the faith was monopolized by monks who had no concern for the mission of saving mankind or even for those religious practices necessary to the attainment of Enlightenment. These reformers, reminding themselves of the original mission of a Buddhist, and reverting to the basic principles of the Path to Buddhahood that Sakyamuni himself had trodden, sought to apply the old spirit to contemporary society. Out of a feeling of profound compassion for the entire human race, they sought to save numberless beings and to purify society. For this purpose they vowed to endure any and all hardships, sacrificing themselves in tireless exertion.

These were the men whose ideal was Bodhisattvahood. They believed that it was only those who followed the Bodhisattva ideal who trod the Path of the Founder, Sakyamuni, and that this way was open to monk and layman alike. They called the contemporary sectarian Buddhism the defective way or vehicle, Hinayana, charging that it twisted the Buddha's teachings in a mean and petty way, and called themselves the followers of the great way or vehicle, Mahayana. With enthusiastic conviction, they threw themselves into a strenuous campaign of proselytization. In order to give a profound philosophic basis to their exposition of the Buddha's doctrine and religious practices, and in order to attract persons of all social stations to their variety of Buddhism, the Mahayanists proceeded boldly to create in the Buddha's name a completely new Canon, rich in the variety of its literary forms, and to spread it far and wide.

The new rivalry between Mahayana and Hinayana enhanced in both parties a spirit of opposition and competition which caused them to vie with each other in their efforts to make new converts. In northwest India and the neighboring countries beyond the border, Mahayana grew in an environment which was predominantly Hinayana. It was in this area that the chief Mahayana scriptures made their appearance about the first century B.C.

It was inevitable that the missionaries of both the Mahayana and the Hinayana persuasions, engaged in a contest in a place so near to the newly opened silk routes, should strike out along these routes to the Central Asian oases and beyond them to China. This was especially true for the adherents of the young Mahayana movement who had taken the Bodhisattva vow to sacrifice themselves in the face of any hardships for the salvation of all mankind. It was only natural that they should set out along the trade routes to assert the universality of Buddhism. China experienced the introduction of both

Mahayana and Hinayana, to be sure, but the preponderant influence of Mahayana and the continued introduction of its ideas as they unfolded laid the foundation and conditioned the development of Chinese Buddhism.

Another important aspect of the Mahayana Buddhism which began to come to China in the first century was the art which came with it. By the latter part of the first century, it had become a common practice in northwest India, where Greek influence had been strong for some time, to make images of the Buddha—a new development, for Buddhists had never before represented the Buddha in human form. The creation of images as objects of worship contributed to the development of temples for the religious ceremonies built around them and, at the same time, furthered the development of painting, sculpture, music, and crafts. The missionary possibilities of a Buddhism complete with its own religious ceremonies and its own art and architecture were much greater since these trappings facilitated the conversion to Buddhism through ritual rather than doctrine. The fact that the Buddhism first introduced into China was a Buddhism equipped with an iconographic art not only aided the cause of proselytization immeasurably, but also determined the direction of Chinese Buddhism from that time onward.

In the second and third centuries the kingdom of Gandhara on the northwestern frontier of India prospered and furthered the cause of Buddhism, both Hinayana and Mahayana, especially during the reigns of King Kaniska and his immediate successors. In 299 a good will mission from King Vasudeva of Gandhara visited the Chinese court at Lo-yang. By that time Nagarjuna had completed his system of Mahayana Buddhist philosophy, and his enthusiastic followers were actively propagandizing his teachings.

Thus it is evident that the many missionaries who came to China were driven by a reforming zeal and were aided in their efforts by a great enthusiasm for their new art and new philosophy. The steady translation of the Buddhist scriptures into Chinese begins in the middle of the second century A.D. with the arrival in Lo-yang of the Parthian missionary Arsaces and the Bactrian missionary Lokaraksha. For the next hundred years we have the names of more than thirty translators and a total of more than four hundred scriptural works which they are supposed to have translated.

Four of these scriptures of Mahayana Buddhism were influential in the rise of Mahayana in India and its spread throughout Asia:

1. The Prajnaparamita Sutras, which deny the substantial reality of all things and attempt to explain the nature of the interdependent existence, which is subject to change and flux; it is an explanation given by means of the theory of dependent causation which is reached by a dialectical method of negation and epitomized in the word sunyata (emptiness, voidness).

2. The Vimalakirtinirdesa Sutra, which sets forth the same doctrine in a literary work centering around the lay devotee Vimalakirti.

3. The Saddharma Pundarika Sutra which, by resort to some very clever parables, asserts that the Mahayana is adaptable to persons of all schools of thought, and which in particular appears to be aiming at the conversion of persons engaged in the then very dangerous business of international trade.

4. The Sukhavati Sutra, which tells of the Buddha-land open to believers of every class.

What then was the situation in China in those three centuries as the missionaries were coming with their new doctrines, their images, rituals, and newly translated scriptures? The Latter Han Dynasty was declining. Its hold over the Western regions had been lost, and it had fallen prey to civil war which culminated in its collapse in A.D. 220. China was then divided into three kingdoms until it was reunited by the Western Tsin Dynasty in A.D. 281. This dynasty also fell prey to civil war, the two capitals of Lo-yang and Ch'ang-an were sacked, and it collapsed in A.D. 316. This was an age characterized by great social unrest in which many lives were lost through slaughter and famine, and the uncertainties of life reached a peak. It was also an age in which great changes were wrought in the worlds of learning and thought.

The Han Dynasty, which reigned from the second century B.C. to the beginning of the third century A.D., had established a culture based on the canonical writings of the ancient sages as arranged by Confucius. Official positions were conferred upon persons who had studied the Confucian classics. The basis for the evaluation of good and evil in politics and ethics was sought in these classics and on them was constructed an absolute system of relationships between lord and subject, father and son, and senior and junior officials. Society was constructed and stabilized around the family system.

The policy of the Han Dynasty established the sainted position of the mythical emperors Yao and Shun and the mythical kings Wen and Wu, as well as of administrators such as the Duke of Chou and Confucius himself, and the authority of the classics ascribed to them was widely accepted. The ruling class, that is, the class which was at once the intelligentsia and the bureaucracy, was dominated in thought and controlled in all its activities by the heavy restraint of the classics. The classics reinforced in them a stubborn respect for antiquity and a feeling of superiority toward other nations. It was no easy matter for Buddhism, a religion originating with a people regarded by such a society as barbarian, to be introduced into the China of that time.

Since the authority of the Confucian classics persisted in China until the recent ideological revolution ushered in by the Republic in the twentieth century, Chinese Buddhism throughout its history was subject to the pressures of Confucian ideology and Confucian politics. It gained in strength when Confucianism weakened or receded—for Confucianism in China never utterly perished—and, by altering Indian Buddhism in such a way as to conform to Chinese thought and life, assured itself a continued existence as a distinctively Chinese Buddhism. The latter half of the second century A.D., the period in which Buddhism in Chinese translation had its start, was a time in which the authority of Confucianism was in decline and new modes of thought could gain acceptance.

At that time the study of Confucian classics had become highly formalized and had degenerated into a specialized art of exegesis in which "a text of five characters required a commentary of twenty or thirty thousand words." Furthermore, the Confucian scholars, who were supposed to be rationalists, had grafted onto their interpretations of the classics such things as Yin and Yang, the five elements, prophetic writings, and omens. It was fashionable to explain matters of state and human phenomena by relating them to the phenomena of nature. In addition, the society of that time accepted superstitious belief in spirits, demons, soothsayers, tabus, and the like.

In this period the great families with inherited wealth annexed to their own estates the small holdings of the poor peasantry, reducing the common people to slavery and serfdom and maintaining their authority by the high official positions which they held. The mass of the peasantry, left to wallow in ignorance and extreme poverty, was faced with mounting anxiety and discontent and turned to superstition, magical arts, and soothsayers for refuge.

In such a society, the mythical Yellow Emperor and Lao-tzu became the central figures in the cult of the never-dying, never-aging guardian spirits. The school of Lao-tzu, Taoism, which had once held its own with Confucianism, had declined, after Confucianism became the official doctrine of the state, to the level of popular beliefs and popular superstition. The Yellow Emperor and Lao-tzu had become in the popular mind immortal spirits dwelling in heaven and conferring upon their believers longevity and escape from calamities. This cult, claiming the art of healing, acquired in the space of little more than ten years several hundreds of thousands of followers and attempted a rebellion in A.D. 184 which hastened the fall of the Latter Han Dynasty.

Into the society of the Latter Han Dynasty came Buddhism with its golden images and its ascetic monks and lay devotees who burned incense and chanted Sutras before those images. In the latter part of the first century A.D. the younger brother of Emperor Ming worshiped Buddha images alongside the images of the Yellow Emperor and Lao-tzu. Emperor Huan (147–167) erected in the palace at Lo-yang a magnificent altar for the worship of the Yellow Emperor, Lao-tzu, and Buddha. Apparently the Buddhism which was received into the China of the Latter Han Dynasty was received by all classes, high and low, as a sort of religion of charms and incantations, seeking longevity, relief from misfortune, and good luck from the Buddha who had attained the status of a Guardian Spirit in India—in the sense in which the believers in the Yellow Emperor and Lao-tzu understood the nature of guardian spirits.

In Chinese society until very recent times a huge illiterate population was ruled by a small bureaucracy with a high degree of classical education. Among these illiterate masses there was current an ineradicable belief in spirits, popular gods, and magical charms. Buddhism, making its compromise with this Taoistic, polytheistic, magic-ridden religion of the Chinese masses, spread throughout China and maintained itself until recent times.

On the other hand, the Buddhist scriptures in Chinese translation, containing the philosophical doctrines of Indian Buddhism, became accepted in the course of time by China's educated classes and came to be studied in the light of the classics attributed to China's own saints and sages. In particular, there emerged from the midst of the Chinese nation influential monks and nuns who, seeking release through Buddhism and aiming to purify society and save mankind, were devoting themselves wholeheartedly to the study and practice of their religion. From the standpoint of both doctrine and works they were providing the educated classes with new leadership. This is what produced the so-called Northern Buddhism which eventually achieved a dominant role in the philosophy and religion, arts, and sciences of China's cultural vassals, Korea and Japan.

It must be borne in mind that the period following the collapse of the Latter Han Dynasty in A.D. 220 provided a set of circumstances favorable to the growth of Buddhist faith and doctrine.

First of all, the change in the habits of thought and learning favored the growth of Buddhism. A new age was dawning in which there was a recession in the authority of Confucianism and the intelligentsia were turning to a study of Lao-tzu and his disciple Chuang-tzu. New schools of thought, led by young scholars, were beginning to carry the learned world with them. These young scholars were rebelling against the hair-splitting and formalized interpretations of Confucianism and were demanding liberation from their bonds. Typical of the young scholars of the time is Ts'an Hsun, who, raised in a Confucian home, said to his father and elder brother in A.D. 230, "The six Confucian classics, which say nothing of the origin of change in all things and of the basis of human life, are but the chaff of the Sages!"

It was at about that time that Yen Ho and Wang Pi studied Lao-tzu and developed a theory describing his "nothingness" (*wu* in Chinese) as the basis of all existence. Their metaphysical system made them in one leap the darlings of the learned world of their time. This system made Confucius a sage superior to Lao-tzu, but only because he had completely mastered the meaning of Lao-tzu's nothingness. Wang Pi said, "Although Heaven and Earth are broad, nothingness is their heart. Although the Sage-King is great, emptiness is his chief." Such ideas as these had a tendency similar to that of the Buddhist scriptures in Chinese translation which were being presented to the Chinese public at this time. This tendency is seen specifically in the Prajnaparamita and the Vimalakirtinirdesa Sutras which stressed emptiness (sunyata) and taught that only one who has mastered this emptiness can become a true Buddha.

Those learned persons who were fond of Lao-tzu naturally went on to study Chuang-tzu, who develops the ideas of Lao-tzu. About A.D. 300, studies of Lao-tzu, Chuang-tzu, and the classical *Book of Changes* came to dominate the thinking of the intelligentsia, creating a system of metaphysics known as "dark learning" in China. Upper-class society became full of sophisticated discussion groups devoted to "pure talk"—that is, talk of a nonpolitical nature, but at the same time just pure talk—whose members were experts in dark learning. Such discussions welcomed the philosophical doctrines and rich literary and mystical wisdom of the Prajnaparamita and other Buddhist Sutras as absolutely necessary to their thought.

A second factor facilitating the spread of Buddhism was the emergence of a new mood which, in conjunction with the growing fashion of Taoist studies, opposed the fetters of Confucian propriety. It was a mood which sought man's liberation into a life beyond the sphere of all restraints, a life in which a man might act, think, and speak freely according to the dictates of unfettered human emotion. Typical of this mood were the famous Seven Sages of the Bamboo Grove. Society came to admire as "gentlemen beyond the limits," or "gentlemen in retirement," the men who took no political office, who divorced themselves from the cares of lay life and immersed themselves in study, thought, and contemplation in the placid surroundings of mountains and forests. Such a mood could easily be transformed into admiration for the followers of Buddhism who left the household life in quest of the true Path. The learned and virtuous men of the monastic world were in fact likened to the Seven Sages of the Bamboo Grove and honored in the same way.

A third factor to be remembered in explaining the spread of Buddhism in China is that, as we have mentioned, the end of the Latter Han and the following period was a time of political cataclysms and wars in which life and property were constantly exposed to the great dangers of famine, pillage, and massacre. It was an age in which religious salvation was keenly desired. Hsi K'ang, for instance, who lived from A.D. 221 to 262 and was the leader of the Seven Sages of the Bamboo Grove, gave strong evidence of a profound insight into the impermanence of all things and of a religious seeking, through disciplines, for the state of the never-aging Spirit. A social situation existed in which the interest of the thoughtful could easily turn toward Buddhism and could readily accept a doctrine which preached the painfulness and impermanence of human life.

At the same time, in addition to the missionaries from India, there were Central Asians of Chinese birth who came to China to proselytize effectively by preaching and translating the scriptures. Their knowledge of Chinese and Western languages stood them in good stead. Dharmaraksha (Fa-hu Chu), who was from Bactria, spent forty years in China and by the time of his death in A.D. 314 had translated over fifty Buddhist scriptures.

By the fourth century there were already some outstanding native Chinese monks with many followers. Typical of such leaders were Tao-an (312–385) and his disciple Hui-yuan (344–417). Up to the time of Tao-an, Chinese Buddhist monks had used surnames indicating their masters' nationalities—for instance, Chih for a Bactrian master, Po for a Kuchan, Yu for a Khotanese, and Chu for an Indian. Tao-an suggested that all should take the surname of Shih, since all were disciples of Sakya. (*Shih* is the first syllable of Shih-chia, the Chinese transcription of *Sakya*, which at that time was pronounced in a fair approximation of Sakya.) His suggestion has been the practice among Chinese Buddhist monks ever since.

Tao-an also worked out the rules of religious life which have been followed in all Chinese temples since his time. The Chinese Buddhists who had been under the guidance of monks from Western countries came to regard themselves as belonging to the same order as their teachers and as serving the same Buddha, and thus they began to lead their own religious life independently. The Chinese religious body grew away, one might say, from its non-Chinese parent. Tao-an also built up a large monastery which was described by a Confucian scholar in a letter to the prime minister of the Western Tsin Dynasty:

Teachers and disciples total several hundred, and of fasting and study there is no wearying. There is no dazzling of the eyes and ears of common men by resort to magical tricks, nor is there any trampling on the differences among the lesser monks by resort to threats or authority. Furthermore, teachers and pupils courteously respect one another. It is a magnificent sight, and one such as I have never seen before.

Tao-an's disciple Hui-yuan spent the last thirty years of his life on Mount Lu, south of the Yangtze in what is now Kiangsi Province, in the monastery of the Eastern Grove as the head of a group of earnest monks and laymen. There they formed the White Lotus Society, a religious group of 123 monks and laymen who united in a vow to be reborn in the western paradise of the Buddha Amitabha. That organization left its indelible mark on the future course of Chinese Buddhism for it was the origin of the Pure Realm (Ching-t'u) movement in China.

In the third century A.D. the Prajnaparamita was the scriptural text most in vogue among the Chinese intellectuals who had been discussing the ideas of Lao-tzu and Chuang-tzu. The quest for the real meaning of the Prajnaparamita's concept of sunyata—commonly called prajna study—was pursued with the greatest vigor. The Chinese intellectuals had at their disposal several translations made in the preceding century, rendering the Buddhist scriptures into a language and script fundamentally different from the Indian originals. They sought to understand the Buddhist scriptures by comparing the translations and by interpreting them in the light of their dark learning and pure-talk methods. In this way it was very easy to depart from the original meaning and it was inevitable that key passages would be subject to a variety of interpretations, just as was the case with the Chinese classics.

Tao-an found himself in the midst of this type of prajna study and became aware of the incorrectness of interpreting the Buddhist scriptures in the light of the Chinese classics. He became convinced that it would be possible to understand the true meaning of Buddhism and to tread the true Path of the Buddha only if they could clarify the meaning of the original words. While aware of the difficulties involved, he devoted his whole life to the careful study of the Prajnaparamita Sutras. He collected as many as possible of the Chinese translations of the Buddhist scriptures and did his best to compare the various translations with one another. Tao-an's prajna study is credited with having come rather close to an understanding of the meaning of the original, but even so the research of the Chinese Buddhists, who lacked the necessary knowledge of the Indian originals, had serious limitations.

For a solution to the misunderstandings created by their faulty methods of study, the Chinese Buddhist world had to await the help of a foreign monk trained in prajna doctrine and thoroughly conversant with the original languages. This role was filled by Kumarajiva, who was welcomed to the capital at Ch'ang-an, in 401, sixteen years after the death of Tao-an.

Kumarajiva was born in Kucha of an Indian father and a mother who was a royal princess. Kucha at that time was completely dominated by Hinayana Buddhism, and Kumarajiva as a child accompanied his mother to Kashmir where he studied Hinayana. Later, however, upon becoming acquainted with the Mahayana Buddhism of the school of Nagarjuna, he came to the conclusion that this school alone represented the true doctrine of the Buddha, a doctrine distorted by Hinayana. Thereafter he devoted himself exclusively to the study and propagation of Mahayana, becoming widely famous as a Kuchan Mahayanist.

At this time an invading army from China defeated Kucha and took Kumarajiva off as a captive of war, holding him against his will for eighteen years in what is now Kansu Province. It was fortunate both for him and for the development of Chinese Buddhism that during this period he had with him gifted scholars who were masters of the Chinese language and who remained by the master's side throughout his life and assisted him in his translations. They received directly from the master Nagarjuna's doctrine of sunyata which Kumarajiva was propagating and were able to overthrow the generally accepted method of understanding Buddhism in the light of Lao-tzu and Chuang-tzu.

In 401, Kumarajiva was welcomed as a national preceptor at the capital at Ch'ang-an. The king assembled for him all the Buddhist scholars of his kingdom and instituted with their cooperation a great translation project at government expense. The quantity of material translated by this epoch-making project is listed by an eighth century catalogue as seventy-four items, totalling 384 rolls. This group of scholars retranslated in a joint project those scriptures which had always been the most beloved and studied by Chinese Buddhists, the Prajnaparamita, the Vimalakirtinirdesa, and the Saddharma Pundarika Sutras. It also translated the works and biographies of the first and greatest organizer of Mahayana doctrine, Nagarjuna, and of his pupil Aryadeva. It acquainted China with their vigorous religious activities and announced far and wide that this and only this was the essence of Buddhism.

Thanks to the cooperative nature of the project, first-rate scholars who had gathered from over the country were able to go home as authorities equipped with the best translations and the most authoritative interpretations of the Buddhist scriptures. Their ability to propagate the teachings of Nagarjuna fulfilled what Kumarajiva regarded as his mission in life. Most of his pupils eventually understood that Buddhist sunyata is neither Lao-tzu's universal elemental substance nor absolute vacuity, but rather that sunyata refers to the relativity of all forms of existence, that is, to dependent causation; consequently, sunyata signifies a religious consciousness that makes clear the denial of the independent substantiality of things. Thus was pointed out the approach to the understanding of fundamental Buddhist ideas without benefit of comparison with Lao-tzu and Chuang-tzu.

Another point to note is that Kumarajiva, who was honored by China's Buddhists as the most trustworthy authority on Buddhist doctrine, was a former Hinayanist who had rejected Hinayana in favor of Mahayana and who had gone so far as to say that the Hinayanists misunderstood Buddhism while Mahayana alone was the true doctrine of the Buddha. As a result of this, China's Buddhists became believers in Mahayana and developed their own doctrines on a Mahayana base, and thus the Buddhists of Korea and Japan also became exponents of Mahayana. Kumarajiva, therefore, laid the foundation for the conversion of eastern Asia into a Mahayana land.

Mahayana Buddhism was not introduced into China by Kumarajiva alone, to be sure. Kumarajiva's arrival was followed by the translation of such important scriptures as the Avatamsaka, the Mahaparinirvana, and the Lankavatara Sutras, both by Chinese monks who had studied in India and Central Asia and by foreign monks as well. In addition, the writings of Asanga and Vasubandhu, who had organized and propagated the new Mahayana doctrine of Vijnanavada-Yogacara after Nagarjuna's time, were also translated and widely circulated in China.

BUDDHIST SECTS IN CHINA

Although many of these Mahayana scriptures had taken a long time to develop in India and were the products of differing sets of circumstances, the Chinese, with their deeply ingrained confidence in the written word, accepted the Buddhist scriptures in Chinese translation as the literal word of the Buddha. They treated all the Buddhist scriptures, including the Hinayana Canon, as the record of the forty-odd years of Sakyamuni's preaching career. In what order, then, did Sakyamuni preach these sermons? What is their relation to one another? Which sermon was the apex of Sakyamuni's doctrine? These and other questions, peculiar to Chinese Buddhism, were now raised, and the Chinese Buddhists were at pains to arrange the numerous scriptures of the Mahayana and Hinayana Canons so as to fit them into the one lifetime of the Buddha.

Each person who sought to arrange the Buddhist Canon would single out the one scripture which in his opinion was the apex of the Buddha's doctrine, place upon it the highest value in Buddhism, arrange the whole Canon in such a way as to lead logically to this one work, and declare the rest of the Canon in its entirety to be no more than an introduction, a religious educational approach, to the scripture chosen. The result of this classification was the beginning of the Chinese Buddhist sects. At this point we see the birth of a new Buddhism, different from the Indian parent. Most of the Chinese Buddhist sects were founded during the period of unity under the Sui and T'ang dynasties from the end of the sixth century through the eighth.

THE T'IEN-T'AI SECT

This sect was founded by Chih-i who lived from 538 to 597. His father had what appeared to be a promising career as an official under Emperor Yuan of the Liang Dynasty at the capital at Chiang-ling. But in 554 a northern army came south and captured Chiang-ling, killed the emperor, carted off several tens of thousands of nobles, officials, and common folk as slaves, and conducted a large-scale slaughter from which only some three hundred families managed to escape. Having lost both his father and mother in this famous massacre, Chih-i found himself a war orphan at the age of seventeen and turned aside from a life of bureaucratic honors to a career of Buddhist religious practice.

He had his eyes opened to the faith by Hui-ssu, who had been rebuffed for trying to tell the scriptural scholars of North China that contemplation and practice are the most important things in Buddhism, and had come south to avoid persecution for his views. Eventually Chih-i parted with his master and entered the capital of the Ch'en Dynasty—the present Nanking —where he attacked the Buddhist community for the way in which its members vied with one another in subtlety, asserting that first of all one must have a religious experience through the practice of contemplation. He gradually gained followers, but he found after some years that although his disciples increased in numbers, those who had true religious experience did not. In spite of the fact that he had won the support and faith of the ruling house and many of the aristocracy, he resolved to give up his temple and retired to Mount T'ien-t'ai to live an austere religious life.

His religious experience, deepened by contemplative practices which were characterized by a denial of reality, self-criticism, and penance, led him beyond the absolute denial of relative reality to a state of mind of absolute affirmation. In the light of this religious experience he read the Saddharma Pundarika very carefully and arrived at the firm conviction that in this Sutra lay the final goal at which the entire preaching career of Sakyamuni Buddha had been aimed. Accordingly, he took over with modifications the various studies of this Sutra which had been done by other Chinese scholars, as well as various theories for the arrangement of the entire Chinese Buddhist Canon, and set forth a new Buddhist system with the Saddharma Pundarika at its center. His central teaching was called *The Recondite Doctrine of the Saddharma Pundarika*. He also wrote *The Great Quiescence and Perception* in which he explains the practices by which one may attain to the state of mind which he was constantly striving to perfect. These two works are studied to this day as basic texts by his successors—called T'ien-t'ai in China and the Tendai Sect in Japan—since they are the classics that set forth the doctrines and the religious practices of this sect.

Chih-i regarded the vast Buddhist Canon as the record of the Buddha's education of all beings, the process whereby in his profound mercy he set forth his teachings. He believed that the Buddha began with the attainment of Enlightenment and proceeded from the shallow to the profound with due regard for the spiritual shortcomings of his listeners. The purpose of these teachings was to convert those who did not yet believe and to enable those already converted to attain to the state of Buddhahood.

The Buddha, as soon as he had attained Enlightenment, preached the Avatamsaka Sutra in which he set forth the content of his perception exactly as he perceived it—the so-called First Period. In the Second Period, since the state of Enlightened One could not be understood by persons whose Buddhist training was as yet only in its elementary stages, the Buddha went on to preach the Hinayana scriptures, the Tripitaka, thus enabling them to mount the first step. Next, in the Third Period, for the benefit of those persons who, having mastered Hinayana doctrine, were firmly convinced that they understood Buddhism, he preached the Vimalakirtinirdesa and other Mahayana Sutras which admonished and rebuked them, telling them that this was not the road to true Enlightenment.

In the Fourth Period the Buddha preached the Prajnaparamita Sutras, which set forth the doctrine of sunyata as an antidote to all fixed notions. Finally, in the Fifth Period, he preached the Saddharma Pundarika and the Mahaparinirvana Sutras, the ultimate doctrine, intended for those who were religiously enlightened and advanced, stating that all men, without distinction of Mahayana or Hinayana, will attain to the state of the Buddha. Chih-i held, then, that the preaching of the Saddharma Pundarika was the final goal of the Buddha's career on earth, and expounded a doctrine based primarily on that Sutra.

In spite of the assertion that the Saddharma Pundarika Sutra is the core of Chih-i's system, his doctrine is an expression of the theories of Nagarjuna as transmitted by Kumarajiva. It is, so to speak, the Chinese expression of the Buddhist theories of the Indian Nagarjuna. Chih-i's doctrines are an expression of the appropriate application of three kinds of mental activity. The first is the act of direct affirmation, called establishment or illumination. Second is the act of denying the first, called abolition or obstruction. And last is the act of embracing, then surpassing the first two, called the double illumination and double obstruction.

Chih-i believed that all things are "perfectly coalescent within the three truths" of emptiness, temporariness, and middleness. Of the things that exist, nothing exists independently and of itself; all things are mutually interdependent and interrelated. In other words, they are empty. But the concept of emptiness, which is a denial of substantial reality, is not a declaration of nonexistence. It refers to the "temporary existence" of things which exist in a state of constant, interrelated flux. Emptiness and temporariness are neither simply the one nor simply the other. They are a negation accompanied by affirmation, an affirmation accompanied by negation. That is what leads one to a perception of the truth of middleness, which contains and yet at the same time surpasses the first two truths of emptiness and temporariness.

According to Chih-i, emptiness, temporariness, and middleness are not three separate things. On the contrary, emptiness in and of itself is both temporariness and middleness; temporariness in and of itself is both middleness and emptiness; middleness in and of itself is both emptiness and temporariness. The fact that all things have an existence on both the empty and temporary levels is what is meant by middleness; it is the true nature of things. By arriving at the intuition of this "perfect coalescence within the three truths," all of the phenomenal differentiations which have been denied are now absolutely affirmed in their very phenomenal state—and consequently the daily life of the layman is the road to Buddhahood which all must tread. Thus is attained that religious state which is expressed in the words "life and death are Nirvana," or "this world is quiescent brilliance, Nirvana."

Chih-i grew up under South Chinese dynasties at a time when the Buddhism there was centered in the study and exposition of doctrine. But he, having learned that Buddhism without practice and experience is meaningless, attacked and criticized this super-intellectualized Buddhism and brought it back into the realm of practical religion. And yet he was equally severe in his strictures against that minority of Buddhists who ran only to practice and whose religion had no theoretical base. With such phrases as "the eyes of wisdom and the legs of practice" and "doctrine and contemplation both carried out," he stressed the weakness of wisdom without practice and the dangers of religious practice lacking the eye of wisdom. Chih-i held that it was only through the joint practice of study and contemplation, each acting upon the other, that one could reach the road to Buddhahood. In his own life he lived up literally to what he preached.

Chih-i understood and experienced through the earnest conduct of contemplative practices all the doctrines that he taught —the truth of emptiness, temporariness, and middleness; that everything is the product of dependent causation; that all things are interdependent and interrelated; that there is no controlling force, no "I"; that all, without distinction of religious approach, will attain Buddhahood. In the light of his religious experience, gained through earnest contemplative practice, he subjected the teachings of Nagarjuna and the Saddharma Pundarika to searching analysis and on that basis built the doctrine of the T'ien-t'ai sect.

THE THREE TREATISES (SAN-LUN) SECT

This sect was founded in South China by the monk Chi-tsang (549–623), who was a younger contemporary of the founder of the T'ien-t'ai sect. Chi-tsang was the son of a Chinese mother and a Parthian father who lived first near what is now Canton and then moved to the capital city, now known as

Nanking. At the age of seven he was placed under the tutelage of a monk at the Monastery of the Prospering Empire near his home, and there he studied the Three Treatises, that is, Nagarjuna's Madhyamika and Dvadasanikaya, and the Sataka by Aryadeva, Nagarjuna's disciple.

Some years later he fled from the disorders that attended the end of the Ch'en Dynasty and took up residence in the Monastery of Good Omen, where he worked out the doctrines of what was later to be the San-lun sect. That is why he is best known as the Great Master of the Monastery of Good Omen. At the invitation of the emperor he moved to the capital at Ch'ang-an where he was recognized by the T'ang emperors as one of the ten great monks of the city. There he occupied himself with the propagation of his doctrine until at the age of seventy-five he passed away just after completing his *Essay on Not Fearing Death*.

Chi-tsang held that the Buddhist scriptures are all like the medicine prescribed to the beings to cure them of their false views concerning the differentiation of things. He held that since the goal of each of the scriptures was to bring all beings to a right view free of attachments—that is, to the Middle Path —there was no justification for distinguishing some of the Buddha's doctrine as primitive and some as sophisticated, nor could one particular scripture be elevated above all the rest. This may be interpreted as a criticism directed at the contemporary Buddhist world in which a rivalry was growing up among the several schools, each based on one particular scriptural text.

Chi-tsang felt that the writings of Nagarjuna and his disciple Aryadeva set forth clearly the very heart of Mahayana Buddhism, that is, the method by which the Buddha sought to enable all beings to break free from differentiation and false views and to bring them into the sphere of right views and the Middle Path. Accordingly he lectured on the Three Treatises more than a hundred times, composed commentaries on each of them, and wrote *The Recondite Doctrine of the Three Treatises (San-lun hsuan-i)*, in which he set forth in a unified form the doctrine contained in all three of the works he had studied since his childhood.

Chi-tsang grouped the numberless fixed ideas to which we mortals are subject under eight headings: birth, extinction, one, different, going, coming, impermanent, and permanent. The thoroughgoing denial of these eight false views, the elimination of these persistent ideas through the assertion of eightfold negation—no birth, no extinction, et cetera—is in itself Enlightenment, that is, the perception of the Middle Path. However, if one were to think that one first eliminates false views and then attains to the truth of the Middle Path, that itself would be a false view, which in turn would have to be eliminated. There is no truth apart from the elimination of false notions; the elimination of falsehood is in and of itself the manifestation of truth. The Middle Path of eightfold negation and the identity of the elimination of falsehood with the manifestation of truth are the principal goal in the religious practices of the San-lun sect.

Chi-tsang's life was in itself a carrying out of the principles of a religion which demands constant introspection in the light of the eightfold negation, constant scrutiny of every actual moment, an endless exertion. There is no Chinese sect in modern times which embodies his teachings, but his doctrine is still studied by the followers of many sects.

THE CONSCIOUSNESS-ONLY (YUI-SHIH) SECT

About the time that Chih-i and Chi-tsang were teaching the Mahayana Buddhism of Nagarjuna in South China, the study of the newer type of Mahayana propounded by Asanga and Vasubandhu had come into vogue in North China. Hsuan-tsang (602–664), who had spent some years in study in monasteries in North China, determined to study the Yogacara (Yui-shih) philosophy of Asanga and Vasubandhu directly under the guidance of an Indian teacher. Since he could not obtain permission to make the trip, he slipped illegally through the west Chinese customs barrier and set out alone on his perilous journey to India in quest of the Dharma. This was in 629, shortly after the death of Chi-tsang.

After an extremely difficult journey, Hsuan-tsang went to the great monastery at Nalanda in India, the very fountainhead of Buddhist learning at that time, and there he studied both Mahayana and Hinayana doctrines. In particular, he acquainted himself with the conflicting views of numerous scholars on the theories of Asanga and Vasubandhu, studied the new logic, and visited the chief monasteries and pilgrimage places of India. He returned to the capital city of Ch'ang-an in 645, bringing with him many Sanskrit texts of the Buddhist scriptures.

The T'ang Dynasty at that time, under the able leadership of the enlightened Emperor T'ai-tsung, was in the full bloom of its strength and about to take a more direct hand in governing its western territories. T'ai-tsung accordingly gave Hsuan-tsang a warm welcome and asked him for a detailed written account of everything he had seen and heard in the kingdoms of Central Asia and in India. This is the origin of *The Record of the Western Regions,* in which Hsuan-tsang has described his experiences and made his acute observations on the people and customs of Central Asia and India. It is a work of undying value for the study of Asian civilization.

Soon after his return, the government encouraged and supported Hsuan-tsang and many other scholars in a project to translate the Sanskrit texts which he had brought from India—some seventy-six items which came to 1,347 rolls in the Chinese version. Among the works translated were some of the well-studied and oft-chanted scriptures formerly translated by Kumarajiva, such as the Mahaprajnaparamita, the Vimalakirti-nirdesa, and the Sukhavati Sutras. Hsuan-tsang's faithful translations of the Buddhist scriptures, which were made possible by his thorough knowledge of Sanskrit, were undoubtedly authoritative renderings of the original meanings, but so much of the theory and practice of Chinese Buddhism was by that time based on Kumarajiva's translations that Hsuan-tsang's new ones were unable to replace them.

However, Hsuan-tsang's translation of the Prajnaparamita-hridaya was widely accepted. The Mahaprajnaparamita (The Great Discourse on Perfect Wisdom) was available in translation, but it is a very long work which fills 600 rolls in the Chinese version, while the Prajnaparamitahridaya (The Essence of the Discourse on Perfect Wisdom) is a greatly condensed summary which because of its brevity is suitable for daily use. Many commentaries on it were written, and its use as a text for daily reading by both monks and laymen has remained great even to the present day.

Hsuan-tsang's aim was to spread the knowledge of the Indian Yogacara (or Vijnanavada) theories. With his beloved disciple K'uei-chi (632–682) he translated the Vijnaptimatratasiddhi, a work which gives the basis for the Yogacara doctrine. He adhered for the most part to the interpretation of Dharmapala, but took into account other scholars as well. K'uei-chi composed a summary and a commentary which provided the basis for the Consciousness-Only (Yui-shih or Fahsiang) sect. K'uei-chi resided at the Monastery of Mercy and Loving-kindness, which was built for his mother, and thus the sect is sometimes called the Mercy and Loving-kindness sect (Tz'u-en).

According to the doctrines of this sect, all phenomena are the products of consciousness. Consciousness is divided into eight kinds, of which the eighth—fundamental, or storehouse, consciousness (alayavijnana)—is the most basic and the source from which arise all the phenomena of the universe and the human conditions of error and Enlightenment. All existence is classed in five grades and further subdivided into one hundred dharmas. By arriving at an understanding that everything is consciousness only (Yui-shih), one can, according to this view, advance to the state of Enlightenment.

This new system, which attempted to explain religious phenomena psychologically and rationally in accordance with the logical discipline that had been developing in India, evoked a new interest in the Chinese learned world. But the Chinese intelligentsia, having a rich tradition of exegesis and, being deficient in religious enthusiasm and the practical aspects of religion, had already reached a point at which their own Buddhism was Chinese in theory and practice, and this pure Indian transplantation could no longer wield great proselytizing power. However, it was widely studied as Buddhist doctrine and as phenomenology, and as such it had a considerable influence on Oriental thought. It is still studied, but is not followed exclusively by any Chinese sect. Even in the Republic of China there was a revival of Consciousness-Only study among intellectuals, and comparisons of this branch of Buddhist thought were made with Western philosophy. In Japan it was known as the Hosso sect.

THE HUA-YEN SECT

This sect gets its name from the Avatamsaka Sutra (Hua-yen) which gives an account of the first three weeks after the Buddha's Enlightenment and sets forth the practices for a Bodhisattva. In Japan the Sutra and sect are known as Kegon.

In China it was commonly supposed that of all the Mahayana scriptures the Avatamsaka, describing the contents of the Buddha's great perception, was the first Sutra he preached, and the Mahaparinirvana was the last before his passing away. Under the circumstances it was inevitable that the contents of these two scriptures, regarded as the first and last sermons of the Buddha, should acquire particular importance in the eyes of devout Chinese Mahayanists. Both were translated into Chinese early in the fifth century and gradually came to be regarded by many as the scriptures preaching the most important and profound doctrines to be found in all the Mahayana scriptures. A school of thought centering around the Mahaparinirvana reached the peak of its influence in the sixth century, but from the seventh century onward it ceased to exist as an independent sect.

The most important doctrine preached by the Avatamsaka —or Hua-yen—Sutra is that all beings without distinction have the Buddha-nature, that is, all beings have the inherent properties which will lead them to the attainment of Buddhahood. This became a fundamental article of faith common to all Chinese Buddhists. In the realm of religious practice, too, this Sutra was important, for its prohibition against the eating of meat became a part of the Buddhist discipline in China and is recognized as valid by both monks and laymen to this day.

Early in the sixth century a translation was made of Vasu-bandhu's commentary on one chapter of the Avatamsaka Sutra, the chapter setting forth the ten stages of a Bodhisattva. The commentary was widely read and accepted, and there grew up a systematized Avatamsaka doctrine which became the basis of the Hua-yen sect. Fa-tsang (643–712), who organized the Hua-yen sect, held that it was incorrect to judge the relative value of the different Buddhist scriptures on the basis of their chronological order, as urged by the T'ien-t'ai sect. He urged that the relative value of each scriptural work be judged on its own merits with reference to the entire Buddhist Canon.

As an example of the kind of analysis recommended by Fa-tsang, one might consider the development of ontology, with particular reference to phenomenon and substance, proceeding from the simplest and most primitive to the most advanced theories. There are ten steps in this analysis, beginning with (1) the simple theory that both the perceiving subject (atman) and the perceived object exist. (2) One goes on then to the view that the perceived objects exist but the perceiving subject does not. (3) Perceived objects exist in the present but have no existence in past or future. (4) Even objects perceived in the present are of two kinds, those with real existence and those with but temporary existence. (5) Only supramundane objects are substantially real. (6) The concept of supramundane can exist only in antithesis to that of mundane, and therefore it is a mere name.

These first six steps trace the development of ontological concept in Hinayana. Mahayana, however, proceeds from the concept of substance to (7) the idea that subjective concepts of differentiation are devoid of real basis and that there is an undifferentiated substance to all things. (8) Substance is the "suchness of being" and when wrong notions fade away the suchness of beings exists in its pristine purity. (9) Both the external form that is perceived and the internal thought that perceives it are beyond verbal expression. (10) Finally we come to the ideas expounded in the Avatamsaka which are the culmination of all ontological theories. According to this Hua-yen doctrine, each differentiated phenomenon—thing—is complete within itself, each phenomenon is a subject with relation to all other phenomena, and thus each experience contains all experiences within itself in an interdependent, mutually complementary relationship.

For example, if one were to attach a bright jewel to every intersection in a net, each one would reflect the sparkle of all the others. Each reflected sparkle in turn would contain the reflection of all the other jewels. So it would go without limit, each sparkle blending with, entering into, depending upon, and complementing all the others. That, according to Hua-yen philosophy, is the nature of all existence. The attainment of this intuition is the goal of the Avatamsaka, and this is the meaning of Enlightenment in Hua-yen Buddhism.

As a result of the continued speculation on the meaning of the Buddhist scriptures in Chinese translation, both the T'ien-t'ai sect of south China and the Hua-yen sect of north China went beyond the absolute denial of reality to its absolute affirmation. The Chinese Buddhists were dissatisfied with the negative expressions of emptiness and substancelessness so essential to Mahayana Buddhism, which stands squarely on the rock of dependent causation and denies that anything that has only dependent existence can have substantial reality. The Buddhists of China laid special emphasis on the notion that the religious state at which they aimed must be a state of mind in which concrete reality is absolutely affirmed. This is what makes Chinese Buddhism Chinese.

One would be safe in saying that Indian Buddhism was transformed into a philosophy and religion in keeping with Chinese ideas. When it was adopted by a Chinese society with a deeply ingrained habit of thought that set much more store by concrete facts than by abstract ideas, it was changed from a negative expression of emptiness to a doctrine of absolute affirmation. The theories of Hua-yen Buddhism continue to be studied and accepted, but there is no one sect devoted to this doctrine in modern times.

ESOTERIC BUDDHISM

Very shortly after Fa-tsang's death (712), three Buddhist missionaries came to the capital city of Ch'ang-an from India, bringing esoteric Buddhism with them. Buddhist charms and incantations had been coming into China gradually over a long period of time, but esoteric Buddhism in the real sense came with these three men. It was not exactly the same as Tantra-yana which became so popular in Tibet, but it was closely related. The principal scripture of esoteric Buddhism is the Mahavairocana Sutra, which was translated into Chinese and became the basis for making the images and conducting the ceremonies of this branch of Buddhism.

The three missionaries gained the confidence of the T'ang court, where they conducted ceremonies for the banishment of misfortune and the attraction of good luck. For a time esoteric Buddhism flourished under the auspices of the court, but it went into complete abeyance after the persecution of Emperor Wu-tsung (845) and the fall of the T'ang Dynasty in 907. Some of its rituals were adopted by other sects and have continued to the present time, but it has had no continuing existence as a sect in China. Needless to say, the belief in all kinds of charms and incantations remains to this day both in the temples and among the people of China, where it is very real and very strong. As a sect, it has continued in Japan where it is called Shingon.

All of the above sectarian systems except esoteric Buddhism were organized and developed by Chinese monks. All of them were of a high order of philosophic sophistication, and their doctrines and practices were of a kind that could be grasped and performed by specialized monks, but they could scarcely become the religion of laymen, particularly the illiterate Chinese masses. More or less contemporaneously with these philosophic sects there arose two more practical, more popular, thoroughly Chinese sects which became the two most important tendencies in Chinese Buddhism and continue as the most popular and influential in modern times. They are the Ch'an (Meditation) and Ching-t'u (Pure Realm) sects.

THE MEDITATION (CH'AN) SECT

The practice of meditation (dhyana) is a characteristic not only of Indian Buddhism but of all Indian philosophic and religious systems. The Chinese word *Ch'an*, however, refers to a system which, while having its roots in Indian dhyana, gradually moved away from the quiet Indian contemplation to a specifically Chinese religious practice. The word itself derives from *jhana*, the Pali equivalent of *dhyana* and in T'ang times was pronounced almost the same way. In Japan it became Zen.

The Chinese Ch'an sect is supposed to have been founded by the Indian monk Bodhidharma. According to Ch'an tradition, he had an audience with Emperor Wu of the Liang Dynasty (502–549), who was typical of the devout Buddhist ruler, and told him flatly that for all his Buddhist good works he had accumulated no merit. This tradition, of course, can scarcely be regarded as historical fact. And yet, from the words and deeds of the reputed founder, which were invented and recorded by the Ch'an sect, one can catch a glimpse of that sect's attitude toward the contemporary realities of the Chinese Buddhist community.

Bodhidharma's biography as preserved by the Ch'an sect consists mostly of legends, but we are told that early in the sixth century he visited Lo-yang, then the capital of the northern dynasty. The magnificence of the temples of Lo-yang and the elaborate ceremonies with which the anniversary of the Buddha's birth was celebrated are described in detail in *The Record of the Monasteries of Lo-yang*, which was written about A.D. 450. In these handsome temples the study of the Buddhist scriptures was carried out in great earnestness, and the monks vied with one another in the race for fame as learned Buddhist scholars.

Bodhidharma, who had obtained his food by begging and had made contemplation in a quiet place his daily practice, turned to the Chinese Buddhists of Lo-yang and said:

The scriptures are but the finger that points to the moon of Enlightenment. When one can see the moon, there is no further use for the finger. But to become lost in the study and interpretation of the scriptures, in other words to forget to look at the moon, to forget about attaining to Enlightenment, is to set Buddhism on its head. Both the Buddha and the common man have the true nature. To see this clearly, practice dhyana. When you arrive at the unshakable conviction that "the common man and the saint are one and the same," you will have no further need to follow after the written teachings of the scriptures.

So saying, he ascended Mount Sung, there to practice seated contemplation.

Among the learned Buddhists of northern China, there were very few who were willing to practice serious contemplation in accordance with the teachings of Bodhidharma. But one monk did persist resolutely in Bodhidharma's way until he attained Enlightenment, and the line of his successors continued down to Hun-jen (602–675). Hun-jen had two outstanding disciples who became leaders of the northern and southern schools of Ch'an. The northern school centered at Ch'ang-an and Lo-yang, where it was favored by the court and much of the aristocracy and continued to grow until a rebellion overthrew the emperor and Lo-yang was captured. After that the northern school went into a decline.

The southern school was led by Hui-neng, a poor and unlettered son of a family which sold firewood for a living. He settled in southern China, and his followers built up houses of contemplation throughout central and southern China which flourished and eventually submerged the northern school. He was recognized as the Sixth Patriarch, the true follower of Bodhidharma. In the course of time his school of Ch'an was divided into several subschools which spread all over China and converted many temples and monasteries into Ch'an centers.

By this time Ch'an was manifestly different from the Indian dhyana which Bodhidharma had brought to China. It made use of new methods unknown in India, such as the study of paradoxes, beating the practitioner with a rod, shouting "Ho!" at him, and other devices calculated to bring him nearer to a grasp of Enlightenment. This sect became known as Zen in Japan, where it also continues as an influential Buddhist sect. We shall leave the Ch'an sect now, since many translations of Ch'an texts and original studies of the subject have been appearing in English and French over the last few years.

THE PURE REALM (CHING-T'U) SECT

In Mahayana Buddhism the true Buddhist, the Bodhisattva, takes a vow to rescue all beings from woe and to create a society which is pure in the Buddhist sense. To that end—which is identical with the attainment of Buddhahood—he must work at the six perfections: while living a proper moral life, he must practice charity, endure all things with equanimity, practice contemplation, perfect his understanding, and strive without backsliding until his goal is achieved. A Buddha, according to this view, is one who for this purpose has taken his vow, worked at the six perfections, and carried his vow to completion.

The Buddha Amitabha (or Amitayus) is a Buddha of this present age who took and kept a vow to save those beings who have lost the way to Enlightenment because of sin and folly. He is now carrying out the salvation of the beings in the Sukhavati world, "the extremely pleasant pure realm"—called *chi-lo ching-t'u* in Chinese, hence the name Ching-t'u for the sect.

The scriptures preaching faith in Amitabha were translated into Chinese in considerable numbers from an early period, and the Amitabha cult in China can be traced back as far as the fourth century. In A.D. 402, as we have seen, Hui-yuan and 103 of his followers formed a society on Mount Lu for meditation on the name of Amitabha. For that reason Chinese Buddhists have traditionally regarded Hui-yuan as the founder of the Pure Realm sect, but actually the doctrine was systematized and spread far and wide by T'an-luan and his successors in the early seventh century.

T'an-luan was a Buddhist scholar who was planning an overall commentary on the scriptures when illness halted his work. At first he made a study of indigenous Chinese elixirs and practices for longevity, and in an effort to regain his health and lengthen his life, went south and studied under a Taoist master. On his way home he encountered the Indian monk Bodhiruci who told him that, no matter how much or little he might be able to add to his life span by performing the practices which he had learned from the Taoist master, human life remained a transitory thing. When he learned for the first time that Buddhism also had a doctrine of limitless life—for that is the meaning of the Sanskrit *amitayus*—T'an-luan was roused from his error and became a believer in the Pure Realm. He studied Vasubandhu's commentary on the Sukhavativyuha Sutra and wrote a commentary on it entitled *Notes on the Treatise on Rebirth in Paradise* and spread the Ching-t'u faith even among the peasantry of his province.

Some thirty years after T'an-luan's death, Emperor Wu of the Northern Chou Dynasty instituted a thoroughgoing persecution of religion, decreeing the destruction of all Buddhist and Taoist monasteries and popular shrines, and compelling all monks to return to lay life. The emperor declared:

> We are putting an end to temples and monks only in order to clarify the true doctrine of Sakyamuni and to prosper his religion. The essence of Sakyamuni's doctrine, that is, the Mahayana, lies in undiscriminating mercy. But in the monasteries of today self-interested monks, in other words Hinayana monks, while making a pretense of Mahayana, are monopolizing honor and glory. Therefore the only way to prosper the true religion of the Buddha is to destroy these religious bodies that are violating the original spirit of Buddhism.

This, of course, was an excuse devised by a non-Buddhist emperor to stave off some of the opposition of the Buddhist faithful to his policies.

Among the monks who were forced back into the laity, however, were some earnest followers who searched their souls to see whether they had not in fact forgotten the meaning of undiscriminating mercy. Hsin-hsing (540–594) was one of those who repented his past and gave thought to what the Buddhism of the present emergency and the future must be. He realized that, although he was a monk, he had not kept the monastic discipline, that in fact he had not been able to keep it. He not only felt that he was a sinner, but also that he did not have the intelligence to understand the profound meaning of the scriptures, that as far as the scriptures were concerned he was stupid, "congenitally blind." He felt that this was true of all his contemporaries as well as of himself; they were all sinners and blind men.

The contemporary society, in Hsin-hsing's eyes, was full of sin; it was a society in which there was no Buddha, not even a Bodhisattva like Nagarjuna. To the sinful fools in a sinful world the road to Enlightenment was blocked. The Buddhists were busy deciding the relative degrees of profundity and shallowness in the various scriptures, selecting one particular scripture as the absolute truth and deprecating the others as temporary expedients, extraneous, and shallow. Each sect was vaunting itself; each sect was claiming the superiority of its own philosophy over all the others. This was the arrogance of people who were guilty of the terrible sin of maligning the word of the Buddha. The type of religious practice which in antiquity had proved capable of saving such a sage as Nagarjuna was not the sort of thing that might save a person in this day and age.

Nevertheless, the Buddha had preached that all living beings have the Buddha-nature. Even we sinful fools have the Buddha-nature; we are the Buddhas of the future to whom Buddhahood has been promised. What then is the doctrine conferred upon the sinful fools of this sinful age?

The Buddhist community of that time generally believed that fifteen hundred years had passed since the passing away of the Buddha, and they accepted the well-known prophecy that fifteen hundred years after the Buddha would come "the final decay of the Law" when society would degenerate, the monks would violate the commandments, the laity would persecute the faithful, and there would be none who would attain Enlightenment. Hsin-hsing, accepting that chronology and prophecy, and seeing the persecution and civil turmoil around him, gave the entire matter very profound thought. He came to the conclusion that it was no time to be sifting out degrees of sophistication in the scriptures, nor a time to distinguish degrees of excellence among the many Buddhas and Bodhisattvas in order to choose one's favorite scripture and Buddha.

Hsin-hsing decided that it was a time when all Buddhas should be honored and worshiped equally. All men must perform every manner of good works as an expression of the will of the Buddha for the sake of others, for the sake of society. All living beings, as future Buddhas equipped with the Buddha-nature, must be respected alike. In oneself one must see wickedness and folly, and toward all others one must show respect, for that is the Buddhism of the age of final decay. This was Hsin-hsing's teaching.

When the Sui Dynasty replaced the northern Chou and began an enthusiastic policy of Buddhist revival, Hsin-hsing preached his doctrine in the capital at Ch'ang-an and gained many devoted followers. However, shortly before his death he was condemned as heretical by the Buddhist community in the capital, and the emperor decreed the dissolution of his sect and forbade the teaching of his ideas. The opposition was due to his assertions that in the era of final decay rulers must not punish even those monks who violate the discipline but must respect all equally, and that those who were at such pains to establish sects were guilty of the great sin of not knowing their own place and of maligning the Law of Buddha. Even though he had been condemned, earnest Buddhist monks in quest of the truth could not ignore his declaration that men must search their souls to see what sort of religion could provide equal salvation to the sinful members of a sinful society.

Tao-ch'o (562–645), although a monk well schooled in philosophy, was impressed at the age of forty-eight with T'an-luan's Ching-t'u faith of fifty years before and came to believe that, since the present was the evil age of final decay, sinful and foolish mankind could be led to the gate of Enlightenment only through faith in Amitabha's Pure Realm. He began to practice and teach exclusive meditation on Amitabha.

Shan-tao (613–681), a disciple of Tao-ch'o, was one of the most important leaders in the growth of the Pure Realm sect. He composed a commentary on the Amitayurdhyana Sutra, the Sutra outlining the process of meditation on Amitabha, and he further systematized the Pure Realm doctrine. He was active at the imperial capital of Ch'ang-an at the very time in which Hsuan-tsang had returned from his travels in India.

Shan-tao began by saying, "I am a sinful, lowly person, eternally involved in error, shut off from salvation." He degraded himself and sank into the pit of despair. But in that pit of despair he felt the very mercy, that limitless mercy which embraced him. He realized that for men, as long as they live in this society, it is impossible to wipe away the three poisons of greed, anger, and folly which bind them to a never-ending, vicious circle of sin and error. But the salvation of the sinful common man who has lost the way to Enlightenment is provided by the vow of Amitabha. A life in keeping with Amitabha's vow is one in which one thinks exclusively of Amitabha Buddha, never forgetting him for a moment, whether one may be walking, standing still, sitting up, or lying down, whether the time be long or short. It is a life in which thoughts of Amitabha fill one's mind constantly. By living such a life, the sinful common man basks in the light of mercy, he is purified, and in the very midst of his involvement with greed, anger, and folly he is enabled to live forever in this "now," this present moment, filled with joy and courage.

Shan-tao described the life of the Amitabha devotee with the clever parable of the two rivers and the white road. A traveler who has crossed a great open space on his way to visit a friend who lives far to the West is pursued by wild beasts and highwaymen until he comes to a great river. On the right side of the river great flames are roaring and on the left side mighty waves are raging; between the waves and the flames there runs only one thin road, a white road four or five inches in width. If he tries to cross, he may fall into the flames or into the waves. If he turns back, he is certain to be killed by the wild beasts or the highwaymen. Stalemated, the man takes one step down the narrow road in the direction of his friend's country in the West. At that very moment he hears two encouraging voices, one from the farther side of the river saying to him, "Come! I will protect thee. Come straight down the line!" The other voice from his side of the river says, "Go! Thou shalt surely be saved." Suddenly he is filled with unshakable determination. Although the flames lick his feet from the one side and the waves from the other, nothing daunted he sets his feet firmly on the narrow white road and proceeds. The highwaymen call out invitingly to him, "That road is dangerous! Come back! We are your saviors." But his mind made up, he pays no heed to them and single-mindedly proceeds down the white road, taking strength from the sound of "Come!" and "Go!" until he reaches the farther shore. There the hand of loyalty is extended to him by the dear friend he has come to visit.

The fire in this parable represents our angry heart. The water represents our covetous heart. The narrow white road between them represents the heart that seeks after truth in the very midst of a daily life characterized by anger and greed—it is the road to faith. Step over the sin-laden reality of death and tread the road to faith! The voice crying "Come!" is Amitabha Buddha's merciful protection. The voice crying "Go!" is Sakyamuni Buddha's encouragement. Once one's mind is made up, there is no more yielding to the blandishments of superstition, and although the covetous and angry heart does not vanish, the determined journey to the ultimate ideal is completed. The Amitabha devotee, according to Shan-tao, is the traveler who proceeds down life's white road.

Shan-tao illustrated in picture form the contents of the Amitayurdhyana, which is based on the tragedy of Bimbisara, king of Rajagraha, and his queen. He collected many hymns and conducted his followers in a daily service of penance and hymn singing. In this way, the Pure Realm doctrine was spread far and wide among the monks, laymen, and laywomen.

After Shan-tao's time, many members of the Ch'an Sect, as well as members of the Hua-yen and T'ien-t'ai sects, called upon the name of Amitabha and believed in the Pure Realm. In this way Pure Realm doctrine became adulterated with Ch'an, T'ien-t'ai, and Hua-yen elements. But the cry *Nan-wu A-mit'o-fo*—from the Sanskrit *Namo Amitabhaya-Buddhaya*, Homage to Amitabha Buddha!—echoes from every temple, every village, and every home in China to this day.

Thus, we have considered the origins of the chief Buddhist sects in China. In modern times, the distinction between sects is not clearly made, as it so often is in Japan. Many priests practice several points of view. The majority of the temples in China belong to the Ch'an sect, but without making a clear distinction between the doctrines which have blended in a distinctively Chinese manner. T'ien-t'ai, Ch'an, and Ching-t'u or Pure Land are the sects which have survived to modern times.

All of these sects played their part in the history of Buddhism in Japan.

BUDDHISM AND TRADITIONAL CHINESE THOUGHT

Chinese Buddhism in its prime was subjected to severe persecution three times by emperors named Wu. In each case the conflict between Buddhism and traditional Chinese thought was in the background.

The first of these persecutors, Emperor T'ai-wu of the northern Wei Dynasty, followed the advice of his Taoist advisors and decreed in A.D. 446 that the Buddhist religion was to be wiped out, that not one monk, not one scriptural text, not one image was to remain in existence. That policy continued for seven years until the emperor and his ministers died. The new emperor immediately instituted a revival of Buddhism, and the Buddhists who had been in hiding betook themselves with a new fervor to restoring Buddhism. The world-famous Buddhist caves of Yun-Kang were constructed in commemoration of the event.

Sixty years after this Buddhist revival there were 13,727 temples in the northern Wei territory alone, and some twenty years after that the temples numbered more than thirty thousand, and there were more than two million monks and nuns. This unexampled increase in the Buddhist community, achieved in so short a time, caused learned men to sigh in amazement.

The increase in the Buddhist community under the southern dynasties, south of the Yangtze, was also very great at that time. In the Sung Dynasty (420–478) there were 1,913 temples and 36,000 monks and nuns, while in the Liang Dynasty (502–556) there were 2,864 temples and 82,000 monks and nuns. In the southern dynasties, as in the northern, Confucian scholars and Taoists frequently argued that Buddhism, an alien faith, was both harmful and unnecessary in China. Many of them advocated its suppression and outright abolition, but it never came to a complete prohibition in the southern dynasties as it did in the northern.

In 574, as we have seen, Emperor Wu of the northern Chou Dynasty decreed a complete suppression of religious organizations. The emperor had frequently assembled Confucian, Buddhist, and Taoist scholars with the hope that he could reconcile and unite them, but the mutual recriminations, particularly between the Buddhists and Taoists, only became more violent. Emperor Wu was bent on perfecting the fighting power of his entire realm in order that he might defeat his eastern rival, the northern Ch'i Dynasty, and unite all of China. He decided to return to lay life the monks of the Buddhist and Taoist communities and enroll them in the lists of public and private workers, and to destroy their temples and all places of worship not provided for by the Confucian ritual canon. It is worthy of note that he sought not only to destroy Buddhism, but to make Confucianism the official religion of the government.

In 589 Emperor Wen of the Sui Dynasty overthrew the northern Chou and immediately restored Buddhism and Taoism. Of the two, Buddhism experienced an extraordinarily quick revival and prospered more than ever before. From that experience, as we have seen, there arose the practical Buddhist movement of the Pure Realm, basing itself on the "here and now."

The ruling house of the T'ang Dynasty (618–907) considered themselves to be descendants of Lao-tzu and gave Taoism a position of honor above Buddhism. Nevertheless, the Buddhist community grew both in numbers and influence far more than did Taoism. In the imperial capital of Ch'ang-an, for instance, in the early eighth century there were ninety-one Buddhist monasteries and nunneries against sixteen for the Taoists. For the whole country, the figures at this time were 1,677 Taoist temples and 5,358 Buddhist. Buddhist temples increased from this time on, and so did their holdings of fields, mountains, forests, banks, pawnbrokerages, mills, tenant farmers, and slaves. The Buddhist community became the equal of the great wealthy aristocrats, which had the unfortunate result of attracting more and more persons into the monasteries simply for the sake of a guaranteed livelihood. Edicts aimed at restraining the growth of the monasteries were promulgated from time to time, but the goal was not one easy to achieve.

Finally, the Taoist Emperor Wu-tsung, who reigned from 841 to 846, attempted to reduce the power of Buddhism by decreeing in 845 that there could only be four temples in each of the capital cities and one in each of the provinces, and all other temples were to be deconsecrated and the monks returned to lay life. The government deconsecrated more than sixteen hundred officially recognized temples and more than forty thousand unofficial temples; they returned 260,500 monks and nuns to lay life, confiscated vast areas of farm land, and took over 150,000 slaves who had been the property of the Buddhist community.

The succeeding emperor permitted the restoration of Buddhism, and the number of temples and monks immediately increased. But the T'ang Dynasty was declining, civil wars were following one upon another, the monks were producing no outstanding personalities, and the only sects that were flourishing were the practical ones like the Ch'an and Ching-t'u. The Sung Dynasty, which came to power in 960, adopted a policy of playing down the arts of war and cultivating the arts of peace. It instituted at state expense a project for the translation and publication of the Buddhist scriptures which made the doctrines of the philosophic sects available again. The Buddhist community continued to grow, as is seen from the fact that in 1021 there were 397,615 monks and 61,240 nuns in China.

At this time, Confucianism experienced a revival, and government by Confucian bureaucrats became stronger. This Confucianism was a new Confucianism which had absorbed some Buddhist philosophy and grafted onto itself some metaphysical ideas which before that time had been absent. Confucianism had always had a superior attitude toward the doctrines of non-Chinese peoples. Now that it had incorporated into itself some of the philosophic doctrines of Buddhism, it more than ever regarded Buddhism as a useless nuisance and tried, inevitably, to do away with it. In addition, the Khitans

and Juchens, two non-Chinese peoples from Manchuria, occupied north China at this time and their dynasties were harassing
the Sung. That resulted in the Confucian ultranationalism becoming even more pronounced. Neo-Confucianism became
the official doctrine of the Sung Dynasty and was the basis for
constant efforts to do away with Buddhism, the barbarian
faith.

The Mongols, who overthrew the Sung Dynasty in 1280,
were believers in Tibetan Buddhism and thus protectors of
Buddhism in China. But when the Ming established a purely
Chinese dynasty again in 1368, the Neo-Confucian philosophy
became again the official doctrine of the state, and opposition
to Buddhism greatly increased. This state of affairs continued
until the Ch'ing Dynasty when the first two of the emperors
were devout Buddhists. But the third emperor, who ruled in
the latter half of the eighteenth century, had this to say about
Buddhism:

This is not a religion to be venerated by the Middle Flowering
Land, particularly by its officials. But since this religion has a long history and doing away with it utterly and immediately might produce
social unrest, since also the clergy are but one part of the stupid populace who have lost their ability to live as useful members of society,
we will permit them, as befits the compassion of the Son of Heaven,
to dwell undisturbed in their mountain and forest retreats, isolated
from officials and common folk, there to practice their religion, that
no harm may be done to the nation or to society. However, it is desirable to decrease gradually the number of monks and temples and
ultimately to do away with them altogether.

That became the policy for the bureaucracy. Thus, for example, early in the nineteenth century a funeral service in
honor of a Manchu official was forbidden on the grounds that
the deceased had been a Buddhist and the ceremony might
have an undesirable effect upon the people. On another occasion, there was a considerable to-do when it became known
that a number of civil officials and young men who had passed
the civil service examinations had been present at an ordination
service in a Buddhist temple. With the Buddhist religion forbidden to officials and declared undesirable even for common
folk, and the monks confined to an ascetic religious life within

the temples and cut off from secular society, the effectiveness of Buddhism as a popular religion could only wane.

BUDDHISM IN CONTEMPORARY CHINA

The centuries-old, traditional, bureaucratically enforced Confucian theories of Chinese superiority were broken down by the might of the modern European powers. Some of the progressive intellectuals in China at the end of the nineteenth century felt that China must reform speedily by instituting a new system of education containing elements of Western learning. As an emergency measure they recommended that the temple buildings and lands that were to be found in every city and village be converted to the use of this new system of education. This recommendation immediately found many supporters and was put into action; and the corrupt officials, war lords, and local bosses, who abounded in China at the time of the late Ch'ing and early Republic, took advantage of this situation to oppress the helpless monks and to convert the temple properties to public—and even private—use.

In the Republic of China, which overthrew the Ch'ing Dynasty in 1911, there arose a movement to put an end to all cultural features that impeded scientific progress, including the ancient authority of Confucianism. That movement, which sought the abolition of all kinds of superstition, developed into an antireligious movement under the influence of Marxism. The two medieval religions, Buddhism and Taoism, also came under fire. Popular images that had been worshiped in the temples were destroyed, ceremonies in honor of the ancestral spirits were banned, and a struggle between the temples and the authorities grew up all over the land. Increasingly, demands were made that all temple properties should be confiscated and turned over to the public.

The monks, in order to defend themselves against these attacks, were obliged to take stock of themselves and embark on their own reform movement. In 1912 a group of Buddhist monks organized the New Buddhism Movement and requested the government to protect temple properties. Under the leadership of T'ai-hsu, who died in 1946, their activities developed into a powerful reform movement throughout all of China. They were keenly aware of the need to re-educate the monks in order to reorganize the outmoded Chinese Buddhist community and make it an effective vehicle of salvation in the modern era. They created such institutions as the Wuchang Buddhist Institute to train progressive monks and propagate Buddhism in society at large. They published a journal, the *Sound of the Tide*, issued appeals to Buddhists throughout the world, established the World Library of Buddhist Learning at Wuchang and the Sino-Tibetan Institute of Buddhist Doctrine at Chungking, and sent students to study Buddhism in Tibet, Thailand, Japan, and other countries. All this work was carried on by disciples of T'ai-hsu who shared with him the hope of establishing new Buddhism in China.

Another person worthy of mention is Yuan-ying who was an advocate of the preservation of tradition and strove for the unification and organization of Buddhism throughout China. He established the Chinese Buddhist Society at Nanking, helped in the formation of charitable groups and educational institutions throughout China, and gave his all to the service of the people and their conversion to Buddhism. According to the statistics compiled by branches of the Chinese Buddhist Society in 1930, there were 267,090 temples, 738,000 monks and nuns, and 3,890,000 lay devotees in the Buddhist community. While it is true that these figures are not accurate and it is impossible to know how many of the alleged temples and monks are really active, nevertheless one can gather that the Chinese Buddhist community is still large.

Mention must also be made of Yin-kuang, who, rather than take to the political or social limelight like T'ai-hsu or Yuan-ying, renounced the path of social organization and chose to exert himself in a life of austere religious practice. He sought to gain followers among the monks, the officials, and the common people by his virtue and faith, and to set an example of Buddhism in practice. In the violent upheavals of modern China and the vicissitudes of the Buddhist community under the Republic, the presence of Yin-kuang was a veritable beacon. A believer in the Pure Realm, he propagated his own faith and, turning to a China and a world torn with endless strife, continually preached mercy and peace.

In addition to the few who have been mentioned, there were several score monks who contributed to the reform and revival of the Buddhist community under the Republic, but the number is very, very small.

TEMPLE LIFE

There are both small and large temples in China. The small temples are usually poor in resources and manpower and are transmitted by the resident monk to a disciple whom he has trained very much in accordance with his own inclinations. They are appropriately known as hereditary temples since the disciples in turn transmit the temple to their disciples for generation after generation.

The large temples are wealthy in resources and house several score, sometimes several hundreds, of monks. They are known as "thickets and groves of the ten sides," that is, gathering places housing persons from everywhere. The resident monk who is in charge of the temple is chosen by the community of that temple from anywhere in China, and any properly qualified monk may be admitted if he has come for the purpose of practicing the Buddhist faith. The resident and other leading monks assign their respective duties to the members of the community, manage the affairs of the temple, and guide the daily religious life of the monastery. Among the 260,000 temples in China, the number of large temples, the "thickets and groves of the ten sides," can be numbered in tens. There are even fewer in which, under the leadership of outstanding priests, several hundred earnest monks are leading a serious religious life.

The temples are also classified according to their principal activities as contemplation temples, study or doctrinal temples devoted to a particular sect, and disciplinary temples devoted principally to the study of monastic disciplines. In addition, there are temples devoted primarily to the Pure Realm sect or to esoteric Buddhism, but Chinese temples have no sharp lines of sectarian distinction such as are found in Japan. The contemplation temples, associated with Ch'an Buddhism, are the most numerous. In all temples the invocation Nan-wu A-mi-t'o-fo, Homage to Amitabha Buddha, is pronounced, the esoteric incantations are used, and a common monastic discipline is followed. As a general rule, in the morning various incantations are recited, followed by a reading of the Prajnaparami-tahridaya, and at dusk the Sukhavativyuha is read, followed by penance and the recitation of Nan-wu A-mi-t'o-fo.

The monastic discipline is based, for the most part, on a set of regulations known as Paichang's Pure Rules. They were first composed by a monk named Pai-chang Huai-hai (720–814) as a set of regulations appropriate to the peculiar practices of the Ch'an sect and underwent considerable alteration during the tenth to the fourteenth centuries. The fact that a set of regulations specifically designed for the Chinese clergy was formulated and supplanted the Indian regulations indicated that the practical side of Indian Buddhism had become Sinicized in China.

BUDDHAS AND BODHISATTVAS

The objects of worship in Chinese Buddhism are in general the same in all the temples. Temples dedicated to Maitreya, Sakyamuni, Amitabha, and Avalokitesvara are the most common. In Chinese Buddhism as in Indian Buddhism, from an early period, it was believed that Sakyamuni was the seventh Buddha to appear in this world. Chinese Buddhism also took over the belief that in the distant future Sakyamuni's successor, Maitreya, would appear in the world and convert the sentient beings. In the Buddhist caves and statuary carved in the fifth and sixth centuries there are not a few statues of Sakyamuni with images of the six Buddhas of the past above his head, and there are many images of Maitreya—who dwells in heaven as a Bodhisattva until he emerges as the Buddha of the future. Faith in Sakyamuni and Maitreya continues to this day.

Mahayana Buddhist thought included not only this world of ours but many other worlds besides. The Mahayanist universe consists of many distinct worlds like our solar system, in each of which they imagined a Buddha converting the beings of his own particular world. Typical of these Buddhas of other worlds are Akshobhya and Bhaishajyaguru in the East and Amitabha in the West. Ever since the scriptures describing these worlds—called Pure Lands, or Pure Realms, by the Chinese—had been translated into Chinese, the Buddhas of those lands were objects of devotion in the Chinese Buddhist community. But of all of them it was the worship of Amitabha that flourished most and continues to flourish to this day.

A Buddha is no different fundamentally from any of us. If a man but perceives correctly, he is a Buddha. All human beings have the Buddha-nature, which is also known as the "mind pure in its very nature." It may also be referred to as Tathagatagarbha—the womb of "him [the Buddha] who has gone the same way as all others who have attained Enlightenment." Any human being, by perceiving this originally pure mind is, by that fact, a Buddha. If we could but perceive that the inner pure mind is one and the same with the Buddha, and that the Buddha and the common man are at bottom no different, we should be Buddhas ourselves and should have attained our freedom. It is like water as calm as a mirror (the pure mind), which, when wind (ignorance) blows upon it, forms countless waves (the differentiated world), but which, when the wind stops, returns to its original mirror-like state.

The Buddhist is one who awakens to the pure mind within himself, vows to save all beings, and exerts himself in the performance of those acts that will make him a Buddha. That is the definition of a Bodhisattva. The acts which will make him a Buddha are summed up under the six perfections—generosity, adherence to discipline, forbearance, exertion, meditation, and wisdom. The Bodhisattva deprecates the Hinayana Buddhist as one who is intent only on the attainment of his own personal Enlightenment and is content to rest within it once he has attained it. He calls such a person "self-seeking." The Bodhisattva, on the other hand, out of a feeling of the great mercy of the Buddha—a feeling beyond differentiation, a feeling that regards oneself as empty—identifies his own mind with the mind of the Buddha that strives for the salvation of all. In an effort to rescue all beings from suffering, the Bodhisattva sacrifices himself in continual religious practice.

Just as the Buddhas may be conceived of in incalculable numbers, so there are incalculable numbers of Bodhisattvas. The Mahayana scriptures that have been translated into Chinese mention many Bodhisattvas, but those most worshiped in China are Avalokitesvara, Manjusri, Kshitigarbha, and Samantabhadra. In recent times the Buddhists of China have dedicated Mount P'u-t'o in Chekiang Province to Avalokitesvara, Mount Wu-t'ai in Shansi Province to Manjusri, Mount Chiu-hua in Anhwei Province to Kshitigarbha, and Mount O'mei in Szechwan Province to Samantabhadra. Many temples have been built on these mountains, and monks and laymen make pilgrimages to them.

Of these four Bodhisattvas, Avalokitesvara—known in Chinese as Kuan-yin—is the most widely worshiped and has come to be believed in by monks and laymen as the goddess of compassionate love who rescues mankind from present ills and lavishes good fortune upon the world. It is interesting to note that the Chinese have converted a Bodhisattva, who in Indian Buddhism can only be a male, into a goddess. Kshitigarbha, along with the so-called Ten Kings—who judge the souls of the dead—is regarded by the Chinese masses as the savior of beings in hell.

POPULAR BUDDHISM

Buddhism, while clearly understood by the intelligent thinker to be atheistic, is taken by the general mass of the people to be a polytheistic religion.

Chinese society consisted of a mass of common people, most of whom were engaged in agriculture, who were left to wallow in incredible ignorance and poverty, and were ruled over by a minority of intellectuals with an essentially Confucian education. Even in recent times the common people have been left in their ignorance, with an extraordinarily low standard of living. For such people, in general, there can be no security in life without reliance on some supernatural power. Such a society requires gods to pray to, and a polytheistic religion can be easily manipulated by supplication. Spirits, gods, shamans, and magic became bound up with the life of the Chinese people. Buddhism, which was received into this society and became its religion, would have been much too sophisticated for common acceptance if it had remained a philosophic system confined to the monastic groups.

We have seen how, when Buddhism first came to China, Sakyamuni, the religious practitioner, was turned into an immortal golden god like Lao-tzu and the Yellow Emperor, to be worshiped because he possessed a mysterious power to confer blessings and avert misfortunes. But that alone would not have enabled Buddhism to push aside traditional Chinese faiths and capture the hearts of the Chinese masses as rapidly as it did. Buddhism, through its points of contact with the traditional Chinese religions, shook the spirit of the Chinese people with great force. This was chiefly due to the doctrine of rebirth based on good and bad deeds, running like a thread through past, present, and future.

In the latter half of the fourth century, the famous historian Heng Yuan stated in his *Record of the Latter Han* that Buddhism preaches, "Although man dies his spirit does not perish, but takes on a new form. All the good and evil which he did in his lifetime is repaid." He went on to say that even among aristocrats and scholars, "when they behold the limits of life and death and retribution, there is none who does not feel terror in his heart and lose himself in it." The Chinese people to whom this new doctrine of rebirth was preached also thought of some sort of continuation of the spirit after death, but since they were concerned primarily with scholarly speculation and tended to concentrate their attention mainly on the present life and particularly on politics, they had done no profound thinking on the question of the hereafter and had no systematic theories about it.

It was disturbing for people who had only vague ideas about life and death to be told that the present is a result of the good and evil deeds of a former birth and that the good or evil deeds of this life are an invisible force—karma—pregnant with the good or ill fortune for tomorrow and determining future rebirths. When they are told that these future births might be in the form of men or even demons or wild beasts, then these persons, even those among them who had hitherto lived with a very rosy view of human life, could scarcely help turning their thoughts to the baffling question of life and death, nor could they avoid experiencing the disquieting effects of fear.

A tiny number of leading monks and intellectuals understood rebirth and karma correctly. They knew that the Indian ideas of karma and rebirth caused the religious practitioner Siddhartha to become aware of the fundamental facts of human life—birth, old age, sickness, and death—and to use them as a jumping-off place for passing beyond to that free sphere of release that has put an end to the round of life and death, there to dwell secure in the realization of dependent origination, the understanding of the interrelation and interdependence of all things. They realized that, in Buddhism, karma and rebirth are significant as the call to an inner awakening, not as something that puts an end to the subjective nature and objectivizes it, nor as an explanation of the various spheres of existence.

Nevertheless, when the doctrine of karma and rebirth was preached to the masses, calling their attention to the woes of human life, it could not help becoming objectivized and vulgarized. The majority of the Chinese took from Buddhism first and foremost the strange, yet easily understood, objectivized doctrine of reincarnation in the six states of existence —as denizens of hell, hungry demons, beasts, spirits, human beings, or gods. Fear-stricken with the idea that from men they could be reborn as beasts, or demons, or gods, or men, in a never ending cycle, they took to performing Buddhist good works for the sake of their own souls and those of their deceased relatives and friends. They constructed images of the Buddhas and Bodhisattvas, made offerings to the Buddha and monks, and performed religious ceremonies.

The Indian doctrine of reincarnation was accepted by the Chinese masses as the most representative doctrine of Buddhism and spread rapidly among them. It became identified with the family system, the very basis of Confucian society, and with the obligations of filial piety. Buddhist ceremonies for the welfare of seven generations of ancestors, as well as one's near dead, became very common—thus contributing to the prosperity of the temples and monks but becoming at the same time the cause of their corruption and decline.

As Confucian ideas became dominant in the government and the feelings distinguishing the Chinese from the barbarians gained in strength, Buddhism became separated from the ruling class, the intelligentsia, and the monks were forced to turn to the ignorant populace. To acquire the confidence of the masses, the monks had to do what the people wanted, that is, chant scriptures, particularly for the benefit of the souls of deceased kinfolk. The Buddhism of the people became inextricably interwoven with Taoistic beliefs, and the Buddhas and Bodhisattvas themselves became objects of worship akin to the popular gods of Chinese tradition, to whom one prayed for salvation and good fortune.

The Bodhisattvas, however, preserved some of their Buddhist character, since they were for the most part "gods of loving-kindness," while China's traditional popular gods were "gods to be feared." Avalokitesvara, who had the greatest number of devotees of all the Bodhisattvas worshiped in popular Chinese Buddhism, became identified with the legendary third daughter of King Miao-chuang. She refused the marriage arranged by her father, became a nun, and later healed her father's illness by giving him her own hands and eyes. Then she attained Enlightenment. As the goddess of mercy and compassion she was fervently worshiped by the general populace during the Ming and Ch'ing Dynasties. There were Avalokitesvara halls in the major monasteries and Kuan-yin shrines in every village, and frequently shrines to the goddess of mercy in the home. The believers were particularly numerous among the wives and mothers, who prayed to Kuan-yin for recovery from illnesses, for the protection of their children, and for the gift of good children.

Some of the leading monks in the late Ming period warned that there was nothing in the Buddhist Canon proper that said that the daughter of King Miao-chuang had turned into Ava-

lokitesvara, but even the monks fell in with this popular belief, encouraging the cult of the female Kuan-yin and striving
to gain adherents for it. As can be seen from this one example
of the Avalokitesvara cult, the temples and clergy, cut off from
the educated classes, were obliged to turn for support and for
their very livelihood to the Buddhist faith of the ignorant
masses. Consequently, they vulgarized their teachings and
interlarded them with superstitions, and their acquaintance
with the true doctrine of Buddhism sank so low that they
could no longer propagate the true teachings of Buddhism.

Although modern China could boast more than 700,000
monks, the majority of them had no education in Buddhist
doctrine. Their level of general knowledge was very low, they
were cut off from modern civilization, and it is an ill-concealed
fact that they were not equipped to assume religious leadership
in the modern world. Most of the temples had lost their potential as centers of Buddhist education. In the face of the
impotence of the temples and the monks, it was the lay devotees who upheld the cause of Buddhism in recent times, and
their proselytizing exceeded that of the monks.

LAY DEVOTEES

Two laymen who exerted a great direct influence on Buddhist life in recent Chinese history were P'eng Chi-ch'ing and
Yang Jen-shan. P'eng Chi-ch'ing (1740–1796) had his philosophic base in the doctrines of the Hua-yen sect, but his energetic religious and evangelistic activity were in the Pure Realm
tradition. He pronounced the formula Nan-wu A-mi-t'o-fo
thirty thousand times a day and has left the world several
written works encouraging the Pure Realm faith which have
been very effective in recent times.

Yang Jen-shan (1837–1912) also believed that one should
look to the Hua-yen for doctrine and to Amitabha for practice. His mission was to spread the Buddhist faith among intellectuals. He established the Chin-ling Scriptural Press, which
published more than two thousand rolls, thus laying the foundation on which the revived Buddhist learning of the Republican era was built.

One of his disciples, Ou-yang Chien, founded in 1918 in Nanking the China Institute of Internal (Buddhist) Studies which conducted specialized research in Buddhist doctrine, principally the Consciousness-Only school of Yogacara. A similar institute, the Three Eras Study Society, was also founded in Peking for the study of Yogacara doctrines. It should be pointed out that the Institute of Buddhist Learning at Wuchang also laid the greatest stress on the study of the Yui-shih philosophy. It is an interesting fact that the Yogacara philosophy was singled out by the Buddhist scholars of the Republican era as a system capable of holding its own with Western philosophical thought. Many studies of Yogacara doctrine, traditional studies as well as those with new interpretations in the light of Western philosophy, were published by these lay scholars.

Lay societies were organized in Shanghai and later in all the major urban centers of China, numbering among their members Buddhist laymen holding high positions in economic and political life. They kept the five commandments—not to kill, not to steal, not to commit adultery, not to lie, and not to take intoxicants—and they studied religious doctrine, practiced meditation, invoked the name of the Buddha, and gave much time to the propagation of Buddhism as well. Buddhist libraries and book stores were maintained. Since most of the lay Buddhists were believers in Amitabha, groups were organized throughout the country for the performing of Pure Realm practices—known as "lotus societies" or "pure deed societies."

As a result of these activities, there came to be a considerable number of influential persons in the economic, political, and intellectual worlds of the Republic of China who entered Buddhist temples for a fixed period each year, or even for several years, to keep the commandments, study the doctrine, and give themselves up to the earnest practice of meditation and the invocation of the name of the Buddha.

In spite of the vulgarized beliefs of the ignorant masses and the pressure of criticism in the ideological, political, and social confusion of the early Republic, thanks to the awakened monks and influential lay devotees, Buddhism in China began to show signs of revival that became more evident with the passage of the years. The collapse of the Confucian state and society was in the process of becoming a blessing for Mahayana Buddhism with its universal and intellectual character. With the coming of the Communist government, some of the lay leaders fled to Formosa, while those who have remained in China are cut off from the rest of the Buddhist world. On the basis of available information, it is not possible to form a scholarly judgment as to what is happening to Buddhism in China at the present time.

KOREAN BUDDHISM

The flowering of Buddhism in China in the latter half of the fourth century carried the religion into Korea and from then on the fortunes of Korean Buddhism, like those of Korean politics and ideology, were closely related to developments in China. Korea at that time was divided into three kingdoms, all of which welcomed Buddhism. Three centuries later, in 668, the kingdom of Silla completed the conquest of the other two kingdoms and set up a dynasty which continued until 935.

Under the Silla Dynasty the Buddhism of T'ang China entered Korea very readily. Many Korean monks went to China to study, some rendering distinguished service to the Chinese Buddhist community, others proceeding to India for further study. One of the outstanding monks of the period was Wonhyo who was an active preacher in the mid-seventh century, writing a great deal and laying the foundations of Korean Buddhist doctrine. His works are held in high esteem in China and Japan as well, where their influence has been considerable. It was in the latter part of the seventh century that the Hua-yen doctrine that all beings without distinction have the Buddha-nature was first introduced and flourished for a time. At about the same time a Korean monk was active in the learned circles of T'ang China which were studying the Consciousness-Only doctrines of Yogacara, and as a result the Yui-shih (pronounced *Yusik* in Korean) doctrines spread in Korea among the scholars.

The building of temples proceeded apace, and there survive in the area of Kyongju, which was then the capital, relics of these structures. The stone Buddhas of the Sokkuram (stone cave hut), for instance, show us even now how outstanding was the Buddhist art of the Silla era.

In A.D. 935 the Silla Dynasty was overthrown and replaced by the Koryo Dynasty which had its capital at Kaesong. During the next two centuries the ruling house was profoundly devoted to Buddhism, with the result that both learning and practice flourished greatly, giving rise to the period of greatest prosperity for Buddhism in Korea, in the eleventh century. Toward the end of that century the son of the king became a monk, studied in China, and returned to spread the T'ien-t'ai teachings in his own country. He also persuaded the king to gather Buddhist texts from Korea, China, the Khitan realm, and Japan and to publish 1,010 separate items, totaling more than 4,740 rolls.

Ch'an Buddhism spread widely in Korea during the Silla Dynasty and then in the twelfth century became very popular in the variety taught by the monk Chinul. In the course of time Korean Buddhism, like the Chinese parent, became primarily Ch'an (called *Son*), and the other disciplines of the Hua-yen, T'ien-t'ai, and Pure Realm sects were blended into it.

As the government of China turned to Neo-Confucianism, the Korean rulers began to encourage the Confucian teachings and adopted a policy of suppressing Buddhism. The beginnings of opposition in the thirteenth century revealed the decadent state of Buddhism in Korea. The Buddhist community, which had long before ceased to be an earnest religious body, declined further under the weight of the oppression which was adopted as state policy in the fifteenth century. The social position of the monks waned until they were rated as one of the eight classes of the common people, and the faith became vulgarized. This policy of suppressing Buddhism was in line with an identical policy pursued in China—which from the fifteenth century on was officially Korea's suzerain—and the decline of the Buddhist community in Korea was similar to the lot of Buddhism in China.

As a result of the Sino-Japanese and Russo-Japanese wars, Korea came more and more under Japanese domination until in 1910 it was annexed by Japan. According to statistics compiled in 1926, Korea had 1,363 temples and 7,188 monks and nuns. All temples were under the jurisdiction of thirty-one parent temples, of which four or five were most influential. The educational level of the monks is very low; scarcely half of them could be considered capable of doing the work of religious conversion in the present age of rapid technical advance.

The Japanese Buddhist sects vied with one another in spreading their activities to Korean soil, building temples, instituting social work and educational programs, and the like, but their efforts to remake Korean Buddhism in the Japanese image met with almost no success. Nevertheless, impelled to some extent by the example of Japanese Buddhism and by the tiny handful of Korean monks who had been educated in Buddhist institutions of learning in Japan, the Korean Buddhist community began to feel the need of raising the educational level of its own leaders. The thirty-one parent temples united to form a Buddhist Institute at Seoul, but the task of reforming the decadent Korean Buddhist community was no easy one. Before there could be any results from their efforts, the Pacific War broke out, and the chaos of the following years makes it impossible to judge the status of Buddhism in Korea at the present moment.

CHAPTER SIX

Buddhism in Tibet

Lobsang Phuntsok Lhalungpa

Buddhism came to the snowbound land of Tibet in the seventh century A.D. By that time the Doctrine of the Buddha had been established for centuries in China on the east and Kashmir and Khotan on the west, with Buddhist traders, pilgrims, and soldiers going back and forth along the borders of Tibet. Many efforts had been made to introduce Buddhism to the Land of Snow, but conditions were not favorable until the country was united under a strong central authority and the ancient religion—Bonism—had declined.

Bonism was characterized by the worship of heaven and the spirits of mountains, rivers, trees, and other aspects of nature. In ancient times it practiced human and animal sacrifices, and even today some ritual offerings to spirits and natural objects are made. Bon opposition to Buddhism continued for some centuries after the Dharma was accepted in Tibet, but such Bon practices as are followed today are intentionally incorporated into Tibetan Buddhism in order to preserve the ancient culture.

The strong central authority which made possible the introduction of Buddhism was established by the father of King Songtsan-Gampo. When Songtsan-Gampo, or Just-Powerful-Dignified, came to the throne in A.D. 642, he found it necessary to assert his authority by campaigning through his newly acquired kingdom which borders on China, Nepal, and India. As he traveled along his borders, he was attracted by the many reports he heard of the civilization of those countries. Finally, he set off on a military expedition to Nepal, where he was received by the king and given the daughter of the royal family in marriage. The new queen, a devout Buddhist, brought with her as part of her dowry an image of the Lord Buddha, and Songtsan built for her a great temple which is now popularly known as Jokhang, the House of the Lord Buddha.

Songtsan's next move was to send a group of Tibetan students to India to study Buddhism. Unfortunately, all of the first group died because of the burning heat of the plains, but of the second group which made its way through Kashmir to India, one member survived and returned to Tibet with many Sanskrit books. Aided by Indian and Chinese teachers, he invented for the Tibetan language a new script modeled upon the Western Gupta script of India and translated several Sutras from Sanskrit into Tibetan. It is possible that the celebrated sandalwood image of Avalokitesvara, the Lord of Compassion, which is now worshiped in the Potala, the Palace of the Dalai Lama, was originally brought to Tibet by the Indian teachers who helped make the early translations.

Tibet at this time was a warlike nation, and Songtsan's military power was so formidable that he compelled the Emperor of China to give him in marriage a lady belonging to the imperial court, Princess Water-Lotus. She, also, was a devout Buddhist and brought to Tibet the famous Buddha image now enshrined in the Temple of the Lord, the chief temple of Lhasa.

King Songtsan was a model ruler who built temples in almost every part of his empire during the thirty years of his reign. He was deeply concerned with the cultural development of the country, with social reforms, and the protection of his people. He prohibited killing as a sport and forbade the custom of painting the face with red paint which had been common in Tibet. He redistributed the land and pasturage of the country, encouraged agriculture, weaving, masonry, carpentry, painting, sculpture, and the manufacture of paper and ink for books. The king himself became a pupil of Thonmi, the man who had studied in India, and encouraged many people to become literate. He gave the people a new civil law, made Buddhism the state religion, and saw to it that Buddhist principles were widely taught.

The king is said to have instructed the people in Buddhism, encouraging honesty, humanitarian works, the living of a pure and simple life, respect for learning, and love of the motherland and one's fellow men. No wonder, then, that to the Tibetans he is not only their national hero but also the inspired founder of the nation, the giver of civilization and, above all, the living spiritual guide of Tibet. Memorial statues and portraits of this great ruler are found everywhere in temples, government offices, and private shrines, and he is worshiped as one of the incarnations of the Lord Avalokitesvara.

During the next few generations the kings of Tibet encouraged the translation of Sanskrit works into Tibetan. The scholars were well versed in Chinese and Sanskrit as well as the dialects of Kashmir and Nepal and by coining a number of new words were able to develop the rough Tibetan language into a polished and expressive literary medium.

The next great king who helped to lay the foundations of Buddhism in Tibet was King Trisong-Detsan, or Fair-Throne, Powerful-Key, who came to the throne in A.D. 765. He sent an envoy to China in search of scriptures and brought from India the great Indian teacher Santarakshita. Unfortunately, before Santarakshita could accomplish very much, an epidemic broke out in Tibet and the Bonists stirred up the people against Buddhism by alleging that the importation of a foreign religion and foreign teachers had provoked the wrath of the gods. The Bonists were aided by the powerful support of the king's uncle, a minister in the government, and their opposition was so strong that Santarakshita had to retire to Nepal and some temples were destroyed. Eventually the king and his supporters overcame the difficulty by sending the uncle to a distant place where he was assassinated, depriving the Bonists of their most powerful support.

When Santarakshita returned to Tibet, he suggested that the king invite the great tantric teacher Padmasambhava to Tibet because it was thought that he would make a strong appeal to the ritual-loving Tibetan people. Padmasambhava possessed great supernatural powers by means of which he is said to have subdued many powerful spirits. He was the founder of the Old Tantric school, or Old Translation school, now erroneously called the Red Hat Sect by Western scholars. He visited many parts of the country conferring tantric initiation and expounding tantric doctrines. As a compromise with Bonism, he incorporated many of its gods and goddesses into the lowest grade of tantric guardian deities. This did not, of course, in the least affect the doctrinal integrity of Buddhism. He replaced the Bon cult of animal sacrifice with symbolic worship and its practice of black magic with inner purification.

The higher aspects of tantric teachings were communicated to only a select few, including the king himself and some of his ministers and newly ordained monks who were considered to be sufficiently advanced in spiritual insight and psychic power. The Samye monastery, undoubtedly the greatest ever built in Tibet, was established at the suggestion of Padmasambhava, and Santarakshita officiated at the ceremony of laying the foundation. It contains many different shrines dedicated to various tantric deities and disciples of the Lord Buddha and has a large library of Sanskrit and Tibetan books.

Santarakshita and Padmasambhava collaborated in teaching the Tripitaka, the philosophy of the Yogacara system, and tantric teachings. The first seven Tibetans were ordained by Santarakshita according to the rules of the Theravada school, and after that many more young men joined the Order. Many scholars were engaged in translating the Tripitaka into Tibetan.

In the meantime, the envoy who had been sent to China and had been in retirement because of the Bon uprising handed over to the scholars the books he brought from China. Also at this time a Chinese monk, who belonged to the "abrupt" or Ch'an branch of Chinese Buddhism, began to teach the people a system of meditation which discarded all thoughts and actions and stressed the importance of annihilating all concepts whatsoever. This doctrine was inconsistent with Buddhist philosophy and ethics and led to the organization of a religious debate between the Chinese monk Kamalashila and a disciple of Santarakshita, who had been trained in dialectics at Nalanda. The debate aroused widespread interest and was attended by members of the royal family, scholars, and the common people of Tibet. Even before the most important part of the debate was reached, the Chinese monk was defeated and sent back to China.

The king then issued a decree that henceforth the people must follow the conservative system of the Sarvastivadins in monastic discipline, the Mahayana systems of Madhyamika and Yogacara in philosophy, and tantric doctrine in meditative practices. Thus came into existence the cooperation between Hinayana, Mahayana, and Tantrayana.

The establishment of official relations with Nalanda in India led to a series of visits from Indian scholars and visits of Tibetan scholars to Nalanda, which went on without intermission for four or five centuries. The people as a whole were convinced of the truth of Buddhism and of the sincerity of the efforts made on its behalf, and both people and scholars held the Indian pandits in high esteem. As soon as they had taken the noble teachings and profound philosophy of Buddhism into their hearts, the people of Tibet were transformed from great warriors and gallant fighters into peaceful religious devotees. Abandoning arms, they produced many great spiritual teachers, competent scholars, able linguists, and devout practicers of meditation. The scholars were masters not only of Tibetan lore but also of the rich Sanskrit literature.

The third king who made memorable efforts to further the consolidation of Buddhism in Tibet was King Repachen who ruled from 817 to 836. In the first year of his reign he called a Great Council which was attended by Indian and Tibetan scholars who discussed ways to propagate Buddhism in Tibet. As a result of that council a number of scholars cooperated in revising the language, inventing figures of speech, polishing the literary style, coining new words, accurately defining logical and philosophical terms, and formulating rules for writing and translating books. The result was the creation of an elegant and accurate language, replete with precise philosophical terms and beautiful figures of speech, thanks to which the perfect authenticity of the texts translated into Tibetan was now ensured. Sutras, Tantras, and the writings of Indian scholars were translated, as well as noncanonical literature dealing with astrology, medicine, poetry, drama, fiction, etymology, Sanskrit grammar, political science, and the art of invocation.

King Repachen also encouraged the spread of Buddhism by preaching, by the establishment of temples, monasteries, and libraries, and by supporting the Buddhist arts of painting and image making. However, just as the king's tremendous activities for the spread of Buddhism were reaching their climax, the great work received a terrible and unexpected setback. As a result of a Bonist conspiracy led by the minister Tiger-Nose and Yong-Bull, the king's elder brother, King Repachen was assassinated. Although the people themselves harbored no anti-Buddhist feeling, for by this time the Indian religion had gained the confidence of the great majority of Tibetans, the Bonists held power for five years until the king's brother was assassinated. After that, there were no more kings in Tibet whose influence for Buddhism was comparable to Songtsan-Gampo, Trisong-Detsan, and Repachen.

In the period of political disorder which followed the two assassinations, the monastic organizations quietly grew in strength, and at the same time there grew up an unorganized movement carried on by individual lay Buddhists who were followers of the Old Translation school. They not only invented doctrines of their own but claimed to be the discoverers of hidden literature which they said had been buried in various places by Padmasambhava. In addition, many non-Buddhist tantric teachers came from India and Kashmir and interpreted the tantric teachings literally, teaching the people that they might freely indulge in the enjoyment of wine and women. This, far from being a contribution to the cause of Buddhism, was in fact a definite disservice.

By the eleventh century, that state of affairs caused grave anxiety to the scholars of Tibet, so much so that they dedicated themselves wholeheartedly to the restoration of Buddhism. A special envoy was sent to Nalanda to persuade the great pandit, known to the Tibetans as Atisha, to come to their assistance. He arrived in A.D. 1042 and settled first at Tholing monastery, then lived at many other monasteries where Tibetan scholars from all over the country came to study with him. They found in Atisha an Indian pandit who was master of all forms of Buddhism and possessed deep spiritual insight. This combination of knowledge and insight, together with his serene and pleasant disposition, his admirable personality and, above all, his loving and compassionate heart, accounts for the success of his mission.

Atisha's first step toward the revival of Buddhism was the composition of a short treatise in Sanskrit which was translated and published widely. This work is a synthesis of the essential teachings of Hinayana, Mahayana, and Tantrayana, based on the conception of the one great Path consisting of various stages. At each stage a different spiritual principle reaches full development and serves as the foundation for the next stage. Human beings are classified as belonging to the elementary, intermediate, or advanced stages of the Path. In this scheme, the term *Hinayana* is used to describe the first stage, not in the derogatory sense of the "Little Vehicle," but in the sense of the necessary first stage, or *yana*, of the Path. Mahayana is the intermediate stage, and Tantrayana is the superior stage. Atisha pointed out that the practice of tantric doctrine should be undertaken only after passing through the previous stages of ethical training and philosophical reflection of Hinayana and Mahayana.

The actual practice of tantric doctrines, he maintained, was a purely spiritual activity. Consequently, the use of a female counterpart, or of intoxicants, or the resorting to tantric practices for worldly or selfish purposes, must be given up entirely. Atisha traveled far and wide teaching the simplest and most fundamental form of Buddhism, the taking of the Three Refuges, the observance of the ten golden precepts—which are protection of life, alms-giving, chastity, speaking the truth, spreading the Doctrine, mediating between enemies, contentment, love for all beings, holding right moral and philosophical views—the practice of self-sacrifice for others, and the development toward all beings of a love like that of a mother for her only child.

Atisha refused to give philosophical expositions to intellectually ambitious persons and would give them only the teaching about purity of heart and love. He encouraged the worship of the Bodhisattva Avalokitesvara and the Goddess Tara the Deliveress; he taught the repetition of their mantras, meditation, fasting, and living occasionally in silence. His system is known as the Three Stages—Hinayana, Mahayana, and Tantrayana, based primarily on the Tripitaka; and the Four Deities—the Lord Buddha, the Bodhisattva Avalokitesvara, the Goddess Tara, and the deity known as "The Immovable One." It was his view that every single teaching of the Lord Buddha must be realized for the attainment of Enlightenment.

Atisha's mission to Tibet is notable for the founding of the Kadampa school, which became the basis for the Gelukpa school and brought about in his time a higher standard of learning and a stricter observance of rules throughout the country. His mission is also notable for the inspiration which he brought to a great many scholars and spiritual masters in all schools of Buddhism and for rescuing the people of Tibet from the wrong practice of the Teaching. After remaining in Tibet for seventeen years the great pandit died in Nyethang monastery, where his tomb still stands. Today he is worshiped throughout the country as a living spiritual guide, and his works are even now widely read.

The great Buddhist renaissance in Tibet in the eleventh century is associated with the names of Atisha, Marpa, and Marpa's disciple, Milarepa. Although Marpa could not be called a follower of Atisha, he had studied with him at Nalanda and continued to teach in Tibet for some time after Atisha died. Marpa was the founder of the Kagyupa school, which is one of the major sects in Tibet today.

Marpa deplored the disputes concerning tantric doctrine which were so prominent in his day and resolved to become a master of Tantrayana. He studied first in Tibet, then on three different trips through Nepal visited India where he studied under 108 pandits. His most inspiring spiritual teacher was the great pandit Naropa, who had left Nalanda University to follow tantric practices in lonely places.

Marpa evolved a most effective method of training disciples which produced a great many scholars, preachers, hermits, and spiritual teachers who together formed the Kagyupa school, or the School of the Successive Order. The Kagyupa school does not attach much importance to learning the Tripitaka and the Prajnaparamita literature or to the monastic life with its strict moral discipline. Instead, it advocates the practice of the essential ethical precepts as the prerequisite to the practice of the actual tantric course which consists of both physical and mental training.

The tantric courses propagated by Marpa were known as the Four Acquired Orders. The first of the Four Acquired Orders is the method of acquiring an illusory body and of transferring the consciousness; it includes the art of dying and obtaining a good rebirth according to the teaching of the Guhyasamaja Tantra. The second Acquired Order is the method of acquiring the power of intuitively realizing the illusory nature of phenomenal existence and of controlling one's subconscious mind when in the dream state so as to overcome the illusory temptations which come in the intermediate state between death and the next life, and thus to take a good rebirth. This method also helps in one's spiritual advancement.

The third Acquired Order is the method of realizing the unobstructed emptiness of subjective and objective self-existence which, if it is practiced with the second method—the illusory body—is the actual means of attaining Enlightenment. The fourth Acquired Order is the method of the mysterious Kundalini, the thermal power of man, which can be used for the attainment of the power of intuitively realizing the Supreme Truth. This method also confers vigorous health, longevity, a brilliant complexion, bodily lightness, and an inexpressible joy beyond that of the senses.

Marpa's disciple Milarepa was asked to devote himself to spiritual practices in the wilderness and to take disciples after attaining realization. During the early part of his life Milarepa had experienced great sorrow. His paternal aunt and uncle refused to hand over the property which his father, shortly before his death, had entrusted to their care. Milarepa's mother, unable to endure the insults and treachery of these relations, resolved to take revenge by sending her son to learn the art of black magic. So proficient did Milarepa become in these studies that he was able to destroy thirty-seven of his enemies, excluding the aunt and uncle, by causing their houses to collapse. This act of violence awakened his sleeping conscience, and in fear of the inevitable consequences of the law of karma he sought the path of peace, solace, and spiritual freedom. So agonizing was his sense of guilt and so strong his spiritual aspiration that he did not allow a moment to pass without thinking of deliverance from mundane existence.

Marpa, his spiritual master, made him undergo terrible ordeals for years before giving him so much as a word of teaching. Eventually, however, he received the necessary instructions, initiations, and directions and thereafter spent years in the wilderness practicing the severe self-mortifications specifically prescribed for him. Later he preached the Dharma among the people, enlightened many disciples, and became the most famous poet-saint that the Land of Snow had ever seen. His chief disciples did tremendous work in spreading the teachings of the Kagyupa school by means of preaching, writing, and establishing monasteries. They in turn had many disciples, some of whom created the subsects of the Kagyupa school.

The many subsects of the Kagyupa school were created because of the establishment in different monasteries of different teachers, each with his own methods and his own instructions for the practice of the Doctrine. In spite of the differences in details, they taught in common the realization of the transitoriness of beings and the world; cultivation of the thought of deliverance; the importance of leading a purposeful and creative life with a pure mind and unselfish motive; recollection of the effects of the law of karma; faith in the doctrine of Enlightenment; development of right understanding, concentration, meditation, compassion, and love like that of a mother; and the practice of yoga together with the double comprehension of the emptiness (sunyata) of all beings and phenomena. They recommended to the laity such humanitarian works as building temples and maintaining religious institutions; they encouraged carving images, painting thang-kas—the pictures which serve as the object of meditation—and building mani-walls on which the six-syllabled mantra, *Om Mani Padme Hum,* is inscribed.

Another influential school which started in the eleventh century was the Sakya school—so called because its first monastery, founded in A.D. 1071, was built on a patch of gray-colored earth (*sa-kya*) and therefore known as the Gray Earth Monastery. The school was started by Koncho Gyepo Khon, a married teacher who was deeply disturbed by the debaucheries indulged in by followers of the Old Translation school and the corrupting influence of the yogins from India and Kashmir. While the Kagyu schools primarily emphasized meditation, the Sakya school from the beginning laid great stress upon the systematic study of Buddhist literature in order that the course of spiritual practice should bring about a perfect realization that would not be confused with mere development of the natural powers of the physical body or of the lower mental faculties. The Sakya school gained a high reputation for learning and for authentic spiritual attainment, which is the reason its hierarchy later found itself in a position of political power.

By 1220 the teachings of the Sakya school had spread through all of Tibet even though the country was divided politically into small kingdoms. Its leader at this time was the great Kunga-Gyetsan, a most outstanding scholar in Buddhist literature, logic, philosophy, and Sanskrit as well as a master of the non-Buddhist philosophies of the Brahmans and the Jains. With his great knowledge of the non-Buddhist systems he was able to defeat a Brahman philosopher in debate by disproving the six theses of the Hindu school of logic, thus converting the

Brahman to Buddhism by means of the right method of argument. He was able to lay a firm foundation for the revival of the Dharma by demonstrating in this way the purity, authenticity, and correctness of the Buddhist position.

When the Mongol army invaded Tibet, Kunga-Gyetsan was invited to Mongolia by Godan, in 1247. Thanks to his scholarship, spiritual insight, and effective propaganda he soon gained great influence over the Mongol king and people, and as a result close ties were established between Mongolia and Tibet. He was accompanied on his visit to the Mongols by his nephew Phakpa, a most brilliant and talented personality who inherited the learning and noble qualities of his uncle and became an outstanding scholar. Kublai Khan was so satisfied with Phakpa's teaching that the Great Khan invited him to the imperial court and appointed him the first Imperial Preceptor and gave him authority over all of Tibet. Thus Phakpa became the first Lama sovereign of the country, which by this time had been reunited under the Mongol army with the Sakya monastery as the headquarters for the central government. Despite the Great Khan's request that he should declare the Sakyapa system as the state religion and suppress all other schools, Phakpa was so tolerant of differing views that he declared instead that there should be complete freedom to follow any of the systems included within the mighty framework of Buddhism. During this time a new impetus was given to Tibetan Buddhism and standards of learning were raised in every branch of Buddhist literature and art.

Although the political power of the Sakya hierarchy came to an end in A.D. 1326, the office was hereditary and his successors were able to maintain their religious prestige and preserve their estates. Since he is the descendant of the first Lama King of Tibet, the head of the Sakya monastery today holds an official rank equal to that of the Regent and enjoys the rare privilege of riding in a palanquin. These hierarchs are reported to possess great authority over lesser, wilder goddesses, as well as over female spirit-mediums. Doctrinally, the Sakya school is based on a synthesis of the Tripitaka called "The Course of the Path and Fruition," and on the Chatur Tantra of the New

Translation school which incorporates one or two Tantras of the Old Translation school, but interprets them in its own way.

The most remarkable achievement of the Sakya school was the compilation of the scriptures of Tibetan Buddhism, the Kagyur and the Tangyur, in 329 volumes. This great work was done in the fourteenth century, based on a catalog compiled in the eighth century.

By the middle of the fourteenth century, four schools had arisen in Tibetan Buddhism. The Old Translation school (*Nyingmawa*), which started with Santarakshita and Padmasambhava, had continued to exist, but with no marked increase in influence. The Kadampa school founded by Atisha had declined in importance during these years, but Atisha's teachings were not forgotten. The Kagyupa school of Marpa and Milarepa was still strong, even though it had divided into many subsects throughout the land. The Sakya school, which had enjoyed political power under the Mongols, had ceased to rule. There was a period of internal political strife in the fourteenth century, and Buddhism declined. But with the coming of Tsongkhapa and his establishment of the Gelukpa school—a reformation of Atisha's Kadampa school—Buddhism was destined to rise once and for all throughout the whole country.

According to Tibetan tradition, the name, monastery, and activities of Tsongkhapa had been foretold by the Lord Buddha. He was born in 1357 and spent his youth visiting different monasteries, studying with most of the scholars of every school. He studied the literature of all the different forms of Buddhism, especially the numerous tantric treatises, the systems of ritual and symbolism, medicine, astrology, and Sanskrit. He mastered all these subjects and received the degree of Doctor of Literature and Philosophy. His search for the correct interpretation of the Madhyamika philosophy obliged him to make a thorough examination of all the relevant scriptural texts and other treatises in Tibetan and Sanskrit and to embark on a course of deep meditation and other spiritual practices. While engaged in those studies and practices he had many visions of deities and developed various spiritual faculties which he regarded as the unavoidable manifestations of one's innate power prior to the perfect realization of the Supreme Reality. With the help of inspiring instructions which he received from the Lord Manjusri, the Bodhisattva of Supreme Wisdom, Tsong-khapa found the attainment of Reality within his reach.

Whatever Tsongkhapa wrote on any subject is precise and accurate, clear in expression, and profound in meaning. His beautiful literary style is unique in Tibetan literature. His practical teaching is extremely systematic, with graded courses embodying the teachings of the three stages of development. He restored the teachings of Atisha which had been neglected for a long time. In order to establish firmly the reformed faith, Tsongkhapa built the Gadan monastery as the spiritual seat of the Gelukpa, the "New Kadampa," school. As the Gelukpa school grew, the disciples built many monastic institutions which were non-tantric in character, known as monasteries which uphold the moral discipline of the Tripitaka, and the two great monastic colleges of Lhasa in which the Tantras are studied and practiced. All these educational institutions are well equipped with the necessary libraries, meeting halls, gardens, and living quarters.

Tsongkhapa insisted upon a thorough study of Buddhist and non-Buddhist literature, but he emphasized that study should not be separated from strict maintenance of monastic discipline and concentration and meditation. He felt that the vigorous practice of meditation, as followed by the Kagyupa school, should not be undertaken without full knowledge of the entire subject, including the experiences likely to occur. He also gave the correct, symbolic interpretation of many Sutras and Tantras, since the literal interpretation of the Tantras had led to wrong practices such as the use of a Sakti or female counterpart, indulgence in sensual pleasures, and the vulgarization of the Tantras for selfish and worldly purposes. The possession of noble moral qualities and the power of controlling the mind were made conditions for receiving instruction and initiation in the tantric teachings. His critics, among whom were some of the best scholars of the time, were silenced after reading his writings and eventually accepted his purified and reformed teaching. Unlike the leaders of the Sakyapa, he never strove for sectarian gains or power.

For some time after Tsongkhapa the Gelukpa school continued to grow throughout Tibet and Mongolia. Once in 1578 and again in 1587 the third Grand Lama of the Gelukpa school went to Mongolia at the invitation of the ruler and converted many of the people of Mongolia to Buddhism. It was there that he was given the title Dalai or "Ocean Wide," by which the incarnate Lama of the Gelukpa school has been known ever since. From that time on, many Gelukpa scholars visited Mongolia and established monasteries, and many Mongolian Buddhists came to Lhasa to study. The fourth incarnation of the Dalai Lama took place in Mongolia, and this was the immediate cause for the strong support which was given later to the fifth incarnation.

As the Gelukpa school grew in importance in Tibet and Mongolia, the oppression of the Gelukpas by the sectarian Red Hat Kagyupa sect became very serious. They were aided by the King of Tsang, the central province of Tibet, until the young fifth incarnation of the Grand Lama sought the help of the Goci Khan. He came to the rescue in 1641 by bringing the Mongol army into Tibet and defeating the petty chieftains and the King of Tsang. After uniting the whole country, he placed the fifth Dalai Lama at the head of the new central government, thus forming the Gelukpa hierarchy and establishing the autocratic and theocratic form of government in Tibet.

The Great Fifth, as he is known in Tibet, after gaining both temporal power and spiritual authority over the whole of Tibet, governed the country through his able prime minister who was a good scholar and astrologer and a capable statesman. It was he who first organized the revenue system by establishing branches of the administration in the provinces, and he also built the famous Red Palace which is still the palace and spiritual abode of the Dalai Lama. The fifth Dalai Lama was a devout follower of the Old Translation school at the same time that he was the Grand Lama of the Gelukpa school. After the Mongol victory he honored his tutor by appointing him the

Head of Tashi Lhunpo monastery near Shigatse and reserving for his exclusive use the honorary title of pandit, or panchen. For this reason the incarnations of this tutor are known as the Panchen Lama.

Since the seventeenth century Buddhism has been the state religion of Tibet with the Dalai Lama as the head of the hierarchy and the government. Buddhism from Tibet has continued in Bhutan, Ladhak, and in Sikkim, where the hereditary head of the religious organization is a descendant of the former kings of Tibet. Many monasteries exist, but they have been reduced to maintaining simple devotional and ritualistic aspects of Buddhism. Bonism still retains a strong hold among the Bhutanese, Ladhakis, and Sikkimese, and the revival of Buddhism there is an urgent need.

Until the Russian occupation of Outer Mongolia, Gelukpa monasteries were flourishing under the direction of the Grand Lama of Urga, all students came to Lhasa to complete their studies, the Tibetan scriptures had been translated into Mongolian, and the spiritual ties between Tibet and Mongolia were strong. Nowadays Outer Mongolia is under the Russians, and Inner Mongolia is under the Chinese Communists, and no new students come to Tibet from Mongolia.

In modern Tibet there are three chief sects. The largest is the Gelukpa school—sometimes called the Yellow Hat Sect by Westerners—which began with Atisha and was restored by Tsongkhapa and is the sect of the Dalai Lama. Next in size is the Old Translation school, which goes back to the time of Santarakshita and Padmasambhava. The third in size is the Kagyupa school, which goes back to Marpa and is represented today by several subsects.

Brief mention should be made of some of the subsects of the Kagyupa school which are found in Tibet today. The successive incarnations of the founder of the Karma Kagyu have continued to the present day, and the present incarnation occupies a high position in the Lama hierarchy. This sect introduced the practice, still very popular in Tibet, of telling instructive stories to the people with the aid of illustrated scrolls. The stories are told in a slow, gentle voice, and the mantra of Avalokitesvara, Om Mani Padme Hum, is recited. The Karma Kagyu followers are distinguished by the red caps which they wear and thus are known as the Red Hat Karmapa. Owing to their sectarian spirit they became antagonistic to the flourishing Gelukpa—so-called Yellow Hat—school and constantly sought to suppress it through the help of the King of Tsang over whom they exercised great influence. This was the cause of the decline of both the Kingdom of Tsang and the Red Hat Kagyu. Today some of the Karmapa monasteries are indistinguishable from those of the Old Translation school since they lost their individual character and distinctive moral, philosophical, and spiritual teachings long ago. The term *Red Hat*, used for the Old Translation school by Western scholars, is misleading and should be given up.

The Dukpa Kagyu school got its name from the fact that on the day its first monastery was consecrated a thunderclap (*duk*) was heard. This sect became the chief one in Bhutan— the Tibetan name for Bhutan is derived from the name of this sect—and continues there to the present.

The Dikhung Kagyu school is centered at a monastery a few miles northeast of Lhasa where they have two incarnate Lamas and a considerable number of monks. Many mountain hermitages were built for the hundreds of contemplatives who practiced a system of yoga derived from the Six Doctrines of Naropa. The more advanced yogins immure themselves in their caves for life with the walls and windows plastered over, with only a small hole in each left open to admit food and air. This is the only Kagyu school which continues to maintain a high standard in the practice of meditation. On a recent occasion a noted yogin of this sect was found to possess the extraordinary spiritual power of multiplying and transforming his personality, as well as transferring himself to distant places in a second. He could read the thoughts of others, and gave symbolical instructions and predicted the future. The stories of his mysterious control over the forces of nature would be sufficient to fill a volume.

Two other sects have had some influence on Tibetan Buddhism. The Jonang school taught tantric courses such as that emphasizing the Wheel of Time, but its philosophy was not in any way in accordance with Buddhism, being strongly under the influence of Hindu Vedanta. It was spread by Taranatha, the great scholar and historian. Today this school has no separate followers.

The other school is the Shiche or Pacification school. By pacification is meant the allaying of the sorrows of the terrestrial and the celestial spheres by the practice of psychological disciplines based on the Prajnaparamita literature. Its founder was the Indian pandit Pha-Dampa, as the Tibetans called him, who visited Tibet many times and China once. He received instruction on the Prajnaparamita Sutra from six different sources, one of which was a revelation from the Lord Maitreya, the Buddha yet to come. His method aimed chiefly at the philosophical understanding and spiritual realization of the Prajnaparamita. He also gave various tantric teachings to his numerous Tibetan followers, most of whom were either noted saints or spiritually advanced persons.

Pha-Dampa's special teaching is known as "the cessation of the false notion of the independent ego." To his male followers he taught the masculine cessation, and to his female followers he taught the feminine cessation. Its most essential teaching is the combination of wisdom and compassion with the creative thought of Enlightenment. The actual practice consists of the transference of one's consciousness to the personal deity and the brief practice of yoga, followed by the consecration, purification, and transformation of one's own body—imagined to be lying dead—into various divine foods which are then offered to one's spiritual master, the gods, the Buddha, and lastly to the spirits. At the same time one analyzes the nature of the ego and meditates upon its unreality and upon the ultimate identity of oneself and others. This practice is popular among all schools, who follow it according to their own conception of the ego-nature.

THE DALAI LAMA

For nearly three centuries the Dalai Lama has been the supreme temporal and spiritual power in Tibet. The present

Dalai Lama is the fourteenth in succession. Tibetans and Mongolians alike look upon him as being anxious to protect them from external enemies and injustices and as being their living Buddha—the one who will help them realize the Buddha and the Bodhisattva ideals. He is honored by all; all put their whole-hearted faith in him; and all love him more dearly than anything else. To the Tibetans the Dalai Lama is not just a ruler or a teacher but a father, guide, protector, and above all, the great Bodhisattva. His words act upon them like magic, while his personality is so holy, so serene, and so forceful that they are thrilled and deeply moved whenever they happen to be in his presence. For his sake they are prepared to make any sacrifice. He is the unifying force of the country and as such is unmatched by any other spiritual teacher.

The Dalai Lama is looked upon as the incarnation of the Bodhisattva Avalokitesvara. According to certain of the twenty-one Sutras of Avalokitesvara—which were the first scriptures to be translated into Tibetan—the Bodhisattva Avalokitesvara made a solemn vow that instead of entering Nirvana he would remain in the world and help sentient beings attain the highest goal. In the Manjusri Mulatantra there is a prediction that Avalokitesvara will appear in the form of kings, spiritual masters, scholars, ministers, craftsmen, and as the followers of various trades and professions. The end of the power of the Tibetan kings and the appearance of rulers who are monks —these being the Dalai Lamas—is clearly mentioned in this prediction.

The Panchen Lama, who spiritually speaking is the second greatest Lama in the land, is known as the spiritual son, while the Dalai Lama is known as the father. This is because from the religious point of view the Dalai Lama is the master and the Panchen Lama is his disciple. Although the Panchen Lama is the head of the Tashi Lhunpo monastery, he possesses no authority over the religious or civil affairs of the country, and his official position is less important than that of the Regent of Tibet. The high regard and respect accorded the Panchen Lama by the people is indicative of their broad-minded and sincere devotion to religion.

The more than 3,000 monks of Tashi Lhunpo monastery, the followers of the Panchen Lama, are very well off in comparison with the monks in other monasteries, getting allotments twenty times as great as those given to the others. They are not dependent upon charity, but are provided for by the estates donated by the government of Tibet. Forgetting all their immunities and privileges, however, some of the followers of the Panchen Lama adopted, some years ago, a truculent attitude and refused to accept even the modified form of taxation imposed by the thirteenth Dalai Lama and sought to gain independence for their monastery. The politically innocent, pure, holy, and simple-minded Panchen Lama, who could not control his followers, was compelled to flee to China. Since then, relations between the Dalai Lama and the Panchen Lama have deteriorated.

The present Panchen Lama is the ninth in succession and was selected jointly by the former National Government of China and the followers of the exiled Panchen Lama. The Tibetans wanted to make the selection according to their own religious tradition which involves a complicated system of checks and counterchecks, but since they were unable to follow this method for recognizing an incarnate Lama, they question the genuineness of the Panchen Lama.

The Dalai Lama is discovered by the united efforts of gods and men, according to the traditional system, and after receiving his education and spiritual training is entrusted with supreme power by the Great National Assembly and the religious and social organizations of the people. As the temporal and spiritual ruler he is a great unifying force, the inspiring teacher and beloved leader of the whole country.

To Tibetans the discovery of a new Dalai Lama is of vital importance for their material and spiritual well-being. The unity and sovereignty of the state depend upon the selection of the right person for their temporal and spiritual ruler. The process of selection is therefore extremely complicated and carefully checked. It rests chiefly on divine guidance given through visions and oracular predictions in which the physical characteristics, moral and spiritual qualities, and abnormal powers of the true candidate are clearly indicated. The first step is to find out from the State Oracle the locality in which the Dalai Lama has reincarnated. As soon as this important fact is known, search parties, which have been selected by lot or by the State Oracle, are sent out. On the basis of their reports the government draws up a list of possible candidates. In the meantime, the Regent of Tibet visits the sacred lake believed to be the abode of the Goddess Kali—for she appeared to the first Dalai Lama and solemnly vowed to watch over all his successors—and there he sees in the depths of the lake a vision indicating the location of the Dalai Lama's new birthplace.

In the case of the present Dalai Lama the vision seen by the late Regent Rading Rinpoche was, it is said, as clear as a movie film, showing not only the locality in which the reincarnation had taken place but the very house. In the second phase of the search the State Oracle gave the names of the parents and the district in which the child was to be found—and these directions coincided with those given by the Regent.

The searching mission disguised themselves as ordinary pilgrims and made their way into Amdo Province in China, and when they found the house they asked for lodging. When the boy turned up, he greeted the men with joy as if he were meeting some of his old followers. He pointed to one of the disguised men and identified him as a monk officer and to another and called him a lay officer, using the Tibetan language which none of his family could speak. The Lama who headed the mission then placed around his own neck two rosaries, one which had belonged to the late Dalai Lama and another which was an imitation. Without hesitation the boy snatched off the genuine one. He then selected the genuine walking stick and drum when they were shown to him, and, holding the stick in his left hand and the rosary and drum in his right, he recited the six-syllabled mantra of Avalokitesvara and retired.

The mission was deeply impressed by the manly character and intelligence of the child as well as by his power of bringing back memories of the past at such an early age. A confidential report was at once sent to the government. It was found that the mission's description of the locality, of the size and shape of the house, and even the color of the red dog there, tallied exactly with the vision seen by the Regent at the lake.

However, complications were caused by an omen which occurred at Lhasa. The horses of the late Dalai Lama galloped to the residence of the Prime Minister whose niece had just given birth to a son. According to the omen-loving people the gods had driven them there in order to indicate that the Dalai Lama had reincarnated in that particular family. At a secret ceremony, attended only by the Regent and the ministers, the State Oracle was asked to exhibit on his own body the sacred signs borne by the Guardian Deity who uses him as a mouth-piece. The Oracle, who was of course in a state of trance, thereupon took off his heavy golden helmet and showed on his head the mark of a sceptre. As another test, a paper containing the questions which the ministers wished to ask the Oracle was given to him rolled up in a scroll so that he could not read them. All the questions were answered point by point in ele-gant phrases such as the Oracle himself would have been quite incapable of composing. On this occasion the Guardian Deities disclosed that the boy at Amdo was the real Dalai Lama, they told his age, the names of his parents, and foretold his success-ful installation.

By way of an additional check, at a brief religious ceremony conducted by specially invited incarnate Lamas, lots were drawn in front of a sacred image of the Buddha. Out of the names of the numerous candidates, the boy's name was chosen. Thus all possible methods of ensuring the right choice were used.

According to Tibetan belief, the selection and installation of the right person is possible only by the combined efforts of men, gods, and Bodhisattvas. Good will among men and a variety of large-scale religious ceremonies are also essential to the success of the undertaking. Throughout the land the gov-ernment and the people held prayers and performed special rites to guide the selection. The whole procedure may be de-scribed as the spiritual election of the spiritual and temporal ruler of a theocratic state, the holy land of Tibet where the lives of men are dominated and shaped by spiritual forces.

Although the mission in Amdo had kept the selection a secret, General Matushi, the Chinese Governor of Chinghai in
whose territory the boy's family lived, suspected his identity
and demanded a ransom of several hundred thousand rupees
which the Tibetan government was obliged to pay. It was not
until they reached Tibet that the child was publicly declared to
be the real Dalai Lama. At every stage of his progress to Lhasa
grand receptions were accorded him by the government and
the people, and he entered Lhasa in the longest procession the
country had ever seen.

After the successful completion of the installation ceremonies the young Dalai Lama was placed in the care of a
picked band of monk officers with a great Incarnate Lama as
his teacher. His program of studies is much the same as that
prescribed for other incarnate Lamas. The daily routine gradually comes to include lessons twice daily, committing to memory a large number of texts, practicing calligraphy, and peri-
odic prayer and meditation. Later on, after he was ordained a
novice, his studies were intensified, and he received the orally
transmitted instructions for the understanding and practice of
the Tantras. After passing the final test in the five subjects he
can assume the title of Doctor of Literature and Philosophy—
Geshe—and then devote himself to the study of the Tantrayana.
When he obtains initiation into all the tantric traditions, which
involves the practice of many daily meditations and a three-
month retreat every year, he is hailed as the Master of the
School of Wisdom and Holder of the Wheel of the Buddha
Dharma.

As spiritual and temporal ruler of Tibet the Dalai Lama
personally propagates Buddhism in general and the teaching of
the Gelukpa school in particular. He governs the country
through an advisory council of ministers and secretaries and
directly appoints the civil administrators and military officers.
Generally speaking, every government department is run by
monk officials and lay officials working in collaboration. Monk
officials do not represent a particular monastery nor are they
necessarily under the Vinaya rules. But, if they should decide
to marry, they must become lay officials.

Justice is administered by three joint civil and criminal courts. Judgments in criminal cases are delivered in accordance with the proclamations of the previous Dalai Lamas and in civil suits in accordance with the merits of the case. Appeals can be made to the Dalai Lama. Capital punishment and extreme mutilation were abolished by the thirteenth Dalai Lama.

The Greater and Lesser National Assemblies are made up of representatives of various grades of officials, monasteries, the military, craftsmen, and other sections of society. They meet only when called upon by the government to discuss measures of outstanding national importance. Final decision is taken by the Dalai Lama in accordance with the recommendations of the National Assembly. During the absence of the Dalai Lama, the National Assembly is responsible for the appointment of the Regent, the choice being made by lot.

The central government is concerned primarily with the education, health, and spiritual requirements of the Dalai Lama, these being regarded as supremely important. In addition, the government deals with such matters as the maintenance of religious institutions, the safeguarding of political independence, keeping down the cost of living, and the preservation of the distinctive culture, social life, and religious traditions of the country.

LAMAS

The Buddhists of Tibet believe that the Buddha has continued to function in the world even after his passing into Nirvana and that, as he assured his followers, he will reappear as a Bodhisattva in innumerable worlds in order to help and to liberate living beings. To the Tibetans the Buddha is not only the supreme teacher but he is also their main support in their efforts to attain the final goal. There are, therefore, numerous Bodhisattvas who choose to remain with beings and share their sufferings in order to show them the true path to liberation. Such Bodhisattvas may be either recognized or unrecognized. In the recognized group belong the incarnate Lamas, the developed or nonincarnate Lamas, and those Bodhisattvas who, although they have acquiesced to the Great Compassion, have not yet acquired the actual state of Bodhisattvahood. The unrecognized Bodhisattvas are those living in various countries where they are destined to alleviate the sufferings of the people and reveal to them the principle of the Law without being recognized as Bodhisattvas.

The highest of all incarnate Lamas, after the Dalai Lama, are those who are possible candidates for the Regency of Tibet. Each of these incarnate Lamas has his own private residence and estates which are managed by selected monks of his own monastery, and each is the head of a prominent monastery. Nearly every monastery in Tibet has an incarnate Lama or Lamas, most of whom are ranked as a Great Incarnation or Middle Incarnation or Lesser Incarnation by the Dalai Lama when he approves their selection as a true incarnation. The Monastic College Incarnations are those who are recognized by their own school and hold no official rank nor approval from the Dalai Lama.

A thorough search for newborn babies who might be incarnate Lamas is made in the directions indicated by the Dalai Lama, the Great Lamas, or oracles. Information is collected regarding the manner of birth, the parentage, the special traits of the candidate, and any unusual signs which might have occurred. This information is then submitted to one of the small number of most highly venerated oracles and to an eminent Lama to determine which of the candidates is the incarnation. The facts of the case are then presented to the Dalai Lama for his decision. As soon as a candidate is recognized as the new incarnation, he will, if he is more than six years old, be taken from his home in a procession and installed in his residence, which may be either inside or outside his monastery. He is cared for by monk attendants, and his personal tutor, who takes the place of the child's father, closely superintends his education and spiritual guidance.

After receiving the lower ordination from the head of the monastery or a high Lama, the young incarnation enters upon the monastic life with great ceremony. He must devote himself seriously to the study of the five principal subjects of his course, which includes memorizing all the basic texts, and many prayers and invocations. He must attend the public debates and the congregational prayers and can give time to subjects not in his regular course only as a sideline. The minimum time in which a clever and diligent student can complete the whole course is thirteen years. No examination is held, but the candidates must appear at a special public disputation which is witnessed by all the Geshes—men recognized as Doctors of the Law. If he comes out successfully from this battle of wits, the student takes up a new subject and continues to review his former work. When an incarnate Lama passes the final contest, he must give a great feast for the college in which he has studied, even if it is necessary to beg the money to meet the huge expense. The chief purpose in giving the very expensive feast is to honor the congregation by making a material sacrifice which indicates the virtue of almsgiving, and, by rejoicing in that sacrifice, to have shown two of the essentials for the attainment of spiritual perfection.

The course of study is regarded as a source of spiritual inspiration and right understanding which will help in the realization of the Supreme Truth—not as a mere cultural training. After taking the degree in literature and philosophy the student must join one of the two tantric monastic colleges of Lhasa to study the vast literature and enormous ritual system of the Tantras. There, under a very strict monastic discipline, the day is fully occupied with study and congregational ceremonies. It is possible for an incarnate Lama to remain all his life in a tantric college, but most of them withdraw after having reached a high level of attainment.

Monks

Under these incarnate Lamas, who are highly respected and honored by all the people, are many thousands of monks who have voluntarily adopted the monastic life. The vows of a monk (monks are called *drapa* or *gedunpa*) are ordinarily for life, but if a monk should decide to leave the monastery he can go to the Lama who is his spiritual teacher and have him recite the mantras, the powerful words, which will release him from his vows. Such an action is not generally approved in Tibet.

After being admitted to a monastery, the monks have to undergo a course of training designed to eradicate what is morally and spiritually wrong and to inculcate a spirit of self-control. This training is generally imparted by the personal teacher of each monk, some of whom are rather tactless and overstrict. Junior monks must perform such services as sweeping the building, drawing water, carrying loads, constructing buildings, and serving food to the congregation. There are three stages—lay devotee, novice, and monk. A monk must observe 253 precepts; a fully ordained nun has to observe 364 precepts.

The study of Buddhist literature and philosophy is confined to the monasteries, and even there it is within the reach of only an intellectually and spiritually gifted minority. There are three types of monastic colleges—those which give instruction in the Tripitaka, those which give instruction in tantric literature and practices, and those which are hermitages for the practice of meditation. The five basic subjects of study for a monk are logic, the Prajnaparamita literature, the rules of monastic discipline (*Vinaya*), Madhyamika literature, and the Abhidharma. Each student monk studies with his own selected teacher besides being under the general supervision of the master of discipline. Basic texts are learned by heart. Daily classes are held in the residence of the tutor with discussion following the explanation, and congregational argumentation takes place almost daily in the monastery gardens. This combination of memorizing, explanation, discussion, and public argumentation is a most effective, constructive, and practical method of attaining proficiency in scholarship. In addition, the monk scholars are encouraged to take up additional subjects in which there are no examinations, such as painting, sculpture, carpentry, sewing, and embroidery.

Fifteen to twenty years must be devoted to the study of Buddhist literature and commentaries. A monk who completes the course of study and successfully passes the public examination is given the title of Geshe, or Doctor in Literature and

Philosophy, and permitted to go on to one of the tantric colleges for study. There he prepares for an examination in tantric literature, ritual, and the making of colored diagrams for the mandalas (thang-kas) which are used as an object of meditation. In addition, he must practice meditation for months and years and then must either retire to a hermitage or spend his time in teaching or preaching to the masses.

In this manner Tibet produces many spiritual masters. Some are incarnate Lamas, some are learned monks, and some are spiritual geniuses—self-developed Bodhisattvas. Monks are given a favored position in society, and respect is shown them by offering them food, money, and other necessities. But the highest honors go to the incarnate Lamas and spiritual geniuses who are the incarnate Bodhisattvas and the self-developed Bodhisattvas of Tibet.

The administration of the monasteries is carried on by the less scholarly senior monks who have shown ability in administrative and financial affairs. The head of each monastery is appointed by the Dalai Lama on the recommendation of its council of senior monks, and he in turn appoints the other officers of the monastery. Social services are not the responsibility of the monasteries, but are rendered by the monks as individuals as part of their practice of the Bodhisattva ideal.

The monk doctors who give medical treatment and dispense medicines receive their training in the two medical colleges of Lhasa and in another college where astronomy and astrology are also taught. The medical system, which owes its origin to the Ayurvedic system of India, was further developed in Tibet until it now takes many years to complete the medical course of study. Medicines are manufactured from fruits, meat extracts, certain internal organs, plants, herbs, metals, powdered precious stones, and wine. Certain pills are ritually consecrated before being given to patients.

Tibet is the Land of Religion where thousands of monks perform the religious exercises and spiritual practices by which they render benevolent service to all beings and seek to attain the summit of Enlightenment.

LAYMEN

In Tibet there are very many oracles who are consulted whenever it is necessary to know something of the future. Rarely are oracles monks; most of them are laymen and a few are laywomen. An oracle is a person who in a trance is connected with a particular spirit or deity and is able to predict future events.

The Tibetan people are highly respectful toward religion, for they regard it as the means for the realization of Enlightenment. Religion is for them the source of their culture, of the intellectual and spiritual illumination which has come to them. Every activity is connected with religion, whether it is a social gathering, leave-taking, building a new house, taking a new government post, concluding a business deal—all occasions of good or bad fortune are preceded by some kind of religious ceremony. Individual devotions are performed morning and evening in one's private shrine, which is decorated with images, offerings of flowers, perpetually burning lamps, and scented or pure water. Books are considered to be more sacred than images, for, while images are only objects of recollection, books impart to us the Teaching. A private library usually consists of a complete set of Buddhist literature in more than 330 volumes.

Both monks and laymen use the thang-ka—which is sometimes called a mandala—as an aid to meditation. It is a picture of a Buddha or Bodhisattva, surrounded by other Bodhisattvas or guardian deities arranged in the form of a diagram which represents the universe, and decorated with symbols designed to aid recollection. In meditation the pictures serve as the object of concentration, and in the higher meditation the devotee concentrates on the higher nature of the deities pictured on the thang-ka.

The recitation of mantras is also prescribed for monks and laymen. A mantra is a word or series of words through which spiritual power is exercised. Some mantras are prescribed in the scriptures for getting good memory or for avoiding misfortune; the most important use is as an aid in concentration. Some mantras, like the six-syllabled mantra of Avalokitesvara, Om

Mani Padme Hum, refer to a particular deity, and the recitation of such a mantra is the calling upon that deity. In Tantrayana, mantras are sometimes used for obtaining spiritual powers.

The prayer wheel is a means of repeating the mantras. Thousands of mantras are written and put in the center of the wheel after having been consecrated by rituals performed by Lamas; the turning of the wheel is the same as the recitation of the mantras. Often the mantras are also recited as the wheel is turned. The turning of the wheel by the wind or a water mill is a continuation of the recitation of the mantras in the wheel. Prayer flags are sometimes Bonist, but when used as a Buddhist devotion the flag has a mantra written on it, and as it blows in the wind it continues the recitation of the mantra.

Three days in every month, including the full-moon days, are holy days on which the people abstain from meat and observe the eight precepts. During the month which commemorates the birth, enlightenment, and passing away of the Buddha —usually in May—no meat is sold and everyone is a vegetarian. There are many festivals throughout the year, such as Sanctification Days, National Day at New Year time, and the big feast which comes after the monks have completed the rainy-season retreat. Bonist ceremonies, which are not associated with Buddhism, are performed by groups of laymen who put on monastic robes. They are presided over by astrologers who perform the ceremonies to propitiate the gods, subdue spirits, avert the evil influences of the constellations, ward off hail, bring luck, and produce rain. Monks regularly perform ceremonies based on the Sutras, and on Tantras which consist of a review of the essential moral and philosophical teachings of the scriptures, followed by a solemn resolve to practice the Bodhisattva ideal. Such ceremonies end with the dedication to all beings of the merits accruing from their performance.

As a result of their deep devotion to religion the Tibetans emphasize the importance of loyalty and trustworthiness. These qualities inspire the community and give a religious significance to social life. Straightforwardness, usefulness, and humility are the qualities favored by Tibetans. Material and moral loss and defeat are regarded as the consequences of one's past evil deeds for which one must accept responsibility. In the daily practice of their religion, the Tibetans seek to practice self-restraint, patience, and self-purification by acting in accordance with the law of karma. To be benevolent and generous in all their activities is their ideal.

Neither the monk nor the layman can attain Enlightenment by himself, however diligent he may be. Everyone must have a spiritual teacher, a guru, a noble and qualified teacher, whose precious instructions are followed with humble submission, wholehearted faith, and solemn resolve. By this means one is inspired and helped to acquire the intellectual and spiritual qualities which lead to Enlightenment.

There are different types of gurus for giving different types of instruction. Every layman has as many as five; Lamas and monks have many more, some of whom give instructions in simple practices, some in philosophy, some give inspiration, and some give training in Tantra. A guru is selected for his moral, intellectual, and spiritual qualities. The Vinaya recommends a teacher who is morally pure and spiritually developed, who knows the Vinaya ceremonies, loves patience, has good disciples, who is ready to assist his pupils morally, intellectually, and spiritually, and who gives timely instructions. The Mahayana Sutras call for more advanced teachers who must be compassionate and able to draw others toward the Bodhisattva ideal. The tantric guru must be still more highly developed morally, intellectually, and spiritually. He must have a thorough knowledge of the Tantras and also know how to give instruction in accordance with the individual temperament and ability of each pupil.

Once a spiritual relation has been established with a guru one must be very careful not to allow it to deteriorate. One must be humble, obedient, vigilant, and faithful. But obedience need be observed only to those teachings which are right and good. The disciple must regard his teacher as the Buddha himself, for he is the living representative of the Supreme Teacher. Therefore the selection of a guru is important, for upon him depends one's intellectual proficiency, religious life, and spiritual attainments. The great sage Naropa said, "There can be no Buddhas without a guru."

The method of training disciples will vary from guru to guru, but their fundamental principles and ultimate objective will be the same. Each guru is supposed to treat his pupil in such a way that he will achieve a highly developed moral character, intellectual proficiency, and spiritual enlightenment. That should result in a sense of responsibility and a compassion which inspires him to render benevolent service to all beings. Mere intellectual understanding, which leads to arrogance, will stand in the way of spiritual awakening, just as spiritual practices without right intellectual understanding and moral practices will be fruitless.

All Buddhists take refuge in the Buddha, the Dharma, and the Sangha. For Tibetans, the fourth refuge is the Lama, the spiritual master for an individual. He is the living embodiment of the Triple Refuge, the physical representative and the source of instruction and inspiration of the Buddha. The mind of one's spiritual master represents the Buddha, his speech is the Dharma, and his body is the Sangha. Such is the nature of the guru who stands at the head of Buddhism in Tibet.

SCRIPTURES

Tibetan Buddhist scriptures consist of the direct and implied teachings of the Lord Buddha together with locally developed ritual traditions and spiritual instructions. These teachings have been transmitted both orally and in writing. The oral instructions are handed down from a spiritual master, or guru, to his disciple—some instructions are never communicated to more than two or three of the most spiritually advanced disciples. The most important of the oral instructions are not imparted by the spiritual master in accordance with his own wishes, but upon the direction of the deities or his own teacher who, though physically dead, is yet alive in his spiritual body. There is also a kind of oral revelation in the tantric system, but not revelation in the dogmatic sense; it is an adaptation of the Teaching to suit different conditions, localities, temperaments, and intelligences with the aim of conveying the Teachings according to the level of spiritual development of the disciples.

In addition to the oral traditions, there is a large body of noncanonical literature which serves as a background for understanding the writings accepted as scriptures. It deals with Sanskrit and Tibetan grammars, with political science, medical science, rhetoric and prosody, history, fiction, drama, songs, poems, biographies, autobiographies, stories about Tibetan heroes, cosmology, genealogy, accounts of travels, guides to places of pilgrimage, and such matters. The writings concerning astrology and astronomy include various treatises for predicting the movements of planets and constellations, methods of averting the evil influences of the heavenly bodies and warding off hail and storms or bringing rain, and guides for the selection of auspicious sites and plans for buildings and for making divinitory calculations.

The canonical scriptures of Tibetan Buddhism include the Kagyur, the Tangyur, the literature of the course of study in monastic universities, the writings of Tibetan scholars who founded schools, the Precious Treasury which is the main literature of the Old Translation school, and collections of writings which consist of numerous ritual texts, summaries of moral and philosophical teachings designed for everyday practice and mental training, guides to meditation, and invocations and classical tales such as the Jatakas, the stories of the previous births of the Buddha.

The Kagyur is made up of the Buddha's teachings as translated in full from the Sanskrit originals. It is published in two editions, one of 104 and the other of 108 volumes, with identical materials. Since the Kagyur embodies the direct utterances of the Lord Buddha, it is the most important and sacred of all the scriptures and is placed on the shrine. It corresponds to what is called the Tripitaka or Three Collections in other Buddhist countries and is defined as the means of avoiding, or overcoming, the evils to which mankind is subject. It includes the Vinaya Pitaka dealing with monastic disciplines and ethics, the Sutra Pitaka or Collection of Discourses, and the Abhidharma

Pitaka or Collection of Higher Doctrine which expounds the basic philosophy of Buddhism.

In addition to the Tripitaka the Kagyur includes the Four Great Tantras: the Tantra of Activities (*Kriya*), the Tantra of Application (*Charya*), the Tantra of Perfection (*Yoga*), and the Tantra of Perfection Supreme (*Anuttara Yoga*). These include the basic texts and commentaries which are very important teachings. They deal with rites, recitation of mantras, concentration, meditation on oneself as identical with the tutelary deity, meditation on the absolute reality of the deity as both vacuity and bliss, and realization of the Supreme Truth by means of the development of intuitive wisdom and compassion.

The Tangyur is a collection of the works of Indian and Tibetan scholars in 225 volumes which ranks next to the Kagyur in importance and is occasionally placed on the shrine alongside the Kagyur. It is made up of commentaries on the Sutras and on the Tantras.

The Literature of the Five Branches (*Tsannyi Yikcha*) is the course of study used in monastic schools covering logic and dialectics, the Prajnaparamita literature, the Madhyamika philosophy, ethics, and the Abhidharma. The Prajnaparamita, or the Discourse on the Attainment of Transcendental Wisdom, consists of seventy sections covering the chief observances of what is known as "the ample practice of the Mahayana teaching." Starting from the various types of creative mental effort, their nature and definition in accordance with the various stages of spiritual progress, it goes on to describe the actual practice of the teachings. It describes and classifies in a systematic manner the Six Transcendental Virtues, which are transcendental almsgiving, morality, endurance, exertion, contemplation, wisdom. It also explains the Seven Instructions on Compassion, which are based on the understanding that every being has been one's own mother and emphasizes that the realization of that fact is the ground for gratitude, affection, love, compassion, and constant exertion to express that compassion. Also incorporated in the Prajnaparamita Sutra are all the essential teachings such as the Four Noble Truths, the Eightfold

Noble Path, the Twelve Causal Links, the Five Aggregates, the Twelve Spheres of Sense, and the like.

The Prajnaparamita Sutra, the Discourse on Perfect Wisdom, is one of the most important of all Sutras in Tibetan Buddhism. Another Sutra of great value is the Discourse of the Passing away of the Lord Buddha, the Mahaparinirvana Sutra. The Way to Enlightenment, or Bodhicharyavatara, a treatise on Buddhist practice by Santideva, is a manual for Bodhisattvas which is equal to the Sutras in importance.

Tantric writings, some of which are in the Kagyur, are given the same status as the Sutras in Tibetan Buddhism. Some of the chief Tantras are:

Guhyasamaja, or Tantra of the Union of the Triple Body of the Buddhas

Chakrasambhava, or Tantra of the Binding Wheel

Kalachakra, or Tantra of the Wheel of Time

Vajrabhairava, or Tantra of the Eternal Destroyer

Vajradakini, or Tantra of the Eternal Goddess

Lamrim-Chimo, or the Great Stages to Enlightenment

Druptha-Chimo, or the Great Philosophical Schools

Ngarim-Chimo, or the Great Stages of the Tantra

Translations of the scriptures were never undertaken independently but were made by learned and able translators working together and in collaboration with Indian pandits. Thanks to definite rules and accurately defined technical terms, the translations made under the supervision of the Cultural Council were done more nearly perfectly than anyone could do them today. Many ancient monasteries have preserved valuable Sanskrit manuscripts, some as old as the sixth century.

The contents of the canonical writings lead mankind from the darkness of ignorance to Enlightenment. They are, it is believed, much more reliable guides than the subjective visions of individuals, however holy. For these reasons Tibetan Buddhists pay respect and homage to the scriptures, either in the form of a book or a few lines of writing, by placing them above the sacred images and by reverently touching them to their foreheads. The correct interpretation of the moral and philosophical teachings in the scriptures is determined by the explicitly stated teaching of the Buddha, logical reasoning, and by the testimony of experience.

THE DOCTRINE

To Tibetans, religion is of all things the most essential; it is the gravitational force which holds together the whole Tibetan people. The spiritual inspiration finds its way into daily life through earnest devotion to the recitation of mantras, the invocation of the Triple Gem and the deities, the repetition of verses embodying the Doctrine, through physical exercises of a religious nature, and meditation. In this way the people's faith and devotion are developed to such an extent that all their thoughts, expressions, and activities are in accordance with religious principles.

An understanding of those religious principles is as important as leading a life of purity, for Buddhism demands a cautious and critical examination of the Doctrine. A strong faith requires a spiritual tradition grounded on the facts of history, the testimony of one's own experience, and an understanding guided by reason and logic. The Tibetan Buddhist is not required to toe the line of any accepted creed—he has perfect freedom to establish his own philosophy or doctrine provided only that he can demonstrate in his own life the results of whatever methods of spiritual training and understanding he advocates. It is because of this tolerant attitude that Buddhism has been able to develop its vast and varied doctrines which are not just differences of opinion but are the different outcomes of a variety of successful experiments.

The Doctrine of the Buddha, the Buddha Dharma, includes the two yanas—Hinayana and Mahayana. From the doctrinal point of view, *yana* means "burden" or "responsibility." Thus Hinayana, which is the doctrine dealing with self-emancipation, is called the Lesser Burden, while the doctrine which is concerned with the attainment of Enlightenment for the sake of all sentient beings is known as the Greater Burden.

After the Lord Buddha passed away, the Hinayana divided into many sects which, because of their greater prominence, claimed to be in the line of direct descent from the Buddha. Their Canon of the Buddha's teachings was written down in Pali in the first century B.C. The Mahayana followers, on the other hand, were more scattered and had neither organizations nor recognized institutions of their own for some time. Tibetans believe that the Mahayana teachings were handed down orally from generation to generation until they began committing them to writing in the first century B.C., beginning with the larger Prajnaparamita Sutra and the Saddharma Pundarika Sutra. The Mahayana came to include the yana based on the Prajnaparamita and the yana of the tantric teachings. Thus there are three yanas in Buddhist doctrine—Hinayana, Mahayana, and Tantrayana.

The different moral, psychological, and philosophical teachings of the three yanas are not mutually antagonistic, nor do they in any way disrupt the unity of the Buddha Dharma, which is free from internal contradictions. They are simply different expedients suited to people of different temperaments and mental capacities. The Buddha had the spiritual faculty of recognizing in a person whether or not he possessed the "meritorious seed of Emancipation," which is the potentiality of Emancipation attained by past good deeds. By this insight the Buddha could judge the capacity of the aspirant and expound the Doctrine in accordance with the disciple's potentiality. What he teaches a devout monk disciple is not the same as what he teaches a householder or a king.

It is obvious that the Buddha did not preach the various yanas in their present fully developed form, but he surely did originate the idea that there could be different yanas, each having the same unique objective, designed for different persons according to their different degrees of understanding and stages of spiritual development. It is from those different levels of instruction given by the Buddha that Hinayana, Mahayana, and Tantrayana developed.

As foretold by the Buddha, Nagarjuna discovered the Prajnaparamita literature and propagated the Mahayana teachings by his writings. As a result of his study of the Prajnaparamita and his practice of meditation, he gained insight into the fundamental nature of reality. Since his teaching avoided the two extremes of asserting of reality that it exists or does not exist, the new school which he founded became known as the Madhyamika, or the School of the Middle Way. In the same way, Asanga was the founder of the Yogacara, or Vijnanavada school. But though they were the first organizers of their respective schools, it would be a mistake to think of them as being the original authors, for the author was the Buddha himself.

The interpretations of Nagarjuna and Asanga gave an impetus to the study and practice of the yanas as successive stages of a single path. After flourishing in India for centuries, this method of study and practice was introduced into Tibet where it was encouraged and kept up by all schools. The most comprehensive of the texts studied in Tibet is Tsongkhapa's *The Great Stages of Enlightenment* (*Lamrim Chimo*), which is a comprehensive work in which all the yanas are explained.

Practically speaking, Hinayana, Mahayana, and Tantrayana are interlinked in their essential principles and are the successive stages of one path. Each depends upon the others and serves as a stepping stone for the next higher. It is impossible to achieve the highest realization by sticking to one particular yana. Just as Mahayana is futile and dangerous unless it is based on the essential principles of Hinayana, so Hinayana is an incomplete approach to supreme realization unless it finds its consummation in Mahayana doctrines. Neither Mahayana nor Hinayana can claim to be independent of the other or superior to the other, for they are of equal importance for the attainment of Enlightenment.

The Saddharma Pundarika rightly says, "In the Buddha lands of the universe there is only one yana, neither a second, nor a third. The exhibition of a variety of yanas is only a means adopted by the Great Sages." Hence there is ultimately only one yana, which is neither Hinayana nor Mahayana but is constituted by them, and which can therefore best be called what the Lord Buddha called it, the Buddhayana. As the Buddha said in the Saddharma Pundarika, "The Dharma has been preached with reference to one yana only—to the Buddhayana, which leads to the attainment of supreme Enlightenment."

The attitude of the Tibetans toward the Southern Buddhism of Ceylon, Burma, Thailand, and Cambodia is invariably appreciative and friendly. The general idea of Theravada teaching is of course known through the Tripitaka literature. Tibetans believe that the Theravada teachings are like the foundation of a house and Mahayana is like the superstructure. Just as both the foundation and superstructure are necessary to a building, so are both Theravada and Mahayana necessary to the Buddhayana. Furthermore, Tibetans are highly appreciative of the strict observance of monastic discipline which prevails in Theravada countries. Not only do they agree that a high standard of ethics contributes to perfection, but Tibetans openly declare that if the monasteries of their own country were equally scrupulous in this respect they would have a higher standard of scholarship and spirituality. This is the attitude of the Tibetans, based on their understanding and devotion to the three yanas.

THE THREE PRECIOUS ONES

The Three Precious Ones, that is, the Buddha, the Dharma, and the Sangha, have been known to the whole Buddhist world ever since the beginning of Buddhism. In temples and private shrines Tibetan Buddhists take devout and heartfelt refuge in the Three Precious Ones in the presence of their respective symbols, that is to say, before the images, the scriptures, and the congregation. This taking refuge in the Triple Gem is the most fundamental belief and most widely accepted practice in Buddhism. It precedes all other religious acts such as the reading of scriptures, making of solemn vows, receiving ordination, performance of ceremonies, and practice of meditation.

Tibetan Buddhists place great emphasis on the good intention preceding the taking of the Three Refuges rather than on the formal act of taking refuge. The intention must be of a sincere and benevolent nature, supported by a strong resolve, and the vow itself must be constantly borne in mind while performing any religious practices. Finally, whatever merits may accrue to one from the taking of the Three Refuges, or from any other spiritual exercises, must be dedicated to the happiness and enlightenment of all beings.

The taking of the Three Refuges includes within its scope the taking of all the principles of Buddhism; one who does not take the Triple Gem is not a Buddhist. The taking of the Three Refuges is a vow to exert oneself for the realization of the Supreme Truth, which is the ultimate refuge. It is a gross misunderstanding of Buddhism to say that it teaches the attainment of emancipation merely by taking the name of the Lord Buddha or by reciting mantras. The ignorant, not fully understanding the operation of karmic law, seem to attribute a protective power to the Triple Gem in a mundane sense. According to Tibetan Buddhism, the Triple Gem cannot protect us from natural calamities, accidents, or the consequences of evil deeds if we do not have in ourselves the seeds of goodness. Nor can the spiritual inspiration and power of the Buddhas or the Bodhisattvas deliver us from natural calamities. They can only help us indirectly by bringing our merits to maturity so that the good karmic effects of these merits may give us whatever protection we need. The inspiration given by the Triple Gem serves as an efficient cause from which arise the consequences of our good and benevolent deeds.

The Tibetan formula for taking refuge clearly emphasizes the fact that the practice of the Doctrine is for the sake of all: "I take refuge in the spiritual master, The Buddha, in the Dharma, and in the Sangha, until I have attained Supreme Enlightenment. By the merits gained by my practice of the Six Transcendental Virtues may I attain Enlightenment for the benefit of all sentient beings."

THE BUDDHA

When a Tibetan takes refuge in the Buddha he is vowing to attempt to reach Buddhahood, to follow the career of a Bodhisattva. There have been in the past, are now in the present, and will be in the future, many Buddhas. When a human being has attained the highest development possible of the love, wisdom, intuition, resolution, spiritual power, and other qualities of a Buddha, such a human being can only be compared to other Buddhas. Bodhisattvas are those who have reached the middle stages of attainment, possessing the Buddha qualities to an extent which no ordinary human being can imagine. Tibetans believe that the Lord Buddha is still spiritually active and that he continues to guide, inspire, and protect the spiritual life, as do also the Bodhisattvas who appear again and again on the earth for the good of humanity.

The role of every Buddha which appears as a human being is the same as that of Buddha Sakyamuni—they appear on earth in the same manner and expound the same truth. In this cosmic period three other Buddhas appeared before Sakyamuni, and a fifth, Buddha Maitreya, is still to come. Those three Buddhas, like Sakyamuni, in the first stage of their careers made a solemn promise to liberate all beings, but each of them decided to make his appearance at a favorable time and place. They avoided the present age of conflict because they knew that it is the worst age of all, the age in which humanity would reach the climax of hatred, doubt, suspicion, fear, and all evils. The Sakyamuni, then a Bodhisattva, felt a profound pity and therefore accepted this period. From that time onward, he practiced the Bodhisattva virtues ceaselessly in all his existences, right up to the one in which he was born as Prince Siddhartha in the Sakya clan and attained Buddhahood. Both the Jataka tales and the Sutras show us how he made further progress in spiritual attainments and renewed his Bodhisattva vows in each existence.

Throughout all these lives the keystone in the arch of his aspiration was his solemn devotion to the practice of the means of attaining Supreme Buddhahood so that he might serve all beings with love, compassion, and wisdom in action. Then, when he was born as Siddhartha Gautama, he was a man like us. But after attaining supreme Enlightenment he was endowed with the highest physical, mental, and spiritual attributes and thus transcended the level of ordinary humanity and even of the spiritually advanced. Upon his body he bore the thirty-two major and eighty minor signs of a Buddha. With his acquired power the Buddha had control over matter and space, the laws of the material universe ceased to function in relation to his body, and he transcended the operation of the law of karma. He could have shown his acquired state if he had wished to, but the Buddha did not care to make a display of anything that might seem miraculous lest it create a wrong impression in the minds of his followers.

The Buddha deliberately remained on the level of ordinary humanity, showing in his body all the possible effects of karma, such as disease and death. Another important physical characteristic of the Buddha was his serene and tranquil demeanor and his affable personality. His speech was simple yet profound, with a beneficial effect on the lives of his followers—it was indeed the voice of Supreme Truth. Tibetans generally claim that the Buddha's speech possessed sixty distinct perfections, all of which could be heard simultaneously and understood in as many different languages. Though generally taken literally, this belief could very well mean that one saying of the Buddha can be interpreted in various ways.

Although the Mahayanists, like the Theravadins, believe that the Buddha was a man who reached the highest state of human perfection, they at the same time hold a different view that upon attaining the supreme Enlightenment he became one with the Triple Form of the Enlightened one (*Trikaya*). At that point he ceased to be an ordinary man physically, mentally, and spiritually. This conception of the Triple Form, or Three Bodies of the Buddha, is a doctrine of paramount importance for understanding the Mahayana conception of the Buddha, and the ultimate goal of man.

The Triple Form includes the Earthly Body (*Nirmanakaya*), the Subtle Body (*Sambhogakaya*), and the Unmanifested Body (*Prajnadharmakaya*). Therefore a Buddha may be defined as one who possesses these Three Bodies, together with all the qualities necessarily associated with them.

The Earthly Body (Nirmanakaya) appears in three different ways: as the Earthly Form of the Buddha proper, in various emanations as Bodhisattvas, and in concrete created forms.

When the Buddha himself appears in an Earthly Body, he bears upon his body the thirty-two major and eighty minor

marks of an Enlightened One which are the result of his meritorious deeds in former existences—such as a curl of hair on the
forehead, a knot of hair, and so on. But since his Earthly Body
was in reality transcendental and not subject to the operation
of natural law, including the law of karma, these marks only
seem to be the result of his previous good actions. In reality
they were deliberately assumed for the purpose of increasing
the faith of his followers. This Earthly Body of the Buddha
was mind-made and could be multiplied and transferred from
place to place at will. It was majestic and dignified in appearance and clearly expressed gentleness and love. The Earthly
Body plays the role of supreme spiritual guide, and as such
plays a vitally important part in the progress and spiritual welfare of humanity.

The second aspect of the Earthly Body is the Bodhisattva. So
great is the responsibility of the Buddha that he does not rest in
the state of Nirvana but appears in the world again and again
as an ordinary man who, inspired by universal love, compassion, and wisdom, shows the Path to all. A Buddha emanates as
such Bodhisattvas as many times as he thinks necessary. Although Bodhisattvas are subject to the operation of natural law,
there is no possibility that they can resort to evil deeds and
wrong conceptions out of ignorance and selfishness. Their
role, like that of the Buddhas, is to show the right Path to
erring humanity, for they love to live in the world and serve
beings. The numerous Bodhisattvas serve and direct mankind
with motherly love and wisdom, and in all that they do they
maintain without exception the course of natural law and are
ready to suffer its conseqences, however painful.

The third aspect of the Earthly Body is the concrete created
form, of which there are very many. The concrete created
forms can appear as paintings, images, or any other objects of
religious art, or even as inanimate things such as hills and trees.
The Buddha has stated in many Sutras that he would appear in
the form of kings, ministers, priests, craftsmen, farmers, or
even as birds and beasts.

The Subtle Body of the Buddha (Sambhogakaya), which is
the second Body, is infinite in radiance, endowed with all the

specific qualities of a Buddha, and sublimely beautiful. It is adorned with the splendid thirty-two major and eighty minor signs, all of unimaginable size. Although it is beyond the reach of human eyes, it appears to the highly developed Bodhisattvas. Aside from the fact that the Subtle Body immeasurably surpasses the Earthly Body in glory, the only difference between them is in location and duration and the relative scope of their duties. Of the different aspects of the Subtle Body one of the most difficult to understand is the fact that within it are contained all Buddhas. That is, in every particle of every Buddha can be contained all the other Buddhas, without there being any increase in the size of the particles or any decrease in the size of the Buddhas. This conception, which had its origin in the meditations of highly developed Bodhisattvas, is by no means easy to grasp until one has attained the same level of meditation. It is a way of saying that the Supreme Reality and all the specific qualities of the Buddhas are in essence identical.

The influence of the Subtle Form of the Buddha is so great that it extends over 10,000,000,000 worlds. Its work is nothing less than the liberation of all beings, including those Bodhisattvas who are not yet fully emancipated. Its tremendous task is summarized in the Five Perfect Attributes:

1. The Subtle Body perfectly manifests all the acquired qualities of a Buddha.
2. Its abode is the whole universe.
3. It remains in manifestation until the end of existence of all beings.
4. It appears only to highly advanced Bodhisattvas.
5. It imparts to the Bodhisattvas the highest form of Mahayana doctrine.

The activity of this Subtle Body of the Buddha is perfect and incessant. It is a mistake, however, to think of it as governing the universe, or protecting beings from the consequences of their own deeds, or of forgiving evil deeds. All its actions, through its countless emanations as Bodhisattvas, aim at leading beings along the Path of the Buddha to the ultimate Enlightenment.

The third Body of the Buddha, the Unmanifested Body (*Prajnadharmakaya*), is difficult to define but something at least may be said concerning the complexities of its nature and functions. It is the Enlightened Mind in the sense of Supreme Reality, Supreme Wisdom combined with Infinite Compassion, and freedom from any obscurity caused by emotional defilements or false conceptions. The Supreme Reality of the Unmanifested Body is devoid of self-nature; it includes the other two Bodies of the Buddha. The Unmanifested Body is identical with the essential nature of all beings and things; within it there is no distinction, no origination, no cessation, no growth, no cause, no effect, and no condition. It is the Absolute Nature or the Supreme Reality of all individual persons and things, the goal to be realized through transcendental wisdom. It is to be attained by following the right Path shown to us by the Buddha on the basis of his personal experience.

The Unmanifested Body of the Buddha is endowed with a vast number of attributes which are the goal to be attained by those who follow the Path of the Buddha. Chief among the attributes in addition to Supreme Wisdom, Compassion, and Spiritual Power, are the Five Spiritual Faculties:

1. The Essential Wisdom, which perceives the Supreme Reality of all things and is devoid of growth and cessation
2. The Mirror-like Wisdom, which is pure and clear and free from obscurity
3. The Equality Wisdom, which frees the mind from all impediments
4. The All-discerning Wisdom, which sees things intuitively without going through the process of reasoning
5. The All-performing Wisdom, which accomplishes its purposes

All these attributes are the common heritage of all sentient beings. The attainment of the Triple Body of the Buddha is the goal of every form of life, the aim of every Tibetan Buddhist.

All schools of Tibetan Buddhism recognize that there are many Bodhisattvas in the world who are conscious reincarnations of previous Bodhisattvas and spiritually advanced persons. There are numerous Bodhisattvas not only in Tibet, but throughout the world, since Bodhisattvas may follow not only the ethical and philosophical teachings of Buddhism but of any similar teaching. There are many passages in the Sutras which tell of the two types of Bodhisattvas, those who vowed to lead mankind by exemplifying the ideal of the Buddha in a Buddhist land and those who vowed to help humanity in different ways and by different means in non-Buddhist lands. The schools in Tibet recognize and honor the leaders of their own hierarchy as emanations from one or another of the members of the Mahayana Bodhisattva trinity of Avalokitesvara, the Lord of Compassion; Manjusri, the Lord of Wisdom; and Vajrapani, the Lord of Power.

The Sutras contain accurate predictions concerning the appearance in India and Tibet of certain prominent Bodhisattvas, especially concerning the incarnations of Avalokitesvara. Once the Buddha was asked by a disciple the reason for an unprecedented light that filled the universe, and he replied that there was a world situated far to the West of this one, known as the Lotus World, and that the Buddha Amitabha and the Bodhisattva Avalokitesvara lived there. The light was caused by the departure of Avalokitesvara to take up his abode among men to help sentient beings. In other Sutras it is said that Avalokitesvara would incarnate himself as King Songtsan in Tibet, and again as King Trisong-Detsan. And later, as we have seen, he has incarnated himself as the Dalai Lama.

DEITIES

The deities of Tibetan Buddhism are classified in three groups: the Supreme deities, the Higher Guardian deities who have reached at least the seventh of the ten stages of the Bodhisattva path, and the Lower Guardian deities who have reached any of the first six stages.

The Supreme Deities (*Yidam*) are numerous, each representing particular characteristics which are symbolized by colors, such as white for a peaceful aspect, and so on. They all belong to the Subtle Body of the Triple Body of the Buddhas of the past, the present, and the future. Their ultimate origin, according to tantric doctrine, is the Unmanifested Body of the Buddhas whose infinite motherly love and unlimited power were personified as the Deity of Compassion (Avalokitesvara), the Deity of Wisdom (Manjusri), and the Deity of Power (Vajrapani). From this trinity emanated the other Supreme Deities. All schools of Mahayana Buddhism accept the assembly of Buddhas and deities in which the Earthly Body (Nirmanakaya) of the Buddha occupies the central place. These take precedence, being meditated upon at the beginning of all religious ceremonies, both public and private.

In this assembly of deities are included Goddesses like Kurukulli who represents power, the White Tara who represents longevity, Parnasavari who protects from epidemics, the Green Tara who liberates from sorrows and dangers, and Sarasvati who is the patroness of wisdom, poetry, and song. Buddhists believe that all these divine forms have the same origin, that all of them are manifestations of the Unmanifested Body of the Buddhas.

The Guardian deities of the higher class possess all the qualities of a Bodhisattva—compassion, wisdom, and power. Their role is nothing less than that of the Bodhisattva. While the Bodhisattvas help and lead human beings in the sphere of real life, the Guardian deities render the same service from the realm of the spirits. The aspect of the higher Guardian deities is generally of a terrifying nature, symbolizing both the power of wisdom to crush ignorance and the active opposition of these deities to the enemies of human happiness and welfare. They originate from the Supreme deities, each of whom emanates a Guardian deity having a special duty in looking after the spiritual welfare of the devotee and the happiness of human beings. Avalokitesvara, for example, emanates Mahakala, the Great Black One or the Protector; Manjusri emanates Yama; Vajrapani emanates Vaisravana, the Guardian deity of Wealth.

Of the lowest class of deities, those who assume gross forms and associate intimately with men, some are in the first six stages of the Bodhisattva Path, others have not reached even the first stage, and many are non-Buddhist in origin. Such

Guardian deities cannot be compared in all respects with those mentioned above. Their duties, which are comparatively limited, relate to the worldly and spiritual welfare of human beings in general and devotees in particular—they may be described as spirits rather than gods. Some are of Indian origin and entered Tibet at the time of the introduction of Buddhism. Kali, for instance, belongs to the lowest class of deities and has nothing to do with the meditation or spiritual progress of the devotee. A devotee worships such a deity in the same way that he welcomes a friend or asks him for help.

Most of the lowest class of deities are of Bon origin. These deities may be communicated with through the medium of an oracle. Some have become guardians of the state, and their oracles are honored by the government. Important matters concerning the Dalai Lama and the nation are referred to them for advice, and their words influence the decisions finally made. Each such oracle has a temple and a monastery in which daily services are conducted. Among guardian spirits receiving such honors are Pehar, who came from Bihar in India, and the chief spirit Dorje-Draden, who acts as the adviser and personal guardian of the Dalai Lama. Both of them are emanations of Buddha Amitabha.

Among the spirits not recognized by the state is Gyechen-Shukdan, or Great Powerful King, who is said to have been an eminent disciple of Tsongkhapa who pledged himself to assume such a form for the protection of the Gelukpa school. After several births as a great Lama he became a powerful spirit who is honored by all Gelukpas as a guardian and serviceable friend. The Gelukpas also honor all the deities found in the Four Great Tantras. The Old Translation school, the Kagyupa school, and the Sakyapa also have their special deities based on their Tantras and commentaries.

Minor oracles are found in almost every province. Usually they are poor people who have scarcely any spiritual qualities and who allow themselves to be used as oracles simply to gain a livelihood. Apart from these, there are many ancient spirits who either constitute the retinues of the higher or lower Guardian deities or who are independent. Tibetans also believe in the existence of good and evil spirits of the mountain peaks and passes, of water, of the locality, of the family, and of animals. In the case of the inferior kind of spirits, offerings are made to them as a sort of almsgiving. A morally weak and impure person is said to be the victim of evil spirits. This is not punishment, but one could not be harmed by them unless he were already weak or impure.

COSMOLOGY

The conception of the universe in Tibetan Buddhism is the same as that held in other Buddhist lands. The universe is of infinite extent, comprehending all things; yet it is neither existent nor nonexistent, but formless and uncreated—like sentient beings it is without beginning or end. It is neither identical with beings, nor a whole of which beings are the component parts. Within this vast, limitless space are contained all the possibilities and potentialities that beings can explore. Buddhist metaphysics does not attempt the solution of so abstract a question as the origin of the universe or beings.

According to Buddhist theory, the worlds evolved as the effect of previous karmas, both gross and subtle, collective and individual, good and evil. Since beginningless time the essentially pure consciousness of beings has been obscured by ignorance, due to which they succumb to defilements such as lust and hatred. The karmas produced by these defilements are the chief causes of the multitudinous worlds with all their differences in size, beauty, pleasantness, and so on. The superior classes of beings, such as human beings and gods, despite the sufferings to which they are subject, have the possibility of attaining a higher stage of realization.

The Abhidharma and the Kalachakra Tantra agree that the universe is so full of worlds that it is impossible even for a Buddha to enumerate them all. Wherever the universe reaches, there worlds and beings exist. According to the Abhidharma, the universe consists of three planes—the formless plane, the plane of bodily existence which consists of seventeen regions, and the six spheres of desire. The countless subdivisions of each plane, with the exception of those of the formless plane, all constitute separate worlds.

The duration of one particular world system is equal to one great cosmic period. One cosmic period consists of twenty intermediate cosmic periods. Twenty periods are required for the evolution of a world system, twenty for its duration, twenty for its gradual destruction, and twenty for its annihilation. The twenty cosmic periods of gradual destruction are equal to the time it takes for the length of human life to decrease from eighty thousand years to ten years at the rate of losing one year at the end of every century. The origination and destruction of a world system both start with the lowest world.

On the plane of Bodily Existence there are five worlds inhabited only by Bodhisattvas who receive there the highest form of the Teaching directly from the Subtle Body of the Buddha. The rest of the worlds are inhabited by sentient beings who are classified as belonging to six different realms of existence. The beings of the first three realms, that is, the gods, demigods and men, are in many ways superior; those beings of the other three realms are the inferior beings, the constant sufferers, the spirits, and the animal beings. All beings are perpetually subject to three kinds of suffering:

1. Their existence is bound up with calamities such as old age, disease, and death, which are the result of their own ignorance and folly.
2. Their happiness is impermanent, being transformed into sorrow at the very moment of its origin, so that what gives pleasure at one instant gives pain the next.
3. For many human beings, and most beings of the inferior classes, life is an uninterrupted succession of miseries and afflictions of every kind.

All six realms of existence, and all the inhabitants of those realms, are the result of the law of karma.

The human realm of existence is the highest and most important, having the greatest advantages and the greatest dangers. With proper training, the intellectual and spiritual potentialities of man are capable of reaching the summit of perfection. Without proper training, man might develop a gigantic brain but it would be full of lust, hatred, and ignorance and would be only a source of suffering. Man must, therefore, make a momentous decision on which depends his fate both here and hereafter. Because man occupies this central position in which he can make a decision, he occupies a central place in Buddhism.

Just as there is a process of evolution for individual beings, so there is an evolution for the world systems. The last phase of one world system, the phase of annihilation, is succeeded by the first phase of the next world system, the phase of origination. Upon the gradual destruction and annihilation of the worlds, the beings inhabiting them are transferred to other worlds. When a new world is evolved, first there is produced an atmospheric disc which has the capacity to support the earth; from the atmosphere clouds are produced, and from the clouds rains. From the rains are produced tiny particles of matter, and from these the earth is formed.

In addition to the different worlds in the universe there are innumerable Buddha-fields, or Buddha-realms. These Buddha-fields are not to be compared with our gross material world which has evolved because of the effects of the collective karma of beings. They are invisible to anyone who is not either a Buddha or a Bodhisattva. Although they are numerous, they are in every respect identical, since they have evolved out of subtle elements. They are intangible, radiant, and free from physical defects. Unlike our own world, the Buddha-fields have neither sun nor moon, but are self-luminous. They are inhabited by Bodhisattvas over whom the Subtle Body of the Buddha presides. In the Buddha-fields disease, decay, and death are unknown; there is no heat nor cold. Everything is beautiful and perfect there; no labor is required, for the beings of those realms do not have to face such problems of existence as are common here on earth.

In the Buddha-realms every object symbolizes a high ideal or principle which is understood by the Bodhisattvas; even the wind breathes forth high ideals. The Bodhisattvas of one Buddha-field can travel to the Buddha-fields of other worlds without any conveyance because they all possess the power of arriving in a place the moment they think of it. But however wonderful these Buddha-fields may be, they are only a stage through which the Bodhisattva must pass on his way to final liberation. Since these realms have only a relative existence, they are still within the reach of the law of karma, though not of evil karma.

The Sutras mention many Buddha-fields. There is the Buddha-field of the Subtle Body of Buddha (Sambhogakaya). The Field of the Great Rejoicing presided over by the Earthly Body of the Buddha, and the Field of Turquoise Leaves, presided over by the Goddess Tari, are both situated in the East. Avalokitesvara presides over the Buddha-field called the Checker Board, which is in the South, and the Blissful Realm of Buddha Amitabha is in the West.

The Tushita heaven is not included in the Buddha-fields, for it is a much inferior place located on the plane of desire, inhabited by various gods and goddesses. It is in the Tushita heaven that each of the 1,002 Bodhisattvas of the present cosmic period is born to prepare himself for his great mission on earth.

The relations of beings in the earthly realm to the planets in our world is not mentioned specifically in the Abhidharma, but the Kalachakra Tantra, in describing the material universe, mentions ten planets and twenty-eight constellations. Among the people of Tibet the belief in the influence of certain planetary conjunctions is very widespread, and the need for counteracting the influence of unfavorable conjunctions by the performance of certain rites is recognized. The influence of the planets, which may be either good or evil, affects only people of average attainments, however, for the spiritually developed are not harmed by evil planetary influences, nor are the very wicked benefited by good influences. It is said that spiritually weak persons cannot afford to ignore the influences of planets since they are one of the conditions for bringing to maturity the meritorious or demeritorious fruits of karma.

The Four Characteristics

The basic principle of Buddhism, which sums up the fundamental nature of existence and the goal of human life, is formulated as the Four Characteristics:

1. All compound things are suffering.
2. All compound things are impermanent.
3. All things are without self.
4. Nirvana is the only peace.

It is clear that these Four Characteristics are very similar to the Four Noble Truths. The first two Characteristics are the same as the first Noble Truth of suffering; the third Characteristic implies the second Noble Truth concerning the cause of suffering. That is, beings under the influence of ignorance have wrongly assumed the existence of a self in themselves and have attributed the same selfhood to other beings. From that arose self-attachment leading to hatred, lust, and the other defilements. And finally, the fourth Characteristic, that Nirvana is the only peace, is the same as the third and fourth Noble Truths concerning the cessation of suffering and the way to attain it.

Thus it is clear that the Mahayana Buddhists of Tibet have no hesitation in accepting the Four Noble Truths of Theravada as the foundation for Mahayana and Tantrayana.

The Mahayanists accept the Four Characteristics, or the Four Noble Truths, as an elementary course before proceeding to the practice of their own distinctive teaching that things are in reality empty and possess only a relative and nominal existence, like that of a mirage, or the reflection of the moon on a pool of still water. The Mahayana practice aims at the cessation of the notions of existence and nonexistence and the realization that all things, since they are mutually conditioned and dependent, are in reality empty. The realization of this truth destroys the wrong conception of separate individual selfhood. The dual conception of the intuitive insight into emptiness and the practice of the Great Compassion toward all beings, has for its aim the realization of the Triple Body of the Buddha for the sake of all beings.

THE TWO TRUTHS

The Threefold Body of Enlightenment is to be realized by following the twofold Path consisting of the practice of an elaborate ethical teaching and the cultivation of wisdom. In the cultivation of wisdom there are two kinds of truth, or two points of view from which the universe may be regarded—relative truth and Absolute truth.

There are various schools of Buddhist philosophy which have discussed the doctrine of the two truths, propounding different views according to their different stages of enlightenment. Here let us consider the universally accepted views of the Prasangika school. This school owes its origin to the Buddha himself; for its abstruse philosophical teaching was discovered by Nagarjuna, and the Buddha had prophesied that Nagarjuna would be his chief exponent in philosophy. To this school Tsongkhapa of Tibet contributed yet another inspiring and clear view on the conception of sunyata, voidness.

The first of the two truths, the relative truth, refers to the entire world of objects as perceived by the unenlightened mind. Asanga, the great Yogacara teacher, advocates the use of the term *apparent truth* since the existence of things is denied only from the standpoint of Reality. According to the Yogacara school, that which exists only in appearance cannot be Absolute truth. Absolute truth is Reality itself as perceived by one who has reached a high stage of development through the acquisition of Wisdom and the tranquillization of the mind through meditation. According to the Yogacara school, the mind which has acquired Wisdom through meditation sees the whole of phenomenal existence and the Absolute Reality as interdependent, but not one.

Some who argue against the view that the relative and absolute are interdependent say that they are identical, that whatever constitutes the real nature of phenomena is at the same time the Reality of the Absolute. If, however, they are identical from the relative point of view, the eradication of defilements in the relative phenomena would at the same time be eradication of Reality. It would also imply that the Absolute truth would be imperfect, just as the relative phenomena are imperfect.

According to the Prasangika school the difficulties which arise when seeing the relative and absolute as interdependent or as identical can be avoided by the Two Truths. Everything, from the Unmanifested Body of the Buddhas to existing beings and things, can be regarded simultaneously from the point of view of Absolute truth and relative truth—there is nothing outside the scope of the Two Truths. Thus the two extreme views are avoided. The relative truth avoids the wrong extreme of self-dependent existence, while the Absolute truth avoids the extreme of annihilation.

The view that phenomena have only a dependent, a merely nominal, existence is the exact and pure relative truth. The Prasangika branch of the Madhyamika school holds that whatever things are compound are subject to causes and conditions and consequently have only a nominal and conceptual existence; there are no phenomena which have absolute independent existence. Even uncompounded principles come within the scope of dependent existence and are contingent, for their existence is dependent on causes and conditions and is not real existence. Thus the real nature of things and beings, which avoids the extremes of independent existence and of annihilation, is identical with the Absolute truth. Therefore, the Absolute truth is sunyata, which can be realized through the relative truth with the help of Wisdom and tranquillity of mind.

Although the exact nature of sunyata, voidness or emptiness, is difficult to describe in words, it can be explained and realized. Consequently it is wrong to say that the Absolute is beyond the comprehension of the mind—for the conception of the Absolute has itself only a relative and nominal existence. If the Absolute were incomprehensible, the Absolute would be reduced to the level of a barren abstraction. At the same time it remains true that no ordinary mind can realize the Absolute without first attaining Wisdom by means of right knowledge which is based on the Two Truths known through both reason and personal experience of meditation. Thus it is that the Buddha's teachings are the means for the realization of Truth.

SUNYATA

In Tibet the two best known schools which interpret the meaning of *sunyata* are the Yogacara, or Consciousness-Only school, and the Prasangika, or Critical school, which is a branch of Madhyamika. The Prasangika school adheres faithfully to the teaching of the Lord Buddha which was revived in India by Nagarjuna and was later given a fuller explanation by Tsongkhapa by means of the scholarly researches and spiritual practices he carried on under the inspiring directions of Lord Manjusri, the Bodhisattva of Wisdom.

Sunyata may be realized by means of the relative truth of the doctrine of dependent origination. The nature of sunyata is that beings have no individual existence in reality. This truth can be realized, with the help of reason, by those whose minds have become tranquillized and have developed Wisdom. The following line of thought may help one get a rough idea of what is meant by saying that beings and things have no self-existence.

If personality, for instance, really did exist, attachment to it could not be avoided, and therefore the attainment of enlightenment by means of spiritual practice would be impossible. But a thing does not have absolute existence nor a being have real personality because they both originate in dependence upon causes and conditions in the phenomenal world; they both possess only a relative or nominal existence. From the point of view of Absolute truth things are empty because they have no self-nature; from the relative point of view they are empty because they are dependent. That this dual conception was the ultimate view of the Buddha has been demonstrated by Nagarjuna.

The principle of dependent origination makes this clear. From the relative point of view it is possible for one thing to be produced by another. For instance, if the necessary conditions are present, a plant may grow out of a seed. But it does not grow in reality. Strictly speaking, it is not born of itself, nor of others, nor of both, nor is it born without a cause. It is impossible for a thing to be born out of itself, for in that case it would be in existence before its birth. Even the seed and its fruit are not regarded as a single entity. Things which are born out of cause and conditions, like a child from its mother or a plant from a seed, are called natural objects. If the cause could be independent of its own conditions, then the effect could be independent of the cause. Cause and effect are therefore mutually dependent. All phenomena exist within a space-time, causal framework and are destroyed only from the relative viewpoint of dependent origination. In their true nature they are beyond all such conceptions. Thus the conception of the emptiness of things from the Absolute point of view and that of their birth, duration, and destruction from the phenomenal point of view, are not opposed. Only in their relative nature are things subject to birth, duration, and destruction.

It is through the understanding of the dependent origination of phenomena that the Buddhist conception of sunyata can best be realized. When it is realized that beings and things do not have a self-nature, it is understood that they are relative and conceptual and do not exist from the Absolute point of view. The outstanding characteristic of sunyata is that it does not stand for the annihilation of things but merely for the negation of the false idea of their independent self-nature. It affirms the relative, conceptual existence of phenomena. He who realizes sunyata in this way understands the action of the law of karma, the effect of evil actions performed through ignorance. This is why the Bodhisattva, who realizes sunyata, is filled with compassion and seeks to lead mankind into the right Path.

The Nature of Man

The understanding of sunyata makes it possible to understand the nature of man. Man, according to Buddhism, consists of the five aggregates or skandhas, all of which are subject to change from one moment to another until the process of birth and death ceases in Nirvana. This compound called man is made up of one material and four mental aggregates—body, feeling, perception, volition, and consciousness. While the compound holds together, it experiences sensations which it likes or dislikes, it perceives the world around it, it desires, it thinks.

The compound of five aggregates aspires, resolves, remembers, contemplates, has faith, is heedful, tranquil, vigilant, and detached—and the opposite of each. It is subject to twenty-six defilements, all coming ultimately from ignorance. Due to its desires it becomes attached to its own aggregates, and from that come sufferings of every kind, and the other defilements such as hatred, pride, doubt, anger, jealousy, greed, hypocrisy, cunning, laziness, unchastity, heedlessness, distractedness, and the like.

This compound of aggregates, this man, is dependent upon the six organs of sense—eye, ear, nose, tongue, body, and mind. They in turn are dependent upon those sense objects in the changing world around them which can affect the six senses. In this aggregate, the "I" or the "self" cannot be identified with any one of the parts or with the total of the parts. The self or ego possesses only a nominal existence. Neither individually nor collectively do beings possess any independent ego or unchanging central principle. Man is a compound of aggregates brought together by the action of the law of karma, and what he becomes will be determined by the way in which he reacts in this existence and future existences which will also be shaped by the law of karma.

KARMA

The common people of Tibet know little of philosophy, but they at least know that it is futile to approach philosophy without an understanding of the law of karma. Their entire understanding and practice of the Teaching are the result of their constant awareness of karma and its inescapable consequences. It is this consciousness of the law of karma that produces patience, nonviolence, kindness, generosity, loyalty, and holiness in the lives of the Tibetan people.

Karma means action. The results of actions will be experienced, even after countless ages. Everything is caused by and dependent upon the law of karma—it is the law of nature. The good and bad qualities of the material universe and the happiness and sufferings of beings are all due to the law of karma. All the differences between beings, from the highest state of human perfection to the level of the most inferior beings such as insects and spirits, are conditioned by the law of karma. Karma is not the will of any god, nor a purposive plan. It is a universal principle which applies to all existing things, whether they recognize it or not. Karma may be defined as the inevitable sequence of cause and effect. He who understands the action of karma will understand the true nature of beings and things.

Tibetan Buddhism summarizes the characteristics of karma under four principles:

1. The consequences of karma are inevitable.
2. The consequences of karma are constantly on the increase, to however small an extent. That is, an evil act increases the evil and a good act increases the good, and the tendency continues unless it is checked by a more powerful karma.
3. One can never attain the desired result without acting upon the appropriate cause.
4. The results of one's actions will never be lost. Actions never annihilate themselves; even after the passing of hundreds of cosmic periods, their effects will come to maturity as soon as there is a conjunction of the right conditions.

From the point of view of human beings, karma is performed through the physical body, the vocal organs, and the mind and is meritorious or demeritorious. The ten demeritorious actions are killing any sentient being, taking things not given, indulgence in adultery, lying, slander, speaking abuse, gossip, thoughts of hatred, thoughts of craving, holding wrong views. Obviously, the results of these actions will vary according to the circumstances. If done by a lay devotee, a novice, a fully ordained monk, a Bodhisattva, or a tantric devotee, the demeritorious acts will produce graver consequences than if done by an ordinary person. Similarly, the same karma will have different consequences if done by a wise man than if done by a fool, for the wise man will undertake the practice of mental purification while the fool will ignore such a procedure.

Karma may mature through the consequences of being reborn in the animal kingdom, the spirit world, or in lower worlds, or it may mature after being born as a human being. For instance, the residual karmic consequence of killing is the unnatural death of the person who committed the act; it determines one's birth in a country where wars, diseases, and similar conditions will bring one's life to a speedy end. In the next birth there is a reawakened inclination to resort to the performance of the same action which determined that birth—whether the determining karma was killing or compassion.

Meritorious actions—such as almsgiving, chastity, speaking the truth, propagation of the Dharma, mediating between enemies, contentment, love for all beings, and holding right moral and philosophical views—will also mature in rebirth as a human being who will enjoy long life and health, spiritual progress, and life in a family and country which is peaceful and happy.

Some karmas bear fruit in the same life in which they occur. These include actions committed out of extreme selfishness or generosity, or as a result of antagonism against or faith in the Three Refuges, the guru, one's parents, or the common people. Whichever karma is strongest will bear fruit first, some in this life, some in the immediately succeeding one, and some in remote future lives.

Without having understood the nature of karma, it is hardly possible for one to realize the Supreme Reality. It is closely related to the Buddhist doctrine of the dependent origination of all things, for beings and things arise in dependence on the causes and conditions which bring them into existence, and they are really devoid of any selfhood. By understanding the law of cause and effect one can understand the relativity of all things and thus see that all phenomena are empty, that they possess only nominal existence. Thus the law of karma is the necessary consequence of the doctrine of dependent origination. It is also due to the law of karma, the reality of the inevitability of the results of our actions, that it is possible for us to act in such a way that we can follow the Path which leads to Enlightenment.

REBIRTH

Since there is no soul in beings, there cannot be any transmigration in the sense of an unchanging soul or ego moving from body to body. The rebirth is determined by the meritorious volitions of past lives, just as the plant grows from the seed. The actual process has been explained in the Buddhist doctrine of the twelve links in the chain of causation. In Tibetan Buddhism it is illustrated in the Wheel of Existence, which gives a vivid pictorial representation of how consciousness, obscured by ignorance, goes on accumulating all sorts of life-affirming activities. The Wheel of Existence symbolizes the unbroken circle of births and deaths which goes on in the various worlds.

In addition to the results of actions in past and present lives, the immediate cause determining the kind of rebirth one obtains is in each case the nature of the dying thoughts. If evil thoughts have defiled the consciousness at the time of dying, one will suffer rebirth in an inferior state, just as pure thoughts will bring rebirth in a superior state among men or the gods.

Those people who have committed neither highly meritorious nor highly demeritorious karma—whose consciousness is like a dried seed that needs heat and moisture—instead of being reborn at once, remain for some time in an intermediate state known as the Bardo. Such people, having failed to think good thoughts at the time of death, will have to experience subjective states which arouse emotions of fear, desire, and alarm, and these states partially determine the nature of their succeeding rebirth because they bring about the ripening of evil actions previously committed. The length of sojourn in Bardo varies from one week to seven. Tibetan Buddhists believe that while the consciousness is in this state it can be assisted by those with whom it had spiritual or physical relationship while on earth. It will be helped if such people will spend their property for the spiritual and material welfare of the masses and will perform various types of religious ceremonies for the benefit of the consciousnesses in Bardo.

The Old Translation school has a book called *The Liberation from the Intermediate State*—translated into English as *The Tibetan Book of the Dead*—which is read in front of the dying man or in front of the dead body by a celibate Lama. This practice is based on the Tibetan belief that after death the consciousness of the deceased person remains in or near the body for a week, or at least for three days, so that communication with it is still possible by means of the vibrations set up by the recitation of inspiring scriptures of this type or by the power of a spiritual genius.

According to the Abhidharma, beings in the intermediate state possess five subtle senses and live on odors, and therefore Tibetans make burnt offerings of barley flour, honey, sugar, milk, sandalwood powder, and fragrant herbs. At the conclusion of this ceremony the merits accruing from its performance are dedicated to the deceased. This ceremony is performed once a week by a monk and daily by a member of the family.

Since the mental state of a dying person is, as it were, the steering wheel which guides the karmic vehicle to its destination, Tibetans attach great importance to what they call the art of dying, the transference of consciousness. This is one of the tantric practices. The people who are advanced in tantric practice can choose their deaths and rebirths at will. The friends and relatives, and his own Lama, have the special responsibility of giving the dying man the moral support which will enable him to restrain anger and tranquillize his disturbed mind. They must use all possible means to make sure that only good and pure thoughts are present in his mind. Any object or person for whom he has either a strong liking or dislike should be removed from the room. A faithful friend should assure him that he should not be anxious about his family, for the friend will look after them as if they were his own. The spiritual master should give instructions in the art of dying. The dying man is asked to have faith in the Triple Gem, to repent his evil actions with a pure heart, to resolve to keep the precepts, to make solemn vows, and to cultivate love toward all beings and a right understanding of phenomena.

At the expiration of his last breath the Lama performs the ceremony called "The Transference of Consciousness."

Thus does the Wheel of Life turn for all beings.

THE GOAL OF HUMAN BEINGS

The highest attainment possible to a human being is liberation from the fetters of ignorance. That state of attainment is Enlightenment; it is Nirvana. It is for the sake of that liberation that one follows the Path of the Buddha.

This Path is not followed in order to save one's soul, for there is no soul to be saved. It is not followed for the sake of the development of one's personality or for self-improvement, for there is no self to improve, no personality to be developed. Nor is the Path followed for the sake of rebirth in paradise, although the idea of such rebirth makes a strong appeal to the ignorant masses. Strictly speaking, the popular idea of rebirth in a paradise stands in the way of the proper practice of the Dharma for the sake of liberation from the fetters of ignorance. However, the principle of gradual spiritual development through a series of lives does admit the possibility of a temporary existence in paradise as a means of attaining the final goal—but it is not, of course, the goal itself.

The first objective of a human being is to insure, under the law of karma, a series of human lives which will make possible continuity of effort toward the realization of the goal of liberation from ignorance. Spiritual progress depends upon the accumulation of merits and step-by-step advancement in the acquisition of intuitive knowledge. Lack of the necessary understanding very often causes a good devotee to become, after death, a powerful spirit. In this state there are few opportunities to realize the truth, which is why it is considered to be an inferior, miserable kind of existence. Since human life is the one and only approach to the Path of Deliverance, it is supremely important to live so that successive rebirths will bring one nearer to that goal.

The central theme of Buddhism is that man's destiny lies in his own hands and that he can attain Enlightenment by adopting the course that ultimately sets him free from the bondage of existence and leads to the realization of the Supreme Truth. The moral and philosophical teachings of Buddhism aim at the development of wisdom and compassion to their fullest extent in order that a man may gain Enlightenment not for himself alone but for the sake of all sentient beings. The practice of morality and meditation are the characteristics of the Path which leads to Nirvana.

THE SIX TRANSCENDENTAL VIRTUES

The Six Transcendental Virtues are a most comprehensive, creative, and inspiring formula. They constitute the Path of Supreme Enlightenment and are an effective means to moral purification and spiritual perfection. These virtues, which embody the highest ethical principles and the most beneficial intellectual training, were exemplified by the Lord Buddha in the course of his human career. They are: Transcendental Almsgiving, Morality, Endurance, Exertion, Contemplation, and Wisdom.

The practice of each virtue must be preceded by taking a sincere refuge in the Triple Gem, understanding the law of karma, and by the practice of the basic moral precepts, the realization of the impermanence of all beings and things, and the firm resolve to live a life which follows the Path of the Buddha. These practices include the Four Noble Truths, the Noble Eightfold Path, and an understanding of the Twelve Causal Links. In addition, one must develop compassion and love for all beings by remembering that during countless lives beings have all been one's own mother and that, like oneself, they are subject to suffering.

Transcendental Almsgiving includes giving of one's personal property whenever asked to give, giving useful and beneficial instructions to others, protecting all life and aiding the unfortunate by all possible means, and kind and compassionate treatment of others. Transcendental Almsgiving is perfected when one has a will power and compassion so strong that he is ready to sacrifice even his own life for others without the slightest hesitation or fear.

Transcendental Morality is made up of abstention from evil practices, practice of the positive and creative precepts of Buddhism, and benevolent and altruistic practices for the benefit of all beings.

Transcendental Endurance is endurance of antagonism and suffering trials and sacrifices in the pursuit of the realization of Supreme Truth—endurance which is free from hatred, bitterness, or envy.

Transcendental Exertion is action motivated by a strong resolve and solemn vow to serve all beings and liberate them from the bondage of mundane existence; it is the optimistic and creative practice of the six virtues without despair; and it is the removal of all laziness, sense of inferiority, lack of confidence, and attachment to things or evil actions.

Transcendental Contemplation is the means of gaining control over one's mind so that one gains tranquillity, calm, and a disciplined mind.

Transcendental Wisdom is the wisdom acquired by learning, reflecting, and meditating on whatever concerns the path of right and wrong and the destinies of beings here and hereafter. It is, undoubtedly, the most effective weapon for cutting away that attachment to one's own existence which is incompatible with the attainment of Enlightenment. It is acquired primarily through the practice of meditation.

MEDITATION

Meditation has occupied a central place in all forms of Buddhism. It is the effective means of eradicating skepticism and wrong views and of developing the intuitive knowledge, wisdom, and compassion which make it possible to have the insight which leads to Enlightenment.

Meditation must always be preceded by morality and concentration. The moral disciplines are designed to create mental purity, right motive, vigilance, watchfulness, patience, and diligence in order that the practice of concentration might be possible. Religious devotion is the first stage of moral discipline. For ignorant people a good start is worship of the Triple Gem, recitation of verses illustrative of moral and philosophical teachings, the recitation of Sutras and mantras, prostration before an image, offering water, flowers, and lamps, and confession. The aim of religious devotions is the bringing about of a spiritual awakening and the development of moral character.

The second preliminary step before meditation is concentration, which is the means of getting rid of one's evil actions, habits, thoughts, and emotions in order to attain tranquillity. Through concentration one gains full control over one's thoughts and feelings, thus making meditation possible. The objects of concentration may be the Triple Gem, mantras, symbolic implements, one's own nerve centers, the breath, or the Kundalini—the internal coiled-up energy. The object of concentration may be used later as the subject of meditation.

If the different deities have been used as objects of concentration, they may also serve for meditation. Corresponding to the different manifestations of each deity there have been evolved specific ways and means of meditation. A peaceful and beautiful aspect, white in color, is indicative of the blissful state of the Buddhas and of the cessation of all evils. A fearful aspect, either black or dark blue, represents the power of wisdom to destroy ignorance. Some aspects are both peaceful and fearful; and if yellow, they represent the power of maturing sentient beings; if red, they stand for the power of influencing all beings. These deities are of great value for meditation; through worship a devotee may gain inspiration for his spiritual development. The recitation of a deity's mantra helps to concentrate the mind, but meditation upon one of the aspects of the deity is more important. The choice of a deity as an object of meditation is made on the recommendation of the guru.

Without meditation liberation from the bondage of existence and the practice of the Bodhisattva ideal is impossible. Although Tibetan Buddhism follows some forms of meditation which are taught in the Sutras, it is predominantly tantric. In tantric meditation the lower aspect of a phenomenon is transformed into the higher aspect by means of the constant awareness of its fundamental reality. This is the basic principle of tantric meditation.

Three of the four collections of Tantras advocate religious devotion, concentration, and meditation directed to one's own tutelary deity, his mantra and symbols, together with breathing exercises, all of which are to be practiced with the support of Wisdom and right views consciously held. By intensive meditation in this way a devotee can develop within himself spiritual attainments so great that even his physical body is no longer subject to natural law. Such a body can be utilized for the attainment of a higher stage.

The fourth Tantra, the Supreme Tantra, teaches two main stages of meditation—the stage of self-spiritualization and the stage of spiritual perfection. The first stage consists in meditating upon oneself and one's tutelary deities as spiritualized and transformed into a higher nature. As the devotee progresses in this practice, he meditates upon a tiny radiant disc in which he visualizes the deity in the full size and shape of a man without affecting the size of the disc or the man. Here, as always, the devotee must be conscious, to the extent that his development in Wisdom permits, of its illusory nature on the one hand and its absolute reality and compassion on the other. At this stage there is another meditative process which aims to spiritualize the ordinary process of the Wheel of Life and transform life, death, Bardo, and birth into the Triple Enlightenment.

Among the accompanying actions of tantric meditation are rendering devotion and homage to the Triple Gem and to one's personal spiritual master and his lineage, taking the Bodhisattva vows to work for the benefit of all beings, mental sanctification, the purification and dedication of offerings to the deities, invocation of spiritual blessings on all beings, confession, admiration for the Buddha Ideal, recitation of prayers and mantras, and the transference of one's individual merits to all beings.

The second stage of meditation in the Supreme Tantra is the stage of spiritual perfection. It utilizes the subtle body, the "channel of spiritual energy," various nerve centers, the creative power released from the Kundalini, the retention of the breath, and various bodily postures. It proceeds then through six stages:

1. The purification of one's physical body and its transformation into a subtle illusory form.
2. Purification of the lower nature of the vocal organ and its transformation into a spiritualized eternal voice.
3. Purification of every kind of wrong view, attachment, and desire and the realization of the absolutely true and blissful nature of the Triple Form of Enlightenment.
4. While using various forms of breathing exercises, meditation centers on the psychic body with constant awareness regarding its spiritualization.
5. Meditation for the simultaneous realization of the Absolute and of the Supreme Bliss.
6. This stage aims at the attainment of the perfect but still dual state wherein the illusory body is manifested from the perfected mind which has realized the Absolute Reality. After this stage one attains the state of inseparable union with the Triple Body of the Buddhas.

Throughout all these stages of meditation the practice of yoga is carried on in a way which utilizes the natural psychic or spiritual powers of man. It is an excellent means of gaining a high stage of spiritual enlightenment rapidly. Tibetan tantric practice is strictly guarded against intellectual ambition or materialistic tendencies because psychic powers obtained without moral qualities and spiritual motives, without a humanitarian orientation through Wisdom and Compassion, are likely to be used for vulgar and evil purposes.

Tantric practice never aims at the acquisition of such powers as floating in the air, transforming oneself into various shapes, multiplying personality, transferring one's own or another's consciousness into a different body, thought reading, and the like. Psychic powers are of little importance. What is important is the attainment of Supreme Enlightenment for the sake of all sentient beings.

NIRVANA

Nirvana is identical with Supreme Enlightenment, with the gaining of the Threefold Body of Buddhahood, and with the cessation of birth. Nirvana is the complete cessation not only of sorrow, but also of its cause. It is the cessation of delusion, attachment, hatred, and of the holding of inconsistent views; it is the cessation of all clinging to the false idea of an ego-personality.

The nature of the perfect Nirvana being difficult to conceive or explain, one has to realize it for oneself. It is a subjective state of purity produced by the complete cessation of mental defilements. In it there is no place for either attachment or nonattachment, either to the self or to the not-self. It is not an objective reality into which men enter and rest, nor is it a particular mental state. It is pure, eternal, unchanging, unextended, nonsubstantial, quiescent, attributeless, unacquired, and devoid of unsupported cause and condition. It is emptiness but not nothingness, calm but not compassion, selfless but not the Supreme Reality. It is not consciousness (for it is devoid of the five skandhas), nor unconsciousness, nor both, nor neither. It cannot be spoken of as existent, for it is noncompounded, nor nonexistent, for within the sphere of subjective experience it is a reality. At the same time it transcends the limits within which distinctions are made between elements and between space and time. Furthermore, if it were nonexistent the practice of good deeds, contemplation, and meditation would be fruitless.

The negation of both existence and nonexistence must be cognized either empirically or by means of transcendental intuition (prajna). Empirical knowledge needs some tangible attributes to take hold of—but Nirvana has no such attributes. Transcendental intuition has only the void, essencelessness (sunyata) for its object—consequently it cannot cognize Nirvana as being either existence or nonexistence, for such a characterization constitutes a definite essence. Being without origination, formless and indescribable, Nirvana is not to be cognized even as the negation of existence and nonexistence. Nirvana really consists in the avoidance of the notion that "Nirvana exists."

Although Nirvana is not produced by the Path, it can be attained by following the Path. In the ultimate analysis, the following of the Path and the attainment of Nirvana are illusions having no basis in reality. One should take as one's aim simply the getting rid of all misconceptions about the existence and nonexistence of beings and things and the realization of the essentially nondual nature of all phenomena whatsoever. Nirvana is not to be eradicated like the passions, nor attained like the fruits of saintship. It consists in the avoidance of all notions of eradication and destruction—so long as the mind continues indulging in such notions there can be no Nirvana. Once this is realized, all attempts at particularization and definition cease. Nirvana is the complete disappearance of all figments of the imagination. Unless the ego-conception in all its forms is eradicated, beings will continue to assume the existence and nonexistence of things, which will result in endless suffering. When the ego-conception in all its forms is finally eradicated, that is Nirvana, that constitutes the Triple Form of Enlightenment—the Highest Goal of Tibetan Buddhism.

CHAPTER SEVEN

Buddhism in Japan

Shinsho Hanayama

Included in this chapter are sections on Shin and Jodo
Buddhism by Mitsuyuki Ishida, Zen Buddhism by Reiho
Masunaga, and Nichiren Buddhism by Shobun Kubota.

The earliest historical records concerning Buddhism in
Japan, compiled in the eighth century, differ as to the date
on which the envoy from the ruler of Korea introduced
Buddhism to the Emperor of Japan. Whether it happened in
538, the most widely accepted date, or on October 13, 552,
it is likely that the many Koreans who had been coming to
Japan for some time had already introduced Buddhism among
the common people.

The ruler of the small western kingdom in Korea presented
to the Imperial Household in Japan a gold-plated image of
Sakyamuni Buddha, together with some other Buddhist articles, some Sutras, and a letter in which he praised the Buddhist
faith. In that letter the Buddha's teachings are referred to as
the Supreme Truth which will bestow boundless rewards upon
the believers in the Dharma and will guide people to the state
of Enlightenment. The letter describes the transmission of
Buddhism from India through China to Korea and says that
the ruler is now introducing this supreme religion to Japan in
fulfillment of the prediction of the Buddha that his teachings
would be transferred to the East.

According to the record of the Imperial Household, the
emperor was greatly pleased and exclaimed, "Never have I
heard of such an exquisite teaching. Never have I seen anything so radiant and beautiful as the Buddha's face." It is not

difficult for us to see the reason for these words of the emperor. The culture of Japan at that time was very low and unrefined, and for this reason it can be easily imagined that the people were astounded at the solemn beauty of the image of the Buddha and the profundity and mysteriousness of the teachings of Buddhism. When the emperor consulted his court as to the advisability of accepting Buddhism, the leader of the Soga clan replied that if Buddhism was being practiced in various countries throughout the world, there was no reason why it should not be accepted in Japan. But the leader of the Mononobe clan opposed the suggestion on the ground that the emperor of Japan had always paid homage to the various gods at every season of the year and, if this foreign Buddha were accepted, it would rouse the wrath of the gods who had been protecting the country. Since agreement could not be reached, the emperor presented the image to the leader of the Soga clan to worship freely.

Such opposition to Buddhism as was expressed at that time was due more to political rivalry between these two clans than to a struggle between Buddhism and Shintoism. At that time, Shintoism was still in a primitive stage and was undoubtedly far below the cultural level of Buddhism as it had developed in all the countries of Asia.

The first of the Mikados to put his faith in Buddhism was Emperor Yomei who assumed the throne in 585. Unfortunately, soon after becoming emperor, he became ill and passed away. During his illness, a man named Tasuna left his home and relatives, renounced the world, and became a priest in order to pray for the recovery of the emperor. This is the first record of anyone in Japan becoming a Buddhist monk. Even though his motivation was not his own salvation, as was the case in early Buddhism, from the Mahayana point of view, which aims at the Enlightenment of all forms of being, it was permissible.

As the illness of the Emperor progressed, he requested that an image be made of Bhaishajyaguru, the Buddha of the East, who is the Buddha of Healing, known for his vows to cure all kinds of sickness and spiritual illness due to ignorance. Although the emperor died before the image was completed, the work went on under his younger sister, the Empress Suiko, and was installed in the world-famous Horyuji Temple at Nara, where it may still be found today. The first temples to be built in Japan by the state were Hokoji in 596 and Horyuji in 607. Horyuji, "a temple for the development of the Buddha Dharma," is generally regarded as the oldest wooden building in the world today.

PRINCE SHOTOKU

Empress Suiko, the first Empress of Japan, took over the throne in 592 in order to end the confusion created by the assassination of the emperor, her brother-in-law. She immediately appointed Prince Shotoku, the son of Emperor Yomei, as her successor and made him the Regent. He was nineteen years old at that time, and for the next thirty years he governed the country wisely, laying a firm foundation for the government and devoting his efforts to the elevation of the cultural life of the people.

At the beginning of his regency Prince Shotoku adopted Buddhism with the conviction that it was the world trend of philosophical thought of his time. He expanded school facilities, dispatched envoys and students to China to bring back the highly developed culture of that country, compiled the first history of Japan, promulgated the first constitution for the country, encouraged industries, improved transportation and communication, provided medical care for the ill, saw that kind attention was given to orphans and the weak, and instructed the people to extend the same degree of kindness to animals. Indeed, the accomplishments of Prince Shotoku made his regency a brilliant era in the history of Japan.

On the first of February, 594, Prince Shotoku issued an Imperial Ordinance supporting and urging the development of the Three Treasures—the Buddha, the Truth (Dharma), and the Brotherhood (Sangha). The year that this Ordinance was promulgated is considered to be the date of the establishment of Buddhism in Japan. It marks the end of the half century of struggle between opposing clans and the beginning of the period in which the people throughout the nation were united into one as followers of the Buddha's teachings. According to the official history of that period, the officials competed with one another in the building of Buddha temples in appreciation for the blessings and privileges bestowed upon them by the Emperors and the ancestors of their clan.

Such temples had not been known in Japan before the arrival of Buddhism. In India the first temples (viharas) had been built as training centers for followers of the teachings of the Buddha, and later as buildings to house the images of the Buddha, but in Japan the temples were built by the people primarily as a means of expressing their feelings of gratitude toward the emperors and their ancestors. This attitude toward the temples has continued to modern times. The temples of the various sects in Japan have functioned as centers of religious studies, as training centers for religious practices, and as centers for spreading Buddhism, but most temples have also as a matter of course served the primary function of having funerals and memorial services for their followers and keeping custody of their family graves. This is evidence of the fact that the family system and the relation between the people and the Imperial Household determined the way in which they accepted the teachings of Buddhism.

The Constitution which Prince Shotoku gave to the people in 604 was based on the principle that harmony among the people should be the aim of any human society. Recognizing the difficulty of carrying out this principle, the Constitution stipulated that the actual means for realizing the aim was the revering of the Three Treasures. It was pointed out that the wrongs which were being committed daily in the lives of men could be corrected only by observing and accepting the way of life of the true Dharma of the Buddha which had been highly respected by the people of the world throughout the ages.

Two years after the promulgation of the new Constitution, Prince Shotoku lectured for the first time on the Srimaladevi-simhanada Sutra, the Sutra which is a sermon delivered by a princess, a laywoman, and which was sanctioned by the Buddha. Later in the same year, he gave a lecture on the Saddharma

Pundarika, *The Lotus of the True Law*, which sets forth the doctrines of One Vehicle and the Eternal Buddha. These lectures were the beginning of the practice of venerating and lecturing on the Buddhist Sutras in Japan. It was also at this time that Prince Shotoku decided to preserve the lectures for posterity by writing commentaries on the Sutras.

It may not be too far from the truth to conclude that it was because of his resolve to write the commentaries that he sent the first envoys to China in 607 and again in 608, to bring back important Buddhist books. Because of the difficulties of transportation, it is not likely that the three most important longer Sutras were the first ones available in Japan—that is, the Mahaparinirvana Sutra, the Avatamsaka Sutra, and the Prajnaparamita Sutra. It is much more likely that the first Sutras to be translated and circulated in Japan were the three which Prince Shotoku selected for his commentaries—the Saddharma Pundarika Sutra (Hokekyo in Japanese), Vimalakirtinirdesa Sutra (Yuimakyo in Japanese), and the Srimaladevisimhanada Sutra (Shomangyo in Japanese). These three are classified as shorter Sutras; although they are much shorter than the others, they have practically the same importance from the standpoint of contents.

The Vimalakirtinirdesa Sutra praises the Mahayana way rather than the Hinayana. The other two shorter Sutras teach the principle of Ekayana (One Vehicle) which is a harmony achieved on a higher plane, rising above the problem of the superiority or inferiority of the Mahayana or Hinayana ways and avoiding the undesirable discrimination between the two schools of Buddhism.

The Ekayana way, which is the supreme way, is the method of following the Path by which Enlightenment may be achieved by all forms of life universally and equally, whereby all good actions are given equal value and the final goal of attaining the realm of the absolute Buddha can be attained by all beings. The final objective is the absolute Buddha, the Awakened One with boundless life, with boundless mercy, compassion, wisdom, and light. The absolute Buddha is called the Dharmakaya Buddha, and the historical Sakyamuni is considered to be a realization of the Dharmakaya. The absolute Buddha transcends the limitations of time and space and is in actuality the Dharma (Truth) itself. The absolute Buddha is free from all changes of the cycle of life and death and is the final ideal objective of all beings. All modern schools of Buddhism in Japan consider themselves to be followers of Ekayana.

Prince Shotoku worshiped this Dharmakaya Buddha and put his faith in Ekayana, the Buddhism of one Great Vehicle. In his practice of the Ekayana way he made no distinction between the ways of laymen and priests. He taught the way of practicing the Ekayana in everyday life and saw no need for the followers to leave their wives and children to pursue the way by profound meditation in solitude as practiced in Hinayana Buddhism. This attitude of Prince Shotoku toward religious practices gave rise to another characteristic of Japanese Buddhism, the Buddhism practiced in family life, which became typical of the Buddhism of Japan.

Prince Shotoku wrote his commentaries as an expression of his firm belief in the teachings of the Buddha. He interpreted the Mahayana philosophy and practices, not according to the literal meaning of the words, but rather according to the underlying meanings based on a thorough understanding of the Buddha's spirit. Through his envoys he obtained many commentaries on the Mahayana Sutras which had been written by the most authoritative Chinese philosophers of his time. He has indicated in his commentaries the mistakes which had been made by the Chinese translators and has commented on some of their mistaken interpretations. He also expressed his own confident, sometimes arbitrary, interpretations on various problems raised by other commentaries on the Sutras.

Prince Shotoku died in 622, greatly mourned by the people of Japan. According to the ancient records, "So deep was the sorrow of the people that it was identical with the sorrow of the aged man who was deprived of his only child, of the child which has lost its compassionate parents; the heaven and earth seemed to have fallen, and the heavenly bodies of the universe had ceased to glow." It is not difficult for us to understand the sorrow expressed in the ancient records. The image of the

Sakyamuni Buddha enshrined in the Golden Hall of Horyuji temple today was made in memory of Prince Shotoku a year after his death and was made to stand just the same height as the prince.

NARA BUDDHISM

The Nara Era, as defined in the historical records, was from 710 to 783, but all early Buddhism in Japan centered around Nara and may conveniently be referred to as Nara Buddhism. It was in the vicinity of Nara that the first transcriptions of the Tripitaka were made, the first commentaries written, the first distinctively Japanese festivals originated, and the first sects arose.

Following the death of Prince Shotoku the country was disturbed by rebellion until the Taika Reformation in 645, but fortunately the attitude of the state toward Buddhism was unchanged. The number of priests had increased so much that it now became necessary for the emperor to appoint ten state Buddhist masters to guide the priests and monks in their study and practice of Buddhism. The emperor also turned his energy to completing the temples and other memorial buildings which had been delayed by the unsettled conditions during the civil strife.

One of the first festivals to grow up in Japanese Buddhism was the Urabon-E, commonly called Bon. It began with the emperor calling all the court officials and subjects to the temples to read the Avalambana Sutra—called Ullambana and then Urabon in Japanese, hence its name. The Bon dance originated with the story of Moggaliputta, the disciple of the Buddha who, on the day marking the end of the rainy-season retreat, made offerings to the large gathering of Bhikkhus and was filled with joy when he saw that the offerings had saved his mother from horrible suffering in the land of the hungry devil (one of the six worlds of suffering). The dance is an expression of joy at the release of a person from one of the worlds of suffering. Thus the Bon dance is usually conducted today in temple grounds and participated in by many people to express their feeling of happiness. In Japan Bon is based on the belief in the obligation to console and make offerings to the spirit of the parents and ancestors who have passed from this life.

Another religious festival which originated at this time and was continued as one of the most important Buddhist affairs for several centuries—though not very widely observed in modern times—was the Yuima-E. It is based on the Vimalakirtinirdesa Sutra which is called the Yuimakyo in Japanese. It originated when an ancestor of the Fujiwara clan was stricken with illness and the emperor sought to aid and console him by having the Yuimakyo read to him. Because of the spiritual consolation given to him by this reading, he fully recovered and in the following year built a temple where the Sutra was read and studied every year. The temple, Kobukuji, still stands and is regarded as the headquarters of the Hosso sect.

The Ninno-E, or Ninno Service, was first held at this same period in the latter half of the seventh century. It was built around the study and chanting of the Prajnaparamita Sutra, called Ninnohannyakyo in Japanese. This Sutra is one of the state-protecting Sutras which protects against natural calamities and thus brings peace to the lives of the people. This service gradually gained popularity among the people, and the Prajna-paramita Sutra was widely studied and chanted throughout Japan. For some centuries it was a national custom for the emperor to hold a Great Ninno Service at least once during his reign, but that custom is not continued in modern times.

During the latter half of the seventh century the emperors and their families were influential in propagating Buddhism throughout Japan. Services within the palace with many priests participating were held more frequently, temples were built in the regional government centers, and Buddhism was introduced to the most remote districts of Japan. Ordinances were issued governing the conduct of men and women priests, and state Buddhist Masters were appointed to guide the priests and people in their quest for the teachings of the Buddha. The day that an emperor passed away was designated a National Mourning Day, and other days were designated for Buddhist ceremonies. During this period the Tripitakas were copied and studied. It was also at this time that the common people began the custom of releasing birds and fish which had been captured, as a means of practicing the pity to animals which is an expression of the spirit of compassion taught in Buddhism.

During the two centuries after Prince Shotoku, many students returned to Japan after having spent years in China studying Buddhism. It was these students of Chinese Buddhism who introduced the various sects which became prominent in the Nara Era. By the beginning of the ninth century the government officially recognized six Buddhist sects—Sanron, Hosso, Kegon, Ritsu, Jojitsu, and Kusha. An understanding of these sects will give a clear picture of the development of Buddhism in Japan during the first few centuries after it was introduced by the Korean envoy.

Two of these sects, while recognized in the official lists, did not have a significant separate existence. The Jojitsu sect was based on the study of the Satyasiddhi Sastra (Jojitsuron in Japanese), which was closely related to one of the Three Treatises of the San-lun sect in China. It was only natural that as San-lun came to Japan as the Sanron sect, those who were interested in the Satyasiddhi Sastra turned to the wider field of study offered by the Three Treatises. The other minor early sect was Kusha, based on the Abhidharmakosha of Vasubandhu (Kusharon, in Japanese). As the Hosso sect grew in importance, since its doctrines included those expounded in the Abhidharmakosha, followers of the Kusha were absorbed in Hosso. Thus there are only four sects of importance in the Nara period, Sanron, Hosso, Kegon, and Ritsu.

THE SANRON (THREE TREATISES) SECT

The Sanron sect of Japan was the San-lun sect in China, based on the Three Treatises—the Madhyamika and Dvadasanikaya of Nagarjuna and the Sataka, written by Aryadeva. According to the records, the Sanron sect was introduced to Japan from Korea in 625. Some time later they sent scholars to China for further study, and under their leadership the teachings became broader and more profound. There was a tendency toward the development of subsects as different scholars returned from China and won followers to their teaching.

The few writings which we have today from the early scholars of the Sanron sect indicate that they had made an intensive study of the Madhyamika philosophy of Nagarjuna and of the Vijnanavada doctrines which became the characteristic teachings of the Hosso sect in Japan. They show evidence of careful study of the major treatises of Mahayana and of the Hinayana treatises, Abhidharmakosha and Satyasiddhi, which were favored by Kusha and Jojitsu. Since the scholars of this school wished to be freed from all attachments, they refrained from calling their faith by any sectarian name.

Although they were called Mahayana, they used the term not in the sense of opposition to Hinayana but in the highest sense of the word as transcending the sectarian positions of both Hinayana and Mahayana. The basic principle of their doctrines was that the highest realization is to be grasped through the passive expression of sunyata, emptiness. This belief in passivity led them to criticize the followers of the Hosso school for their close relations with the officials and executives of the government. They were also very critical of the Hosso doctrine which classifies human beings in five categories and designates one class of human beings as people devoid of the Buddha-nature, who could never attain Buddhahood. The Sanron scholars strongly maintained that the true meaning of the Buddha's teaching is that all forms of being are equally entitled to become enlightened Buddhas.

The Sanron sect does not exist in Japan as a separate school in modern times, but its doctrines are still studied.

THE HOSSO (CONSCIOUSNESS-ONLY) SECT

The Hosso sect in Japan developed from the Consciousness-Only school of Hsuan-tsang in China, based on the writings of Asanga and Vasubandhu. The scholar Dosho was the first to introduce the doctrines of Hosso in Japan, about 660, at a time when the doctrines had not yet been fully formulated in China. He is believed to have brought some Chinese translations to Japan and upon his return is said to have devoted himself to promoting the welfare of the people, especially through the building of wells along major roads, and improving transportation and communication through building bridges. When he died, his followers obeyed his directions and cremated his body.

The cremation of Dosho introduced to Japan a custom which had originated in India and was based on the teachings of Buddhism, that since the human body is merely a compound of the four elements of earth, water, fire, and air, it is destined to return to those elements. The spread of the practice of cremation was to some extent a measure of the spread of Buddhism. But one strong motive was without doubt the desire to cut down the expense of burial rites and the cost of building large mausoleums. The adoption of the practice of cremation thus freed funds which would have been used for mausoleums so that they could be used for the construction of temples which spread the teachings of Buddhism among the people. It also helped to overcome some of the primitive beliefs of the common people which had been based on fear of death and a reverence for the dead body.

After the time of Dosho, other scholars followed his example and went to China where they now were able to study the completely established doctrines of the Hosso school. They brought back with them a great many excellent copies of the Sutras which were then copied and distributed widely among the people. Some of those copies are now designated as national treasures, not only because of their age and religious importance, but also for their beauty as artistic creations.

Gyogi (670–749) was a student of Dosho who followed the example of his master by going about in Japan building bridges, embankments, ports, and free inns for travelers in an effort to promote the welfare of the people. Thus he practiced the spirit of the Bodhisattva, for which he was highly respected by the people. He also participated in the erection of the Daibutsu, the Great Buddha image, and for his virtuous actions and achievements was given at the time of his death the title of Bodhisattva. This was quite unusual, for in Japanese history only a few people have been given the honorable title of Bodhisattva.

The doctrines of the Hosso sect were very much the same as those of the Consciousness-Only school in China, with the emphasis on the fact that the true nature of the Dharma lies outside the realm of logical explanations and must be sought in the realm of consciousness only.

As we have seen, there was some controversy concerning the Hosso principle that human beings are classified in five groups, one of which cannot attain to Buddhahood. It has long been the desire of human beings to become enlightened Buddhas themselves and to help other forms of life eventually attain Buddhahood, this being the great compassion of the Buddha. However, it must be admitted that there are people who are very wicked and possibly cannot be freed from all types of evil. Certainly, there are incongruities between the ideal and the actual in life. When the law of karma is applied to all people, there seems to be an element of truth in the Hosso doctrine that there are some people who can never hope to become enlightened Buddhas, people who are devoid of even a vestige of goodness. It is not surprising that in the class-conscious Nara Era there were people who accepted this teaching of the Hosso sect.

However, this must have been incompatible with the other principle taught by the Hosso sect, based on the Brahmajala Sutra, that all forms of existence in the six worlds—the worlds of hell, hungry demons, beasts, spirits, human beings, and gods —are indeed one's parents through their existence in previous births. One of the great Hosso teachers, Zenju, stressed this point when he said that the ordinary concept of filial piety, which requires that we meet hatred with hatred, is like trying to quench a flame with grass, while Buddhism requires that we "face hatred with love and this is like putting out the flame with water." Thus the widely accepted concept of filial piety which implied that a son must take revenge for an injury to his father was changed to a broader attitude toward all beings.

The Hosso sect exists in Japan today as a small sect with about twenty ancient shrines, but the doctrines which it taught concerning Consciousness-Only are a part of the principles of many sects.

THE KEGON SECT

The Kegon sect is based on the Avatamsaka Sutra (called Kegon in Japanese and Hua-yen in Chinese). This Sutra, in eighty volumes, was copied in 722 in memory of the former emperor, but it was not until 740 that a Korean priest began to lecture on the Sutra and founded the Kegon sect in Japan. Although the sect grew for a time during the Nara Era, there were no new doctrines developed in Japan.

Kegon in Japan accepted the classification of the scriptures in five levels, as had their predecessors (the Hua-yen sect) in China, with the Avatamsaka Sutra as the apex of the teachings of the Buddha. This was expressed as the teaching of Ekayana, the One Vehicle, which transcends both Hinayana and Mahayana and is the highest, the final truth. They held that the principle established in the Avatamsaka Sutra that all beings in the universe can and will be enlightened is the highest principle in Buddhism.

Although the Kegon principles were widely acceptable in Japanese Buddhism, shortly after the sect was established the capital was moved from Nara to Kyoto, and Kegon gave way to the new religions which arose there, the Tendai and Shingon sects. Today, Kegon has its traditional headquarters at Todaiji in Nara—the temple of the Great Buddha—but the sect exists only as a custodian of the ancient traditions.

THE RITSU SECT

The Ritsu sect was concerned primarily with the Vinaya Pitaka, the code of discipline which governed the ordination and conduct of members of the Sangha. The problem of ordination of the monks and priests was especially difficult since it required that the ceremony be attended by ten masters fully qualified to give the precepts, and that it be performed in a place set aside for that purpose—the seema of Theravada Buddhism, called the *kaidan* in Japan. The difficulty was that in the eighth century in Japan there were no masters qualified to conduct and witness the ceremony of giving the precepts. The scholars who visited China realized the importance of these ceremonies, and some of the Chinese scholars who visited Japan also pointed out the need for proper ceremonies, but there were not enough qualified masters to assist them.

Two Japanese scholars went to China in 733 and invited Ganjin to make the journey to Japan to perform the ceremonies required by the code of discipline. Ganjin asked for volunteers among his followers to go to Japan to introduce the precept rituals, but none of them would leave their master. Thereupon, Ganjin decided to cross the China Sea and visit Japan himself, and then his followers decided to go with him. It took them eleven years to get to Japan because of government opposition, storms, and the menace of pirates. Finally, after a very difficult journey, they reached Japan and received the nation's enthusiastic welcome at Nara.

In April, 754, a kaidan was erected temporarily before the temple of the Great Buddha, the Daibutsu, at Nara, and there Ganjin and his followers gave the Bodhisattva precepts to many members of the Imperial Household and their ministers, and to 440 novices and eighty priests who received the precepts and were ordained again. After that it was possible to perform the ceremonies of the code of discipline properly in Japan.

Ganjin and his followers brought with them commentaries on the Vinaya Pitaka and many commentaries of the Tendai sect. It seems likely that the rituals of ordination were conducted in strict adherence to the rules of Hinayana, but their teachings were Mahayana. This is understandable, for it is to commit a fallacy to think that the precepts of India could be applied to Japan without alteration, for there is a great difference in geographic conditions, climate, and customs in Japan.

Ganjin's successor made it clear in his instructions that the beings who follow the precepts of the Bodhisattva will attain the highest form of Enlightenment. He showed how the 250 precepts of the Bhikkhus and the 500 precepts of the Bhikkhunis are only preliminaries to the precepts of the Bodhisattva, which are far superior.

The instructions given in the ethical precepts of the Vinaya, however, must have influenced the ethics and moral life of the priests and laymen. In explaining the Five Precepts of the code of discipline, for instance, emphasis was put on the need for a spirit of gratitude toward the master, a sense of thankfulness to parents, and the virtues of compassion and of limiting one's wants so that one is satisfied with what is given. The leaders of the Ritsu sect also taught that no matter how small and insignificant the forms of life might be, they all were born with the Buddha-nature. By preaching that Buddha's compassion extended equally to all beings, they refuted the Hosso teaching of the five classes of human beings. They also, influenced by both Chinese morals and the Vinaya, dealt with many minor problems in everyday life such as how to conduct oneself when eating with the master, the seating arrangement when people gather together, or the rules to observe when a follower walks down a road. These teachings were later taken into the everyday life of the people and constitute even today an important part of the system of conduct in the life of the Japanese people.

The Ritsu sect did not continue as an influential force in Japanese Buddhism after the other sects had their own kaidans for ordination, but indirectly it had great influence on the development of Buddhism in Japan. In modern times only a few historic shrines are claimed as belonging to the Ritsu tradition.

THE END OF THE NARA ERA

By the time of Emperor Shomu the country had been unified both politically and spiritually. State masters had been appointed in each province to give spiritual guidance to the people, and at this time the emperor hit upon the idea of erecting state temples in every province to bring happiness to the people by protecting them against natural calamities and the menace of sickness and plague. In the year 741 the Imperial Ordinance concerning the building of state temples was issued, followed two years later by the Ordinance authorizing the making of the image of the Maha Vairocana Buddha. Priests and women priests were assigned to the state temples charged with the responsibility of chanting and teaching the contents of the Suvarnaprabhasa Sutra and the Prajnaparamita Sutra, the state-protecting Sutra.

The images enshrined in the state temples were of the seated Sakyamuni Buddha, while the image enshrined in the great temple at Nara was the sitting image of the Maha Vairocana Buddha which is fifty-three and a half feet high. The Todaiji Temple was the largest temple in Japan, and although the original structure was destroyed twice by fire, it remains the largest wooden temple in the world.

The Maha Vairocana Buddha is considered to be the central Buddha of more than one thousand times ten billion Buddhas, which are all like the historical Sakyamuni Buddha. Just as the Sakyamuni Buddha appeared in India to save the people of this earth, so Buddhas like the Sakyamuni Buddha appear in each of the other 10,000,000,000 worlds like this earth and preach the Dharma. These Buddhas are called minor Sakyamuni Buddhas. The Buddhas who preach to these minor Sakyamuni Buddhas are called the major Sakyamuni Buddhas. The Maha Vairocana Buddha in turn preaches to these major Sakyamuni Buddhas. The literal meaning is that the Maha Vairocana Buddha is the greatest Buddha who prevails everywhere and gives forth the most brilliant light. The Maha Vairocana Buddha appears as a thousand major Sakyamuni Buddhas in accordance with the time and place, and then each one of the major Sakyamuni Buddhas in turn appears as the 10,000,000,000 minor Sakyamuni Buddhas in the actual worlds to teach the Truth to all forms of being.

Thus, under Emperor Shomu, the Daibutsu, the great image of Nara, represented Maha Vairocana Buddha, the main image in each of the sixty-four state temples represented the major Sakyamuni Buddhas, and the images in the other temples throughout the land represented the minor Sakyamuni Buddhas. The political unity of Japan was further strengthened by this faith in Buddhism. Of the various periods ruled by the emperors in Japanese history, there is no era which saw such a strong and perfect unity in Buddhism and in government as the period ruled by Emperor Shomu. This golden period is called the state of perfect peace; it was the time when the ideal method of government was carried out in accordance with the ideal of the Dharma.

Empress Koken, the daughter of Emperor Shomu, left the Imperial throne to devote herself to the study and practice of the teachings of Buddhism and then assumed the throne again. The relation between the government and Buddhism became even closer when she chose priests as ministers to aid her. One unfortunate result of this was that those who wanted to win fame, glory, and benefits by being ordained into the priesthood increased in number, and this led to internal corruption among the priests. This corruption, together with financial problems of the state, caused the downfall of the government at Nara. It then became necessary to move the seat of the government from Nara and to renovate the spirit of the people by starting a new government. In the year 794, Emperor Kanmu decided to establish the government at Heian (Kyoto), away from all the temples and priests of the old city of Nara.

BUDDHISM IN THE HEIAN ERA

In the Heian Era (794–1184), the period in which the capital remained in Kyoto, two new sects arose—Tendai and Shingon. Emperor Kanmu issued Ordinances again and again in an attempt to arouse the priests from their degenerate ways and in the hope that he could find and encourage priests with noble moral virtues. It was this encouragement which aided the rise of the two new sects.

Most of the emperors who ruled during the Heian Era put their faith in Buddhism and sought to assist the development of the religion by building temples and being ordained. During this same period the power of the Fujiwara family became so great that it is said to have surpassed the power of the Imperial Household. A study of the diaries written by noblemen of this period shows that a great deal of time was given to building temples and holding memorial services in the temples. Both the Imperial Household and the leading families encouraged works of art and literature during this era.

The problem of conciliation between Shintoism and Buddhism, which had become increasingly conspicuous during the Nara Era, approached solution in the Heian Era. The first step in the conciliation was made by calling the ancient gods Bodhisattvas and referring to them as the temporary forms which have appeared in this world. A second theory which aided this conciliation was the theory of the leaving of imprints in Japan —that is, the belief that the Buddhas and Bodhisattvas came from their original land to Japan and left their imprints as the ancient gods to enlighten the people. The Buddhists traced the origin of the imprints back to Sakyamuni in India and thus explained the relation of Buddhism to the ancient gods. The people generally accepted this explanation without any doubts whatsoever.

Today in Japan there are many Shinto shrines in which the image is the Great Bodhisattva of Hachiman. It was widely believed that the god enshrined at the Great Shrine at Ise was an incarnation of Avalokitesvara. In the Buddhist temples and Shinto shrines, the priests and shrine keepers were always on good terms and cooperated in leading the spiritual life of the people. It was not until the late nineteenth century that the close relationship was ended by decree. In modern times it is the custom for most homes to have a family altar on which the image of the Buddha is enshrined and where there are tablets bearing the names of the deceased. There are also family Shinto shrines where the names of the gods are written on paper or wood and enshrined, and there it is customary to worship morning and evening.

It is now the custom of the Japanese people to worship at the Shinto shrines on happy occasions like weddings, or when a baby is born, and also at the spring and autumn festivals of planting and harvesting. They go to the Buddhist temples for memorial services or funerals, for the Bon festival, and for the spring and autumn equinox services. The financial support for these temples and shrines is borne by the people as a natural responsibility. This conciliation of Shinto and Buddhism shows that Buddhism did not remain an imported religion based on foreign rules and doctrines, but became a Japanized religion in every sense of the word.

That same tendency to develop a distinctly Japanese Buddhism continued in the sects which arose during the Heian Era, and especially in the sects which grew up later. The Tendai and Shingon sects, which came into being during the time that the government was in Kyoto, were reactions against the Buddhism centered in Nara. In the Nara Era, since the everyday life of the priests was closely related to the political and economic life of the laymen, there was an inevitable corruption of the morals of the priests. Therefore the young priests who wished to follow the way in earnest secluded themselves in the deep mountains or along the ocean in an attempt to get away from the attachments of the city and pursue their quest for the truth in the Buddha's teachings. These young priests were given protection and benefits by the new government in Kyoto, and among them there were some who became leaders in the new sects of Buddhism. Those founders, who had the courage to pursue their quest by retiring to remote and secluded sites, deserve our deepest respect.

THE TENDAI SECT

The Tendai sect was founded by Saicho who studied at Nara and at the age of eighteen left the city and retired to Mount Hiei near Kyoto, where he lived alone for twenty years, studying and practicing Buddhism. In the seventeenth year of his life of seclusion he accepted an invitation to lecture to the priests of Nara and on that occasion established himself as a great scholar.

The Saddharma Pundarika Sutra, The Lotus of the Wonderful Law, had been interpreted by the Nara priests according to the doctrines of the Sanron and Hosso sects, but their interpretations were incorrect, according to Saicho. They erred because they either tried to look at the Sutra from the standpoint of sunyata, the voidness theory of Sanron, or from the standpoint of the five classifications of human beings of the Hosso sect—and these interpretations tended to hide the real spirit of the Sutra. Saicho emphasized the belief that all forms of life stand on an equal basis in attaining Buddhahood and brought the Ekayana Buddhism back to the forefront.

Emperor Kanmu was so impressed by the teachings of Saicho that he wanted to appoint him to the task of giving spiritual guidance to all the people. But Saicho asked permission to go to China to study at Mount T'ien-t'ai where he could clear up his doubts concerning the doctrines of the Tendai sect and could obtain new books not yet known in Japan. With the Emperor's permission, he went to China in 804 and there studied both Tendai and esoteric Buddhism (*Mikkyo*). He returned in the autumn of 805 with numerous books about Tendai and Mikkyo, as well as Buddhist items to be used for the esoteric rituals of Mikkyo. In January, 806, Saicho was given Imperial permission to establish the Nihon Tendai sect, the Japanese form of Tendai.

During the next twenty years of his life, Saicho struggled constantly to establish his new sect. In addition to the problem of defining the doctrines and practices of the sect, he found himself involved in a controversy with the scholars of the Hosso sect, and burdened with the problems related to introducing Mikkyo Buddhism, which was not his central concern. But most of all he was burdened with practical problems. He had to invite followers from a considerable distance and found it hard to persuade them to accept the life of seclusion at Mount Hiei, and then, when they had been instructed, he was not able to ordain them since the only recognized kaidan was in Nara. When he sent disciples to Nara to receive the precepts according to the Hinayana rites, he found that some of them preferred to stay in the city and others were won away from his teachings by the Hosso priests.

That situation led to an important revolution in Japanese Buddhism. In order to retain the scholars he had trained at Mount Hiei, Saicho decided that it was necessary to establish an independent kaidan, an independent ritual for ordination of scholars in the Tendai sect. Not only was there a practical necessity for this step, but it was theoretically necessary as well, for it was to Saicho a fallacy to follow Mahayana studies and Mahayana practices but to insist that one should follow Hinayana precepts in ordination. Therefore, he fought for an independent Mahayana ritual for giving the precepts, based on Mahayana beliefs.

This revolution is one of the greatest since the establishment of Indian Buddhism; it is an unprecedented outcry against a life of following the precepts which had been established at the time of the Sakyamuni Buddha and had been strictly adhered to by the Buddhist Sangha for more than 1,300 years. This insistence upon a consistent following of Mahayana beliefs was an act of unexcelled courage on the part of Saicho, and his theory was one which could not be refuted by anyone. If by *Mahayana* we mean a way of thought which believes that the manifestations of Truth are not uniform but that they differ according to the passage of time and place and the geographical limitations of a country and the racial differences of a people; and if by *Hinayana* we mean just the opposite, that Truth is always manifested in the same way regardless of differing circumstances—then clearly Saicho's position was the Mahayana way.

More than 1,200 years ago Saicho taught with courage that the three factors of Precepts, Practice, and Doctrine, which were practiced in India centuries before, need not necessarily be practiced to the letter everywhere throughout the world. Of course the Buddhist community at that time was vehemently opposed to this thought, and Saicho was persecuted. He carried on his struggle with Nara Buddhism until the time of his death, and it was not until a week after his death, in 822, that the emperor gave permission to establish a kaidan at the top of Mount Hiei. Thus the Tendai sect was freed from the shackles of Nara Buddhism and was able to train its scholars according to the ways proper to Tendai teachings, to unite the temple and the teachings in one harmonious whole.

After Saicho, there were two outstanding Tendai leaders— Ennin (794–864), and Enchin (814–891). Both men studied in China and returned as masters of Tendai thought and the rituals of Mikkyo. During the ninth century there was a great deal of study and practice of esoteric Buddhism with different masters imparting their secret rituals to their followers and adding to the complexity of the secret doctrines and mystic rituals. At this time there arose two subsects in Tendai, one following Ennin and the other following Enchin.

Tendai doctrines have developed in Japan, so they cannot be said to follow exactly the pattern of Chinese T'ien-t'ai. The basic Sutra is the Saddharma Pundarika, and the original emphasis upon practice is reflected in a continuing research in Mikkyo, the esoteric aspect of Buddhism. Tendai also uses the state-protecting Sutras and Sutras which are commonly studied by the Zen and Jodo (Pure Realm) schools.

Tendai has continued in modern times, but not as one of the leading sects in Japanese Buddhism. Some Tendai doctrines have been adopted by all other sects, and Tendai in Japan today includes aspects of Zen, Shingon, and Jodo beliefs and practices. According to the latest census figures, there are about 4,000 temples and 750,000 followers in the Tendai sect in modern Japan.

THE SHINGON SECT

The Shingon sect was founded by Kukai, who is also often called Kobo Daishi, the Great Teacher Who Spread the Dharma. When Kukai (774–835) was young he studied Confucius and Lao-tzu at Nara; then he turned to Buddhism and after a time went to live along the ocean where he tried to find Truth by turning to the natural world. In 804 he went to China in the same party with Saicho. There he studied esoteric Buddhism—the two schools of Mikkyo—learned Sanskrit, drew Buddha images, and painted mandalas, that is, pictures of the Buddha's Enlightenment. He received his instructions in Mikkyo from a famous master and made such progress that the master, on his deathbed, instructed him to return to Japan and spread Mikkyo Buddhism there. He had intended to stay twenty years in China, but he had progressed far beyond his expectations, so he returned to Japan in 806 and devoted the rest of his life to establishing the Shingon school of Buddhism.

Kukai used all the knowledge and facilities at his disposal to spread Mikkyo Buddhism in Japan. He had studied the teachings of Confucius and Lao-tzu in his early manhood, and the teachings of Indian philosophy, the various doctrines of Hinayana and Mahayana Buddhism as taught by the Kusha, Jojitsu, Hosso, and Sanron sects, and the Ekayana teachings of Tendai and Kegon—and he used all of these studies as a background for organizing the Mikkyo doctrines he taught. He pointed out that religious development begins with a simple, uneducated human being driven by physical desires who is then given ethical training which is required for social life, and then reaches the level of religious awakening which can be developed from a relatively limited outlook to the highest stages of insight.

Religious doctrines, according to Kukai, may be classified according to the degree of profundity:

1. A state of no doctrines at all
2. The teachings of Confucius and Lao-tzu
3. The Sankhya and Vaiseshika schools of Indian philosophy
4. The Kusha sect (Abhidharma)
5. The Jojitsu sect
6. The Hosso sect
7. The Sanron sect
8. The Tendai sect
9. The Kegon sect
10. The Shingon sect, the highest religion with the highest practices and doctrines

The Shingon sect is considered to be the highest form of religion, because all other sects taught doctrines suitable to each form of life while Shingon alone teaches the absolutely true doctrines as preached by the Dharmakaya Vairocana.

Esoteric Buddhism had been introduced to Japan before Kukai, but in an incomplete form. Mikkyo had originated in India, where the tantric rituals practiced among the people had been adopted by Mahayana Buddhism and then taken directly from India to China. In China, Kukai's master had received the esoteric teachings from Indian teachers. Thus the Mikkyo of Kukai was most perfect and complete. He taught the Mikkyo as the truth which lies inherent in all human beings and is the supreme wisdom of the Buddha which the human being should cultivate, develop, and accomplish. It was natural that the people who were tired of the Nara Era Buddhism should be interested in the impressive Indian rituals of chanting mantras, of the symbolic bending of the fingers of both hands, and of the clasping of both hands while the mind rests in tranquillity. Many people came to believe that the newly introduced mystic Buddhism would bring greater benefits than the Buddhism of

Nara which taught the chanting of Sutras and the real understanding of the teachings.

Shingon taught that it is not necessary to have unlimited future time and rigorous austerities to attain Buddhahood, but that the human being in this human body born of parents could, by these esoteric practices, attain the highest Enlightenment. Furthermore, it taught that only by means of the rituals of Mikkyo could such Enlightenment be attained. In addition, Shingon taught that the practices of Mikkyo would avert natural calamities, illness, robbery, and invasion and would realize the wishes of all men.

The primary purpose in conducting the mysterious rituals of the Shingon Mikkyo was the attainment of supreme Enlightenment in this life. The ritual in which sacred water is poured over the head, for instance, was conducted for the purpose of attaining Buddahood. However, as Mikkyo flourished throughout the Heian Era, these rituals were more and more conducted to satisfy the actual needs of human beings. As a result, the spirit of the original Mikkyo teachings and rituals was gradually put aside, and the result was a degeneration of Mikkyo Buddhism to the lower, praying type of Buddhism which was practiced solely for superstitious, worldly benefits. It is indeed a matter of deep regret that even today this type of belief is actually being practiced in many districts throughout Japan. As long as the people of the world are not given a higher religious education and training, these superstitions will continue to exist.

Although the Mikkyo practices were not embodied in a particular sect in China, the Shingon sect in Japan has continued from the time of Kukai to the present. In the centuries which followed there were many notable teachers, with the result that several subsects developed. In modern times, the census lists fifty-eight recognized sects of Shingon with a total of about 12,000 temples and more than 3,000,000 followers.

BUDDHISM IN THE KAMAKURA ERA

In the latter part of the Heian period there was considerable political unrest which did not end until the Kamakura government was established in 1185. During that period of political struggles the people were deeply impressed by the impermanence and vicissitudes of life as they endured the devastation and spiritual unrest of the never-ending wars. The leading temples maintained their own priest-warriors and fought against each other and even appealed to the emperor at the point of the sword in trying to achieve their ends.

The situation was so bad that the people came to believe that the final age of the decay of the law had come. They believed that the age in which people attained Enlightenment by following the Dharma as preached by the Buddha had passed away many centuries before. The second age, in which people would practice the teachings preached by the Buddha even though they knew that Enlightenment could not be attained, had also passed away decades ago, and they were now entering the period of final decay when there would be no one to practice the teachings of the Buddha. It was decided that the year 1052 was the beginning of the age of final decay. The transmission of the doctrines was carried on only for ideological amusement and for meaningless debates. People entered the priesthood merely to gain a livelihood or to win fame, and few tried to follow the precepts in earnest.

Such was the situation when the new government was established at Kamakura, a government which was unsophisticated but firm, simple but clear in its aims. With the new spirit of independence, Buddhism was given a new life. During the Kamakura Era (1185–1333), three new schools of Buddhism were established—the Pure Realm school of Amida Buddhism (Jodo and Shin), Zen, and Nichiren.

We have asked a recognized leader in each of these three schools to describe the beliefs and practices of his sect.

SHIN AND JODO BUDDHISM

Mitsuyuki Ishida

The followers of the Pure Realm sects of Buddhism seek Buddhahood—that is, Enlightenment—through rebirth in Amida

Buddha's Pure Realm of Highest Happiness. Rebirth in the Pure Realm is attained by faith in the power of Amida's vow to save all beings and by the calling of the Buddha's name in faith.

Amida's vows are recorded in The Great Sutra of the Endless Life, the Sukhavativyuha Sutra, which is the discourse between Sakyamuni Buddha and Ananda on Vulture's Peak at Rajagaha. The Sutra tells us that the monk Dharmakara, the future Amitabha, made forty-eight vows which were to be fulfilled when he became a Buddha. When he became the Buddha Amitabha, these vows became a power which controls the law of karma. The eighteenth vow is of greatest importance for the followers of the Pure Realm. "If the beings of the ten quarters —when I have attained Bodhi—blissfully trust in me with the most sincere mind, wish to be born in my country, and think (one to) ten times, and if they are not so born, may I never obtain the Highest Perfect Knowledge!" From very early times, the word *think* in the vow has been interpreted to mean the calling of the Buddha's name in faith, that is, saying the Nembutsu: "Namu Amida Butsu."

Faith in the Pure Realm Teachings of the Amida Buddha was known at an early time in India and in China and Tibet. (The Pure Realm is sometimes called the Pure Land, or the Buddha Land, or Buddha Field, or Pure Western Land, but Pure Realm is preferable since it avoids the erroneous connotations of a geographic location or a material world.) Faith in the Amida Buddha was common in the Nara Era in Japan and played a subsidiary role in Tendai and Sanron, but it was not the basis of a separate sect in Japan until the time of Ryonin (1072–1132), who formed the Yuzu Nembutsu sect as an offshoot of Tendai. The major move toward forming a sect devoted to the Amida teachings came with Honen (1133–1212) and his disciples Shinran (1173–1262), Bencho (1162–1238), and Shoku (1177–1247).

In Japan today, more than half of the Buddhists belong to the Pure Realm sects, some 18,500,000 people. Of these, seventy-seven per cent are Shin Buddhists, sixteen per cent are

Jodo Buddhists, and the rest belong to the sects known as Seizan, Ji, Yuzu Nembutsu, and Shinsei.

When Honen was forty-two years of age, after years of searching, he came to realize the truth of the Pure Realm teachings. At the outset, he was largely dependent upon the writings of the Chinese master, Zendo (613-681), and the Chinese tradition. The tendency in China had been to emphasize the plight of man who is bound by evil and depravity and by his inability to attain Enlightenment through meditative practices in this age of the decline of the law. Since man cannot accomplish Enlightenment by his own efforts, Chinese Buddhism came to stress the possibility of rebirth to the Pure Realm because of the vows of Amida Buddha, accomplished by reciting the Name of the Buddha. Rebirth in the Pure Realm was regarded as making Enlightenment a certainty through the External Power of that world. Those who think that Enlightenment is possible in this world through their own efforts are said to be following the holy Path of difficult practice depending on the Internal Power, and those who seek to accomplish Enlightenment by rebirth into the Pure Realm by the power of Amida's vow are said to be following the easy way depending upon the External Power.

In Japan, Honen urged mankind to abandon the holy Path and the effort to attain Enlightenment by meditation and the keeping of the precepts. He believed in salvation by the External Power of the Main Vow of Amida which brings about rebirth in the Pure Realm where it is possible to perfect the Enlightenment of a Buddha. The calling of the Name and the Thought of the Buddha, *Namu Amida Butsu*—"Homage to Amida Buddha"—is the practice which gives evidence of faith in the External Power of Amida's vow and brings salvation. The Shin, Seizan, Ji, and Jodo sects in Japan follow most closely the teachings of Honen, putting their whole trust in the External Power and the recitation of the Nembutsu, the Name and Thought of the Buddha. The other sects are much closer to the doctrine of the holy Path of Internal Power which teaches that we can attain Enlightenment in this world by our own efforts.

The teachings of the Pure Realm are based on three scriptures—The Great Sutra of Endless Life (Maha Sukhavativyuha Sutra), The Sutra of Meditation on the Buddha of Endless Life (Amitayurdhyana Sutra), and the Amida Sutra (Lesser Sukhavativyuha Sutra). All Pure Realm sects accept these three Sutras, but they emphasize different sections, and some of them add other Sutras as equally authoritative.

The Great Sutra tells how Dharmakara, when he was still a Bodhisattva striving to become a Buddha, had made forty-eight vows to help ordinary people be reborn to his selfless Pure Realm where they could attain Enlightenment by hearing, believing, and rejoicing in the Merit of the Name and Title of Amida, which is above the natural world and unthinkable. Now that he has become a Buddha his vows are fulfilled and the Pure Realm of tranquil sustenance (which is Endless Life and Boundless Light in the West) is established, and salvation by the great mercy and the power of Amida's Main Vow is available to men.

The Meditation Sutra was preached to Queen Vaidehi who was saddened by the tragedy which was taking place at Rajagaha. Sakyamuni taught that if she meditated on Amida Buddha and kept the precepts or heard the Name and Title of the Buddha, and awakened her faith in the Name and Title and called upon it, many sins would disappear and rebirth would be assured in the Pure Realm of Highest Happiness where she would become a Buddha.

The Amida Sutra explains that Amida Buddha is now in the Pure Realms in the West, beyond numberless Buddha realms, where he casts his light in all ten directions and is preaching to save countless sentient beings. Therefore, Sakyamuni taught that we should always concentrate on the Name and Title—and many other Buddhas also urge this.

In addition to the three Sutras, the doctrines of the Pure Realm are found chiefly in the commentaries of the Fathers of India, China, and Japan—such as Nagarjuna, Vasubandhu, Donran, Zendo, Genshin, and Honen. The different sects value different commentaries according to their own point of view, and especially in the light of the subcommentaries written by the founders of their sects. The most important differences in interpretation are that the Shin sect thinks that the only practice required is the calling of the Name and Title based on faith in the Amida Buddha, and all other practices are to be abandoned. The Jodo sect says that practices other than the calling of the Name and Title are also a way to rebirth to the Pure Realm. The Seizan sect says that meditation and keeping the precepts are part of the merit of recitation of the Name and Thought of the Buddha.

The emphasis of the Shin sect upon the exclusive use of the Nembutsu in faith, rejecting all dependence upon oneself and relying only on the External Power, leads also to the rejection of any concern for lucky or unlucky times, fortunate directions, astrology, or prayer to gods and spirits. All such practices are due to the selfish desire of the unenlightened man and are false and evil, not even to be permitted as accommodations to lower levels of insight.

All branches of the Shin and Jodo teachings have as the object of their religion the attainment of rebirth in the Pure Realm of Amida, which is the Realm of Limitless Life and Limitless Light, and there to become a Buddha equal to him. This Amida, as Dharmakaya, is the ultimate principle and goal of Mahayana Buddhism. It is the world of absolute nonselfishness and nonattachment which reveals existence as it is. This world of Enlightenment is explained by such expressions as: birth and death are Nirvana; one is many and many are one; difference is nondifference, nondifference is difference; birth is death; form is nonform, nonform is form. It is the world where each self is free and yet finds that self and others are not two, but are equal. It is a world in which there is cause and effect and at the same time it is beyond cause and effect, a world of differentiation and nondifferentiation. It is the world of the Body of the Law (Dharmakaya) which has neither color nor form, where ordinary sentient beings and the Buddha are one.

Amida Buddha is that world of Enlightenment which by its very nature, because of its absolute perfection, appeared and took on the form of cause and effect to save the world of sentient beings. Thus, Amida Buddha's Realm appears to save sentient beings who are filled with sin and error and cannot rise above selfish love and hate by themselves. Dharmakara Bodhisattva has fulfilled the forty-eight vows of compassion, summed up when he declared, "I shall not accept Enlightenment unless all beings likewise attain Enlightenment."

Shin especially insists that all beings, filled with reason and passion and completely selfish as the result of past actions from their eternal past, are diametrically opposite to the World of Enlightenment. We are all sinners and evildoers, utterly incapable of realizing Enlightenment by ourselves. At the same time, by the power of the Buddha's vow, we are caused to believe that by the merit of the External Power all sinners are freed and true Enlightenment is perfected. We sentient beings are caused to abandon our confidence in the Internal Power, in our ability to save ourselves, by the light of the bestowal of Amida Buddha's External Power. This bestowal of the External Power causes man to take refuge in Amida, to believe, and to rejoice without a doubting mind.

Thus Shin clearly insists on the complete lack of good in sentient beings and on salvation through the giving of the power of the Main vow. It insists that the perfection of salvation is only by faith and that faith is bestowed by absolute External Power. At the first instant of faith we are given the true merit of the power of the Buddha's vow as inner benefit, and even while we are ordinary men our sins are annihilated and our rebirth and attainment of Buddhahood is fixed. With death, there is rebirth, and at that very instant we become Buddha. Shin teaches that the calling of the Name after the instant of faith is the practice of the Thought of the Buddha in gratitude.

Other Pure Realm sects have different beliefs, such as the Seizan belief that faith must be aroused by sentient beings themselves, or that it is attained by prayer and practices, as Jodo believes. Some sects insist on practices as a condition of faith.

Common to all sects of the Pure Realm tradition is the practice of calling the Buddha's name—"Namu Amida Butsu"—which is to give thanks for salvation, in Shin and Seizan, but is to repent one's sins and pray for salvation in Jodo. It is also customary to have sermons, lectures, and study groups as an aid to understanding the truth of salvation from Amida. Thus there is little tendency to meditation or other practices of a mystical nature.

Shin strongly emphasizes instruction through sermons and lectures. To hear and believe transcends rational thinking. No matter how learned or ignorant a person may be, hearing and believing is still possible and the Nembutsu can be practiced. This is generally true of all schools of the Pure Realm tradition. Sometimes there are special lecture meetings and study societies, but generally the lectures and sermons center in temples where they hear the Dharma, recite the Name of the Buddha, and take part in other religious activities.

Each sect has a number of organized temples with its own headquarters managed by the Monju (Prince Patriarch) and elected delegates from the leaders of the congregations. There are administrative officers who manage schools, hospitals, and other service projects which are an expression of gratitude and thanksgiving and joyfulness for salvation. In some sects, the service activities are looked upon as fulfilling ethical requirements which help toward salvation.

In general, the temple is the place for instruction in the Dharma, for missionary activity, and for festivals and ceremonies. In Shin temples, wedding ceremonies are held, which is unique in Buddhism and emphasizes the special nature of the householder's Buddhism of the sect. It is customary to observe the ceremony of taking the child to the temple soon after birth to hear the reading of the creed and the scriptures. Funerals are held in the temples and memorial ceremonies are also very important. In Shin the most important ceremonies are the services in memory of the death of Shinran, and similar ceremonies are held for the founders of the other sects.

The leaders of the temples are called "neither monk nor lay" since they are married and do not follow the Vinaya discipline, but as householders they devote all their time to religious activities. The believers share the responsibility for providing for the leaders and their families. The leaders supervise the temples, are responsible for temple activities, perform the ceremonies, conduct the funerals and memorial services both in the temple and the homes, preside at congregational meetings, and lecture and preach. When they are ordained as leaders, their heads are shaved and they take part in a ceremony of transmission, which varies according to the sect.

In each temple, as a rule, are placed an image of Amida or a scroll bearing his Name—such as "Namu Amida Butsu"—and the portrait of the founder of the sect. But they are not placed there for idolatrous worship. They are symbols of the contents of salvation. The various services, centering in the recitation of the Name of the Buddha, are performed in front of the Buddha's image or the picture of the founder. In Shin, Seizan, and Ji, this is largely done out of gratitude and thankfulness, but in the other sects it is an expression of the desire for salvation and a deepening experience.

Shin most strongly insists upon pure faith in Amida and completely rejects worship of the gods of Japan—which are used superstitiously as the object of prayers for worldly benefits by many Japanese. It also rejects the worshipful devotion to the Buddhas and Bodhisattvas of other sects, allowing homage to Amida alone. Buddhism has always been tolerant of other religions, and Shin is no exception. Therefore, Shin followers may respect other gods and Buddhas as long as this does not influence the pure faith and loyalty to Amida. That respect is only the homage given to worthy persons who have done good for society, or respect such as is given one's ancestors. Only this attitude of reverence is permitted. Not all Pure Realm sects are as strict in this matter as Shin is.

Music plays an important part in the ceremonies and services of Shin, Jodo, and Seizan, both in the temple and the home, and in both classical Japanese and Western style. In former times, art played a more important part in the tradition of the Pure Realm sects, as is shown by the temples and their art treasures, but such expressions are rare in modern times. Dancing as an expression of joy has always been a characteristic practice of the Ji sect. Noh plays (the traditional lyric dramas which are closely associated with Buddhist thought) have had an important role in the tradition of Shin, and even today there are excellent Noh stages at the headquarters of both branches of the Shin sect—Nishi (Western) Hongwanji and Higashi (Eastern) Hongwanji. There have also been great masters of the tea ceremony in the Shin sect. In this matter of the tea ceremony, it might be pointed out that the spirit of the ceremony may differ according to the circumstances. Zen does the tea ceremony in the spirit of Zen, and Shin does the tea ceremony in the spirit of Shin, which is gratitude.

All Pure Realm schools arose among the masses. They have always demanded freedom of worship, and the government which assures it they consider to be a correct government. Accordingly, it is felt that a proper government policy and a true faith are complementary, that religion should not be used by the government for its own ends, nor should religion subvert the state. Shin has insisted upon this freedom of worship through all its history, but it has not recklessly opposed the state—indeed, it has at times been too cooperative. At all times it has sought to preserve the unique characteristics of the Shin position.

Thus the schools of the Pure Realm have sought through the centuries to live on in the faith of Amida, to establish eternally the Pure Realm of Amida, which means in this world to see others as equal to oneself.

ZEN BUDDHISM
Reiho Masunaga

The Ch'an Buddhism of China was known among the Buddhists of Japan for several centuries before it became established as a distinct sect known as Zen. Eisai (1141–1215) is credited with forming the Rinzai Zen sect in 1191. It has always attracted many intellectuals and members of the ruling class and is an influential sect in Japan today with more than 2,350,000 followers. In 1244, a closely related school, Soto Zen, was founded by Dogen (1200–1253). It spread more widely among the common people and today has over 6,750,000 followers, making it one of the larger sects in Buddhism.

The Obaku school of Zen, which was brought to Japan by the Chinese monk Ingen in 1654, is often referred to as Nembutsu Zen since it is a combination of Zen and Pure Realm beliefs and practices. It has continued in Japan to the present time and has about 100,000 followers today.

The object of Zen is self-enlightenment—the perfection of personality—by means of meditative disciplines, actions in daily life, and earnest work for mankind. It is not enough merely to become enlightened oneself. Man cannot separate himself from society. The Buddha enlightened himself by great wisdom and served all beings by great compassion. Because of great wisdom, an Enlightened One does not linger in the delusive world of birth and death, and because of great compassion, he does not linger in the world of Enlightenment. The follower of Zen must not stop simply in personal tranquillity; he must seek peace and happiness for all beings.

Even though a person who follows Zen attains Enlightenment, he does not neglect discipline and practice. Because the way is endless, he continues to strive even if he becomes a Buddha. Dogen, when studying Zen in China, freed himself from attachment to body and mind, but he continued to teach for the sake of mankind. In Zen, one who clings to the world of Enlightenment is referred to as "a personally enlightened corpse." Therefore the true follower of Zen goes one step beyond the top of the hundred-foot pole and vows to work for others.

In the early days of Zen in China, the practice of Zen was described in these words:

> No dependence upon the words and letters;
> A special transmission outside the classified teachings;
> Direct pointing to the mind of man;
> Seeing into one's own nature.

"No dependence upon the words and letters" means that the words of the Sutras are not taken as final authority. "A special transmission outside the classified teachings" means that systems of teachings based upon the Sutras are not relied upon and that the true law is transmitted by other means. "Direct pointing to the mind of man" emphasizes that we originally have the Buddha-mind and need the actual experience of it. "Seeing into one's own nature" means that the expressing of this Buddha-mind is the same as becoming the Buddha—that you are the Buddha. The true law of the Buddha should be transmitted from mind to mind and from personality to personality.

Therefore, to attain the goal of Zen we must begin by receiving guidance from a true master of Zen who has synthesized understanding and action. Under the guidance of the master—the transmission from mind to mind—we must believe deeply in our original Buddhahood and express this through the Zen meditative disciplines which bring out the Buddha and the patriarchs in ourselves. As we learn to bring out the Buddha and patriarchs in ourselves, we must emphasize living experience rather than the words and letters of the Sutras and transmit the true law of the Buddha and the patriarchs from mind to mind and from person to person. Each of us must regulate our life, both in private and in society, in accordance with monastic rules, not be attached to anything, and not neglect even the smallest detail, but do everything with all our heart. And we must do our utmost for the happiness of mankind and the peace of the world.

Many different methods of instruction have been used by Zen masters. Rinzai Zen masters have tended to use stern austerity and meditation upon the paradoxes (koan). Soto Zen emphasizes silent sitting and meditating on the illumination or insight received while waiting in silence. Other masters have relied upon question-and-answer sessions with disciples, or the use of words suddenly shouted to awaken insight.

Paradoxes are used because it is difficult to express pure experience by ordinary, objective logic. Ultimately, religion is nothing but a way of living and dying, an experience which cannot be described logically. The best way to express our deepest experiences is by the use of paradoxes which transcend the opposites. For example, these are typical paradoxes to be used for meditation: "Where there is nothing, there is all." "To die the great death is to gain the great life." "Drop into a deep chasm and live again after your death." "We have been separated for a long time and have never been apart. We meet each other throughout the day, and do not meet a moment." "If you abandon superior training, you find original Enlightenment in your hand; if you leave original Enlightenment, superior training fills your body." Paradoxes like these bring objective logic to a deadlock, and from there it is possible to uncover the vital way of turning around.

Although the details of meditative practices (*zazen*) will vary within Zen, the general pattern—which is based on methods brought from India by Bodhidharma—is the same. First, you spread a thick square cushion at the place of meditation and place a round cushion on top of it. Then you take either the full meditation position, with your right foot on your left thigh and your left foot on your right thigh, or the half-way position, with only your left foot on your right thigh. You wear your sash and robe loosely and arrange your clothing neatly. Then you put your right hand on your left foot and your left hand on your right palm and place the tips of the thumbs together. You must sit upright without leaning either to the left or right, or forward or backward; your ears must be perpendicular to your shoulder and your nose in line with your navel. The tongue is placed against the palate and the mouth is closed; you keep your eyes open and breathe lightly. When you are sitting comfortably, you exhale sharply and then without motion you think the unthinkable and reach the state beyond thinking. This is the stage of meditation at which you recall a paradox or silently await illumination. When you get up from meditation, you move your body quietly and get up gently.

The mind-to-mind instruction and the practice of meditation are not complete without action. In a Zen monastery, the students are not permitted to sit cross-legged all day. Each one must do his allotted work of cooking, or cleaning, or farming. If the daily work is based on the Buddha-mind, it has the same value as the meditation. Because Zen has infinite meaning for all details of one's daily work, it has spread among the general public.

In Mahayana Buddhism there is no distinction between priests and laymen, except that the priests must undergo special disciplines to enable them to serve as religious leaders. In Zen, the laymen uphold Zen teachings in their daily work. They purify the body and mind and receive the ten precepts—not to kill, steal, commit adultery, lie, sell liquor (in Theravada it is not to drink liquor), not to speak of other's shortcomings, not to praise yourself and blame others, not to begrudge charity whether material or spiritual, not to be angry, not to speak ill of the Triple Treasure.

Laymen come to sit outside the meditation hall at the monastery, they learn to express the Buddha-mind in everyday activities, and they help temples and monasteries financially. The ultimate aims of the discipline of the layman are the receiving of the teaching from a true master and coming into contact with his personality, returning to the Triple Treasure and deepening their belief, receiving the great precepts of the Buddha and the patriarchs, penetrating into the spirit of Zen, and—by expressing Buddhism in their daily life—giving thanks to the Buddha and the patriarchs.

Zen Buddhism does not ultimately depend upon the Buddhist Sutras. This is because the words of the Sutras are nothing more than a finger pointing at the moon or a net for catching fish. But it does not completely reject them. "No dependence upon the words and letters" does not mean no use for the words and letters. Even in Zen temples Sutras are read in the morning and evening. There are different preferences in Zen sects, but all prefer the Mahaprajnaparamita Sutra, The Great Discourse on Perfect Wisdom. The ones closest in spirit to Zen are the Vimalakirtinirdesa Sutra, the Mahaprajnaparamita Sutra, Gandavyuha Sutra, Mahaparinirvana Sutra, Lankavatara Sutra, and the Mahavaipulya Sutra. Zen makes use of these Sutras, but is not enslaved by them. If one is deluded, he does not understand what he reads in the Sutras; if one's mind is enlightened, he practices what he reads; in the highest stages, one is identical with the meaning of the Sutras and has no further need for them.

Zen takes refuge in the Three Treasures of the Buddha, the Dharma, and the Sangha, because Zen is a part of Buddhism. But Zen looks upon the Buddha as the historical personality, Sakyamuni—not as Mahavairocana, Amitabha, or the original Buddha of eternity. This Sakyamuni is the original Buddha before he was divided into the three bodies (Dharmakaya, Sambhogakaya, Nirmanakaya). He can be called the undivided Buddha. This Sakyamuni is the true teacher who leads human beings as a personality endowed with perfect wisdom and perfect compassion. Zen Buddhism refers to him as the practical Buddha, the Buddha who acts historically. He is the Buddha who is immanently identical with the original individual self.

In the early days, the Arahat and Bodhisattva did not differ from the Buddha, but later they became differentiated according to the stage of training. For instance, after the first sermon was preached to the five disciples at Banaras, the Buddha said there were six Arahats. After leaving the home of Yasa, the Buddha said there were sixty-one Arahats—one of them was, of course, the Buddha. But later, as a result of setting up stages of training, the Arahat was given a lower position than the Buddha. Worship of Arahats in Zen Buddhism is centered on the five hundred outstanding disciples of the Buddha. In Zen, priests chant the Sutras for Arahats every morning and hold the worship ceremony for Arahats once a year. Arahats in this sense are those who strive to perfect themselves and who attain their objective. Therefore, they are worthy of respect and deserve the offerings of all. There are many Arahats who are closely linked with the tradition of Zen Buddhism.

The Bodhisattva is a candidate for Buddhahood who seeks Enlightenment and who also tries to save all beings. He perfects himself by working for others. Zen also stresses the Bodhisattva ideal of saving others before oneself. The four virtues which are often associated with Theravada—charity, tenderness, benevolence, and sympathy—are looked upon by Zen in a Mahayana manner, that is, not as individual virtues to be sought, but as a means of saving others, as virtues associated with the Bodhisattva.

In addition to the Buddha, the Arahats, and the Bodhisattvas, Zen respects the patriarchs, the leaders such as Bodhidharma, who have lived in history, and the founders of the different Zen sects and temples.

From the standpoint of Zen Buddhism, the Buddha image must be that of Sakyamuni. But in many Zen temples there are images of Vairocana, Amitabha, and Avalokitesvara (Kwannon) in the central place of honor. This is because, during the time that Zen Buddhism flourished, other sects were changed to Zen and their art objects remained where they had been in the past. In addition, the images of Zen patriarchs are often found in temples. Nevertheless, the main object of honor in Zen Buddhism is Sakyamuni Buddha. Sometimes the Sakyamuni image is attended by Kasyapa, the Buddha of the past, and by Maitreya, the Buddha of the future. Or, the Sakyamuni Buddha may be attended by Manjusri, Samantabhadra, or Ananda.

These images of the Buddha and the patriarchs are definitely not idols—there is no life of the Buddha or of the patriarchs in the images. While concentrating the religious consciousness on the images, the Zen student tries to grasp the eternal and universal truth through the image. Through these images we take refuge in eternal truth. Once, in China, a patriarch on a cold winter morning took a wooden statue of the Buddha from its pedestal and burned it to warm himself. This story shows clearly that Zen rejects the idea of worshiping the statues of the Buddha and the patriarchs. In Zen Buddhism, the superior personality of the master is respected and his portrait is bowed to morning and night. This use of the portrait of the Zen master is the origin of the portrait painting which developed in Zen.

In a Zen monastery, the most important place is the meditation hall since this is the place for giving and receiving the training. The Buddha hall, where the image is located, occupies a secondary place in the life of the monastery. There is often a lecture hall where instruction is given and which is used in ordinary temples as the place for Sutra readings and meditation as well as for lectures. Almost all temples have a cemetery nearby which is visited on memorial days to pay respect to and console the ancestors and the dead. During the persecutions in the latter part of the nineteenth century, the temples in the provinces deteriorated, but they have been gradually restored and have increasingly become centers of culture, education, and social work. The students at the monasteries get up very early in the morning and practice their meditation, read Sutras, listen to lectures, and work. At present, because students in religious universities have increased considerably, there are not so many in the provincial temples. In the religious universities, the students are taught Zen meditation.

Worship in Zen Buddhism is somewhat different in the head temples, special monasteries, and ordinary temples. In the ordinary temples worship takes place in the morning and at night, with salutation—bowing three times before the object of worship—Sutra chanting, and meditation. The morning worship lasts about forty minutes, and the monks chant their favorite Sutras and offer salutation by reading *The Transmission of the Lamp*—the names of the fifty or more patriarchs who have transmitted the teachings, beginning with the six before Sakyamuni and ending with the present teacher, and bowing at the mention of each name. The evening worship lasts about a half hour.

In the head temples and special monasteries, meditation is performed in the early morning and at night, and Sutras are chanted morning, noon, and night. If there are participants, sermons are given at any time. In all the temples, strict attention is given to the details of worship in the three-month disciplinary period which corresponds to the rainy season of ancient Buddhism. Because nowadays there are many participants on Sunday, special Sunday worship is held in all temples and monasteries. The object of these ceremonies is to perfect one's personality and to express gratitude to the Buddha and the patriarchs. This must be done with humility, with piety, and with no thought of profit. In Zen Buddhism, worship is rigidly fixed by monastic regulations. Careful control of conduct is stressed, not only in worship, as is shown by the well-known saying "Everyday action is itself Buddhism and etiquette is itself the essence of Zen."

In addition to the ordinary worship ceremonies, there are many special occasions observed in Zen Buddhism. There are special services on the Buddha's birthday (April 8), the day of his Enlightenment (December 8), the day of his death (February 15), and on the death anniversaries of the founders of various sects and temples. At the time of the spring and autumn equinox, the Higan ceremonies are held praising the Buddha and the 3,000 Buddhas protecting the three worlds; also carried out at the time of the equinox is the ritual remembering ancestors and the spirits of those who are still wandering in darkness without having gained a realization of truth. The ancestors are also remembered at the time of the Bon festival in the summer.

There are also ceremonies on such occasions as admission to the temple, advancement to the next higher stage of understanding, and entrance to a new temple for the three-month period of discipline. Once a year there is a day of abstinence with the ceremony of worshiping Arahats and reading extracts from the Prajnaparamita Sutra. At suitable times ceremonies are held to honor the Buddhas and to pay respect to Avalokitesvara, who is known as Kwannon in Japan. At suitable times, the head of one of the large temples is invited to hold a precept-observing ceremony for three days or a week, and then laymen live with the priests at the temple and receive the precepts of the Bodhisattva.

Zen rituals are carried out with piety and solemnity. It is said that one day a Chinese scholar saw the dining ceremony as he passed by a Zen temple and exclaimed in admiration, "Here is concentrated the etiquette of the three dynasties!" Zen rules are the synthesis of Indian precepts and Chinese manners and have made Zen famous for the solemnity of its rituals and the thoroughness of its training.

Zen combined the intellectual culture of India, the pragmatic culture of China, and the emotional culture of Japan in a movement which influenced architecture, sculpture, painting, calligraphy, flower arrangement, gardening, Noh songs, poetry, music, and pottery. The characteristics of Zen culture are unpretentiousness, profundity, simplicity, and strength. It has vitality and identifies itself with nature. It pours into form while overflowing all form with an easy unconventionality and unrestricted freedom.

Zen art has permeated all phases of Japanese culture. It has had great influence on Japanese temple architecture. In the Noh songs (the traditional recitative chants of the lyric dramas) the quiet fantasy and the inclusion of simple words with meaning beyond intellect were influenced by Zen. Poetry in Japan owes much to the Zen masters of this form of expression. The short poem (*haiku*) sees the world from a moment in time and its profound mood corresponds to the Zen spirit. The art of calligraphy, which is beauty of line, was furthered by many expert calligraphers among the Zen priests; their high talent matched their personalities. In the field of music, it can be said that the lingering notes of the bamboo flute express the profundity of Zen, and that is why Zen priests perfected the playing of the flute.

Tea was introduced to Japan by Eisai, the founder of Rinzai Zen, and the tea ceremony began over six centuries ago. The teahouse, the equipment for the tea ceremony, and the ceremony itself all express profundity in simplicity; they obviously have absorbed the Zen spirit. In the teahouse the host and guest together experience their identity with the universe and taste the pleasure of the oneness of self and others in the great emptiness. The etiquette of the tea ceremony owes much to the tea-drinking rules in Zen monasteries. The four essentials—harmony, respect, purity, and serenity—are also seen in the rules of tea.

The paintings in the teahouse are severe and gain their meaning in emptiness. From the requirements for the pictures in the teahouse grew the monochrome Zen paintings. There were many famous Zen painters who entered into the deepest unity of Zen and painting, expressing an intimacy with nature with strength and simplicity. It was also through Zen, as we have seen, that the art of portrait painting was advanced through the practice of paying respect to the master and the need for pictures as an object of honor.

The teahouse was made beautiful with flowers, and thus grew up the art of flower arrangement. The gardens near the teahouse were also an expression of the simplicity and modesty which are the characteristics of Zen art. Some of the famous gardens of Japan were made by Zen priests. The influence of the tea ceremony on pottery is, of course, evident—creating many art treasures of profound and subtle simplicity.

Zen was also instrumental in the education of the warrior class and stimulated the unique spirit of Bushido, the code of conduct required of the samurai. Zen emphasizes practice rather than theory, which made Zen attractive to the warriors. They adopted those disciplines from the meditative practices which taught control of one's thoughts and the ability to transcend life and death. They also adopted the teachings of Zen which made them satisfied with a plain and simple life, restrained behavior, austerity, and thoroughness in action.

There has been very little relation between Zen and Shinto; Zen has never accepted the concept of incarnations. The relation with Taoist thought is much closer, especially in such concepts as closeness to nature, no attachment to the ego, and the importance of avoiding enslavement by things and events. The rules of Zen also absorbed much of the etiquette of Confucianism.

The view of life and society taught by Zen forms a strong support for the spiritual life of Japan, for Zen always rejects the little path and emphasizes the whole way—it rejects the corner and grasps the all. The meditative disciplines of Zen exercise both body and mind; they synthesize materialism and spiritualism in the practice of the middle way. Zen creates men who transcend their masters. It is a practical religion that enables the common people to live truly in the present moment.

NICHIREN BUDDHISM

Shobun Kubota

The Nichiren sect was founded by the thirteenth-century saint and prophet, Nichiren (1222–1282). In Japan in modern times there are about 2,250,000 followers of the traditional Nichiren teachings and over 2,000,000 followers of subsects which have arisen in recent years.

Nichiren had not expected to be the founder of a new sect, for he had always worshiped Sakyamuni, the founder of Buddhism, and had regarded himself as only a faithful disciple and messenger of the teachings of the Great Master. This deep devotion and love for the Master, coupled with his long and arduous study, convinced Nichiren that the true and only doctrine, the quintessence of Buddhism, was the teaching of *The Lotus of the Wonderful Law*, the Saddharma Pundarika Sutra known as *Myoho-rengekyo* in Japanese. After studying this book from both the theoretical and practical point of view, he came to the conclusion that it should be studied and followed in practice by individuals and nations. All through his life he sacrificed everything in order to live up to the teaching found in this sacred book. It is no wonder that he is called "an ascetic Devotee, who adores and practices the Lotus."

The Nichiren sect, as the name suggests, was so much an expression of Saint Nichiren's faith and experience that the story of his life is a summary of the early history of the sect. When he was twelve years old, he was apprenticed to a nearby Tendai monastery where he studied so earnestly that after four years he had mastered the elements of Buddhism and could recite the Sutras tolerably well. He was ordained a priest on October 8, 1237.

In the thirteenth century, there were ten Buddhist sects in Japan, each claiming to give a true interpretation of the Buddha's teachings. In the temple where Nichiren studied, their practices were eclectic; they took as the chief object of devotion the Vairocana Buddha, they studied the Lotus Sutra, and they followed the Pure Realm practice of repeating the Namu Amida Butsu. Outside the temple, the country was torn by civil wars and the people were enduring a miserable life.

Nichiren, as a new member of the order, felt that it was his duty to become a thoroughly good Buddhist, but he found grave doubts arising in his mind. He wondered if he could find one among the ten sects which would be near to the real spirit of the Lord Buddha and which would bring peace and happiness to the nation. Driven by these doubts and a desire to gain deeper knowledge of Buddhism, he set out on pilgrimages to the chief Buddhist centers of Japan. For ten long years he labored incessantly with heart and soul to master the intricate and erudite teachings of Buddhism before he was rewarded with a clear notion of the Sutra which gives the true teaching and was able to dispel the doubts which had been haunting him. He reached the conviction that the true teaching, the quintessence of Buddhist doctrine, is to be found in the Lotus Sutra, and that if this teaching is followed in practice, it will without doubt bring peace and happiness to both the individual and the nation.

There is a passage in the Lotus Sutra which clearly prophesies a religious persecution to those who dare to spread the teaching of the Lotus during the degenerate days of the decline of the law (*Mappo*). Although the youthful monk knew this, and was aware of the suffering which spreading the teaching would entail, he was overjoyed with the new discovery of the Lord Buddha's real intention and set out alone. Truly he was a lonely but majestic figure with an iron will and firm resolve.

On April 28, 1253, Nichiren decided to make public his view on Buddhism and chose to do it at the spot where he had joined the monastery as a boy many years before. According to tradition, it was on this day at dawn that the young monk stood on the cliff at Kiyosumi Mountain overlooking the Pacific Ocean, and facing East he shouted to the rising sun, "Namu Myo Horengekyo" ("I devote myself to the Sutra of the Lotus of the Wonderful Law"). This is said to be the first time that the name of the Lotus Sutra was recited. In order to commemorate this auspicious occasion, one corner of this mountain is still known as the Forest of the Rising Sun.

When he began to live the life based upon the principles of the Lotus Sutra, the persecutions, which had been prophesied, began to overtake him. However, the suffering and hardship served him well, for they made his resolution stronger than ever before. He realized, because of the persecutions which had been prophesied in the Lotus Sutra, that the teachings of the Lotus are true. Previous to this time he had been known as Rencho; now he formally adopted the name Nichiren. *Nichi* means the sun and *ren* means the lotus flower. As he wrote later in a letter to a friend, "There is nothing so clear and serene as the sun and the moon, and nothing purer than the lotus flowers. The Lotus of Perfect Truth is like the sun and the moon and the lotus flowers. This Nichiren is incessantly emulating the sun and the moon and the lotus flowers." One can understand the mind of Nichiren from these words.

Those words which characterize Nichiren are based on two passages in the Lotus Sutra: "Just as the sun and the moon together are responsible for making the dark places bright, so is the man whose activities in the world bring light and happiness to all living creatures." And the second famous passage admonishes us, "Not to be infected with worldly events but to remain pure like the lotus in a muddy pool."

When Nichiren went to Kamakura, which was then the seat of the government, he met with a hostile reception and continuing persecution, but he also gained several disciples and a growing number of followers. There he published his famous book, *A Treatise on the Establishment of Righteousness and the Security of the Country*. He wrote the Treatise to point out that the social unrest of the period was caused by the utterly chaotic state of the religious beliefs of the people, and that the only way to bring peace to the nation was to follow the righteous teachings enshrined in the Lotus Sutra.

As Nichiren continued his teaching, the bitter opposition of the other sects and of the government increased to such a point that finally he was rewarded with the worst reception imaginable, for he was sentenced to death at the execution ground near Kamakura. But just as he bent his neck to receive the blow of the sword, he was miraculously saved by a great ball of light which caused the guards to be converted to his teachings. He was, however, banished to the island of Sado in the bitterly cold climate of northern Japan. The suffering and hardship he endured there must have been indescribable, but even under those trying conditions his militant spirit never gave in, and he spent his time in further development of his system. It was while he was at Sado that he devised the sacred Mandala, which is the graphic representation of the truth of the teachings of the Lotus Sutra and is the chief object of worship in the Nichiren sect.

After three years of exile he was permitted to leave the island. He returned to Kamakura, but after a short time there he moved to Mount Minobu where he settled with his disciples for the last nine years of his life. There is a beautiful story in connection with his sojourn at Minobu. Whenever Nichiren had a spare moment, he used to climb a hill behind his cottage to a spot where he could see his beloved birthplace, and there he earnestly offered prayers to the departed souls of his parents and teacher. In order to commemorate this deed of filial piety, a tower has been built to remind us of this act.

In 1282, Nichiren fell ill and was advised to go to the hot springs to recuperate. On the way, his condition became serious and he was compelled to stop at the home of a follower. There, on the thirteenth of October, he passed peacefully into the bosom of his beloved and devoted master, the Lord Buddha. Even in his last hours he continued to give a series of talks on his Treatise, which had brought him so much suffering and hardship in his younger days. In his last hour he gave an injunction to a youthful disciple to go to Kyoto where the emperor resided, to preach and spread the teaching and spirit of the Lotus of the Wonderful Law.

Even while he was leading the miserable life of an exile, it is said that Nichiren never lost his composure. Under all circumstances he went about his work with untiring zeal and such hope and cheerfulness that he astonished everybody. Never in adversity or triumph did Nichiren lose his sense of proportion, his calmness, and his serenity. Nichiren demonstrated in his own person the joy and greatness of one who realized in himself the view of life and the outlook on the world which is expounded in the Saddharma Pundarika Sutra.

What sort of a book is The Lotus of the Wonderful Law?

We do not know the exact date of the compilation of the original Lotus Sutra, but it was some time around the first century A.D., in northwestern India. It was translated from the

Sanskrit into Chinese by Kumarajiva in 406. It is made up of twenty-eight chapters, the first fourteen dealing with the nature of man and the second fourteen with the nature of the Buddha.

The first half of the Lotus Sutra explains the real nature of all existence, including the original nature of man. According to this teaching, human nature has unlimited possibilities for development, both for evil and for good. If man chooses the path of wickedness, he has the capacity to reach the lowest bottom of hell, but if he chooses the good, he may gain power of thought equal to a creative deity and may even reach the stature of a Buddha. Thus, one must strive diligently to develop the potentiality of becoming a Buddha. One must also realize that this potentiality of becoming a Buddha, this Buddha-nature, belongs to everything that exists—hence we must respect all beings. One who behaves in daily life as if he fully realizes the Buddha-nature is a veritable Bodhisattva. A Bodhisattva is guided, under all circumstances, by the principle of mercy and always acts with creative altruism.

The second half of the Lotus Sutra, which deals with the Buddha, draws our attention to the fact that the actual Buddha, the historical Buddha, is by real nature the same as the eternal and immortal truth, which in turn is one with the original, Enlightened Buddha. Although this world requires patience and forbearance and is soiled with sin, in reality there is no other world, there is no other paradise. In appearance, this world seems to be made up of the sacred and profane, of ignorance and wisdom in opposition to each other; but these delusive and enlightened elements are not opposed to each other, they are simply two aspects of a single whole. An ordinary person who is obsessed with desire cannot help but feel that this world is full of suffering, but the Enlightened person sees it truly. That is what is meant by the Enlightenment of the Lord Sakyamuni: he became united with the truth, he saw the real aspect of things.

If a man does not live harmoniously with the real nature of the world, he will inevitably be frustrated, restrained by the world. But when man is stirred with profound faith and devotion toward the original Buddha and consciously feels the sense of union with the Buddha's nature, even for a fraction of a second, then his outlook on life and the world is transformed entirely. Then there is no more restraint, no more frustration; there is only freedom. The world which lies outside has not changed, but his own subjective, inner self is changed. With this real awakening, one begins to realize that the world is not a world of suffering, but on the contrary, it is a beautiful paradise. This heavenly abode is not only the habitation for humanity, but for animals and plants and inorganic matter. Such a question as to how plants may develop into Buddhahood cannot arise, for it is seen that plants exist from the beginning in the Buddha world.

The only key sufficient to open the world of the original Buddha is a thought of deep devotion. Herein lies the mysticism of the Lotus Sutra.

Nichiren's religious activity was aimed at the revival of Buddhism based upon the teaching found in The Lotus of the Wonderful Law. After a critical investigation of all the available texts, he chose the Lotus Sutra as orthodox Buddhism. His reasons for choosing this Sutra are known as the Five Principles:

1. The first principle is the Doctrine, that is, what the Lord Buddha taught during his lifetime. In comparison with other teachings, one chooses Buddhism. Within Buddhism, after comparing Hinayana with Mahayana, one's choice falls with Mahayana. Mahayana is divided into the Provisional teaching and the Perfect teaching, and one chooses the latter. Thus, among the Mahayana teachings the Saddharma Pundarika Sutra is chosen as the best.

2. The second principle is called the Endowment, which means the natural qualities of a man. The Buddha's teaching is like a fertilizer which enables the seed to grow into an enormous tree. So it is with man—when he is given the opportunity to study and act in accordance with the teaching of the Buddha, he will eventually become as mighty as an Enlightened One. In this age of the decline of the law, when the Buddha doctrine is almost forgotten and its influence is well-nigh extinguished, the only way to bring people to a conscious

realization of the meaning of life is to give them the doctrine contained in the Lotus Sutra.

3. The third principle which led Nichiren to the selection of the Saddharma Pundarika Sutra is called the Time. On the basis of the periods of time after the Buddha, the present age is the age of the final decay of the law. As the influence of the Buddha has declined with the passage of time, when the living standards of the people differ entirely from those of the time of the Buddha, then the only way to save them is by means of the Saddharma Pundarika.

4. The fourth principle is the Country. There are some nations which do not even know of the existence of the Lotus of the Wonderful Law. There are others which know of the existence of the Lotus Sutra but tend to reject this teaching—and in Nichiren's time Japan was such a nation. But ever since the time of Prince Shotoku the Japanese people had had some interest in this Sutra, and Nichiren considered it very significant that there was a foundation of knowledge of the Lotus Sutra on which to build. Thus, Japan is the country in which Buddhism will grow most successfully and where the Lotus Sutra will flourish.

5. The final principle on which Nichiren chose the Lotus Sutra is known as the Order of Spread of Buddhism. In a nation which has not been blessed with the introduction of Buddhist teaching, any form of Buddhism would be a valuable asset. At the time of introduction, it is desirable to adopt Hinayana, followed by Mahayana. In Mahayana, the Provisional teaching should be adopted first, and then the Real, or Perfect, teaching should be followed. For the individual, at first any sort of Buddhist teacher is sufficient, but later the only proper teacher of the real spirit of the Lord Buddha is one who is thoroughly conversant with the teaching enshrined in the Saddharma Pundarika Sutra. Thus we see why the Saddharma Pundarika Sutra should be regarded as quite orthodox.

In the Nichiren sect, Honmon-No-Honzon, the Supreme Being, one of the Three Great Mysteries, is the object of worship. The Supreme Being is also known as the eternal Buddha as revealed in the Saddharma Pundarika Sutra, none other than the original Lord Sakyamuni Buddha. This is represented in a diagrammatic form, known as the Great Mandala, in which the Sacred Title is surrounded by the Buddhas and Bodhisattvas. It is said that Nichiren gave the final shape to this diagram on May 8th, 1273, a most memorable day since on that day the object of worship for the Nichiren sect was established.

The second Great Mystery is the repeating of the name of the Sutra. It is a great deal more than simply calling out the name of the sacred book. It acts as a reminder of the Lord Buddha, who makes his appearance in the Saddharma Pundarika Sutra, and whose Enlightenment was great and whose power to do meritorious work was wonderful. Thus, if we are willing to repeat the name of this Sutra—Namu Myo Horengekyo—with heart and soul and with great respect, sooner or later we receive a great spiritual benefit. Furthermore, if we wish to turn religious precepts into practice, all we have to do is to receive the precepts gratefully and keep repeating the Namu Myo Horengekyo, "I devote myself to the Sutra of the Lotus of the Wonderful Law." The receiving and keeping of the name of the Saddharma Pundarika is done by repeating the name of the Sutra orally.

It must be clearly understood that repeating the name of the Lotus Sutra is not a simple act like singing. Every human action involves the threefold combination of deed, word, and thought. Thus, when one is uttering the name of the Lotus Sutra orally, he is at the same time combining the word with thinking and doing. This is known as repeating the sacred name of the Saddharma Pundarika Sutra in united action, physically, orally, and ideally. By means of this practice, one progresses on the high road to Enlightenment.

The third Great Mystery is the Kaidan, or sacred place for carrying on mystical rites. In one sense it is wherever a believer in the Sutra lives, and in another sense it is the place where candidates receive the higher teaching; it is usually in a temple, but may be elsewhere. According to Nichiren, all rules and ceremonies are included in the act of receiving and keeping the spirit of the Saddharma Pundarika Sutra. The place where one receives and keeps these mystic precepts is the sacred place of the Lotus Sutra. However, to anyone who worships the right object of worship, has a deep devotion to the eternal Buddha, and repeats the name of the Saddharma Pundarika Sutra, there is no particular sacred place; anywhere and everywhere in this world is the sacred place belonging to the Lotus of the Wonderful Law. Man can only make progress toward the land of the Buddha by the simple acceptance of the three Great Mysteries.

The ethical principles required of the followers of Nichiren are based on the Lotus Sutra, as it has been explained above. Of the five ethical principles given here, the first is extremely important for it expresses in few words the attitude expected of Nichiren's followers toward other Buddhist sects, the nation, and the world in general.

1. Nichiren strongly advised that his followers should make a careful study of his experiences while he lived the kind of life that is expounded in the Saddharma Pundarika Sutra— and that the example set by his life should serve as the ethical base for guiding them in human affairs.

2. Absolute faith and devotion to the eternal, fully-enlightened original master, the Lord Buddha Sakyamuni, is required.

3. The straight path to Enlightenment is the practice of religion by repeating the Name, *Namu Myo Horengekyo*. If one treads this path steadily one will reach the goal eventually.

4. It was Nichiren's ideal to establish a world of the Buddha on this earth by developing and improving the Buddha-nature possessed by all beings. It behooves the followers of Nichiren to do their utmost to realize this ideal.

5. It is an incontrovertible fact that we all possess potential Buddhahood. Such being the case, we must all strive to lead a righteous life.

The chief temple in the Nichiren sect is located in Minobu Machi, the secluded spot where Nichiren spent the last nine years of his life, training his disciples and leading an austere religious life. It is the firm belief of Nichiren's followers that his teaching will spread all over the world from that sacred place.

BUDDHISM AFTER THE KAMAKURA ERA
Shinsho Hanayama

The period after the founding of the Jodo, Shin, Zen, and Nichiren sects was one of great political unrest again. For sixty years the emperor was at Nara and the samurai ruled the country from Kyoto. Then the Ashikaga clan established a rule which continued until 1568, but with many civil wars involving regional rulers. In 1606 the government was established at Edo, the modern Tokyo, which brought peace for a time. The final change in government—before modern times—came in 1868, the time of the Meiji Restoration.

After the Kamakura Era no new major sect was founded in Japan. One important aspect of Japanese Buddhism, however, which was quite widespread but never became the exclusive characteristic of one sect, was the worship of the Bodhisattva Avalokitesvara as Kwannon. The worship of Kuan-yin was brought to Japan from China before the time of Prince Shotoku, and the worship of Kwannon, as she was called in Japan, was common to all sects from that time on. The name of Kwannon appears in many Sutras; images of Kwannon have been placed in a majority of the temples of Japan ever since the Nara Era. Some of the most beautiful images and paintings created in Japan have been inspired by Kwannon, the Bodhisattva of infinite compassion. Even in modern times, Kwannon is honored by the common people of Japan more than any other Bodhisattva.

In the fourteenth and fifteenth centuries there was a considerable growth in the Zen sect with Rinzai Zen spreading among the lords and samurais and Soto Zen practiced by the ordinary people. This was the time of the creation of many works of art, the building of beautiful gardens and temples, and the adoption of the tea ceremony among the people. Confucian influence was strong during this period. It was also a time in which Jodo and Nichiren spread widely among the common people.

In the sixteenth century, two of the rulers made a strong attempt to suppress the priest-warriors of Tendai and Shingon and the sects of Jodo, Shin, and Nichiren.

In the seventeenth century, in order to weaken the religious bodies and bring them under government control, regulations were made by the Edo government which determined the organization of each sect and the relations between temples. Each sect was divided by appointing two head temples, to weaken them by creating rivalries. Thus the influence of the Buddhist institutions and various sects was changed at the will of the government and used by the government for its own benefit. At the same time, measures were taken to link each family with its family temple, and all activities such as births, marriages, deaths, funerals, and even travel by members of the family were registered with the priest in charge of the temple. Thus the temples once more came under state control. As a result, a feeling of stagnation prevailed in Buddhist circles, and the priests chose a way of life which deviated from their original religious aims.

The government suppressed free research in religion and greatly encouraged Confucianism since it was useful in maintaining government power. As civil wars were suppressed and peace prevailed, the people turned to worldly pleasures and the accumulation of material wealth. This concern for worldly pleasures led many temples to begin to cater to the low beliefs of the people and offer to help them attain worldly ends, and some of those tendencies continue to the present day. In spite of all the discouragements, however, the Shin, Zen, and Nichiren sects continued to grow.

The Meiji Restoration in 1868 restored the power of the Imperial Family, ended the policy of national seclusion, and brought the fruits of Western culture to Japan. These new factors greatly influenced the ways of thinking and the religion of the people. Shintoism and Buddhism, which had been closely related, were separated; Buddhist beliefs and worship were banned from the Imperial Household; and the emperor was made the object of worship as the incarnated god of Shintoism. It was a time of crisis for Buddhism. The study of the historical origin of the state led to bitter antagonism based on Shinto practices and even brought about the burning of temples and destruction of Sutras and valuable pieces of Buddhist art. The number of priests who returned to lay life increased, and the priesthood might be said to have reaped the results of their negligence and indolence.

Even though the influence of the priests declined greatly under the pressures of the changes after the Meiji Restoration, the study of the doctrines has continued. The doctrines are the truth expressed in various ways to meet changing conditions of time and place. The study of Buddhism was now conducted as the flower of oriental philosophy to be evaluated in the light of Western philosophy. The students and scholars who studied in Europe introduced the philosophy and systems of thought of England, Germany, and France and also studied Sanskrit and Pali in an effort to modernize the research on Buddhist documents which had been studied for over a thousand years.

In Japan today the various Buddhist sects are conducting an extensive research through their scholars and re-evaluating the material which has been preserved through the ages. At the many great temples of the different sects in Japan are preserved valuable images of the Buddha and the Bodhisattvas, countless Sutras, paintings, and other sacred objects. All these are objects of devout research.

The various sects perform their solemn ancient rituals and chant the Sutras according to the manner of each sect, and members—except those who are educated and live in cities—congregate at the family temple to have the conservative Buddhist annual rites performed. The only time that these city intellectuals go to the temple is to attend a funeral or memorial service. In fact, only a few of these intellectuals have looked in earnest into the problems of life and therefore call on the temple and listen to the preaching of the teachings of the Buddha.

Part of the difficulty lies in the present-day priests who, unlike the priests of Ceylon, Burma, and Thailand, have little worthy of respect in their daily practice of religion. From the standpoint of knowledge and research, the majority of the priests today are far from the honored priests of old who were well-qualified and respected and were able to lead the laymen of their age. From the standpoint of protecting the teachings of the Buddha, there may be much to be learned from the priests of Southern Buddhism.

After the Meiji Restoration it was state policy to forbid the founding of a new sect or the construction of a new temple. The various schools were classified as thirteen schools with fifty-six subsects. During World War II, as a result of the totalitarian policy, there were further restrictions which classified Buddhism in thirteen schools with twenty-eight subsects. The thirteen schools were listed as Tendai, Shingon, Jodo, Rinzai, Soto, Obaku, Shin, Nichiren, Hosso, Kegon, Ritzu, Ji, and Yuzu Nembutsu. After the war the restrictions were totally removed, and many new sects have been formed.

According to the survey by the Ministry of Education in 1951, there were 234 sects in Japan at that time, with a total of 36,000,000 members. In many cases, the new sects have grown out of a revolt against authority or a struggle for power or have developed for financial reasons. It is regrettable that there are not many cases worthy of mention in which the reform of doctrines or faith became the prime motive for establishing a new sect. Most of the new sects have grown up in Nichiren, Shingon, Tendai, and Jodo, while the more united sects like Soto and Shin have had almost no cases of disunion.

At the same time, there has been a growing movement among liberal Buddhists toward cooperation and unification. This tendency was greatly strengthened by the Second World Buddhist Conference, held at the headquarters of the Nishi Hongwanji of the Shin sect in Tokyo in 1952. It was attended by representatives from eighteen foreign countries and all the sects of Japan. This brought about the formation of the Japan Chapter of the World Federation of Buddhists, the All Japan Young Buddhist Federation, and the Japan Buddhist Women's Association. The different schools of Buddhism have sent representatives to many other Buddhist countries to observe practices and confer with Buddhist leaders in the years since the war.

The academic study of Buddhism and the spreading of the doctrines of the various sects is being done in many educational institutions in Japan. There are six major universities supported by different Buddhist schools and six specialized colleges which offer a regular curriculum. In addition, there are short term colleges for young men, high schools, middle schools, and elementary schools operated by Buddhist sects. There are also many social and cultural activities supported by different groups, such as cultural education, medical services, child relief programs, and related welfare services.

The professors and research scholars of Japan are banded together in the Nippon Buddhist Research Association and the Japanese Association of Indian and Buddhist Studies. Their membership is drawn from Buddhist educational institutions and from the various government universities. All these cooperative educational and research activities are indications of the new vitality in Buddhism in modern times. Japan is perhaps unique among Buddhist countries today for the extent of the researches being made with modern methods in the Buddhist literature in Sanskrit, Pali, Tibetan, Mongolian, and Chinese.

In the fourteen centuries since Buddhism came to Japan, there have been many changes; much that is unique has been developed in the new environment, and through the years many men of great spirituality have followed the teachings of the Buddha. The faith and practice of Shin and Nichiren are indeed unique in that they have no counterparts in Buddhism throughout the world, and Soto Zen as developed by Dogen is a religion which can be practiced by men everywhere. The Buddhists of Japan look proudly to the spiritual masters, scholars, and artists of the past and hopefully to the future.

CHAPTER EIGHT

Unity and Diversity in Buddhism

Hajime Nakamura

The estimates as to the number of Buddhists in the world to-day range all the way from 100 million to 500 million, with 150 million the figure which has fairly wide acceptance. There are over 772 million people in the countries in which Buddhist influence is an important factor—Burma, Ceylon, Thailand, Cambodia, Laos, Nepal, Tibet, Korea, Japan, and China. If China is omitted from that figure, on the ground that it is very difficult to estimate the influence of Buddhism in China at the present time, there are 170 million people in the remaining Buddhist countries. Of that number, at least 46 million are followers of Theravada Buddhism and 52 million are avowed followers of Mahayana Buddhism.

Although there is some historical justification for using the term *Hinayana* in describing Southern Buddhism from the Mahayana point of view, for it was the term commonly used to describe all schools which were not Mahayana, it is inaccurate in modern times, and undesirable, since it stresses only the diversity in Buddhism and fails to recognize the large area of unity. Hinayana—the Lesser Vehicle—was used by the Mahayana reformers in a contemptuous sense which expresses their feeling that the older schools were conservative, complacent, and self-righteous. None of those early schools accepted the name or the characterization given to them by the newer Mahayana schools. They continued to go by their chosen names such as Sarvastivada, Theravada, and the like. Of those schools, only Theravada exists today, and it is their strong preference that they be known by that name. For a more general term, describing all the schools which did not accept the Mahayana principles, they prefer *Conservative Buddhism*. Since Mahayana schools prefer to be known as Mahayana, the Theravadins see no objection to that use of the word.

The new, reforming sects called themselves Mahayana because they thought of their system as large and vast, one which can save many living beings, and a system which is superior. Mahayana Buddhism believes that the Doctrine will vary according to the different climatic and cultural situations in which it finds itself, that it will change and develop through the years, and that even at the outset not all of the Buddha's teachings were included in the Canon. Theravada, on the other hand, is proud of itself as the guardian of the true Doctrine of the Buddha which it has preserved without alteration due to time or place. This is a clear point of diversity, but it obscures the amount of unity there is in the two schools, for Mahayana has also treasured much of the teaching which has been preserved in Theravada. Within the two schools, as the preceding chapters in this book have shown, Theravada has maintained a high degree of unity in teachings and practices while great diversity has grown up in Mahayana.

CHRONOLOGY

One minor point of difference between Mahayana and Theravada concerns the date of the life and death of the Lord Buddha. Theravada Buddhists, following the Ceylonese tradition, accept the year 544 B.C. as the death-year and on that basis celebrated the 2,500th anniversary in 1956. Even though scholars have pointed out that they cannot find authentic records for this tradition before the eleventh century, Theravada Buddhists assert that there is no doubt that it is correct because, every year since the time of the Buddha, they have kept an accurate record by reciting as a part of their regular Vinaya ceremonies the number of years and days since his Mahaparinirvana.

European scholars have rejected this chronology as incompatible with the dates known for the kings of Magadha. One of the most moderate opinions was that of the late Professor M. Winternitz, who pointed out that there is sufficient evidence to convince us that the Buddha was a contemporary of King Bimbisara and King Ajatasatru, whom we can place with a fair amount of certainty in the sixth and fifth centuries B.C. Thus, a somewhat later date is required.

One Mahayana theory concerning the correct date is based on the tradition concerning Sanghabhadra, who visited China in A.D. 489. He said that the Indian Bhikkhus made it a rule to put a dot on the Vinaya Pitaka every year at the end of the rainy season retreat and he had counted 975 dots in that year, so the birth-year of the Buddha should be 566 B.C. and the death-year should be 486 B.C. Under the leadership of the late Japanese scholar Junjiro Takakusu, many Japanese Buddhists accepted this date and celebrated the 2,500th birthday in 1932. However, the Jodo, Shin, and Nichiren sects did not join with them since the founders of these sects had adopted the legend that the death-year of the Buddha was 949 B.C., as fixed by the Chinese priest Horin (572–640). Needless to say, even the followers of these sects do not believe this legend literally nowadays.

Dr. Hakuju Ui, adopting the legends set forth in Sanskrit, Tibetan, and Chinese versions of the scriptures, fixed the date of the Buddha as 466–386 B.C. The dates of King Asoka, on whose life he based his computations, have been altered by recent archeological research, so the correct dates would be 463–383 B.C., if his arguments are to be accepted.

Even though there is not agreement concerning the chronology, Japanese Buddhists were glad to collaborate with Theravada Buddhists in their 2,500th year ceremonies honoring the Buddha.

THE MISSION OF BUDDHISM

Throughout these twenty-five centuries, both Theravada and Mahayana Buddhism have recognized their mission to spread the teachings of the Buddha throughout the world. The story of that missionary activity has been told in the first chapter. With a tender compassion for all beings the Buddha set forth "to establish the kingdom of righteousness, to give light to those enshrouded in darkness and to open the gate of immortality to men." (Mahavagga I, 6, 8.) So, soon after the founding of the Order, the Buddha sent out his followers on missionary journeys to spread the Dharma with the command, "Fare ye forth, brethen, on the mission that is for the good of the many, for the happiness of the many; to take compassion to the world; to work for the profit and good and happiness of gods and men. Go singly; go not in pairs."

The Buddhist teachings were universal and all-comprehensive, to be made known to all men for their Enlightenment. This spread of Buddhism was accomplished by the devotion of monks and laymen, and conversion took place only by persuasion. There is no known case of conversion to Buddhism by the use of force. Even King Asoka, one of the most ardent Buddhist rulers, renounced the use of force and sent out missionaries to persuade men to accept the universal truth of the teachings of the Buddha.

BUDDHISM AND THE STATE

It is interesting to note, however, to what an extent Buddhism was aided by friendly rulers or hindered and even exterminated by states which were unfriendly. The important role played by a friendly state is clear when we recall such rulers as Asoka and Kaniska in India, Buddhadasa in Ceylon, Anawrahta in Burma, T'ai-tsung in China, Songtsan-Gampo in Tibet, and Shotoku in Japan. On the other hand, we have seen how an unfriendly government led to the extermination of Buddhism in India, how Mahayana Buddhism was banned by the rulers in Ceylon and Burma, how Buddhism was persecuted by the three emperors called Wu in China, and opposed on several occasions by the government in Japan, especially in the beginning of the Meiji Era. At the present, it is not possible to assess the effect of a Communist government on Buddhism in China.

In early Buddhism, the rights of a king were not considered to be sacred or conferred by the gods. It is said that the Buddha extolled a republican form of government in which the sovereignty of the kings was delegated by the people. But the kings in those days were mostly despotic and oppressive and Buddhists sought to avoid them. The Buddha said, "Kings are like venomous serpents. You should not make them angry. It is better not to come into contact with them." Such an unpolitical attitude could not be maintained, however, and as time went on both Theravada and Mahayana Buddhism were drawn into the political sphere. Frequently the state controlled Buddhism for its own purposes, and such control was always to the great detriment of Buddhism, as has been seen in the history of Buddhism in China and Japan in particular.

In Tibet, the unique amalgamation of Buddhism and political power has continued into modern times with the Dalai Lama regarded by the people as the final authority, even under Communist control. At the present time, Buddhism is the state religion of Thailand, Laos, and Cambodia, and many Buddhists in Burma and Ceylon argue that it should be officially the state religion in their countries. In Japan, the Nichiren sect holds that the state and religion should be identified. Most of the rest of the Japanese sects prefer noninterference on the part of the government. On the question of the proper relation between Buddhism and the state, diversity of opinion is found in both Theravada and Mahayana.

In those countries in which Buddhism flourished it had considerable influence upon the administration of justice. Early Chinese pilgrims found that in ancient India capital punishment and mutilation had been abolished on the ground that they conflicted with the Buddhist attitude of compassion. In Japan in the Heian Era, during the eighth to the twelfth centuries when Buddhist influence was strong, there was no capital punishment. In Tibet, the thirteenth Dalai Lama abolished capital punishment and extreme mutilation.

The use of military force by the state was renounced by Asoka after he became a Buddhist, and there have been many Buddhist emperors since his time who have tried to govern by persuasion rather than by force. The Tibetans were transformed from fierce warlike nomads to a peaceful, friendly people by the acceptance of Buddhism. Some rulers have opposed Buddhism on the ground that its emphasis on compassion tended to make poor soldiers. On the other hand, the samurai class in Japan at one time adopted some of the meditative disciplines of Zen Buddhism as a part of their training to become better warriors. Throughout its history, there has been diversity of opinion within Buddhism concerning the compatibility of Buddhism and military power.

In China and Japan, Buddhism gradually became separated from the ruling class, and the priests were obliged to turn to the ignorant populace for support. In both countries the ruling class became this-worldly. By contrast, in Theravada countries and in Tibet the laymen in the ruling class still hold to their Buddhism and influence the policies and culture of their countries.

TOLERANCE

Tolerance has been an outstanding characteristic of Theravada and Mahayana Buddhism from earliest times. Early Buddhism was filled with the spirit of tolerance. Buddhism has attempted to arrive at the truth, not by excluding its opposites as falsehood, but by including them as another form of the same truth. Although Buddhism was predominant in many Asiatic countries, there is no record of any persecution by Buddhists of the followers of any other faith. They waged no religious war. It is very difficult to have a firm conviction and at the same time to be tolerant, but the Buddha himself and many of his followers have achieved such tolerance.

Buddhists are generally noted for their liberal attitude toward other religions, whether polytheistic, monotheistic, or atheistic. This feature is found in all Buddhist countries. Buddhists admit the truth of any moral and philosophical system, whether primitive or developed, provided only that it is capable of leading men at least part way toward their final goal.

Buddhism has tolerated the various faiths native to the countries in Asia without any clear doctrine of paganism. In Theravada countries, many Hindu gods and goddesses have been included in the religious ceremonies of the Buddhist community, and many Buddhists still observe festivals and customs associated with the nats and other nature spirits of each country. In China, Buddhism has actually been amalgamated with many Taoist beliefs and practices; many shrines are semi-Buddhist and semi-Taoist. The same tolerance has brought about a blending of the various Buddhist sects in China until they are indistinguishable today. In Tibet, as we have seen, Santarakshita compromised with Bonism by incorporating many of its gods and goddesses into the lowest grade of tantric Guardian Deities, without affecting the doctrinal integrity of Buddhism. He replaced the animal sacrifices of the Bons with symbolic worship and taught inner purification in place of black magic. This method was in accordance with the tolerant attitude of the Buddha.

In Japan, the indigenous gods and goddesses were dealt with in the same way that they were in Tibet. In the Nara Era they were assigned rather low positions, but from the Heian Era onward their positions became gradually higher and higher; they were regarded as incarnations of Buddhas and Bodhisattvas. Nowadays the common people do not distinguish between Buddhistic divine beings and Shinto gods. In the past in Japan there were very few shrines that did not have shrine-temples built in their confines where Buddhist priests performed the morning and evening practices of reciting Sutras and served the shrine gods and goddesses together with Shinto priests. The majority of the Japanese pray before the Shintoist shrines and at the same time pay homage at the Buddhist temples, without being conscious of any contradiction.

The Sangha

The Buddha established a religious order which has continued to the present day as one of the oldest and most influential orders of religious brethren in the world. The Buddhist Sangha, and the kindred sect of the Jains, have survived longer than any other institutions in existence today. The Sangha has continued as a celibate, monastic order for monks and nuns in the Theravada countries and in China. In Tibet and Japan some of the religious leaders are celibate and follow monastic disciplines, and some are married and live the life of a householder. Korean priests observed celibacy very strictly for a long time, but in recent years some Korean priests imitated the Japanese priests and got married. In an effort to get rid of everything Japanese, the Korean government has been expelling married priests from the temples. Monks are known as Bhikkhus in Theravada countries (the Sanskrit form is *Bhikshu*). In Burma they are often called Phongyis (*phon* means great, *gyi* means glory). In Japan, the religious leaders are called priests, monks, or ministers and often given the honorary title of Reverend, especially in the Shin sect. The English term *bonze* is a corruption of the Japanese word *bozu*, which means "the head of a monastery," and was formerly an honorary title, but nowadays it is used in a contemptuous sense; people should not address a priest as *bozu*.

In Thailand, Cambodia, and Laos, all Buddhist laymen are expected to spend some time in a monastery receiving instruction in Buddhism; it is possible to be ordained as a monk and then return to lay life without disapproval by the Buddhist community. In Burma it is not uncommon for laymen to spend some time in monasteries, but they do not customarily receive ordination unless they intend to remain. In all other Buddhist countries, the practice of returning to lay life after receiving ordination is not usually approved. The ceremony of ordination according to the Vinaya practices is followed in Theravada countries and was for a long time the custom in Mahayana countries. However, there was another informal self-vow ordination performed by some Mahayanists, called the Bodhisattva ordination and based on the Brahmajala Sutra, which became widely used in Japan. In tantric and esoteric Buddhism the ritual of ordination by anointment is followed.

The practice of remaining in one place for three months during the rainy season was started during the lifetime of the Buddha and is still maintained in Theravada countries, beginning and ending with big festivals. In China and Japan, where they do not have a rainy season, it is very seldom observed, but some festivals continue which were originally connected with annual retreats, and some monastic groups have annual periods of study and meditation.

In both Theravada and Mahayana, the Buddhist community has never been organized around a central authority which could decree doctrines or practices which must be observed by all followers. Buddhist followers of all types have been comparatively individualistic and unwilling to submit to a rigid outer authority. Agreement as to the doctrines to be held and the practices to be followed has been reached by discussion within the community, guided by the scriptures accepted as a basis for their faith. In Theravada countries at the present time, there is great unity, with the different sects playing only a minor role. In Tibet, although there are several sects, the one million Buddhists in the country are united in most matters; such divisions as exist there are more political than religious. In China they formerly had rather marked sectarian differences, but in modern times they have blended into one general form of Mahayana Buddhism. Only in Japan are there marked sectarian differences, as we have seen.

RATIONALISM

According to Buddhism, faith becomes superstition when it is not examined by reason. Gotama was described as one who reasoned according to the truth rather than on the basis of the authority of the Vedas or tradition. Theravada and Mahayana Buddhism have accepted two standards for the truth of a statement: it must be in accord with the scriptures and must be proved true by reasoning. No Buddhist is expected to believe anything which does not meet these two tests.

All schools of Buddhism have presupposed universal laws, called dharmas, which govern human existence and may be known by reason. According to the Buddha, personal relations should be brought into harmony with the universal norms, the universal laws which apply to all existence. The word *dharma* is often used as meaning the Doctrine of the Buddha; in this sense dharma is not dogma, but is rather the Path which is regarded as the universal norm for all mankind, conformity to the nature of the universe.

The acceptance of rational analysis of the nature of human existence has been a continuing characteristic of Buddhism, but it should be noted that metaphysical speculation concerning problems not related to human activities and the attainment of Enlightenment have not been considered to be a proper part of Buddhist rationalism. Thus, the Doctrine of the Buddha is not a system of philosophy in the Western sense but is rather a Path. A Buddha is simply one who has trodden this Path and can report to others on what he has found. We can interpret the appellation *Tathagata*—one who has gone thus—in this sense.

All metaphysical views are only partial apprehensions of the whole truth which lies beyond rational analysis. Only a Buddha can apprehend the whole truth. Rational analysis is useful in making clear the limitations of rationality. The Doctrine of the Buddha transcends comparison; it is neither inferior, nor equal, nor superior to other doctrines. It is by detaching oneself from philosophical oppositions that one is able to grasp the truth. Thus in Buddhism there is no dogma which opposes other dogmas. Of course, Buddhism as a cultural and historical product developed many different systems of thought in the course of time, but it has always sought to avoid obscurantism or coercion to believe what seems to be irrational.

The Buddha taught many doctrines which later scholars elaborated. Sometimes the scholars contradict each other. However, all Buddhists, whether Theravada or Mahayana, agree that they aim to teach the way to realize an ideal life. In Buddhism the entire stress lies on the mode of living, on the saintliness of life, on the removal of attachment to the world. A merely theoretical proposition, such as "There is no ego," would be regarded as utterly sterile and useless. All Buddhists follow the Buddha in wanting to teach how to lead a selfless life. Rational analysis is no more than a tool which is justified in its products. That is why there are so many teachings even on one subject, such as dependent origination.

The Buddha's doctrine is called a vehicle in the sense that it is like a ferryboat. One enters the Buddhist vehicle to cross the river of life from the shore of worldly experience, the shore of spiritual ignorance, desire, and suffering, to the other shore of transcendental wisdom which is liberation from bondage and suffering. Suppose a man builds a raft and by this means succeeds in attaining the other shore. "What would be your opinion of this man?" asks the Buddha. "Would he be a clever man if, out of gratitude for the raft that carried him across the stream to safety, he, having reached the other shore, should cling to it, take it on his back, and walk about with the weight of it?" The monks replied, "No." The Buddha then concludes, "In the same way the vehicle of the doctrine is to be cast away and forsaken, once the other shore of Enlightenment (Nirvana) has been attained." (Majjhima Nikaya, I, 3, 2. No. 22.) Just as the difference in shape, weight, and material among rafts does not matter, difference in teachings does not matter. This point of view is set forth both in Theravada and Mahayana Buddhism.

While such an attitude toward the teachings of Buddhism seems quite contradictory, this attitude can be justified. If one says something, it is justified only by what is called "skill in means." Words like *enlightenment, ignorance, freedom,* and *attachment* are preliminary helps, referring to no ultimate reality, mere hints or signposts for the traveler on the Path, serving only to point out the goal. The wisdom which is sought in Buddhism is not the wisdom of conflicting metaphysical systems; it is the wisdom of Enlightenment as to the true nature of human existence.

FAITH

In Buddhism faith is an introductory means to the attainment of truth, not an acceptance of definite dogmas. When one takes refuge in the Three Jewels, it is a partial turning away from the visible to the invisible; it is some measure of detachment from this world. Faith does not necessarily mean the realization of truth itself. Faith has only a preliminary significance; it is important only insofar as it opens the door of the ideal state. Throughout Buddhist history there have been two currents, the devotional approach and the approach through inner knowledge, insight. The approach through the inner vision has always been regarded as the truer one, while the devotional approach has been more or less regarded as a concession to the common people. The only outstanding exceptions to this have been Pure Realm Buddhism and the Nichiren sect. For them, faith is made supreme.

ESOTERIC BUDDHISM

Esoteric Buddhism has played an important part in Buddhist history. Its aim is insight, the inner vision which leads to Enlightenment. Its emphasis is on practices rather than doctrines. Esoteric Buddhism is variously known as Tantrayana, Vajrayana, or Mikkyo. Mikkyo as practiced in Japan is not fully tantric, but is related to it. Esoteric Buddhism comes from the ancient practices of India as they were modified in the development of Tantra. It had the greatest influence in Tibet where many tantric practices were accepted. In China it was taught for a while, but was never widely accepted. In Japan the ancient tantric practices are preserved in Shingon, but greatly modified. Theravada Buddhism has generally rejected tantric practices. Meditation practices which were originally influenced by Indian yoga have been followed in Theravada Buddhism, in Tibet, and in China and Japan chiefly through the influence of Zen.

STAGES OF THE PATH

It has generally been recognized in Buddhism that there are several stages on the Path to Enlightenment. Theravada has clearly defined the four stages which must be passed through before a man can become an Arahat. Mahayana Buddhism also assumed many steps for getting to Buddhahood. Tendai, for instance, has fifty-two stages which must be passed through before perfect Enlightenment can be attained. The number of stages varies with different Sutras and sects. However, some Mahayanists asserted that they could skip many intermediate steps and attain to Buddhahood directly. Zen, for instance, teaches that Enlightenment comes by means of direct intuition of one's own nature; and Pure Realm Buddhism says that it comes by means of the grace of Amitabha. Differing beliefs concerning the stages leading to Enlightenment have been a point of difference between Theravada and Mahayana and even within Mahayana itself.

THE TEACHINGS

Because Buddhism has existed in so many different places and cultures for such a long time, and has so often been described as made up of different yanas, or vehicles, the unity in belief among Buddhists has tended to be obscured. The very nature of Buddhism has made all attempts to enforce conformity fail, but the persuasive truth of the teachings of the Buddha has won a large measure of agreement in both Theravada and Mahayana. Let us turn now to a consideration of the teachings of Buddhism which have been most widely accepted.

SUFFERING

Always and everywhere through the long history of Buddhism, the fact of suffering has been stressed. Life is suffering. Existence is pain; the struggle to maintain individuality is painful. Buddhists have especially emphasized the fact of death, which overcomes all men. Why do we suffer? It is because of the transiency, the impermanence of human existence. There is sorrow because all things pass away. Our dreams, our hopes, our wishes, our desires—all will be forgotten as if they had never been. This is a universal principle common to all things. "Whatever is subject to origination is subject also to destruction." (Mahavagga I, 23.) Necessary and inexorable is the death of all that is born. There is no substance which abides forever; there is only becoming, change. According to this view, desire causes suffering, since what we desire is impermanent, changing, and perishing.

These desires are caused by ignorance. We are ignorant concerning our true nature and the nature of the universe in which

we live. And we may be freed from our ignorance by following the Middle Path which was taught by the Buddha. This is
not a doctrine of despair. Everyone can be saved finally.
Through the wisdom which comes from reflection on the
transitoriness of life, by following the Path taught by the Buddha, everyone can attain Enlightenment. All this has been accepted by Buddhists everywhere, which is to say that the
whole Buddhist world has always accepted the Four Noble
Truths and the Noble Eightfold Path. Mahayana Buddhism,
even when it looked down on Theravada, has always been at
one with Theravada in developing the purport of these teachings. The only significant variation from this teaching that man
must work out his own salvation, man must tread the Path by
his own efforts, has been the dependence of the Pure Realm
sect upon the help of the External Power.

NON-EGO

So, too, the principle of anatta, non-ego, has been held
throughout Buddhism. Life is nothing but a series of manifestations of becomings and extinctions. It is a stream of becoming.
The concept of the individual ego is a popular delusion; the
objects with which we identify ourselves are not the true self.
The body is only a composite of the five aggregates, skandhas.
Buddhism swept away the traditional conception of a substance called "soul" or "ego," which had hitherto dominated
the minds of the superstitious and the intellectuals alike.

The Buddha clearly told us what the self is not, but he does
not give any clear account of what it is. It is quite wrong to
think that there is no self at all according to Buddhism. The
Buddha was not a mere materialist. As *body* is a name for a
system of qualities, even so *soul* is a name for the sum of the
states which constitute our mental existence. The Buddha did
not deny the soul, but was silent concerning it. Moreover, he
seems to have acknowledged that the true self in our existence
will appear in our moral conduct conforming to universal
norms. The Buddha did not want to assume the existence of
souls as metaphysical substances, but he admitted the existence
of the self as the subject of action in a practical and moral

sense. In the Digha Nikaya, the Buddha says, "He thus abstaining lives his life void of longings, perfected, cool, in blissful enjoyment, his whole self ennobled."

REBIRTH

Belief in rebirth has been general in both Theravada and Mahayana. The only exceptions in modern times would be some liberal, modern thinkers who do not put great stress on the belief. Indian philosophers and religions in general in the time of the Buddha held the doctrine of rebirth, that every being repeats an endless series of worldly existences. After one dies, he is reborn, he keeps his temporary existence for a time, and again dies. The Buddha rejected the sacrifices and the ritualistic magic of the Brahman schools, the animistic superstition of the common people, and the speculations about the ego which were recorded in the Upanishads, but he retained the belief in rebirth. So, too, have the Buddhists ever since.

KARMA

The belief in rebirth had already, before the rise of Buddhism, become a universal conception associated with the doctrine of karma. According to the doctrine of karma, good conduct brings a pleasant and happy result, while bad conduct brings an evil result. All acts, whether mental or physical, tend to produce like acts in a continuing series. Good acts increase in a man a tendency to similar good actions, and bad acts create a tendency toward continuing evil acts of a similar nature. The karma committed with or without previous intention will come to fruition. Some karmas bear fruit in the same life in which they are committed, others in the immediately succeeding one, and others in future lives more remote. The individual is the result of a multitude of causes carried over from his past existences and intimately related to all other causes in the world. The interconnection between one individual and the whole universe is stressed in the Buddhist doctrine of karma. This much of the doctrine of karma has been believed by all Buddhists, through all the centuries.

The most conspicuous diversity in relation to the doctrine of karma concerns the concept of the Bodhisattva. Theravada Buddhism has held that the state of a Bodhisattva is a result of the merits accumulated in his past lives, while the Mahayana schools hold that a Bodhisattva is born in this life freely, because of his own free will. Out of compassion for living beings, by his own intention, and not as a result of past karmas, the Bodhisattva is born among men.

Even the Shin sect in Japan accepts the concept of karma. According to their belief, men can only get rid of the fetters of karma by being born in the Pure Realm through the grace of Amitabha Buddha. The Shin sect differs from the general view of karma in one respect, however. Most Buddhists have agreed with the Indian and Tibetan belief that the immediate cause of determining the kind of rebirth one obtains is the nature of a person's thoughts in the moments preceding death. Buddhists have attached much importance to the way of dying. The Shin sect explicitly denies the importance of such death thoughts, saying that the destiny of each person after death is fixed by his faith during his life.

Belief in anatta, non-ego, and in karma and rebirth at the same time raised a difficult problem for Buddhism: how can rebirth take place without a permanent subject to be reborn? Indian non-Buddhist philosophers attacked this vulnerable point in Buddhist thought. Many modern scholars have also considered it to be an insoluble problem. The relation between existences in rebirth has been explained by the analogy of fire which maintains itself unchanged in appearance yet is different in every moment. The seeming identity from moment to moment consists in a continuity of moments which we may call the continuity of an ever-changing identity. This much is accepted by all Buddhists, but it remains difficult to assume rebirth without an abiding central substance. In order to solve this vulnerable problem, some Buddhists of later days assumed a sort of soul, calling it by different names. This tendency gave rise to the conception of the fundamental consciousness (alayavijnana) of the Yogacara school in Mahayana.

DEPENDENT ORIGINATION

All schools of Buddhism have accepted the chain of causation and the belief in dependent origination as important, but not all have interpreted dependent origination in the same way. Buddhism declares that everything has a cause, or causes, that there is no permanent substratum of existence. There is general agreement that the only true method of explaining any existing thing is to trace one cause back to the next, and so on, without the hope, or even the desire, of explaining the ultimate cause of all things. The universe is governed by causality. There is no chaotic anarchy and no capricious interference. The chain of causation simply says that because of ignorance (that is, lack of knowledge of the causes) we suffer; because of knowledge, we do not suffer.

From that came the concept of dependent origination, of the interdependence of all causes. Scholars of Conservative Buddhism and Mahayana Buddhism used it for anything they wanted to explain. One widely accepted conservative definition was "the interconnection according to causal laws of all the elements cooperating in the formation of life." Vijnanavada, the Consciousness-Only school, occasionally took it to mean "the process of manifestation of all phenomena out of the fundamental consciousness [alayavijnana]." In Mahayana, especially in the Madhyamika school and the Kegon school in China and Japan, dependent origination meant "the interdependence of all phenomena in the universe throughout the past, the present, and the future," or, "the relativity of things and ideas."

SUNYATA

Mahayana Buddhism found in dependent origination the basis for the void, emptiness, sunyata. There is no real existence; all things are but appearance and are in truth empty. Even nonexistence is not reality; everything occurs conditioned by everything else. Voidness or emptiness is not nothingness nor annihilation, but that which stands right in the middle between affirmation and negation, existence and non-

existence, eternity and annihilation. The doctrine of the void
—sunyata—is not nihilism. On the contrary, Mahayana Buddhism asserts that it is the true basis for ethical values. The
void is all-inclusive; having no opposite, there is nothing which
it excludes or opposes. It is living void, because all forms come
out of it, and whoever realizes the void is filled with life and
power and the Bodhisattva's love of all beings. Love is the
moral equivalent of all-inclusiveness, which is nothing but the
void. This is a belief which is very important to Mahayana
thought, but it is not the interpretation of dependent origination which is generally held in Theravada.

NIRVANA

All Buddhists agree that the aim of religious practice is to
get rid of our delusion of ego. By getting rid of this ignorance,
or delusion, Buddhists hope to be untroubled by the transitoriness of worldly life, to be free from the fetters of this mundane
existence. By getting rid of that ignorance, one is said to have
overcome the round of rebirths, one has attained the supreme
goal, Enlightenment. According to Buddhism, the final goal is
not a paradise or a heavenly world. The central theme of Buddhism is that, by following the right Path, one can free oneself
from the bondage of existence and come to the realization of
the Supreme Truth. The attainment of Enlightenment is
identical with Nirvana. All Buddhists agree that Enlightenment is their goal and that it is attained by following the right
Path.

As we have seen, the living process is likened to a fire burning. Through the involuntary activity of one's nature in contact with the outer world, life as we know it goes on incessantly. Its remedy is the extinction of the fire, and the Buddha,
the Awakened One, is one who is no longer kindled or in-
flamed. One who has attained Enlightenment is far from having dissolved into non-being; it is not he who is extinct, but
the life of illusion, passions, and desires. He no longer feels
himself to be conditioned by false ideas and attendant desires.
This ideal state is called Nirvana, "extinction of afflictions."
Nirvana is a lasting state of happiness and peace, to be reached

here on earth by the extinction of the fires of passions. It is the highest happiness, the bliss that does not pass away.

Many poetic terms are used to describe the state of the man who has been made perfect according to Buddhist doctrine: the harbor of refuge, the cool cave, the island amidst the floods, the place of bliss, emancipation, liberation, safety, the supreme, the transcendental, the uncreated, the tranquil, the home of ease, the calm, the end of suffering, the medicine for all evil, the unshaken, the ambrosia, the immortal, the immaterial, the imperishable, the abiding, the further shore, the unending, the bliss of effort, the supreme joy, the ineffable, the detachment, the holy city—and many others. Perhaps the most frequent in the Pali texts is "the state of him who is worthy" (Arahatship).

The phrase used exclusively in Europe to explain Nirvana is "the dying out," that is, the dying out in the heart of the fierce fire of the sins of sensuality, ill will, and stupidity. Contrary to the prevalent European opinion about Nirvana, the craving for extinction in the sense of annihilation or nonexistence was indeed expressly repudiated by the Buddha. Buddhists search not for mere cessation, but for the eternal, the immortal. He who has attained to Nirvana is extolled as being afflicted neither by life nor by death. It is conceptually that Nirvana is negation. *Nirvana* is the word cherished by the ascetics and thinkers of the past, meaning "the ideal state."

Enlightenment can be attained in this life. Emancipation is found in a habit of mind, in being free from craving and illusion. In Theravada Buddhism monks should strive to attain Arahatship; they cannot become Buddhas. Laymen are not expected to attain Arahatship, but may be reborn in one of the heavens. However, in Mahayana, everyone is entitled to become a Buddha finally, although he might have to pass through many births. According to Pure Realm Buddhism, even laymen can become Buddhas by virtue of the grace of Amitabha Buddha; and according to Nichiren, by virtue of the eternal Buddha.

Mahayana Buddhism developed the concept of the realization of Nirvana through the recognition of the true nature of one's existence. Based on this belief, tantric Buddhism and some Chinese and Japanese sects developed the concept of the Great Self, as stressed in the Mahaparinirvana Sutra. This is not found in Theravada Buddhism and is criticized by some as being very close to Vedanta philosophy.

All Buddhists believe that even a most vicious person can ultimately attain Enlightenment. In Theravada, the attainment must come through his own free will and efforts; in Mahayana the efforts may be aided by help given by Buddhas or Bodhisattvas. There is no concept of the eternally damned, although that does not mean that Buddhists deny the existence of many people who are in fact very difficult to save.

THE UNIVERSE

Buddhist beliefs concerning the nature of the universe were shaped by belief in karma and rebirth. This led to the assumption of good and bad places to which people could be born according to their deeds. The three spheres, or planes, are the immaterial plane where pure spirits live, the material plane where beings with subtle bodies live, and the plane of desire which corresponds to our natural world. This belief in the planes of existence has been held throughout all the Buddhist world, although Zen Buddhism in China and Japan has been rather indifferent to it. It is still very widely held in Buddhism, but many Buddhist intellectuals who have been educated in modern science, however devout they may be, do not believe this traditional Buddhist cosmology.

The world in which human beings live, the plane of desire, is made up of four elements—earth, water, heat, and wind—according to the scriptures of both Theravada and Mahayana. The tantric theories add space and intelligence to the list of elements, making six of them. Buddhists in Japan, where there is little illiteracy, do not accept literally the concept of planes of existence and the four or six elements; they accept modern scientific theories concerning the natural world. They think that the theories concerning the planes of existence and the elements are not essential to Buddhism. Theravada Buddhists have not been so outspoken on these matters.

The belief in astrology, in the influence of the planets upon the destiny of individual beings, has at one time or another been widely held in Asia. The Abhidharma literature of India does not mention astrology, but later tantric Buddhism adopted astrology, and it has been highly esteemed by Buddhists in Tibet. There, Buddhists believe in the influence of planetary conjunctions and in the need for counteracting such influences by performance of appropriate rites. Astrology was introduced to Japan along with tantric Buddhism, but nowadays very few Japanese believe seriously in it. The Shin sect forbids astrology as a belief that implies lack of faith in Amitabha Buddha. Astrology is quite common in other Buddhist countries, but there it is observed just as a social custom. Although other forms of divination were prohibited by the scriptures, astrology was not condemned. One can see astrology practiced even in the precincts of the pagodas, but it is not considered to be a part of Buddhism.

LIVING BEINGS

Beings living in the plane of desire are divided into five, and sometimes six, categories: gods, men, spirits, animals, the damned—and sometimes asuras, demons, are added. These categories have been popular among the common people throughout the Buddhist world. One result of this belief has been that the attitude toward animals in Buddhist countries has been one of kindness to a fellow being. In some countries, people visiting temples will release birds or fish which have been captured. The Tibetans have been notable for their kindness to animals as an expression of their Buddhism. There have always been many Buddhists who were vegetarians.

Birth as a human being is essential for the appreciation of the Dharma, for Enlightenment. Gods are too happy to feel a dislike for conditioned things, and they live much too long to have any appreciation for the doctrine of impermanence. Animals, ghosts, demons, and the damned lack sufficient clarity of mind to enable them to overcome their ignorance. Therefore, the human state is in general more favorable than any other for the attainment of Enlightenment. According to Buddhism, man is distinguished from other beings by his aptitude for goodness, a love for the Dharma, and consequently by love or compassion (metta) for other beings. The Buddha was regarded as leading both gods and men alike—therefore he is often called "a Teacher of gods and men." This evaluation of the place of man in the scheme of things has been held in both Theravada and Mahayana Buddhism.

From the time of the Buddha, Buddhism has stressed the equality of man. The Buddha said, "For worms, serpents, fish, birds, and animals there are marks that constitute their own species. There is difference in creatures endowed with bodies, but amongst men this is not the case; the differences among men are nominal only." (Sutta Nipata 602–611.) There was no discrimination among the monks in the early Buddhist order. This sense of equality has been preserved throughout most Buddhist orders ever since the time of the Buddha. In Tibet the successor to the Dalai Lama is not elected by the monks but is selected by divination. In Ceylon, one sect chooses its monks from only one class of society. In Japan the former class status of novices when they were in secular society is taken into consideration in some temples which are patronized by the Royal Family and the nobles. These exceptions are of minor importance; what is significant is that wherever Buddhism has been truly followed, in Theravada and Mahayana countries, the differences among men have been of little consequence, have been nominal only.

ETHICS

The ethics of Buddhism has stressed the universal norms which are constant and apply to everyone. The way of Gotama the Buddha is called the Middle Path because it avoids the extremes of the pursuit of worldly desires or the practice of severe ascetic disciplines. The doctrine of the Middle Way that the Buddha proclaimed is a humanistic ethic which must be adjusted to the infinitely varying circumstances of actual life. In order to avoid the danger of creating detailed and petty regulations which might encroach unduly on the moral autonomy of the individual, the Buddha advised his disciples to follow the spirit of the Middle Way. This fundamental approach to ethical problems has been preserved up to now throughout the Buddhist world.

In Buddhism, the obstacles to the good life have customarily been listed as the Ten Bonds: delusions about the soul, doubt, dependence upon works, sensuality, ill will, desire for rebirth on earth, desire for rebirth in heaven, pride, self-righteousness, and ignorance. The five most heinous crimes have been: matricide, patricide, the murder of an Arahat, the wounding of a Buddha, and the creation of a schism in the Sangha. The ten immoral actions are: killing, stealing, unchastity, lying, slandering, harsh language, frivolous talk, covetousness, ill will, and false views. This definition of the moral problem has been generally accepted throughout the Buddhist world.

Those evil actions are to be avoided by following the Middle Path. Only Pure Realm Buddhism has been an exception, with its belief that all living beings are sinful and are saved by the compassionate grace of Amitabha Buddha.

COMPASSION

The fundamental principle of Buddhist ethics is that all men should develop an attitude of compassion. True wisdom consists not in metaphysical sophistication, but in practical knowledge which is expressed in the attitude of compassion as the fundamental principle in our social life. Compassion or love of one's neighbors is very highly esteemed in Buddhism. Compassion is *metta* in Pali and *maitri* in Sanskrit, both derived from *mitra*, or friend. Thus both words literally mean "true friendliness." If we allow the virtue of compassion or love to grow in us, it will not occur to us to harm anyone else, any more than we would willingly harm ourselves. In this way we extinguish our love of self by widening the boundaries of what we regard as ours, we break down the barriers which separate us from others.

There is a saying in the Tripitaka which is accepted by all Buddhists: "As a mother even at the risk of her own life watches over her own child, so let everyone cultivate a boundless love toward all beings." (Sutta Nipata I, 8.) One should not hurt others. One should not offend others even by speech. Even enemies should be loved. One should have forbearance toward contempt, or bitter and sarcastic comments, or injury inflicted by others. One should forgive them. This very meek and compassionate character was exemplified in the life of the Buddha himself.

This altruistic attitude is attained by meditation on the elements which constitute our "self," that is, our dharmas. Such meditation dissolves oneself and other people into a conglomeration of impersonal and instantaneous elements. By dissolving our human existence into component parts we can get rid of the notion of self, and through that meditation we are led to a limitless expansion of the self in a practical sense—because one identifies oneself with more and more living beings.

The practical results of the development of compassion have been seen in the way that Buddhism has softened the rough warrior races of Tibet and Mongolia, nearly effacing all traces of their original brutality. In Japan, also, according to statistical reports, cases of murder or assault are relatively rare in districts where Buddhist influence is strong. The same quality of compassion is found in the social life of Theravada countries where Buddhism is commonly practiced. The exception in this acceptance of compassion was Ch'an Buddhism in China. There is not a single reference made to the word "benevolence" in the well-known scriptures of Chinese Ch'an Buddhism. Later, that was modified as Ch'an, Tendai, and Pure Realm Buddhism blended into one general Chinese Buddhism; and when Zen was developed in Japan it came to emphasize deeds of benevolence as an expression of Zen.

The difference between Theravada and Mahayana in reference to compassion centered chiefly in the differing conceptions of the Bodhisattva. As a practical ethical ideal for everyday conduct, all Buddhists are agreed upon the importance of compassion.

ETHICAL DISCIPLINES

The disciplines which create a spirit of compassion have always been stressed in Buddhism. The evil passions must be calmed, the senses must be restrained, constant awareness of one's feelings and desires must be developed. Meditation, which is the discipline for the path to Enlightenment, was also adopted as a discipline for the ethical life, as the means for developing the awareness which checks attachment to the senses.

Early Buddhism stressed the necessity for monastic life if one were to be able to follow the disciplines necessary for attainment of the ethical ideal and for attaining Enlightenment. The rules for the layman were far less stringent than for the monk; withdrawal from the life of the householder was considered a necessity if one wished to devote himself to following the Path. The life of the homeless ones was the ideal. This ideal has been based on the belief that involvement in the ordinary worldly affairs is an obstacle too great to be overcome. In the monasteries monks could devote all their time to meditation and study, attachment to food and clothes could be curbed, sexual attachments could be eliminated, all actions could be guarded. Begging was encouraged as a foundation for many virtues. The full code of the Vinaya discipline could be followed. This other-worldly ideal has been preserved in Theravada Buddhism to this day in the Sangha which is still central in Buddhist life. In Tibet, too, although it is a Mahayana country, the monastery has remained as the most important aspect of Buddhist community life and the center for Buddhist disciplines.

On the other hand, some Mahayana scholars argued that the moral disciplines could be followed and the absolute could be comprehended in secular life. It was this type of this-worldly Buddhism which was selected by the Japanese and, to a large extent, by the Chinese. Even when other doctrines were accepted, the Japanese managed to impress upon them their stamp of this-worldliness. Although resignation and nonattachment may have characterized Buddhist life in Asia in general, they were often specifically repudiated by the Japanese, not only in modern times, but also in the remote past.

The Japanese have put heavy emphasis upon activity in human relationships. Even Pure Realm Buddhism, which has stressed the seeking of the other world, has taught that the pure and perfect Realm reveals itself in this world of impurity and the believer must attain the other world within this world. This attitude accounts for the absence of the all-inclusive monastic order in Japan, the disapproval of begging as a discipline, marriage of the priests, and similar practices which distinguish some of the practices of Japanese Buddhism from those of the Theravada countries. It was this attitude which led the Japanese Buddhists to reject the Vinaya disciplinary code in favor of one of their own.

SERVICE

Another distinction between the ethical practices of Buddhism in the southern countries and in the northern Mahayana countries lies in the field of service. The this-worldly character of Japanese Buddhism brought the priests into close contact with the common people and their needs. In the South Asia countries where climate, rainfall, and natural fertility combine to bring harvests without great human labor, the ethics of distribution rather than of production have been emphasized. That is why, for example, almsgiving was considered so important in Southern Buddhism. But in countries like Japan, where production is of vital importance, stress has been placed on the ethics of hard work, of producing the necessary food. Even monks and priests have engaged in productive labor as an expression of their Buddhist ethical principles.

One result of this attitude has been that the responsibility for service in Theravada Buddhism has been placed largely on the individual monk as a personal matter, with comparatively less emphasis on social institutions than has been characteristic of Mahayana Buddhism. Individual householders feel free to come to the monastery for help in time of need in Theravada countries, and many acts of mercy are performed by the Bhikkhus. But in China and Japan there have been many institutions such as hospitals, orphanages, and schools which have been motivated by the Buddhist spirit. Particularly in Japan, Buddhism has always emphasized the idea of working for the people, a concern which is manifested in its vast panoply of social work. In the interests of benefiting mankind,

Japanese priests have been allowed to accumulate money to cure the sick, to build roads and bridges, and perform other similar services for the country.

ETHICS FOR LAYMEN

In both Theravada and Mahayana countries the monks and priests are responsible for the spiritual guidance of the laymen, and the laymen are responsible for the support of the religious institutions. The basic ethics taught to laymen are the same in all Buddhist countries. The laymen should obey the five precepts: not destroy life, not take what is not given, refrain from unlawful sexual intercourse, not tell lies, not drink intoxicating liquors. (But in Tibet and Japan the fifth precept is often minimized.) The duties which are stressed are those between parents and children, pupils and teachers, husband and wife, friend and friend, master and servants, and laymen and monks. The virtues stressed are generosity, courtesy, benevolence, honesty, cooperation, and service—the virtues of a compassionate man. In both Theravada and Mahayana every effort is made to teach these virtues to laymen.

We have up to this point reviewed the major doctrines of Buddhism, concerning suffering, non-ego, rebirth, karma, dependent origination, Nirvana, the nature of the universe, beings, ethics, and ethical disciplines. In all these a large measure of agreement between Theravada and Mahayana can be found even if one does not minimize the points at which they differ. There are two major points, however, on which the divergence is more pronounced—the scriptures which are accepted as authoritative and the concept of the Buddha and Bodhisattvas.

SCRIPTURES

Both Theravada and Mahayana Buddhists have always esteemed the scriptures as the supreme source of knowledge, the standard by which everything should be judged. The only notable exception to this reliance upon the scriptures has been in the Zen sect with its emphasis upon direct insight and its assertion that only silence avoids violating the truth. And even

Zen does not entirely reject the scriptures. One also occasionally finds in Theravada Buddhism a teacher who emphasizes meditation virtually to the exclusion of study of the scriptures, but the general pattern throughout all Buddhism has been one of great reliance upon the scriptures. A very important difference between Theravada and Mahayana centers in the decision as to which of the scriptures will be accepted as authoritative. Even though almost all Buddhists base their faith on the scriptures, there is no one scripture which is accepted as having the same authority for everyone who calls himself a Buddhist.

The attitude toward the scriptures is relatively clear in Theravada Buddhism, for there the Pali Tipitaka is accepted as the final authority. Its contents are clearly defined, the commentaries on its various sections have been reconciled over the centuries, it is available in various vernacular tongues, and it is received by all as the true and complete teachings of the Buddha. Theravada Buddhists reject the Mahayana scriptures as outside the Canon, as later creations which do not reflect the teachings of the Buddha. The Mahayana scriptures which are accepted with great devotion by tens of millions of Buddhists are virtually unknown in Theravada countries, even by scholars. The rejection of the scriptures which are held sacred by Mahayana Buddhism is one of the reasons Mahayanists have persisted in referring to Theravada as Hinayana, the Little Vehicle.

The Sanskrit version of the Pali Tipitaka, also translated into Tibetan, Mongolian, and Chinese, has been incorporated in the Canon of Mahayana scriptures, but is generally regarded as less authoritative than the other Mahayana Sutras. In Tibet it is highly regarded as basic for introductory studies of the scriptures, necessary in the first stage of training. In Japan in recent years the Dhammapada and the Sutta Nipata have been increasingly popular, especially among intellectuals. As a result of the inclusion of the Tripitaka in the accepted scriptures of Mahayana, the Mahayana Buddhists are generally better informed about the beliefs of Theravada than the Theravada Buddhists are about Mahayana. Since Mahayana Buddhism depends upon the Sanskrit rather than the Pali version of the Tripitaka, Theravada Buddhists believe that Mahayana interpretations are liable to error.

The Sanskrit version of the Tripitaka has been preserved intact in Nepal and in Tibet; a small group of Buddhists which remains on the island of Bali also uses the Sanskrit version. In Japan, very few translations of the scriptures have appeared in their own language in the past; people could understand the purport of the Chinese version of a scripture with the aid of diacritical marks. The most important Mahayana scriptures are:

Amida Sutra—a Chinese version of the smaller Sukhavativyuha Sutra

Amitayurdhyana Sutra—setting forth the meditation of Amitabha

Mahavairocana Sutra—the fundamental scripture of tantric Buddhism

Mulamadhyamaka Sastra—a treatise by Nagarjuna, the fundamental text of the Madhyamika school

Prajnaparamitahridaya Sutra—the essence of The Discourse on Perfect Wisdom

Saddharma Pundarika Sutra—The Lotus of the Wonderful Law, setting forth the doctrine of the One Vehicle and the Eternal Buddha

Sukhavativyuha Sutra—the fundamental Sutra of Pure Realm Buddhism

Vijnaptimatratasiddhi—a treatise on Vijnanavada doctrine

Vimalakirtinirdesa Sutra—setting forth Buddhism for laymen

In addition, the Vajracchedika Sutra is important for Zen Buddhism; and two Tantras, Vajrabhairava and Vajradakini, are important for tantric Buddhism.

In Tibet the scriptures are placed on the shrine as an object of devotion; in Japan the Nichiren sect pays homage to the Saddharma Pundarika Sutra; in all the Mahayana countries these Sutras are placed above the Tripitaka as the final authority. This fundamental difference in attitude toward the scriptures is an important area of disagreement which has not yet been reconciled in Buddhism.

The different attitudes toward the scriptures are reflected in the acceptance or rejection of the works of famous Buddhist scholars and commentators. In Theravada Countries, for instance, Buddhaghosha is regarded very highly for his learning and insight, but he is practically unknown in Mahayana countries. Tibetans have been influenced by Dharmakirti, Santarakshita, and Atisha in particular, but these teachers are almost never studied in the rest of the Buddhist world. Kumarajiva and Bodhidharma have had great influence in China and Japan, but not elsewhere. Nagarjuna, Asanga, and Vasubandhu have been most influential throughout the whole Mahayana community, but they are not studied in Theravada Buddhism.

THE BUDDHA

The second major point of divergence between Theravada and Mahayana concerns the Buddha. At the beginning of Buddhism, the Buddha was merely a man and nothing more, but with the lapse of time he came to be extolled more and more highly. Disciples praised him as the Exalted One, the Arahat, the Fully-Enlightened One, Wise, Upright, Happy, World-knowing, Supreme, the Bridler of Men's Wayward Hearts, the Teacher of Gods and Men, the Awakened One. In the Jataka stories the details of the Buddha's lives in previous existences were given. Many miraculous powers were ascribed to the Buddha, such as supernatural memory, levitation, and the like. From the point of view of doctrine, the magical powers were of no great importance, but they played an important role with the common people. Even the relics of the Buddha came to be esteemed for their magical potency.

Buddhism admits the existence not only of one Lord Buddha, but also of other Buddhas. In the Pali scriptures we read of the Seven Buddhas, including Gotama, and in some of the latest books included in the Pali scriptures we hear of twenty-four Buddhas. However, Sakyamuni, the founder of Buddhism, has the most prestige and is the most popular. In Theravada Buddhism devotion is paid almost exclusively to the Buddha

Sakyamuni. Maitreya Buddha, the Buddha of the future, was highly revered in the past throughout all the Buddhist world, but not so much in modern times. Vairocana Buddha, the Primordial Buddha, has been the object of devotion in esoteric Buddhism.

Nearly all Buddhists pay the highest honor to Sakyamuni Buddha. The chief exception is Pure Realm Buddhism which prefers Amitabha Buddha to Sakyamuni, though it pays homage to the latter. The chief difference between Theravada and Mahayana is that Mahayana substitutes the Eternal Buddha for the historical Buddha. According to Mahayana doctrine, his existence in the earthly form is not his true and proper mode of being; his historical existence seems to be quite temporary. Mahayana considers the Buddha under the three aspects of the Triple Body and makes the second Body, the Sambhogakaya, the object of devotion.

Mahayana admits the existence of innumerable Buddhas. The Buddha who works for the benefit of all creatures is not one, but innumerable. There have been innumerable Buddhas in the past, there are many, many Buddhas working in the universe in the present, and there will be innumerable Buddhas in the future. They are engaged in the work of saving as many suffering creatures as they can. A Buddha is regarded as being full of compassion for all suffering creatures; that aspect of compassion is greatly exalted by Mahayana.

While the concept of a savior is not allowed in Theravada Buddhism, it is accepted in Mahayana. The savior does not bring beings directly to Nirvana, but makes the path easier and brings the disciple to a heaven where he may hear the preaching of the doctrine that leads the way to Enlightenment. The only exception to this concept in Mahayana is Pure Realm Buddhism which says that to be born into the Pure Realm is the same as attaining Nirvana. The Buddhas never punish the wicked. A Buddha is compassion itself. Only incarnations of Buddhas may punish the wicked, in order to turn them from their wickedness to the Path which leads to Enlightenment.

Even though there is a distinct difference between Theravada and Mahayana in their beliefs concerning the Buddha, there never has been a belief that a Buddha is the creator of the universe. Buddhism has never believed in a creator-Buddha or a creator-god.

THE ARAHAT

Another point of difference concerns the Arahat. Arahats have always been highly revered in Theravada, and Arahatship is regarded as the ultimate goal of the Bhikkhu. The Theravada Buddhists point out that without perfect unselfishness and loving compassion for those near and dear, as well as loving compassion for the larger human family and all living beings, even the first, second, and third stages of sanctity cannot be reached, and there can be no approach to Arahatship. By his own personal efforts, the Arahat seeks to show that it is humanly possible to reach Nirvana and to encourage others to tread that Path. On the other hand, Mahayana Buddhists have often charged that it is selfish to seek Arahatship, to seek Enlightenment for oneself rather than to work for the salvation of others. This has been a point of disagreement and misunderstanding between Theravada and Mahayana for a long time, and it is in part due to a differing conception of the nature of the Bodhisattva.

THE BODHISATTVA

Bodhisattva means "being destined for Enlightenment." It is often translated as "Future Buddha." A Bodhisattva is originally one who is on the way to the attainment of perfect knowledge; he is a Buddhist saint before attaining the stage of a supreme Buddha; he is a candidate for Enlightenment. In other words, he is nothing but a Buddha in past lives before he became a Buddha. This concept of a Bodhisattva has been retained in Theravada.

In Mahayana the emphasis has been put on the altruistic inclinations and activities of the Bodhisattva. From the outset the Bodhisattva strives toward a plane where there are no differences between his ego and his neighbor's; he identifies his ego absolutely and entirely with that of others. He is extolled as making great efforts to save all suffering beings. He expresses his fervent joy through his good deeds to all beings; he prays to the Buddhas that they may light the lamp of religion for all beings who are in ignorance; he prays for the salvation of all beings and finally offers himself for all beings.

Such Bodhisattvas as Avalokitesvara, Bodhidharma, Manjusri, Samantabhadra, Bhaishajyaguru, and Kshitigarbha are sometimes worshiped more ardently than the Buddhas by their votaries. Kshitigarbha was adored with great devotion in China and Japan because of his vow to save all beings and his refusal to go into Nirvana as long as there is one person left in the depths of this world of sorrow. The images of Bodhisattva Avalokitesvara (known as Kuan-yin in China and Kwannon in Japan) are shaped with a countenance as if he were female. This is because he has been regarded as the supreme Bodhisattva of mercy and compassion, and female features have been regarded as fitter for the purpose of expressing such great compassion. It is this emphasis on compassion in the Bodhisattva and this attitude of great devotion to the Bodhisattva which makes a marked difference between Mahayana and Theravada Buddhism.

Worship

All Buddhists take refuge in the Three Jewels and express their reverence for the teachings of the Buddha through worship. In the early days, Buddhists made it a rule to worship the bodhi tree, the footprints of the Buddha, and the Wheel of the Law as symbols of the Buddha. Relics and personal belongings of the Buddha and the saints were also worshiped. These customs have been preserved throughout all Buddhism and are continued today, although relics are not so common in Mahayana countries since most of them had been placed in Theravada shrines before Buddhism spread to the North. After the practice of making images was introduced, all Buddhists worshiped before the images. Tantric Buddhism accepted the symbols, relics, and images, and added the mandala, a diagrammatic picture representing the cosmic nature of the Buddhas.

It is sometimes thought that the doctrine of self-cultivation is inconsistent with the worship of the Buddha. According to both Theravada and Mahayana there is no inconsistency here, for we should make every effort to realize our true nature in the moral and religious sense, and this ideal is quite compatible with an expression of reverence for the one who has already realized his true nature and gained Enlightenment and shown the way for us. The act of worship before the symbol or image of the Buddha has never been regarded as idolatry by Buddhists; it is simply an expression of reverence for the Buddha, or Buddhas, or Bodhisattvas and a means of concentrating the mind on the significance and truth of the words recited in worship.

Viewed from the theoretical standpoint, and here there is agreement between Theravada and Mahayana, the law of karma is never broken. Neither the spiritual inspiration and power of the Buddha and Bodhisattvas nor the transcendental influence of the Supreme Truth can deliver us from natural calamities; they can only help indirectly by accumulating our merits or by bringing our merits to maturity so that the good karmic effects of those merits may give us whatever protection we need. In practice, common people who do not understand this sometimes pray to Buddhas or Bodhisattvas for worldly help, especially in Mahayana countries. Generally, in Buddhist countries, such prayers for worldly benefits are addressed to spirits of indigenous deities.

The acts of worship are performed at shrines in the home and at temples, monasteries, and pagodas. In all Buddhist lands the devout laymen have shrines in their homes where they perform their individual devotions morning and evening. Such shrines are decorated with images, offerings of flowers, water, incense, and lamps, sometimes with cooked foods, vegetables, and fruits, depending upon the customs of the country. In Japan tablets bearing the religious names of the ancestors are placed beside the image of the Buddha on the family shrine.

From early times, symbols, relics, and images have been placed in stupas, dagobas, pagodas, and shrines as objects of public veneration. Temples are used for private devotions, sometimes as places of instruction, and for the ceremonies and festivals which have grown up in Buddhism. While the images, the pagodas, and the temples all bear the distinctive imprint of the country in which they were made, they have all maintained the common characteristic of expressing in the form of art the highest reverence of the Buddhists who have created them. Wherever Buddhism has been accepted, it has stimulated the creation of great works of art, revered by intellectuals and by the common people.

Music has never been a part of public worship in Theravada countries, where monks and nuns are not allowed to enjoy or sing songs. In China, Tibet, and Japan music has been used as accompaniment for certain ceremonies, and pilgrims customarily sing songs in praise of Buddhas and Bodhisattvas. Some schools of Buddhist music and chanting can be traced back to ancient China. Some effort is being made in modern times to use music more freely in Mahayana worship.

CEREMONIES AND FESTIVALS

Indian Buddhism did not establish a system of ceremonies for family life comparable to those in Hinduism, nor have such ceremonies grown up in Theravada or Mahayana Buddhism. But Buddhism has been associated with death and with funeral ceremonies. In southern countries and in Tibet and Mongolia, people did not practice ancestral worship, and consequently Buddhism did not have anything to do with it there. But in China and Japan, Buddhism has been closely connected with ancestral worship. In China and Japan the ceremonies for the beatitude of ancestors, as well as one's near dead, became very common and nowadays provide most of the temple income, contributing both to the support and the decline of the temples. Throughout the Buddhist world, monks and priests do not officiate at wedding ceremonies, though they are sometimes invited to extend congratulations. The only exception is in Buddhism in Japan, where in modern times some priests have performed the marriage ceremony. The Uposatha ceremony at which the Vinaya discipline is regularly recited has always been performed in Theravada monasteries, but it was given up in Mahayana countries more than a thousand years ago.

Festivals have always played a prominent part in Buddhist life, and, as might be expected, they have been different in each country. In most Buddhist countries the festivals center around the Buddha and incidents connected with him, but in Japan the anniversaries of the founder of each sect are celebrated on a much larger scale than the festivals of the Buddha. Shin and Nichiren, for instance, have elaborate festivals for their founders and pay very little attention to festivals associated with the Buddha. In recent times, the birthday festival for the Buddha (Flower Festival) has been coming to the fore in Japan. Priests celebrate it, not as members of a sect, but just as Buddhists.

In Theravada countries the anniversary of the birth, Enlightenment, and passing away of the Buddha is held on the full-moon day of May. In Tibet it is held a month later. In Japan, the birth is celebrated on April 8, the Enlightenment on December 8, and the passing away on February 15. The chief festival in Tibet is at New Year time, while the New Year festival in Japan is Shintoist, or esoteric Buddhist, and secular.

In addition to participation in the festivals, Buddhists have always been encouraged to make pilgrimages to famous shrines and historic spots associated with Buddhism. This custom continues in all Buddhist countries.

MEDITATION

Although worship before shrines in the home and the temple, and participation in festivals, have been approved in Theravada and Mahayana Buddhism through the years, the most important part of Buddhist worship has always been held to be meditation. In order to acquire the calmness of mind necessary for traveling the Path to Enlightenment, Buddhism has always recommended meditative practices which are derived from ancient yoga, stripped of its ascetic character. The tantric disciplines have never been accepted in Theravada, and in Mahayana have been used chiefly in Tibet and in the Japanese Shingon sect. In Theravada countries meditation is practiced by laymen as well as by monks. In China and Japan it has been practiced by Zen in particular, but the influence of Zen meditation has extended to most other sects. This acceptance of meditation as central to Buddhist practices is a common bond through which it may be possible for Theravada and Mahayana to grow closer together in the future.

BUDDHISM TODAY

Buddhism has been giving evidence of a new vitality in the twentieth century. Challenged by Western culture and by changing forms of government, Buddhism has been forced to a new evaluation of its strengths. It is too early to tell what the results will be from the great changes now in process in Asia, but there are many signs of vitality in the new Buddhist educational institutions, the new research projects, the increase in lay participation, and the many cooperative activities which have started in recent years. Three world Buddhist conferences have been held. The governments of Southeast Asia cooperated in celebrating in May, 1956, the 2,500th anniversary of the passing away of the Buddha in ceremonies in which millions of devout Buddhists participated.

It took Hsuan-tsang a year to make the journey from China to India. In modern times the journey from Japan to Burma or Ceylon can be completed in a day. With the new learning and the new means of communication and travel, it is easy to hope and expect that Theravada and Mahayana Buddhism will grow closer to each other and that Buddhism will once more reach out to bring the people of Asia to the Path of the Buddha.

Bibliography

Translations of Buddhist Writings

Many of the scriptures referred to in this book may be found in *The Sacred Books of the East, The Sacred Books of the Buddhists*, and in the translations published by The Pali Text Society. The following translations of Buddhist writings are of general interest.

BURTT, E. A. *The Teachings of the Compassionate Buddha*. New York: The New American Library, 1955.

CONZE, EDWARD. *Buddhist Texts Through the Ages*. Oxford: Bruno Cassirer, 1955.

———. *Selected Sayings from the Perfection of Wisdom*. London: The Buddhist Society, 1955.

EVANS-WENTZ, W. Y. *The Tibetan Book of the Dead*. London: Oxford University Press, 1927.

———. *The Tibetan Book of the Great Liberation*. London: Oxford University Press, 1954.

———. *Tibet's Great Yogi Milarepa*. London: Oxford University Press, 1951.

FRANCIS, H. T., and THOMAS, E. J. *Jataka Tales*. Cambridge: The University Press, 1916.

HAMILTON, CLARENCE H. *Buddhism, A Religion of Infinite Compassion*. New York: The Liberal Arts Press, 1952.

ROERICH, G. N. *The Blue Annals*. Calcutta: Royal Asiatic Society of Bengal, 1949.

The Shinshu Seiten, The Holy Scripture of Shinshu. Honolulu: The Honpa Hongwanji Mission of Hawaii, 1955.

TAKAKUSU, JUNJIRO. *A Record of the Buddhist Religion as Practised in India and the Malay Archipelago*. The travels of I-Ching. London: Oxford University Press, 1896.

THOMAS, EDWARD J. *Early Buddhist Scriptures*. London: Kegan Paul, Trench, Trubner & Co., 1935.

WARREN, HENRY CLARKE. *Buddhism in Translations*. Cambridge: Harvard University Press, 1922.

General Works

ANESAKI, MASAHARU. *Buddhist Art*. Boston: Houghton Mifflin Co., 1915.

——. *History of Japanese Religion*. London: Kegan Paul, Trench, Trubner & Co., 1930.

——. *Nichiren, the Buddhist Prophet*. Cambridge: Harvard University Press, 1949.

BAILEY, SIDNEY D. *Ceylon*. London: Hutchinson's University Library, 1952.

BELL, SIR CHARLES. *The Religion of Tibet*. London: Oxford University Press, 1931.

BODE, MABEL HAYNES. *The Pali Literature of Burma*. London: The Royal Asiatic Society, 1909.

BRIGGS, LAWRENCE PALMER. *The Ancient Khmer Empire*. Philadelphia: American Philosophical Society, 1951.

BUNCE, WILLIAM K. *Religions in Japan*. Tokyo: Charles E. Tuttle Co., 1955.

CHAN, WING-TSIT. *Religious Trends in Modern China*. New York: Columbia University Press, 1953.

CONZE, EDWARD. *Buddhism, Its Essence and Development*. New York: The Philosophical Library, n.d.

DASGUPTA, S. B. *An Introduction to Tantric Buddhism*. Calcutta: University of Calcutta, 1950.

DAVIDSON, J. LEROY. *The Lotus Sutra in Chinese Art*. New Haven: Yale University Press, 1954.

DE SILVA-VIGIER, ANIL. *The Life of the Buddha*. Illustrated with 160 works of Asian art. London: The Phaidon Press, 1955.

DE VISSER, M. W. *Ancient Buddhism in Japan*. 2 vols. Leiden: E. J. Brill, 1935.

DUMOULIN, HEINRICH. *The Development of Chinese Zen*. New York: The First Zen Institute of America, Inc., 1953.

DUTT, NALINAKSHA. *Early Monastic Buddhism*. 2 vols. Calcutta: Calcutta Oriental Press, Ltd., 1941.

ELIOT, SIR CHARLES. *Hinduism and Buddhism*. 3 vols. London: Routledge & Kegan Paul, Ltd., 1954.

——. *Japanese Buddhism*. London: Edward Arnold & Co., 1935.

FUNG YU-LAN. *A History of Chinese Philosophy*. 2 vols. Princeton: Princeton University Press, 1952.

GETTY, ALICE. *The Gods of Northern Buddhism*. London: Oxford University Press, 1914.

GORDON, ANTOINETTE K. *Tibetan Religious Art*. New York: Columbia University Press, 1952.

GROUSSET, RENE. *In the Footsteps of the Buddha*. London: George Routledge & Sons, Ltd., 1932.

GOKHALE, B. G. *Buddhism and Asoka*. Baroda: Padmaja Publications, 1948.

HALL, D. G. E. *Burma*. London: Hutchinson's University Library, 1950.

——. *A History of South-East Asia*. New York: St. Martin's Press, Inc., 1955.

HEROLD, A. FERDINAND. *The Life of Buddha*. Tokyo: Charles E. Tuttle Co., 1954.

HODOUS, LEWIS. *Buddhism and Buddhists in China*. New York: The Macmillan Co., 1924.

HUGHES, E. R., and HUGHES, K. *Religion in China*. London: Hutchinson's University Library, 1950.

KASHYAP, BHIKKHU J. *The Abhidhamma Philosophy*. Nalanda: Buddha-Vihara, 1954.

KAWAGUCHI, EKAI. *Three Years in Tibet*. Madras: Vasanta Press, 1909.

KEITH, A. BERRIEDALE. *Buddhist Philosophy in India and Ceylon*. London: Oxford University Press, 1923.

KIMURA, RYOKAN. *A Historical Study of the Terms Hinayana and Mahayana and the Origin of Mahayana Buddhism*. Calcutta: University of Calcutta, 1927.

LANDON, KENNETH P. *Southeast Asia, Crossroads of Religion*. Chicago: University of Chicago Press, 1947.

LATOURETTE, KENNETH SCOTT. *The Chinese, Their History and Culture*. New York: The Macmillan Co., 1946.

——. *A Short History of the Far East*. New York: The Macmillan Co., 1947.

LE MAY, REGINALD. *A Concise History of Buddhist Art in Siam*. Cambridge: Cambridge University Press, 1938.

——. *The Culture of South-East Asia*. London: George Allen & Unwin, Ltd., 1954.

McGOVERN, WILLIAM MONTGOMERY. *A Manual of Buddhist Philosophy*. London: Kegan Paul, Trench, Trubner & Co., 1923.

MALALASEKERA, G. P. *The Pali Literature of Ceylon*. London: Royal Asiatic Society of Great Britain and Ireland, 1928.

MURTI, T. R. V. *The Central Philosophy of Buddhism, A Study of the Madhyamika System*. London: George Allen & Unwin, Ltd., 1955.

NYANAPONIKA, THERA. *The Heart of Buddhist Meditation*. Colombo: The Word of the Buddha Publishing Committee, 1954.

NYANATILOKA. *Buddhist Dictionary*. Colombo: Frewin & Co., Ltd., 1950.

PRATT, JAMES BISSETT. *The Pilgrimage of Buddhism*. New York: The Macmillan Co., 1928.

RAY, NIHARRANJAN. *An Introduction to the Study of Theravada Buddhism in Burma*. Calcutta: University of Calcutta, 1946.

REICHELT, KARL LUDVIG. *Religion in Chinese Garment*. New York: The Philosophical Library, 1951.

——. *Truth and Tradition in Chinese Buddhism*. Shanghai: The Commercial Press, Ltd., 1927.

REISCHAUER, A. K. *Studies in Japanese Buddhism*. New York: The Macmillan Co., 1917.

REISCHAUER, EDWIN O. *Ennin's Travels in T'ang China*. New York: The Ronald Press Co., 1955.

ROWLAND, BENJAMIN. *The Art and Architecture of India*. Baltimore: Penguin Books, 1953.

SAUNDERS, KENNETH J. *Epochs in Buddhist History*. Chicago: University of Chicago Press, 1924.

SHEN, TSUNG-LIEN, and LIU, SHEN-CHI. *Tibet and the Tibetans*. Stanford: Stanford University Press, 1953.

SLATER, ROBERT LAWSON. *Paradox and Nirvana*. Chicago: University of Chicago Press, 1951.

SMITH, F. HAROLD. *The Buddhist Way of Life*. London: Hutchinson's University Library, 1951.

STCHERBATSKY, TH. *Central Conception of Buddhism*. London: The Royal Asiatic Society, 1924.

——. *The Conception of Buddhist Nirvana*. Leningrad: Publishing Office of the Academy of Sciences of the USSR, 1927.

SUZUKI, BEATRICE LANE. *Mahayana Buddhism*. London: David Marlowe Ltd., 1948.

SUZUKI, DAISETZ TEITARO. *Essays in Zen Buddhism*. London: Rider & Co., 1926.

——. *An Introduction to Zen Buddhism*. New York: The Philosophical Library, 1949.

——. *Living by Zen*. Tokyo: Sanseido Press, 1949.

——. *A Miscellany on the Shin Teaching of Buddhism*. Kyoto: Shinshu Otaniha Shumusho, 1949.

——. *The Zen Doctrine of No-Mind*. London: Rider & Co., 1949.

TACHIBANA, S. *The Ethics of Buddhism*. London: Oxford University Press, 1926.

TAKAKUSU, JUNJIRO. *The Essentials of Buddhist Philosophy*. Honolulu: University of Hawaii, 1947.

THOMAS, EDWARD J. *The History of Buddhist Thought*. London: Routledge & Kegan Paul, Ltd., 1953.

——. *The Life of Buddha as Legend and History*. New York: Barnes & Noble, 1952.

VALISINHA, DEVAPRIYA. *Buddhist Shrines in India*. Colombo: The Maha Bodhi Society of Ceylon, 1948.

WADDELL, LAURENCE AUSTINE. *The Buddhism of Tibet*. London: Luzac & Company, Ltd., 1899.

WALEY, ARTHUR. *The Real Tripitaka*. New York: The Macmillan Co., 1952.

WARNER, LANGDON. *The Enduring Art of Japan*. Cambridge: Harvard University Press, 1952.

WELLS, KENNETH E. *Thai Buddhism, Its Rites and Activities*. Bangkok: The Bangkok Times Press, 1934.
WINTERNITZ, MAURICE. *A History of Indian Literature*. Calcutta: University of Calcutta, n.d.

The teachings of the Compassionate Buddha, edited by Burtt, and *Buddhism, A Religion of Infinite Compassion*, edited by Hamilton, are the most readily available and least expensive collections of Buddhist writings. Warren's *Buddhism in Translations* is a classic of Theravada writings.

Anesaki's *History of Japanese Buddhism* and Eliot's *Japanese Buddhism* are the standard works in their field; Bunce's *Religions in Japan* was prepared during the war as a concise guide for occupation personnel. Briggs's *The Ancient Khmer Empire* and Le May's *The Culture of South-East Asia* give good background material; Hall's *A History of South-East Asia* is a summary of all that is known about that area; Landon's *Southeast Asia, Crossroads of Religion* is a perceptive and sympathetic study which is a must for understanding that part of the world. Chan's *Religious Trends in Modern China* is an excellent book, full of new information. Although Eliot's *Hinduism and Buddhism* often reveals the author's prejudices and point of view and is not generally accepted by Asian Buddhist scholars as an accurate expression of the spirit of their religion, it is an incomparable mine of information about the whole Buddhist world and an indispensable reference book. No attempt has been made to list all the books which deal with Buddhist art; the books by Rowland and De Silva-Vigier will serve as a good introduction to the history of the arts inspired by Buddhism. Pratt's *The Pilgrimage of Buddhism* is still one of the books which should be read by anyone who wishes to become acquainted with Buddhism. Reichelt writes of Buddhism with understanding and unusual sympathy. Suzuki is generally accepted as the best exponent of Rinzai Zen. Takakusu is not exciting reading, but is accurate and dependable. Stcherbatsky's *The Conception of Buddhist Nirvana* and Wells's *Thai Buddhism* are almost impossible to find, which is regrettable since they are very useful books. Grousset's *In the Footsteps of the Buddha*, which tells the story of Hsuan-tsang's travels, is one of the most delightful books in this field, one which opens up new worlds for the reader. Edwin Reischauer's *Ennin's Travels in T'ang China* is equally interesting.

Glossary

Abhidhamma Pitaka—the third section of the Pali scriptures; the Basket of Ultimate Things; the Basket of Studies of the Supreme Dhamma; a detailed exposition of the Doctrines.

Abhidharmakosha—a treatise by Vasubandhu on the Sarvastivada doctrine; used as an introduction to the Doctrine.

Akshobhya—the Buddha of the East; not a Bodhisattva.

alayavijnana—the foundation on which human consciousness is based; fundamental to Vijnanavada doctrines.

Amida—the Japanese name (Limitless) which combines both Amitabha (Limitless Light) and Amitayus (Limitless Life); a combination which is most important to the Jodo sect. In Japanese Buddhism, Dharmakara became Amida Buddha, the Buddha of the Pure Realm.

Amida Sutra—a Chinese version of the smaller Sukhavativyuha Sutra.

Amitabha—the Buddha of the Pure Realm, of Boundless Splendor. Also known as Amida and as Amitayus, Infinite Duration of Life. In Chinese Buddhism, Dharmakara later became Amitabha.

Amitayurdhyana Sutra—an important Sutra setting forth meditation on Amitayus.

Amitayus—the Buddha of Infinite Duration of Life.

anatta—non-ego; absence of a permanent, unchanging self or soul; substanceless.

Anguttara Nikaya—the fourth part of the Sutta Pitaka in the Pali scriptures.

anicca—impermanent.

Arahat—one who is free from all craving and rebirth and has attained Enlightenment; one who has attained the highest stage, Nibbana.

Asanga—brother of Vasubandhu; he was converted from Sarvastivada and became a master of Mahayana teachings.

Asoka—the ruler of Magadha in the third century B.C. who spread Buddhism throughout India and Southeast Asia.

Asvaghosha—a famous writer at the time of Kaniska in the first or second century A.D., author of the extant Sanskrit text of the *Buddhacarita* which describes the Buddha up to his Enlightenment; his writings are transitional from Sarvastivada to Mahayana, before Nagarjuna, Asanga, and Vasubandhu.

Atisha—came to Tibet in 1042 and founded the Kadampa school.

Avalokitesvara—the Bodhisattva of great compassion, mercy, love; known chiefly as Kuan-yin in China and as Kwannon in Japan, with female features.

Avatamsaka Sutra—a voluminous Sutra setting forth the practices of a Bodhisattva; the basis of the Hua-yen sect in China and Kegon in Japan; assumed in China to be the Buddha's first discourse; teaches that all beings have the Buddha-nature.

avidya—avijja in Pali; ignorance of the true nature of existence; naïve realism.

Bhaishajyaguru—the Buddha of Healing; a Buddha of the East, like Akshobhya.

Bhikkhu—Bhikshu in Sanskrit; a monk.

Bhikkhuni—a nun.

bodhicitta—the Buddha-mind, the Buddha-nature.

Bodhidharma—a famous Indian mystic who came to China about A.D. 520 bringing the yogic disciplines of the dhyana school; regarded as the founder of Zen.

Bodhisattva—a being destined for Enlightenment; a future Buddha; in Mahayana, instead of becoming a Buddha, the Bodhisattva vows to save all beings and works with compassion for suffering beings.

Brahman—the highest Hindu caste; a scholar; Brahmanism is Hinduism. Also, Brahman is the Supreme Being, Ultimate Reality, the sole basis of the universe in Hinduism.

Buddha—the Enlightened One. Also known as the Tathagata, one who has gone thus, one who has arrived from and gone to *thusness*, that is, one who has followed the Path. There were many Buddhas in the past and will be many in the future. The last one of the past Buddhas was Siddhattha Gotama. Siddhattha (Pali) or Siddhartha (Sanskrit) was his personal name; Gotama (Gautama, in Sanskrit) was his family name; he was a member of the Sakya clan, hence, *Sakyamuni* means the wise man of the Sakya clan.

Buddhaghosha—the Indian scholar who came to Ceylon from India and translated into Pali the Sinhalese commentaries on the Three Pitakas; he returned to Burma in the fourth century A.D.

cetiya—a shrine attached to a stupa.

Ch'an sect—the Chinese sect started by Bodhidharma, emphasizing meditation; it became Zen in Japan.

Ching-t'u sect—a Chinese sect known as the Pure Realm, or Pure Land, sect.

Cullavagga—a section of the Vinaya Pitaka of the Pali Tipitaka.

Daibutsu—a Great Buddha image; it often refers to the one at Nara.

Dalai Lama—"Ocean-Wide" Lama; the spiritual and temporal ruler of Tibet.

dhamma—*see* dharma.

Dhammapada—the second book in the Khuddaka Nikaya, in the second Basket of the Pali scriptures; the Way of Truth; a collection of Buddhist teachings.

Dhammapala—an Indian commentator on the Pali Canon whose writings are influential in modern times; he visited Ceylon in the sixth century A.D.

dharani—literally, that by which something is sustained or kept up; the mystic syllables which keep up the religious life of a man; the quintessence of a Sutra; similar to a mantra in Hinduism; the embodiment of a power in a sound.

dharma—dhamma in Pali; truth, law, the principle of righteousness; the consequence of action, of karma; the result of previous action which must work itself out; also, the Doctrine of the Buddha (in this case capitalized); also the universal norms or laws which govern human existence.

dharmadhatu—the world of the cosmic law; suchness; the indescribable source of the truth.

Dharmakara—the Bodhisattva who became the Buddha Amitabha (or Amida) after making forty-eight vows that he would not accept Buddhahood unless the vows were to be fulfilled.

Dharmakaya—the highest aspect of the Threefold Body of the Buddha, the Absolute Nature of the Buddha-mind; the Body of the Law; the wisdom of the void; unmanifested; sometimes called Prajnadharmakaya. In Tibetan Buddhism, Dharmakaya is the abstract aspect of the Absolute Nature, conceived by wisdom; Prajnadharmakaya is the highest spiritual quality embodying all perfections and is acquired.

Dharmakirti—the logician who was influential in Indian and Tibetan Buddhism in the seventh century A.D.

dhyana—jhana in Pali; ultra-mundane experience; contemplation, meditation; sometimes translated as beholding, or absorption, or ecstacy; the basis of Zen in Japan. It is sometimes interpreted as meaning to think closely about an object, or to burn away adverse things which hinder spiritual progress.

Digha Nikaya—the first section of the Sutta Pitaka, the second Basket in the Pali scripture.

dukkha—suffering, misery, sorrow; the true nature of existence.

Ekayana—the one great vehicle which includes Hinayana, Mahayana, and Tantrayana.

Fa-hsiang sect—another name for the Yui-shih sect in China; became Hosso in Japan.

Fa Hsien—a Chinese pilgrim to India in the fifth century A.D.

Fa-hua sect—the Chinese name for the sect founded at T'ien-t'ai; called Tendai in Japan.

Gelukpa school—the sect of the Dalai Lama in Tibet; founded by Tsongkhapa.

Gotama—see Buddha.

Guhyasamaja Tantra—an important tantric text belonging to Mahayana Buddhism; tells of the union of the Triple Body of the Buddhas; occasionally sets forth obscene rites.

Hinayana—a derogatory term meaning Little Vehicle, applied to Conservative Buddhism which is based on the Pali Canon exclusively; Pali Buddhism is represented today by Theravada which does not like to be called Hinayana; Hinayana is the first of the three stages in Tibetan Buddhism.

Honen—twelfth-century Japanese leader who established the Pure Realm teachings as an independent system; the Shin, Jodo, and Seizan sects were founded by his disciples.

Hosso sect—the Consciousness-Only sect, based on the Vijnanavada doctrines of Asanga and Vasubandhu; known as Yui-shih sect in China.

Hsuan-tsang—Chinese scholar and monk (620–664) who visited Afghanistan and India on an extended trip; he brought back and translated many Sanskrit manuscripts and wrote a brilliant record of his travels.

Hua-yen sect—the Chinese sect which became known as Kegon in

Japan; Hua-yen means Avatamsaka and is named for the Sutra; it stresses the doctrine that all beings have the Buddha-mind.

Hui-neng—the sixth Patriarch of the Zen Buddhist tradition in China.

Jataka—the tenth section of the Khuddaka Nikaya of the Sutta Pitaka; a collection of popular stories of the Buddha's previous existences.

jhana—*see* dhyana.

Ji sect—a minor sect of Pure Realm Buddhism in Japan, founded by Ippen.

Jodo sect—the second largest Pure Realm sect in Japan, founded by Bencho.

Kadampa sect—the school founded by Atisha in Tibet.

Kagyupa sect—the school of the Successive Order, founded by Marpa in Tibet.

Kagyur—the chief scripture of Tibetan Buddhism; the Buddha's teachings as translated in full from the Sanskrit originals; it includes the Tripitaka and the four Great Tantras.

kaidan—in Japan, the place for ordination ceremonies, comparable to the seema in Theravada; the Japanese originally followed Vinaya rules for ordination, but later adopted Mahayana rules.

kamma—*see* karma.

Kaniska—ruler of Northern India in the first, or second, century A.D. He was a great patron of Buddhism and Buddhist art.

karma—kamma in Pali; action, conduct; action with inevitable consequences; sometimes the moral law of cause and effect in human activities.

karuna—mercy, compassion.

Kassapa—one of the Buddha's early disciples; also, a Ceylonese commentator on the Pali Canon.

Kasyapa—a Buddha of the past.

Kegon sect—the Japanese sect which was Hua-yen in China; its teachings are based on the Avatamsaka Sutra.

khandhas—*see* skandhas.

Kshitigarbha—a Bodhisattva who has vowed to deliver all people from this suffering world; he especially favors children and the wicked.

Kuan-yin—the Bodhisattva Avalokitesvara characterized by female features in China; known as Kwannon in Japan.

Kumarajiva—missionary from Kucha to China in the fifth century

A.D.; he is famous for his translations, especially the translation of the Lotus Sutra.

Kwannon—the most popular Bodhisattva in Japan; Avalokitesvara with female aspect; known as Kuan-yin in China.

lama—a spiritual leader in Tibet; incarnate lamas are destined to reveal the ideals of the Buddhas and Bodhisattvas; developed lamas have attained Enlightenment through their efforts; a monk in Tibet is called a drapa.

Lao-tzu—regarded as the chief exponent of the doctrine of Taoism in China.

Lotus Sutra—the Saddharma Pundarika Sutra.

Madhyamika—the Mahayana school of Buddhist doctrine based on the Prajnaparamita Sutras and the writings of Nagarjuna.

Mahaparinibbana Sutta—a discourse on the passing away of the Buddha, in the Digha Nikaya of the Sutta Pitaka in the Pali Canon; in a variant version in the Mahayana Canon, it is known as the Mahaparinirvana Sutra.

Mahaprajnaparamita Sutra—a very long Sutra setting forth the doctrine of sunyata, voidness.

Mahasanghika—an early Buddhist sect which grew out of the second Great Council a century after the Buddha; it means belonging to the great order of monks.

Mahavagga—in the Vinaya Pitaka; also a section in the Samyutta Nikaya of the Sutta Pitaka, dealing with the Eightfold Path.

Mahavairocana Sutra—the fundamental scripture of Tantrayana (Vajrayana).

Mahavamsa—the Great Chronicle, a Ceylonese history written in Pali.

Mahayana—literally, the Great Vehicle; the commonly accepted designation for the Buddhist schools which follow the Sanskrit and related scriptures of Tibet, China, and Japan; it accepts a great degree of philosophical speculation, especially concerning the doctrine of dependent origination; it believes that the doctrinal development of Buddhism depends on historical circumstances; it is the second stage of development in Tibetan Buddhism.

Mahinda—the son of King Asoka who took Buddhism to Ceylon.

Maitreya—the Buddha yet to come.

Majjhima Nikaya—the second section of the Sutta Pitaka, the second Basket.

mandala—a pictorial representation of a meritorious deed which
has been accomplished; a symbol of the universe; a diagrammatic picture which represents the cosmic nature of the Bud-
has; used as an aid in meditation; in Tibet it is known as a
thang-ka.

Manjusri—the Bodhisattva of Meditation, or the personification of
Supreme Wisdom.

mantra—in Hinduism, a syllable, word, or verse which has been revealed to a Seer in meditation; an embodiment in sound of a
deity; an embodiment in sound of a power which can effect
spiritual and sometimes temporal results. It is similar to a
dharani in Buddhism.

Marpa—the founder of the Kagyupa school in Tibet in the eleventh century.

metta—universal love, active benevolence, loving-kindness; in
Mahayana it is compassion.

Mikkyo—esoteric Buddhism in Japan; related to tantric Buddhism,
but not fully tantric in its practices.

mudra—a mystic and symbolic gesture of the hands.

Mulamadhyamaka Sastra—a treatise by Nagarjuna; the fundamental text of the Madhyamika school.

Nagarjuna—one of the chief philosophers of Mahayana Buddhism
and founder of the Madhyamika school; probably lived in the
latter half of the second century.

nama-rupa—name and form; consciousness and body; psycho-physical existence; mind and body.

Namu Amida Butsu—the phrase used in Japanese Pure Realm Buddhism to call upon the Name and Thought of the Buddha; it
is called *Nembutsu* in Japan. It is *Nan-wu A-mi-t'o-fo* in Chinese; *Namo Amitabhaya Buddhaya* in Sanskrit. Although it is
sometimes translated "Homage to Amida Buddha," or "I devote myself to Amida Buddha," to translate the phrase raises
questions of Pure Realm dogma. One important distinction is
that *Namu* is part of the proper Name of the Buddha, not just
a word meaning homage.

Namu Myo Horengekyo—the avowal of devotion used in the
Nichiren sect of Japan: "I devote myself to the Sutra of the
Lotus of the Wonderful Law."

Naropa—a tantric master at Nalanda in the eleventh century, a
teacher of Marpa.

Nembutsu—*see* Namu Amida Butsu.

Nibanna—*see* Nirvana.

Nichiren sect—the Japanese sect founded by Saint Nichiren in the thirteenth century.

nidana—cause; hence, the twelve nidanas are the twelve causes in the chain of causation; they become the Wheel of Life in Buddhist art.

Nirmanakaya—the Earthly Body of the Buddha; the Body of Transformations—that is, Sakyamuni Buddha and other Buddhas; the third aspect of the Threefold Body of the Buddha.

Nirvana—Nibbana in Pali; the cessation of selfish desires (or of ignorance) which leaves a man free from the bonds of this life of suffering; freedom from the delusions of ego; Enlightenment; the state of him who is worthy; freedom from all suffering and sorrow; the state of an Arahat after his passing away, a state which is indescribable but is by no means annihilation. The spontaneous attainment of the pure and peaceful realm of mind; the realization of the Triple Form of Enlightenment.

Noh—literally, performance; a lyric drama in Japan, a solemn operatic performance consisting of music, dancing, and recitative chants dealing with historical themes and frequently expressing Buddhist ideas.

Om Mani Padme Hum—a phrase frequently repeated by devout Tibetan Buddhists; *Om* is the Triple Body of the Buddha, *Mani* is jewel, *Padme* is lotus, and *Hum* is a petition for protection.

Padmasambhava—the Indian Bhikkhu who was influential in bringing tantric Buddhism to Tibet in the eighth century.

Pali—the language of the Theravada Canon, believed to have been the language used by the Buddha in the Magadha kingdom.

paramis—perfections; the virtues to be fulfilled by one who aspires to become an Arahat or a Supreme Buddha.

Parinirvana—Parinibbana in Pali; the final, or perfect, Nirvana at the end of earthly existence.

parittas—portions of the sayings of the Buddha which are chanted by Bhikkhus for the purpose of producing a healthy psychic condition which brings relief and confidence to a person who is ill or in danger.

Paticcasamuppada—Pratityasamutpada in Sanskrit; Dependent Origination; Interdependent Causation; the chain of causation.

Patimokkha—the rules of conduct in the Vinaya Pitaka which are recited at the fortnightly services in the monastery.

prajna—wisdom; looking at things as they really are; wisdom destroys all illusions and brings one to spiritual awakening.

Prajnadharmakaya—*see* Dharmakaya.

Prajnaparamita Sutras—a collection of many Sutras; known as the Discourse on Perfect Wisdom, or the Discourse on the Attainment of Transcendental Wisdom; it is the wisdom which has attained the Other World, that is, perfect wisdom that destroys all illusions and brings one to the world of the Awakening.

Prajnaparamitahridaya Sutra—the Heart, or Essence, of the Prajnaparamita Sutras; The Essence of the Discourse on Perfect Wisdom; in this short form it has been widely used in Mahayana countries.

prakriti—the ultimate material cause of the universe; unconscious primal matter; ultimate cosmic energy.

purusha—the principle of consciousness as opposed to matter, or prakriti.

Rinzai Zen—one of the two largest Zen sects in Japan.

Ritsu sect—an early sect in Japan which emphasized the Vinaya rules of discipline.

saddha—confidence, based on knowledge of the truth; it is more than faith.

Saddharma Pundarika Sutra—The Lotus of the True Law, or Wonderful Law, or Good Law; the Lotus Sutra; one of the most important of all Mahayana scriptures, setting forth the doctrine of the One Vehicle and the Eternal Buddha. This Sutra teaches an ethical path which is the way of the Bodhisattva—a life of creative altruism.

Sakya school—a school of Tibetan Buddhism, founded in 1071.

Sakyamuni—*see* Buddha.

Samantabhadra—the Bodhisattva of compassion; one of the chief Bodhisattvas in Mahayana Buddhism.

Samatha—a type of meditation which leads to tranquillity, used in Theravada; a modification of yoga practices, used as a preliminary to the development of insight.

Sambhogakaya—The Body of Enjoyment; the second aspect of the Threefold Body of the Buddha; also called the Subtle Body of the Buddha; the Supreme Enlightened Mind of the Buddha which has taken a merciful vow to live in the empirical world.

samsara—literally, migration; that is, the migration through many rebirths; thus, the world of physical experience, the world of change, the wheel of life and death.

samskara—sankhara in Pali; the innate tendencies of an individual; the karmic formations or results, carried over from a previous existence and from earlier actions.

Samyutta Nikaya—the third section of the Sutta Pitaka.

Sangha—the order of Buddhist monks, founded by the Buddha and continued to the present day in Theravada Buddhism.

Sankhya—a dualistic, realistic school of classical Hindu philosophy.

San-lun sect—the Three Treatises sect in China, founded in the late sixth century; known as Sanron in Japan.

Sanron sect—the Japanese version of the Chinese San-lun sect.

Santarakshita—an Indian Bhikkhu who was influential in establishing Buddhism in Tibet in the eighth century.

Sarvastivada—a sect in early Buddhism which was influential in Northwestern India; it was conservative, close to Theravada; they were philosophical realists.

Satyasiddhi Sastra—one of the treatises ardently studied in the San-lun sect in China.

Sautrantikas—an early Buddhist sect.

seema—a place set aside for ceremonies in the Sangha.

Seizan sect—a minor sect of Pure Realm Buddhism in Japan, founded by Shoka.

Shin sect—the largest Pure Realm sect in Japan, founded by Shinran.

Shingon sect—esoteric Buddhist sect in Japan.

Shinran—the most important figure in Japanese Pure Realm Buddhism, founder of the Shin sect.

Shinsei sect—a minor Tendai sect, similar to Pure Realm Buddhism in Japan.

Shinto—the indigenous religion of Japan.

Shotoku—the Prince Regent of Japan who was influential in establishing Buddhism there in the late sixth and early seventh centuries.

Siddhartha, or Siddhattha—see Buddha.

skandhas—khandhas in Pali; the five aggregates which make up the individual.

Songtsan-Gampo—the ruler of Tibet who first welcomed Buddhism.

Soto Zen sect—the largest Zen sect in Japan.

Sthaviravada—a conservative sect of early Buddhism.

stupa—originally a burial mound for relics of the Buddha and his chief disciples, it developed into elaborate and beautiful structures; also known as a dagoba or pagoda.

Sukhavati world—the Pure Realm; sometimes called the Pure Land, or the Extremely Pleasant Pure Land of the West.

Sukhavativyuha Sutra—the fundamental Sutra of Pure Realm Buddhism.

sunyata—the void; voidness, emptiness; that which denies the viewpoints based on existence or on nonexistence; the all-inclusive; the basis for ethical values; the doctrine that only the whole is real.

Sutra—Sutta in Pali; a discourse of the Buddha or a disciple which is accepted as an authoritative scripture.

Sutta Nipata—Collected Discourses; the fifth section in the Khuddaka Nikaya, in the second Basket of the Tipitaka.

Sutta Pitaka—the Basket of Discourses, the second Basket in the Tipitaka.

Tangyur—the second section of the Tibetan scriptures; a collection of the works of Indian and Tibetan scholars.

tanha—desire; craving; attachment to worldly existence.

Tantrayana—the tantric school of Buddhism; the third, or highest, stage of Buddhism in Tibet; also called Vajrayana. Tantric Buddhism is esoteric Buddhism transmitted chiefly through oral instructions from master to pupil; it emphasizes the methods of attaining supreme wisdom by one's own efforts through meditation on the higher nature with the aid of symbolic rites consisting of gestures, postures, breathing, and the use of the powers of sounds and secret, mystic formulas.

Tathagata—see Buddha.

tathata—suchness, thisness; absolute reality.

Tendai sect—a Japanese sect which was the Fa-hua sect in China.

Thera—elder; the level of ordination of a Bhikkhu after ten years in the Sangha.

Theravada—the Way of the Elders; the Buddhist school based on the Pali Canon; it follows insofar as possible the practices and teachings of the time of the Buddha; it is found chiefly in Southeast Asia.

T'ien-t'ai—sometimes used as the name for the Fa-hua sect in China since its doctrines were first taught on Mount T'ien-t'ai.

Tipitaka—Tripitaka in Sanskrit; the Three Baskets; the Pali Canon, accepted as the complete Canon in Theravada; accepted in its Sanskrit form as the basis for the first stage in Tibetan Buddhism; partially accepted in the Sanskrit version in most Maha-yana sects.

Trikaya—the Triple Body of the Buddhas of the past, the present, and the future; the Dharmakaya, Sambhogakaya, and Nir-manakaya.

Tripitaka—see Tipitaka.

trishna—craving, grasping, clinging.

Tsongkhapa—founder of the Gelukpa school in Tibet in the four-teenth century.

Tushita Heaven—Tussita in Pali; a heaven which is below the level of the Buddha-fields, or Buddha-realms, on the plane of desire.

Upanishads—the Hindu scriptures which elaborate the philosophi-cal and mystical truths of the Vedas.

Upasaka—male lay devotee of Buddhism.

Upasika—female lay devotee of Buddhism.

Uposatha—the fortnightly ceremonies in the Sangha at which the rules of conduct are recited and lapses are confessed; held at the time of the new moon and of the full moon.

Vairocana—the Primordial Buddha; the greatest Buddha, who pre-vails everywhere and gives forth the most brilliant light; the chief object of devotion in the Shingon sect in Japan.

vajra—diamond; solidity, brilliance.

Vajracchedika Sutra—the Diamond Cutter Sutra; important in Zen Buddhism.

Vajradakini Tantra—the Tantra of the Eternal Goddess, important for tantric Buddhism; not a Sutra, but accepted as canonical.

Vajrapani—the Bodhisattva of Power.

Vajrayana—see Tantrayana.

Vasubandhu—brother of Asanga; lived in and near Peshawar, A.D. 280–360; was converted from Sarvastivada by his brother.

Vedanta—a classical school of monistic Hindu philosophy.

Vibhishana—a Hindu deity; the brother of the demon Ravana in the Ramayana epic.

vihara—a monastery in the early days; later used to designate either a monastery or a temple.

vijnana—vinnana in Pali; consciousness, the third link in the chain of causation.

Vijnanavada—the Consciousness-Only school of Mahayana phi-losophy; sometimes called Yogacara, although Yogacara is a somewhat wider school which includes Vijnanavada; emphasizes the fundamental consciousness as the void.

Vimalakirtinirdesa Sutra—an important Sutra setting forth Buddhism for the layman; also teaches the doctrine of sunyata.

Vinaya Pitaka—the first of the Three Baskets, the Basket of Discipline, in the Pali Canon; the code of discipline for Theravada Bhikkhus and Bhikkhunis.

Vipassana—the meditation which leads to insight, used in Theravada; recommended by the Buddha.

visuddhi—purity.

Wesak—the Theravada festival at full-moon time in May which commemorates the birth, Enlightenment, and the passing away of the Buddha.

yana—vehicle, burden, responsibility, duty; the way; it may refer to Hinayana, Mahayana, Tantrayana, Vajrayana, or Ekayana.

Yogacara—see Vijnanavada.

Yui-shih sect—the Consciousness-Only sect in China, introduced by Hsuan-tsang; also known as Fa-hsiang in China and Hosso in Japan.

Yuzu Nembutsu sect—one of the Pure Realm schools in Japan, based on Ryonin's teachings; its early position was close to the Tendai and Kegon sects.

zazen—Zen meditation practices, including postures.

Zen sect—the meditative sect in Japan, derived from Ch'an in China.

Index